AF606974

EMBRACING LIGHT

A YEAR IN ACADIA NATIONAL PARK & MOUNT DESERT ISLAND

SCOTT ERSKINE

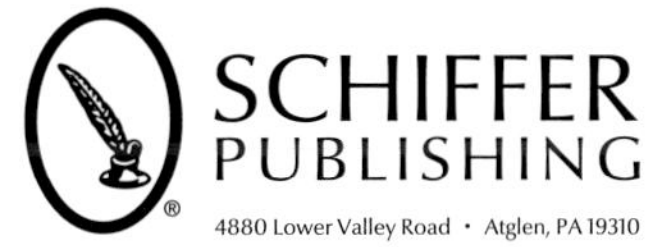

4880 Lower Valley Road • Atglen, PA 19310

Other Schiffer Books on Related Subjects:
Out in Blue Fields: A Year at Hokum Rock Blueberry Farm,
Janice Riley & Stephen Spear, ISBN 978-0-7643-5453-3

Coastal Maine: A Keepsake, Antelo Devereux Jr.,
ISBN 978-0-7643-5575-2

Library of Congress Control Number: 2018958780

Designed by Molly Shields
Type set in Footlight MT Light/ZapfEllipt BT

ISBN: 978-0-7643-5750-3
Printed in China

Published by Schiffer Publishing, Ltd.
4880 Lower Valley Road
Atglen, PA 19310
Phone: (610) 593-1777; Fax: (610) 593-2002
E-mail: Info@schifferbooks.com
Web: www.schifferbooks.com

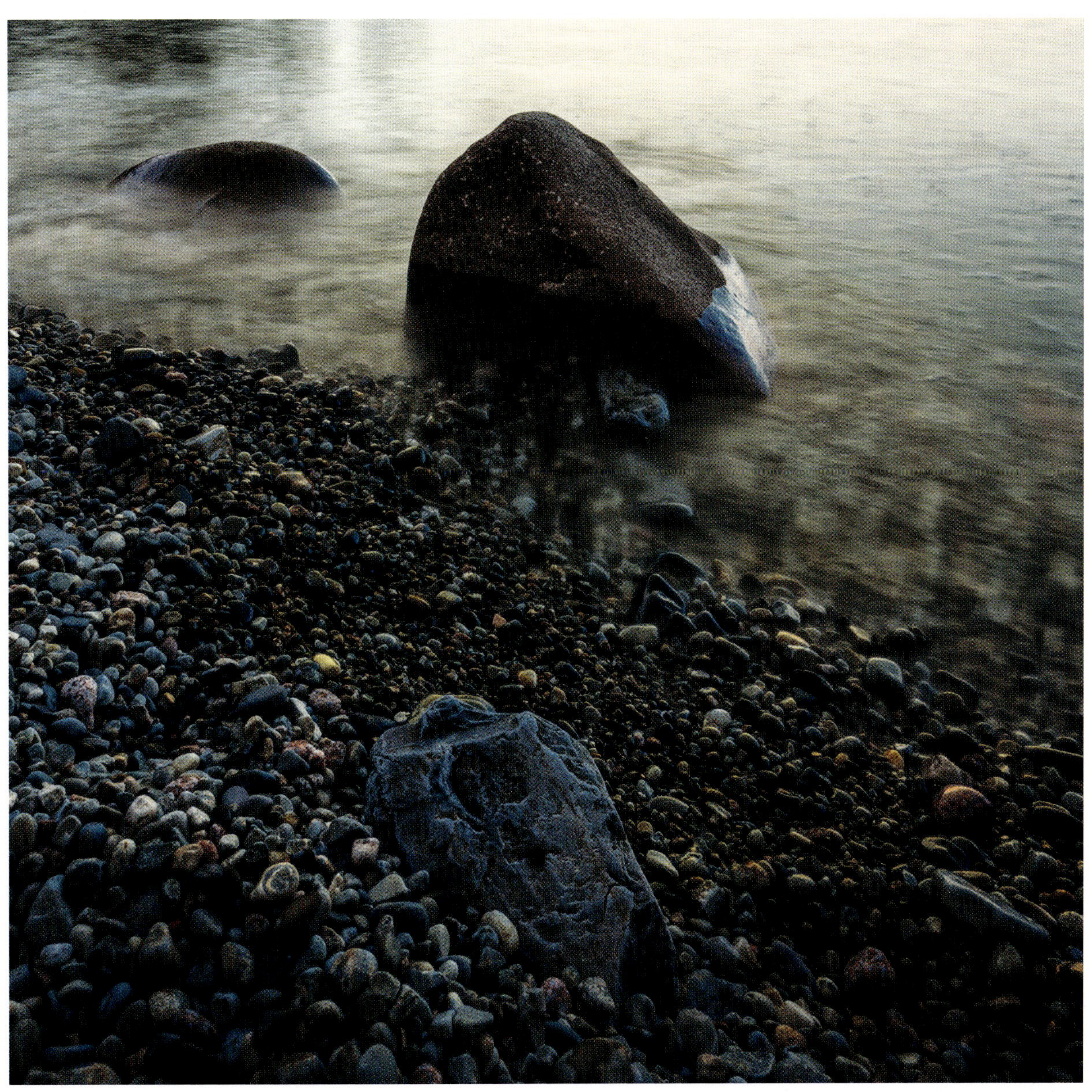

COBBLES, PEBBLES AND BOULDERS, LITTLE HUNTERS BEACH

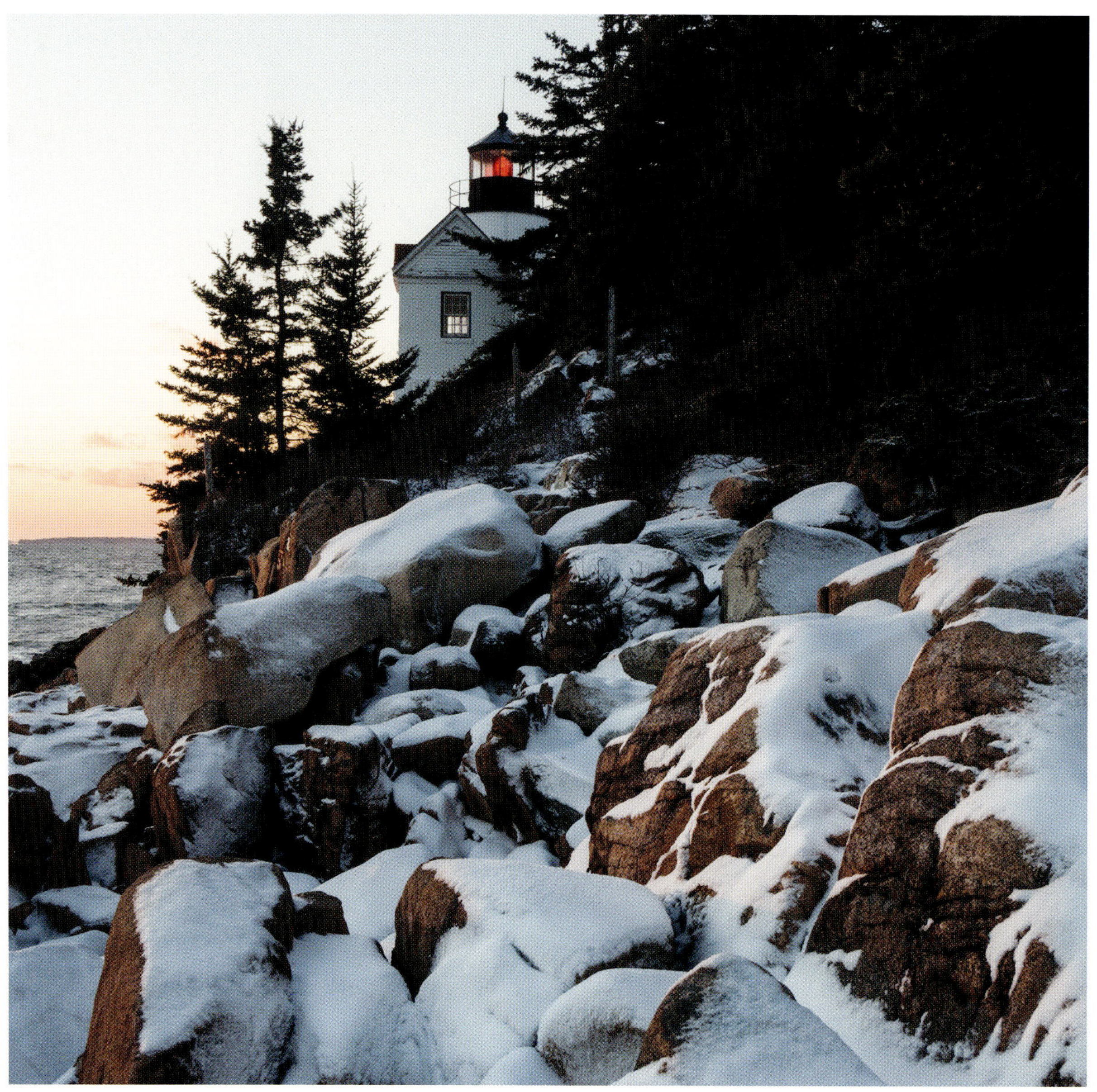

BASS HARBOR LIGHT, WINTER, SUNSET

Contents

Introduction

It's 3:45 a.m. on an early June morning, and I am standing on a cliff 40 feet above the Atlantic Ocean. Small waves break over the rocks below, adding their voice to the early-morning stillness that I share with a few gulls. I have not seen another person, not even another car, since I arrived at this place. The sun is not up yet; I am alone. The lobster boats have not yet started their daily routine of checking the traps. The clouds that brought rain last night are moving off to the northeast and have left behind clean, clear air. The rain has released the aroma of the earth, mixed with the fragrance of the spruce and pines, the decaying leaves from years past, and whatever is blooming. It is a heady mixture; one I can't inhale deeply enough. Walking through the forest to arrive at this place has left my clothes slightly damp from brushing against grasses and bushes along the path. I ponder whether or not the clouds will break enough to give us a glimpse of the sun as it rises. Will there be color in the sky? Will clouds move in from behind the mountains to bring more rain? I cannot control what happens next; I can only stand there and witness it. This experience is the reason I am here rather than asleep in my bed.

A few minutes more and the sky lightens as the clouds take on copper tones. The ocean reflects the light and color back at the sky. The waves continue to wash over the rocks below, although not as much. The tide has risen a few inches. The buoy off Otter Cliffs clangs out its warning of a nearby shoal. Still the clouds remain in place, obscuring the appearance of the sun. I continue my vigil, and anticipation courses through me, evaluating the clouds, the sea, the breeze. And then it happens, at first a tiny rift in the clouds, a quick moment of brightness, and then it slips away. But now the clouds seem more translucent, thinner somehow. Again, a quick glimpse, and then it is gone. We play this game of peekaboo, and then it happens. The clouds reward my patience and give me longer views of the sun. More light spills through; a break provides a spotlight-like ray of light, directly to the rocks below me. This is what I came for, to briefly experience this moment of brightness and wonder. I have found my brief instance of peace and solitude, and I am thankful. I am where I belong at this moment of time. I am in Acadia and I have found my park.

In 2016, the 100th anniversary of the National Park Service, "Find Your Park" was the slogan that was widely broadcast to encourage people to visit and celebrate one of America's greatest ideas. While I have been to many of the national parks, from Maine to Alaska, I already knew where my park was many years ago.

If you drive up Route 1 in Maine, you will come to the small town of Ellsworth. Turn right on Route 3 and head southeast, out of town. Cross a short causeway across Mt. Desert Narrows, and onto Mt. Desert Island, and a few more miles of driving brings you to Acadia National Park. And you have found my park. I've made this trip countless times over the last forty years, and I am always excited by it.

What is it about Mt. Desert Island that keeps me coming back? It's an amalgam of ocean, mountains, sunrise, sunset, stars and galaxies, waves, trees, snow (lots of snow), and the smell of spruce and seaweed and ocean air at sunrise. Hearing the buoy bell off Otter Cliffs from the Tarn, over a mile away, on a foggy autumn day. In the winter, it's the solitude of a snowstorm at Sand Beach, and in the summer it's the ambiance of strolling down Main Street on a warm evening, ice cream cone in hand, watching the fog roll in from Frenchman Bay. Maybe it's being on the rocks at Monument Cove during a hurricane, feeling the wind drive ocean spray in your face, imagining the raw power being exerted in the eternal contest between ocean and rock. Or standing out on the ice on Jordan Pond on a February night, watching the Big Dipper rise above Cadillac Mountain while listening to the ice crack and groan and echo off the surrounding mountains in the darkness. And of course, being the first person to see the sun rise in America on a cold blustery morning. And it's that moment when you are at a popular location and suddenly find you're the sole person to witness the sublime sunset afterglow, because everyone else thought the show was over and left. It's about moments and experiences in which I am the lone witness that matter to me. It's about the experience. In the summer of 2014, I took a new job at the Jackson Laboratory in Bar Harbor, which provided me with the opportunity to be in the park every day. It was a yearlong engagement, but it turned out to be one of the best years I've ever experienced.

The images in this book are about the natural magic and mystery of Acadia and Mt. Desert Island. It can also be sublime in its understated majesty. Acadia doesn't overwhelm the visitor—it seduces you. It is where I go when I feel the need to restore my soul. It's about the timeless quality of the natural world that we briefly are witness to. What was here long before the first people arrived on the island and what will remain after, unchanged in our short blink of time in this universe, is what I seek. And a few lighthouses. Not every day resulted in a great image, but every day was a special experience that I tried to capture with an image. It is my hope that these images inspire you to seek out your own places for reflection and solitude, whether they are in Acadia or somewhere else. Take the time to let your eyes and your mind linger over these images, and try to imagine the stories that might surround them. These are my experiences, and I am happy to share them with you.

The book is organized chronologically, by seasons. My thought was to present the photographs in order as they occurred day by day, to give the reader some sense of how I experienced the progression of the seasons. Some days were very productive, and there are several images that were made in a short time span as conditions rapidly changed, such as the day at Sand Beach when we went from raging blizzard to clear blue sky in ninety minutes. Or during a hurricane, where I rapidly moved from location to location to capture the power of the storm as it battered the coast. Most of the images concentrate on the landscape; however, I am a sucker for lighthouses and the footbridge in Somesville, so several images from these locations are included. Over the course of the year, I made over 18,000 images. Not all succeeded, but all of them contributed in some way to the images presented here. It is not my intention to provide images that are a documentary record of the landscape, but rather an emotional visual rendering of my experiences during my year on Mt. Desert Island. I hope these images convey the intent, and that you are encouraged to get out away from the crowds and create your own experiences.

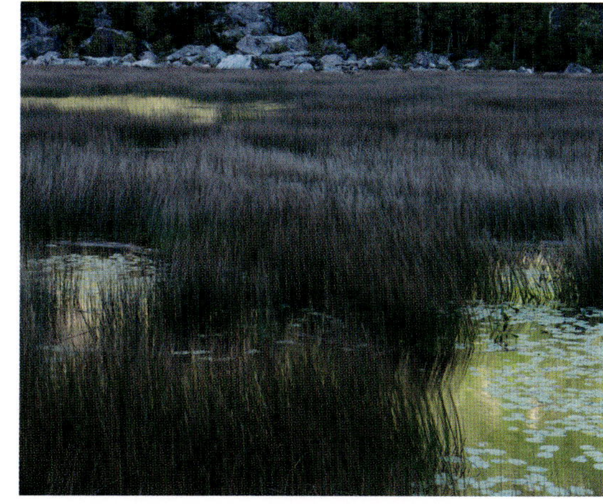

The Tarn, Morning Light Reflections of Dorr Mountain

WHY EMBRACING LIGHT?

Embracing light is a term I use to describe my approach to photography. Someone else probably spoke or wrote those words before me, but that is less important than the idea. I first began to think about embracing light as a title for a photograph I made in the mountains of Vermont a few years ago. I had found a large tree growing around a boulder, its large roots fully exposed, while its canopy overhead was in full autumn color. The sky and air above and around was filled with early-morning fog and thin, puffy clouds that would part briefly to reveal clear blue sky, creating an almost celestial light radiating down on the tree. The tree structure was completely exposed, from the roots emerging from the earth to the leaves at the end of the

EARLY EVENING STARS OVER THE BEEHIVE AND SAND BEACH LAGOON

branches in this ethereal light. It was as if the tree was reaching up and embracing the light, in one last attempt to hold on to the light for one more day before surrendering to the inevitable winter to come. It was a moving experience that lasted only a few minutes, and then the fog burned off, the clouds scattered.

As time passed I thought about that title often, and I began to form ideas about how I photograph all the time, not just in the "golden hours" at the edge of the day, but in any light, at any time of the day, no matter the weather. It was similar to how I approached life after my heart attack in 2012. Just as I made a choice to fully embrace life, pursuing experiences and not things, I was determined to photograph even when conditions were less than favorable, when the light doesn't cooperate, or when the light was too harsh, too soft, or the wind was too constant. The times of perfect, exceptional light come all too briefly, I had to work with the light I was given, not the light I wanted. If I could learn to make meaningful photographs of my experiences in those conditions, how much better would they convey what it is like to be out and about in the world during our brief time on the earth. I was determined to embrace the light that I was given to work with, whenever and however I could. Storms, fog, rain, wind, snow, blizzards, cold, hot, dark, damp, low light, bright light, clear skies; I would work in them all.

There are days when there are heavy clouds over the land and the ocean; when it seems all the color and contrast have been removed from the rocks, the trees, and the sea; when very little light penetrates the thick blankets above. And yet it is still there, revealing the land in a different way, a softer version of itself, as if we had just stepped into a painting by one of the Wyeths. Softening shadows, showing us textures and colors and contrasts in different ways, another view of the world. In New England, we have an expression: "Don't like the weather? Wait fifteen minutes, it'll change." So it is with photography in Acadia—the weather and the elements constantly evolve and dance around us, and if we are still for a few moments, if we observe and contemplate, we will have our own unique experience. Suddenly, the clouds part, the sun peeks through, low in the sky, the longer wavelengths reach out to us, and our experience changes. Now the shadows are a bit deeper, the shapes of objects are more defined and take on substance, and the light is just a bit warmer or colder than it was a minute ago. And if we are quick, if we recognize what is taking place, if we have learned our craft well, we just might be able to capture that momentary experience in a photograph, and we will have embraced the light.

Summer

"If you can't stand the winters, you don't deserve the summers."

—Unknown Mainer

Summers in Maine are quite different from anywhere else I have lived. Warm days and cool nights are typical, with the occasional thunderstorm. Mostly it's quite comfortable, with low humidity, except in late July and early August. The sun rises shortly before 4 a.m. and sets after 8 p.m. Twilight invites us to linger along the coast just a bit longer, waiting to see the stars come out. On moonless nights, they are absolutely brilliant, and it's hard to pull yourself away from the march of the constellations across the sky as the surf provides a background soundtrack. Wildflowers are blooming and all the trees have clothed themselves in green splendor. Wildlife with their newborn offspring can be observed in the meadows and fields, mostly at the edges of the day. And bird species increase as they move along their migration paths.

Tropical storms moving north along the Eastern Seaboard bring high-surf conditions and spectacular waves crashing thunderously into the granite bluffs between Sand Beach and Otter Cliffs. It is no wonder that the rusticators of the early nineteenth century, artists and writers looking to escape the ever-expanding pressures of creating a new nation, ventured into the wilderness to seek relief from the crowded conditions of the new cities. Painters Thomas Cole and Frederic Church and writer Henry David Thoreau all visited here and returned to civilization to tell the story of this Garden of Eden in the wilds of Maine.

Early-morning walks along the shores of Jordan Pond, Eagle Lake, and the Ocean Path are exhilarating, but just stopping in a quiet place and being still for a few minutes also has its benefits, adding to one's enjoyment of the park. I frequently find a convenient rock, slow my breathing down, and just watch. It doesn't matter what—the clouds, the waves, lobster boats, birds. What matters is taking the time to be still. Sense the rhythm of the island. Walk into the forest after a rainstorm and breathe in the smells of the spruce and fir as they mix with the salt air and restore the soul.

This is the time of year when the park and the island receive the most visitors, with the population of the island swelling to over 200,000 on any day. Getting around requires planning, patience, and cooperation, especially between 10 a.m. and 5 p.m. Outside those hours, the crowds thin out, and as the stillness returns, you can begin to get a sense of the island and what the early rusticators experienced.

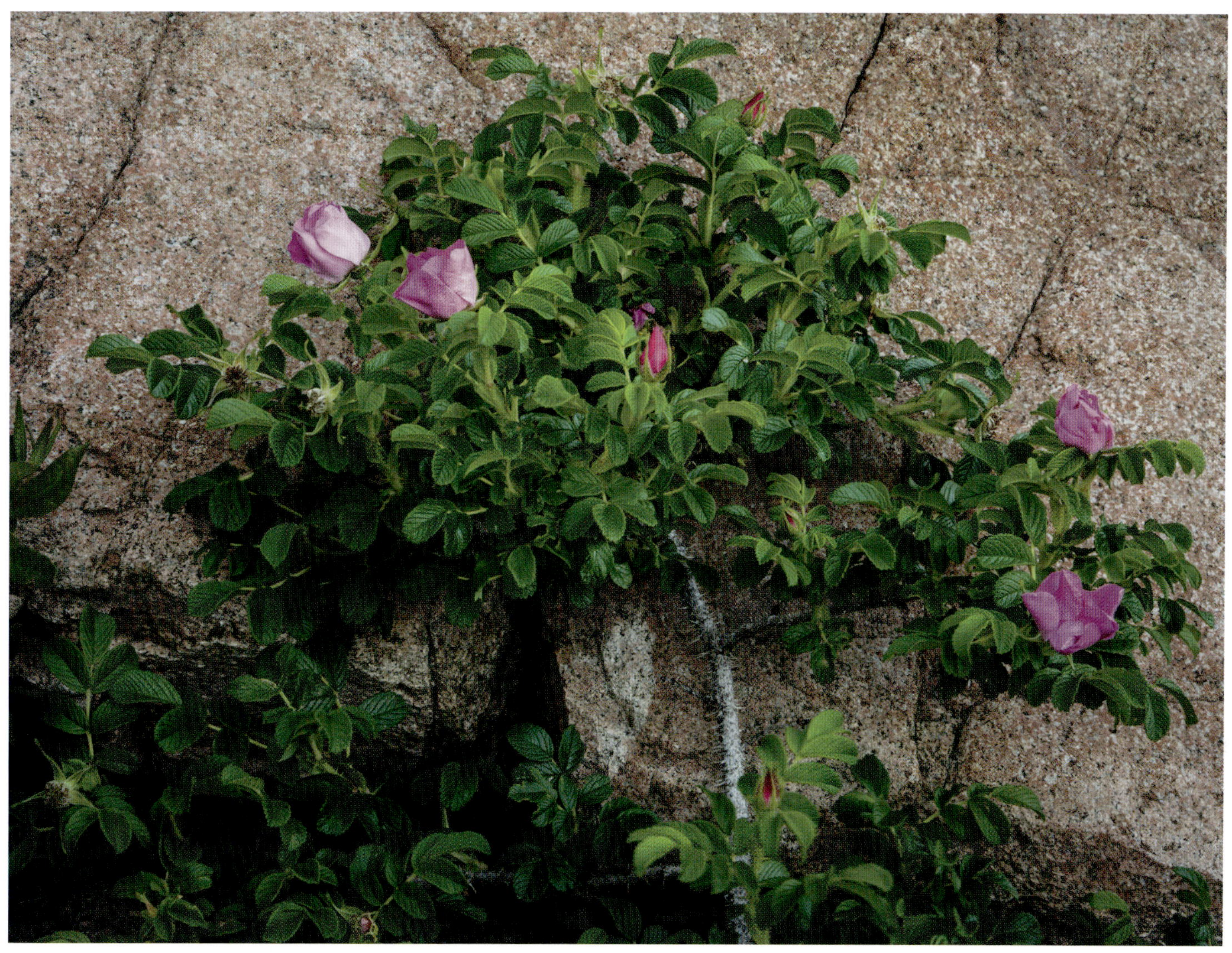

RUGOSA TABLEAU

•

New rugosa blooms open on a background of Acadia pink granite.

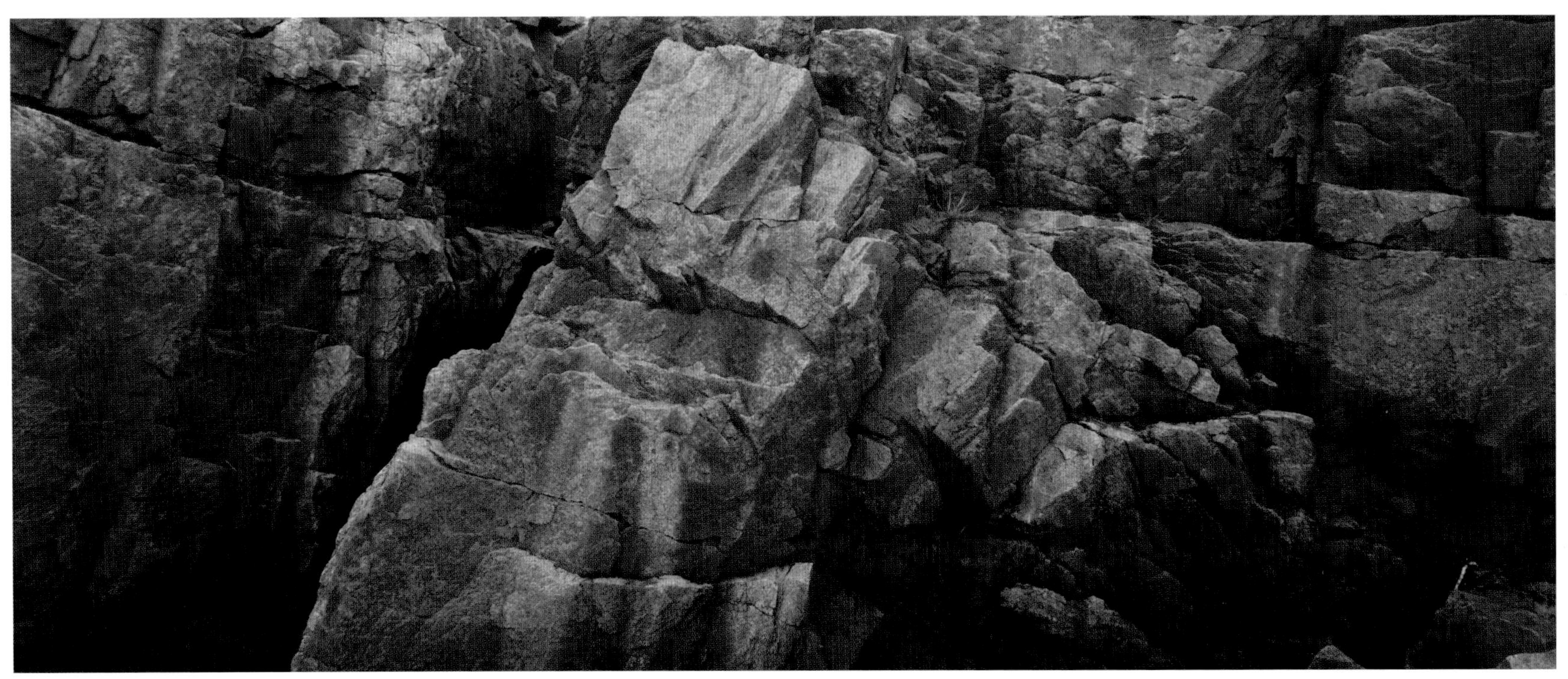

GRANITE ABSTRACT ON A CLOUDY EVENING

•

Overcast skies provided an opportunity to concentrate on abstract intimate images such as this rock face near Thunder Hole.

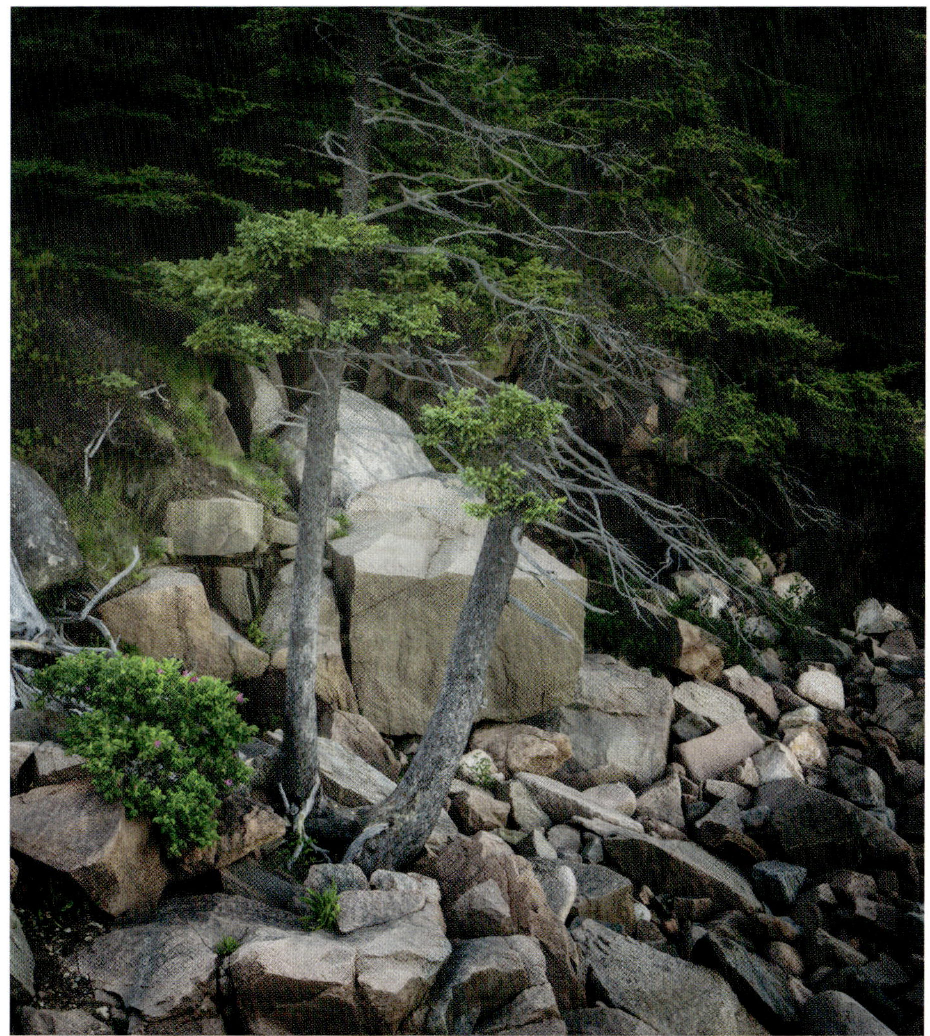

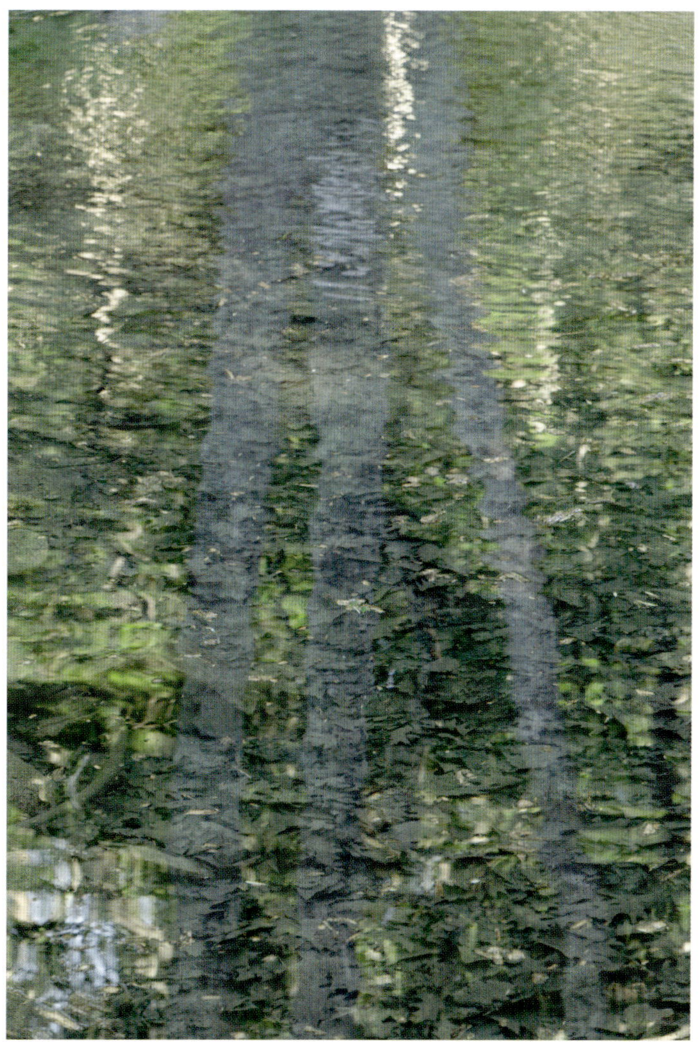

Soft light on a summer's afternoon as fog seeps down into the spruces. Within another thirty minutes the fog completely obscured this view.

A barely perceptible breeze ripples the surface reflections at Sieur de Monts Springs.

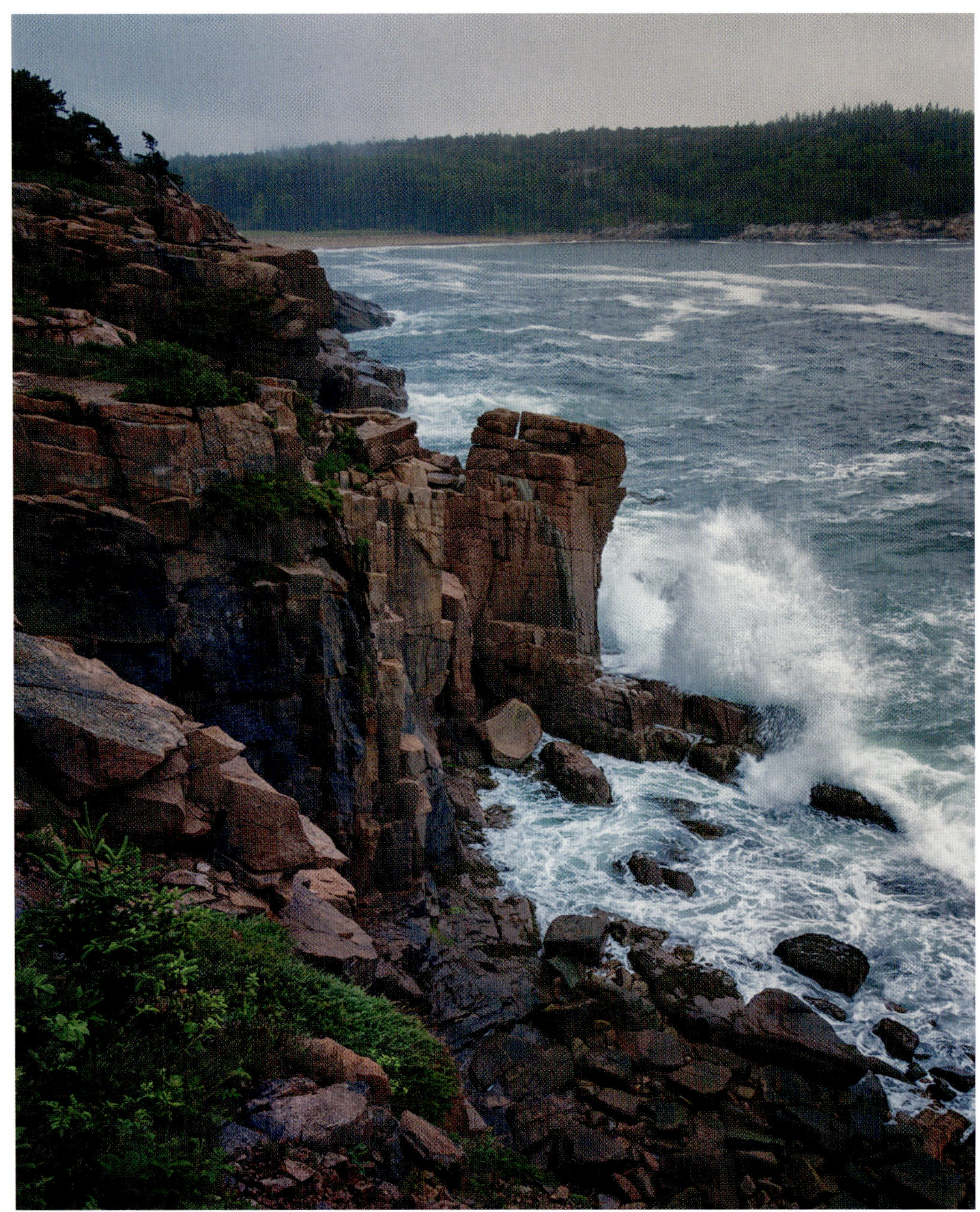

EARLY SUMMER STORM

•

A lone sea stack challenges the might of the sea in late-afternoon light.

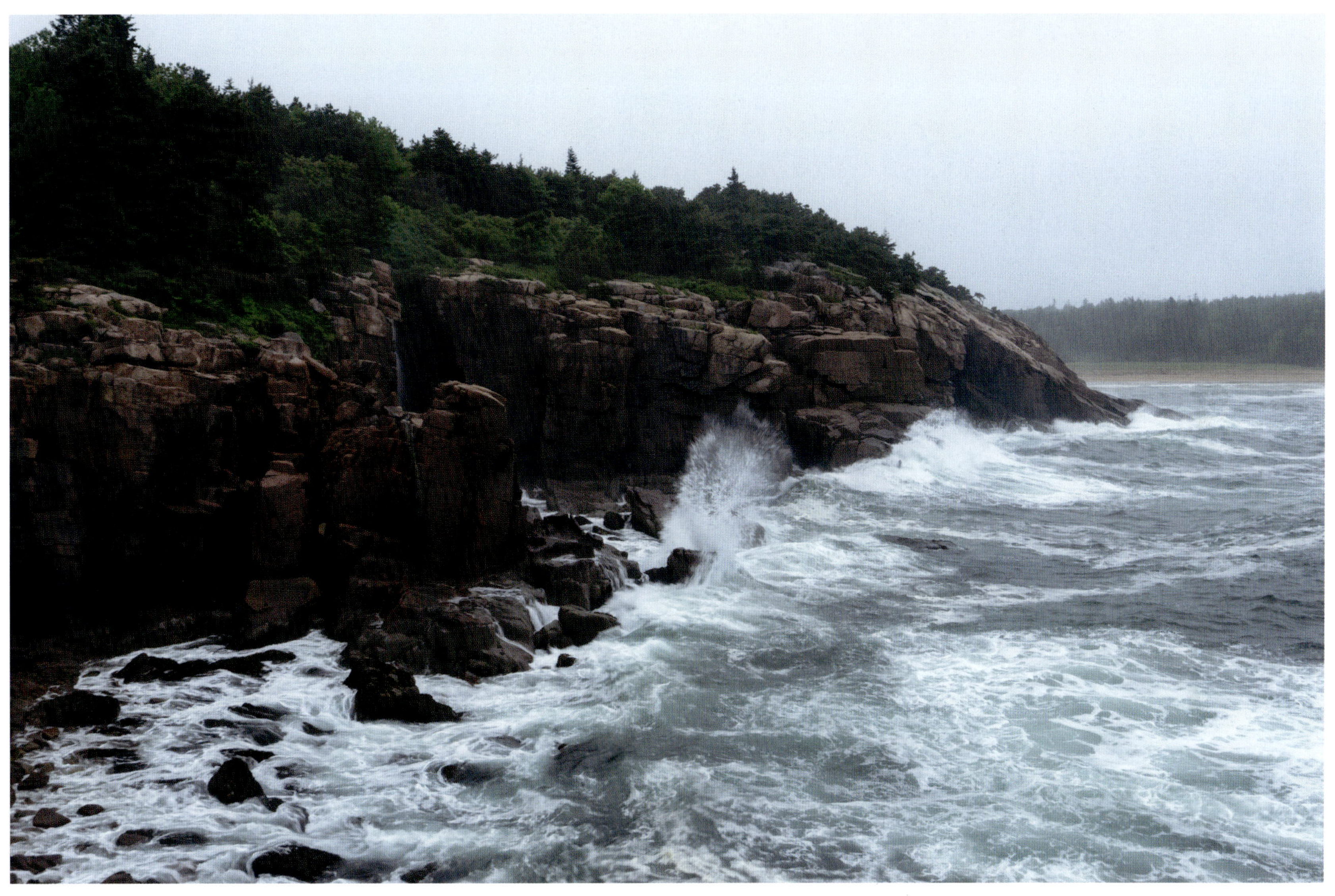

An hour later the contest continues as heavy clouds obscure the day's last light. Fog will soon creep in, closing down the coast.

RUSTED ROCK AND A RISING MOON

Otter Point, sunset, moonrise. On an early-summer evening about an hour before sunset, I stopped to photograph the light on this rock and the surf beyond. Although most of the scene is in shadow, the sun was high enough that it illuminated the distant rocks and the spray from the crashing waves. Most of the light was blocked by large boulders and trees to my right, and the light changed continuously as it filtered through and between them. The clouds were also changing rapidly. At one point an opening in the clouds revealed a rising moon. The Cranberry Islands are in the background on the horizon. I made almost sixty images from this position, trying to get the perfect wave; this is my favorite. Best of all, not a single jet contrail.

I wondered, as I sat and observed the scene before me, how it came to be that this one large boulder, infused with oxidized iron, was in this position, far removed from surrounding rock of similar composition. Most likely it broke off from the cliff face behind my position, not too long ago in geologic time, since its lines and edges were still quite well defined and had not been subjected to hundreds of years of pounding surf, or to storms strong enough to toss it about to grind and crash among the surrounding rock—thus softening its edges, chipping away, bit by bit. Or could there be some unseen, hidden fault line, a secret fracture, waiting for the right number of freeze-thaw cycles and external pressures to cause it to break apart into smaller pieces. It seemed to sit there defiant to all the forces of nature arrayed against it, but knowing that eventually it will still be there, long after current generations have passed on. But for now, it remains, and I am looking forward to visiting this location again.

RUSTED ROCK AND A RISING MOON

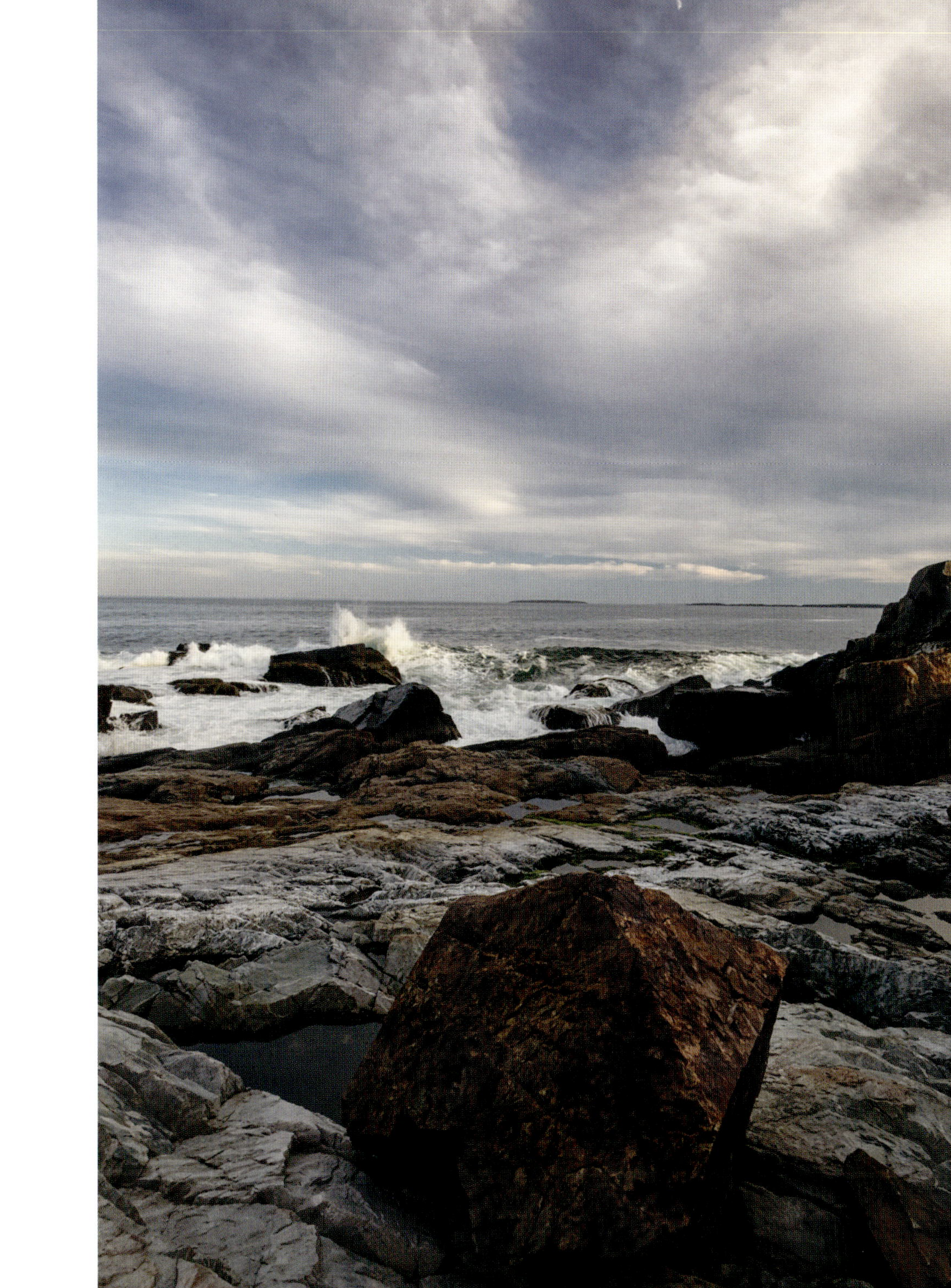

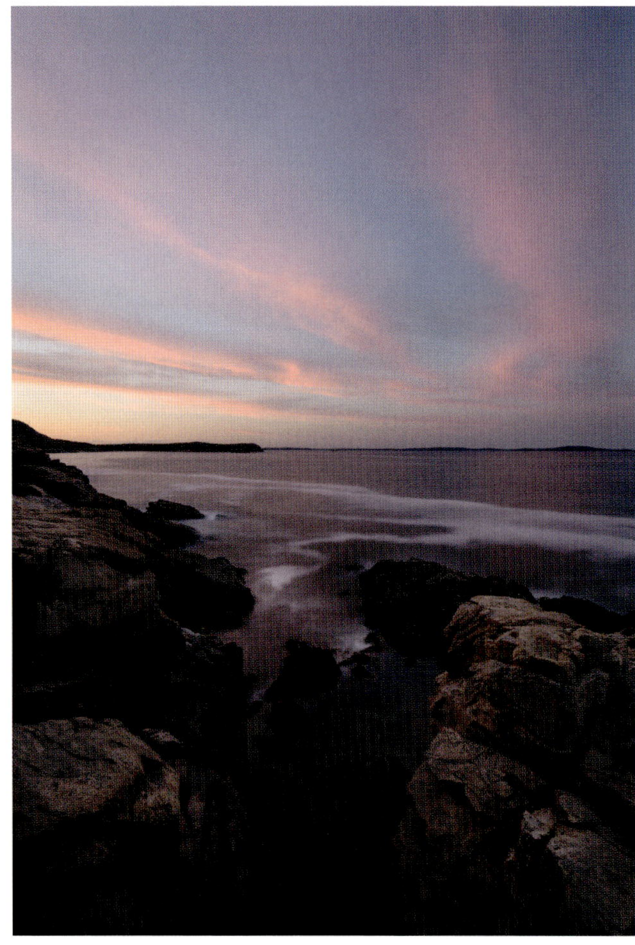

TIDAL POOL SUNSET

•

Between Otter Point and Otter Cliffs you can find several tide pools. This one reflects a cotton candy sky, with Great Head and Schoodic on the horizon. The day's heat was slowly released from the rocks, making this cool evening enjoyable.

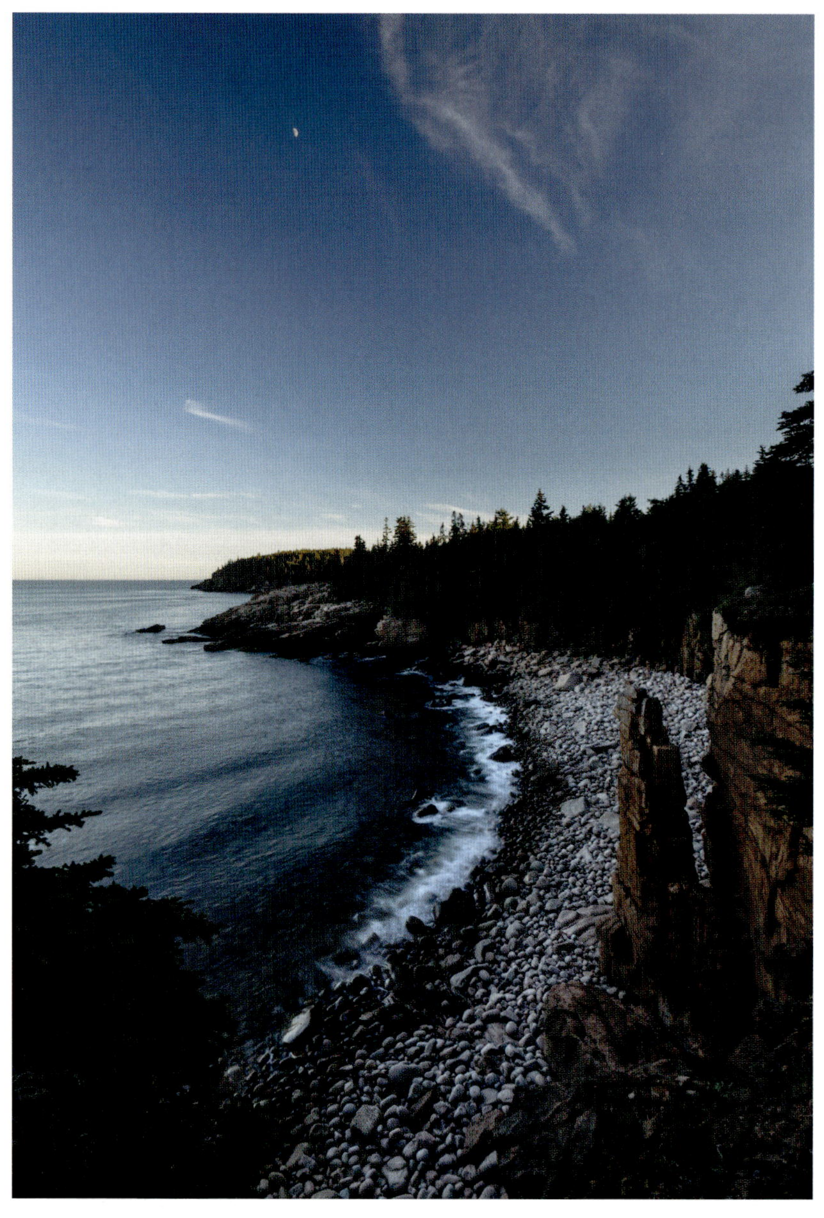

MONUMENT COVE AND HALF MOON, BLUE HOUR

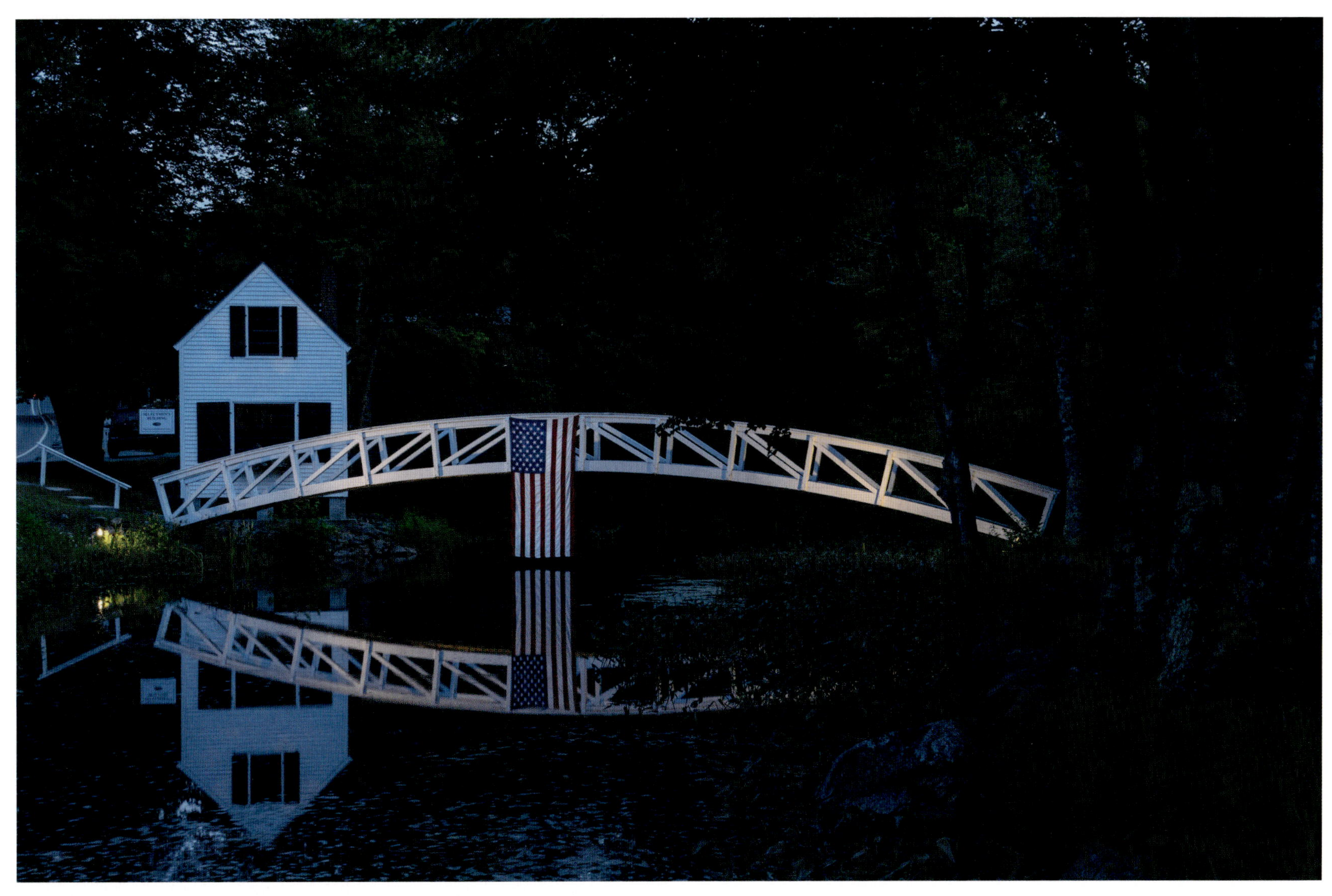

EARLY EVENING AT THE SELECTMEN'S BUILDING, FOURTH OF JULY, SOMESVILLE, MAINE

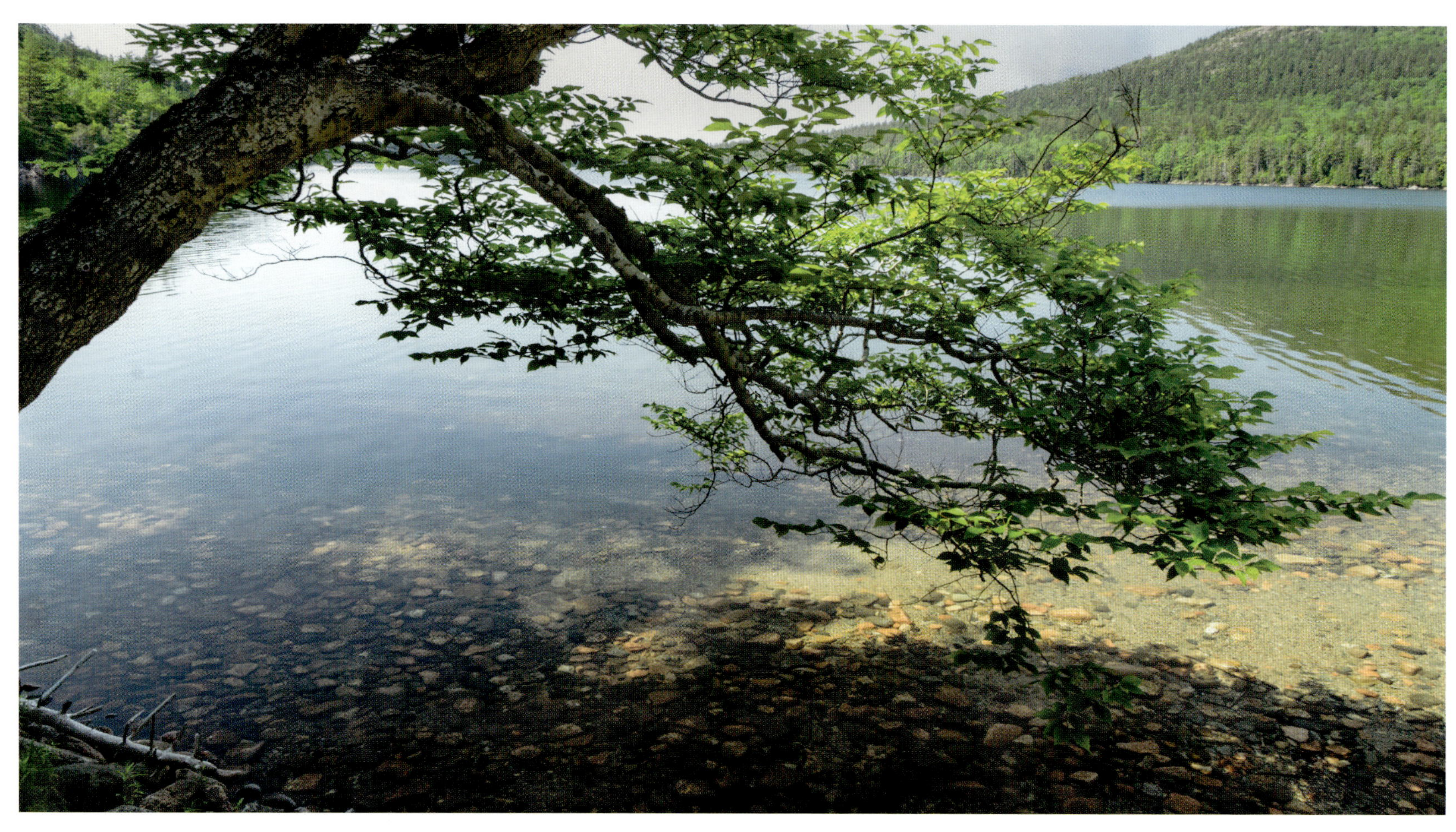

MORNING CALM, NORTH SHORE OF JORDAN POND

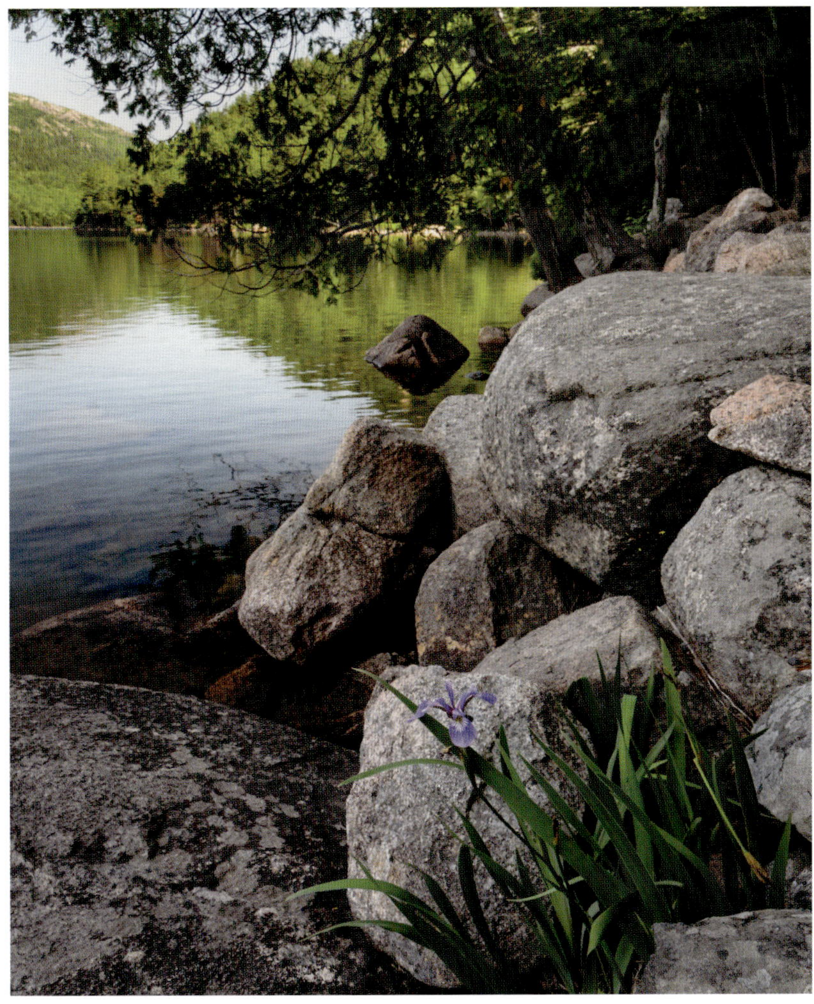

WILD IRIS, JORDAN POND LOOP TRAIL

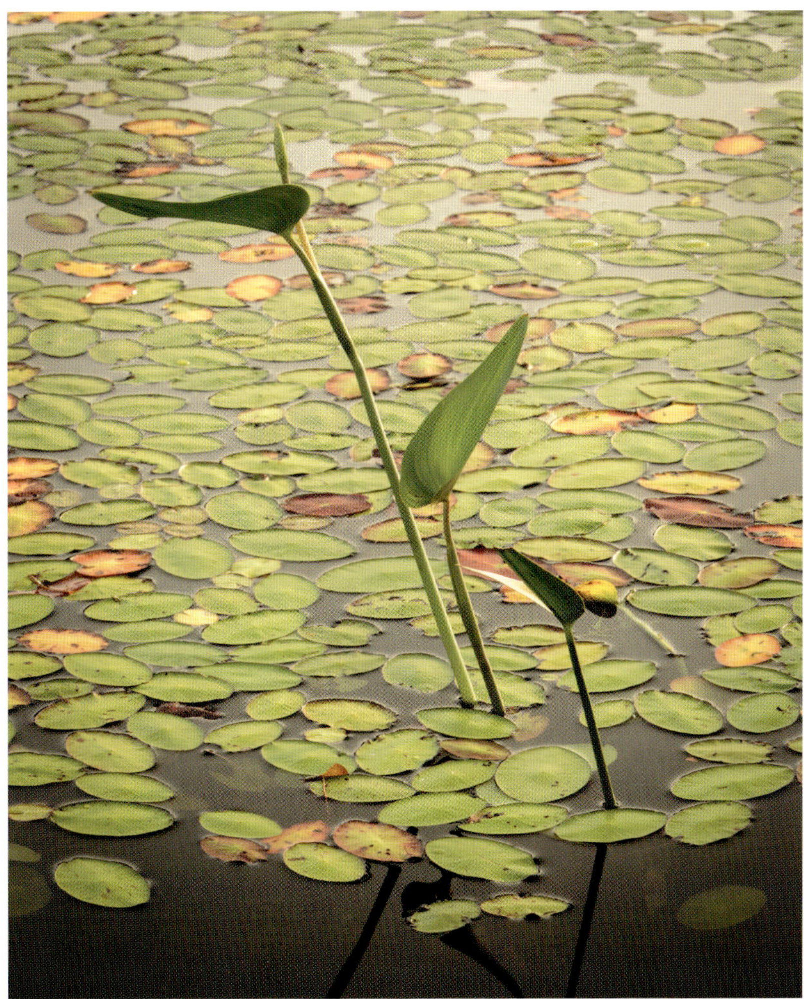

MILL POND AT SUNSET, SOMESVILLE

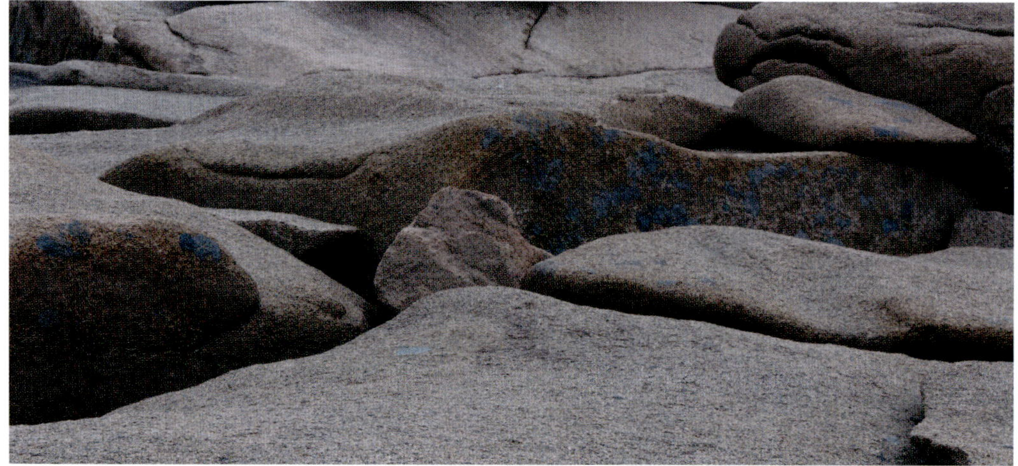

ABSTRACT IN GRANITE AND LICHEN ON A FOGGY EVENING, OCEAN DRIVE

•

These massive granite blocks remind me of the popular game called Jenga. It got me to wondering how many freeze-thaw cycles had occurred? What pressure and stress from rain, wind, heat, salt water, plants, and animals had worked on these granite faces? The granite was formed long before humans evolved, and will most likely remain when we are gone. That is the story portrayed on these hard surfaces. This image was made on a foggy evening, during the blue hour, the period of twilight in the morning or evening, when the sun is below the horizon and residual, indirect sunlight takes on a predominantly blue shade.

•

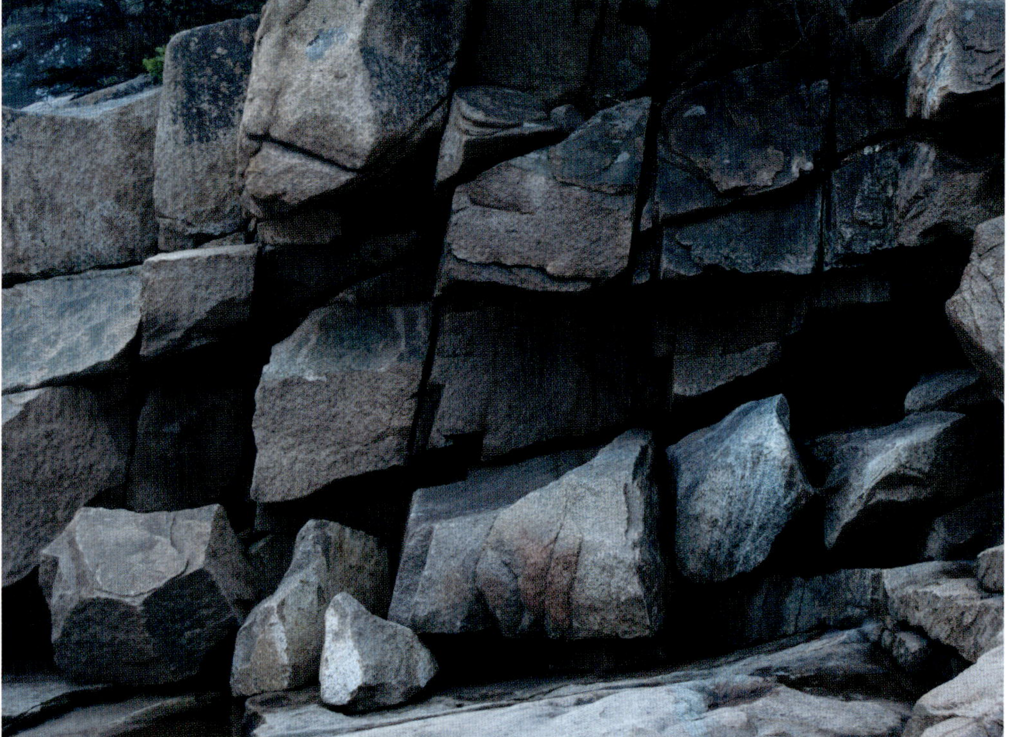

GRANITE BLOCKS AND FOG, EVENING

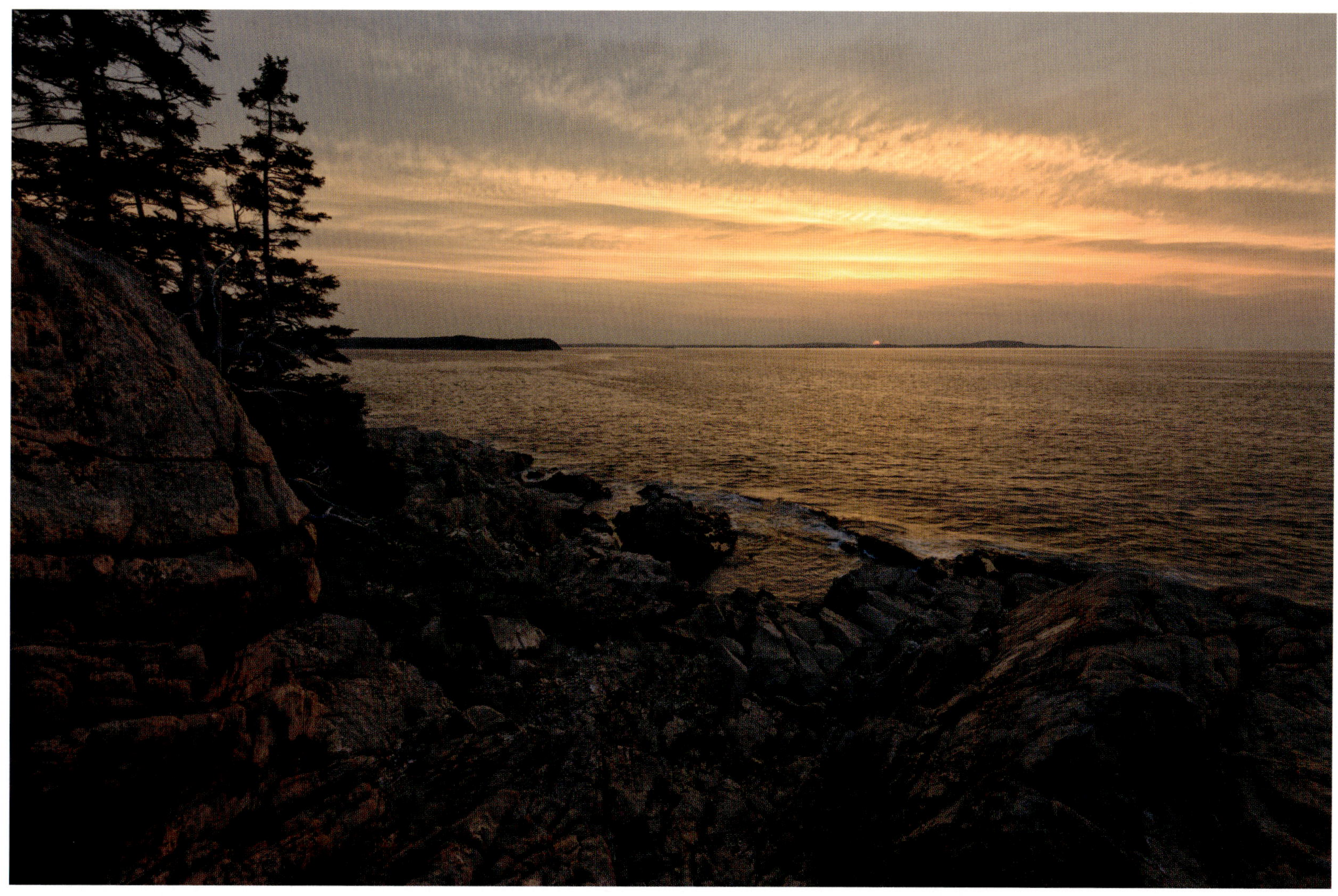

SUNRISE OVER SCHOODIC

•

A storm clears out as the sun rises over Schoodic Peninsula. On mornings like this it's not hard to comprehend how nineteenth-century artists such as Frederic Church found their inspiration.

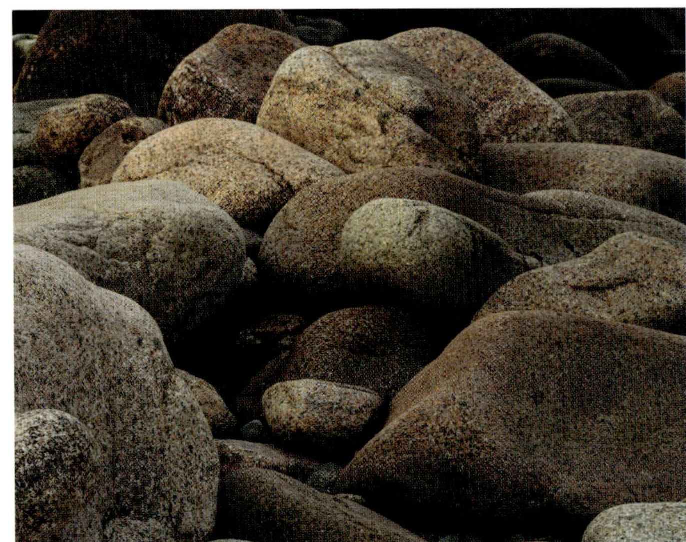

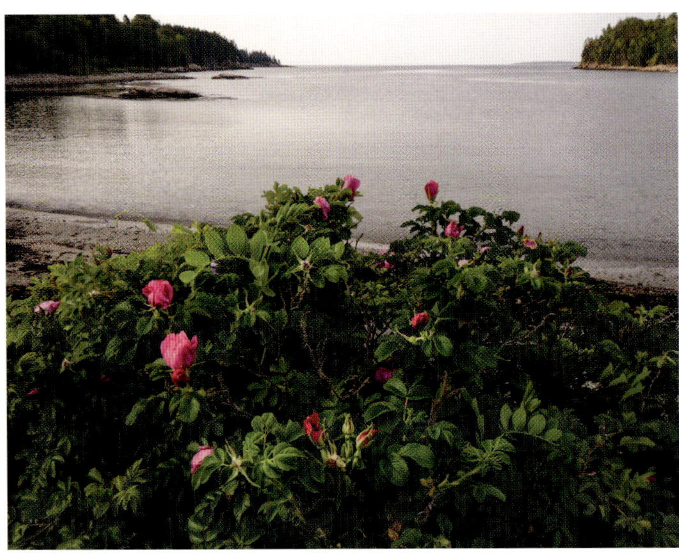

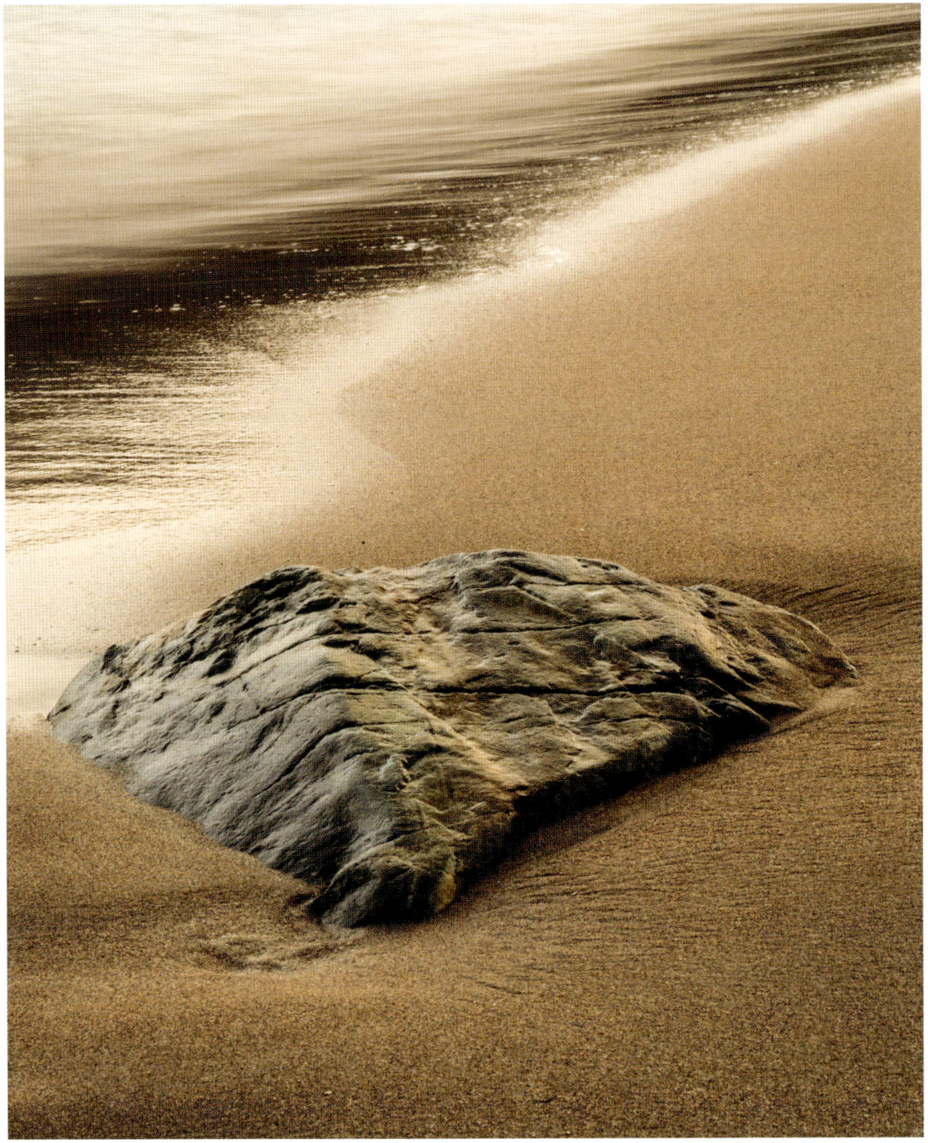

BOULDER PILE AT LOW TIDE, OTTER COVE

EARLY MORNING RUGOSA, OTTER COVE

SUNSET GOLD, SAND BEACH

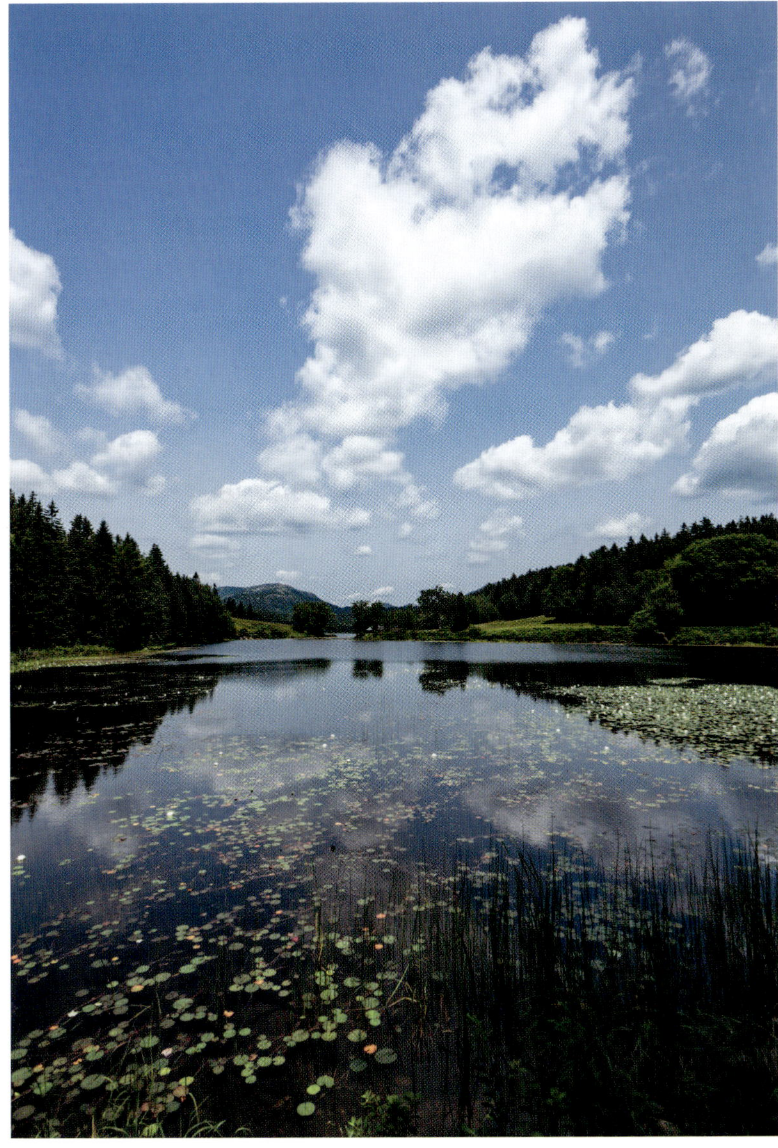

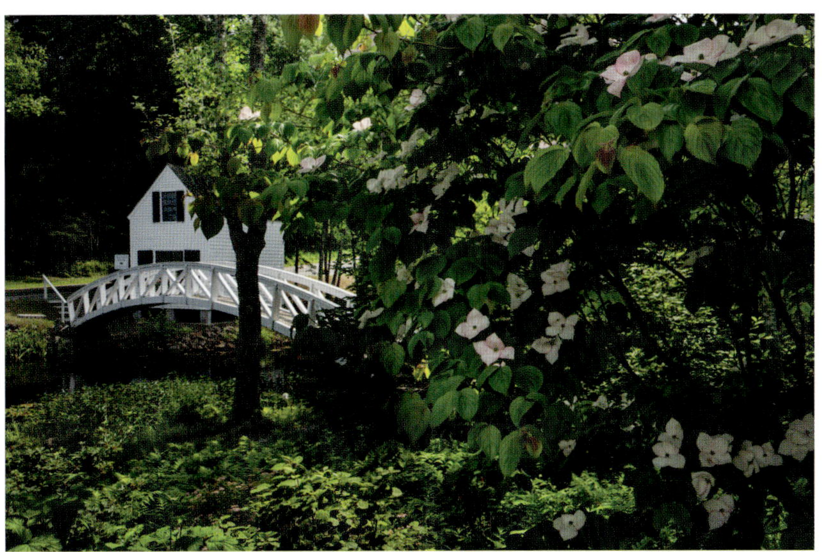

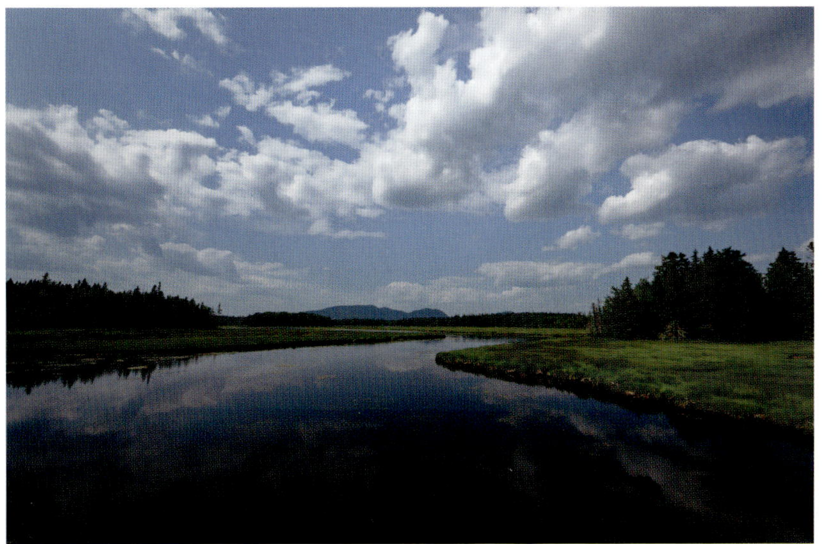

LITTLE LONG POND, JULY AFTERNOON

DOGWOOD, SELECTMEN'S BUILDING AND FOOTBRIDGE, SOMESVILLE

WESTERN MOUNTAIN FROM BASS HARBOR MARSH

SUNSET MOONRISE, BASS HARBOR LIGHT, 10 AUGUST 2014

I had been planning this image for at least five years, but having the supermoon as well was an added bonus. All the images I had seen or made of Bass Harbor Light are from the other side of the building, near the access stairs. But if you want the rising moon, then you need to traverse some very slippery, seaweed-covered rocks so you can look to the east. My initial thought was to capture the lighthouse at sunset, with the moon rising and the rocks glowing a pinkish orange. On a previous visit in the year before, I had noticed that the rocks seemed to "'glow" just as the sun dips below the horizon. However, on this day, clouds to the northwest blocked the sun from illuminating the rock surfaces below the lighthouse. Also at this time of year, the sun sets much farther to the north and wouldn't set in the right position to cause the glow to appear.

The news media was buzzing with stories about the "supermoon" in the first weeks of August. The moon would appear some 14 percent larger and 30 percent brighter than usual. This would be the second of three supermoons that occurred during the summer of 2014. This presents additional challenges, since trying to photograph to maintain detail both in the shadows in the rocks as well as the surface of the bright moon would exceed the limits of the camera's sensor. Because the moon is also in motion, long exposures greater than five seconds couldn't be used since the moon would appear as a white streak in the sky and lose detail. Finally, it was low tide when I arrived at 7 p.m., but by 7:20 the moon had begun to rise. As it rose, clearing the atmospheric haze just above the horizon, it was also moving to the right. I had to frequently shift my position to the right to keep the moon's reflection on the water, while at the same time keeping my eyes on the rising water covering the rocks to my right and limiting my movements. Fortunately, the ocean was calm and there were only slight but gentle waves. By 8 p.m. I had to abandon my position to make it back to the stairs safely. Negotiating those slippery rocks in the dark with a rising tide was not in my plans.

When I first arrived, there were many other photographers and tourists who were climbing over the rocks; however, since the sunset was not very colorful because of the clouds to the north, they soon departed. I knew that I had to get this shot right, and coming back on the next night wouldn't work because the moon would rise an hour after sunset. My next chance to make this image would be in September.

It had been quite a day, I had driven six hours to get to Bar Harbor from my home in Massachusetts, grabbed some supper, checked into my hotel, then drove across the island to Bass Harbor in time for the sunset. By 8:15, my gear was packed up and I headed back to Bar Harbor with what I was sure would be a great image.

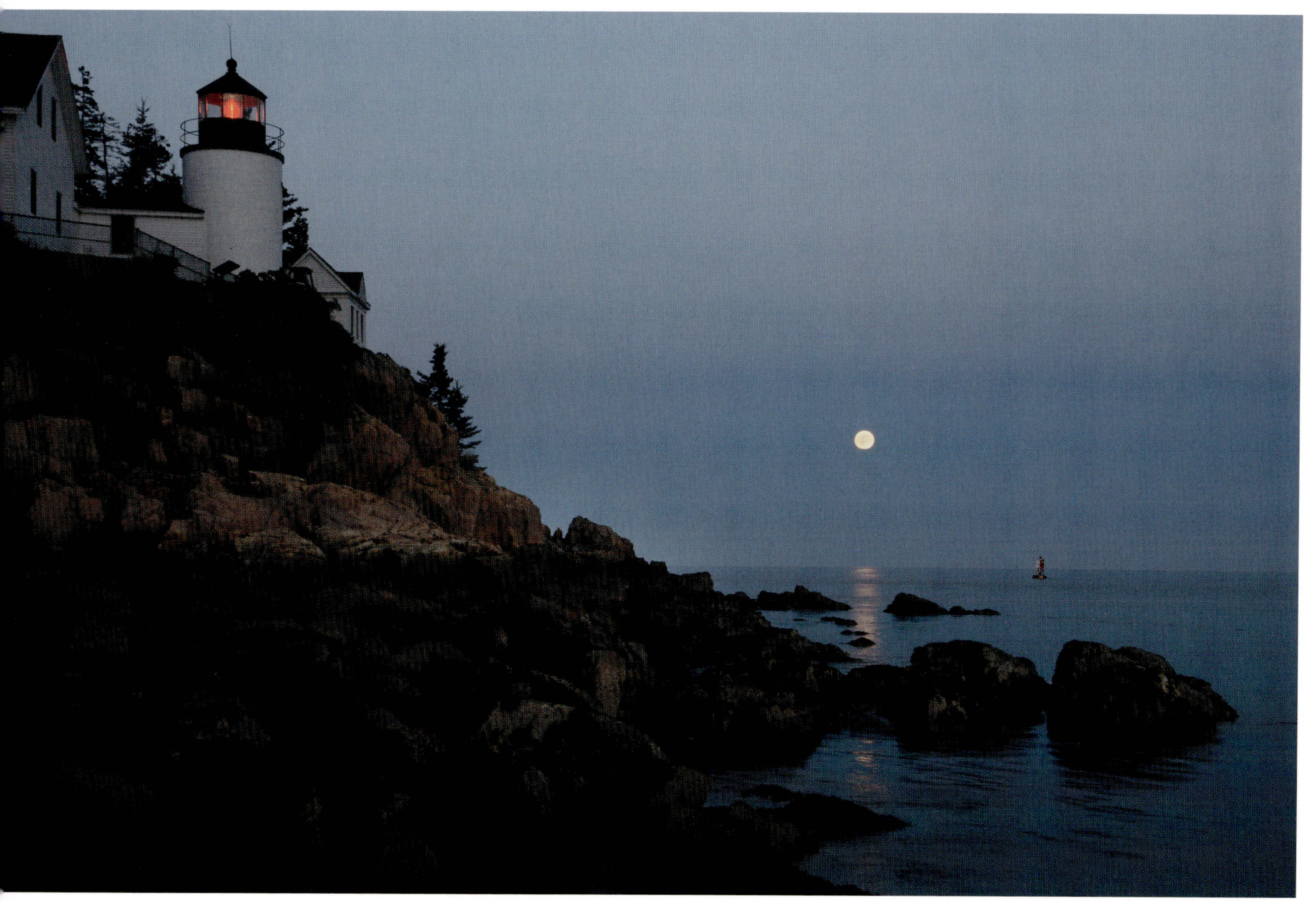

AUGUST MOONRISE, BASS HARBOR LIGHT

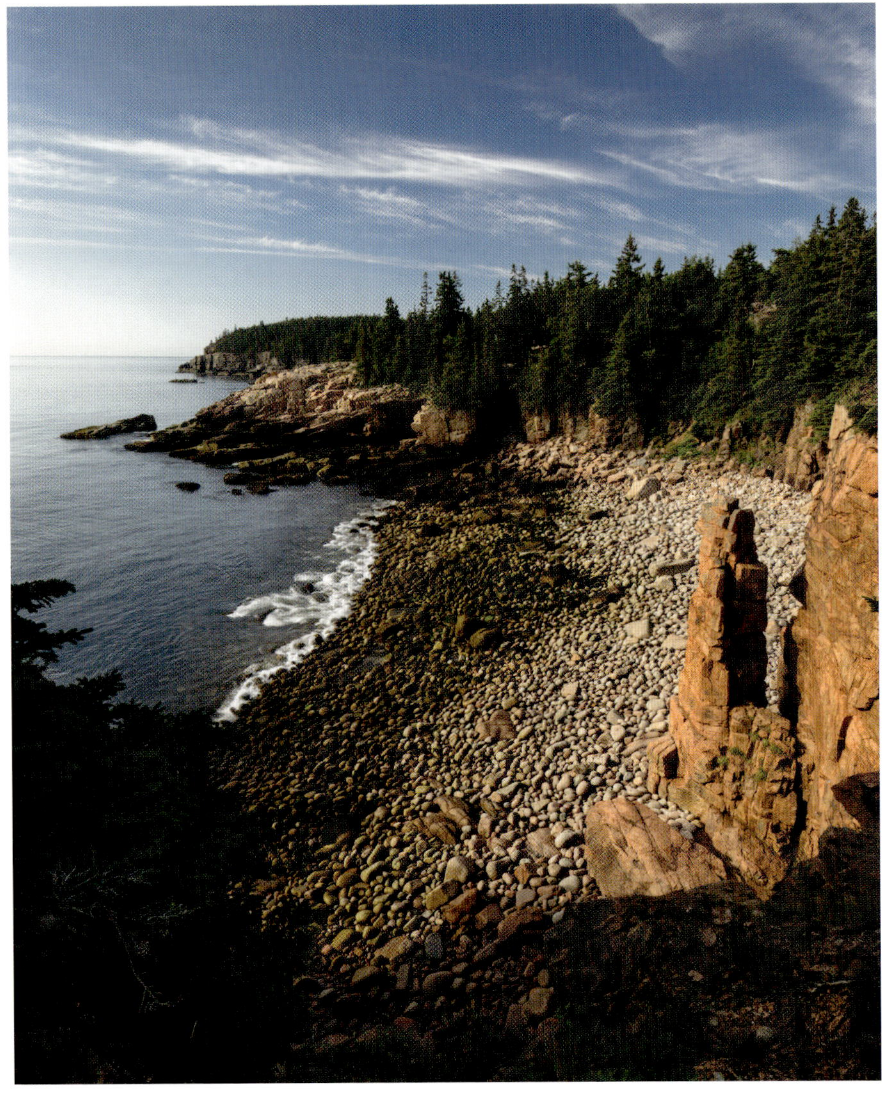

MONUMENT COVE, EARLY MORNING

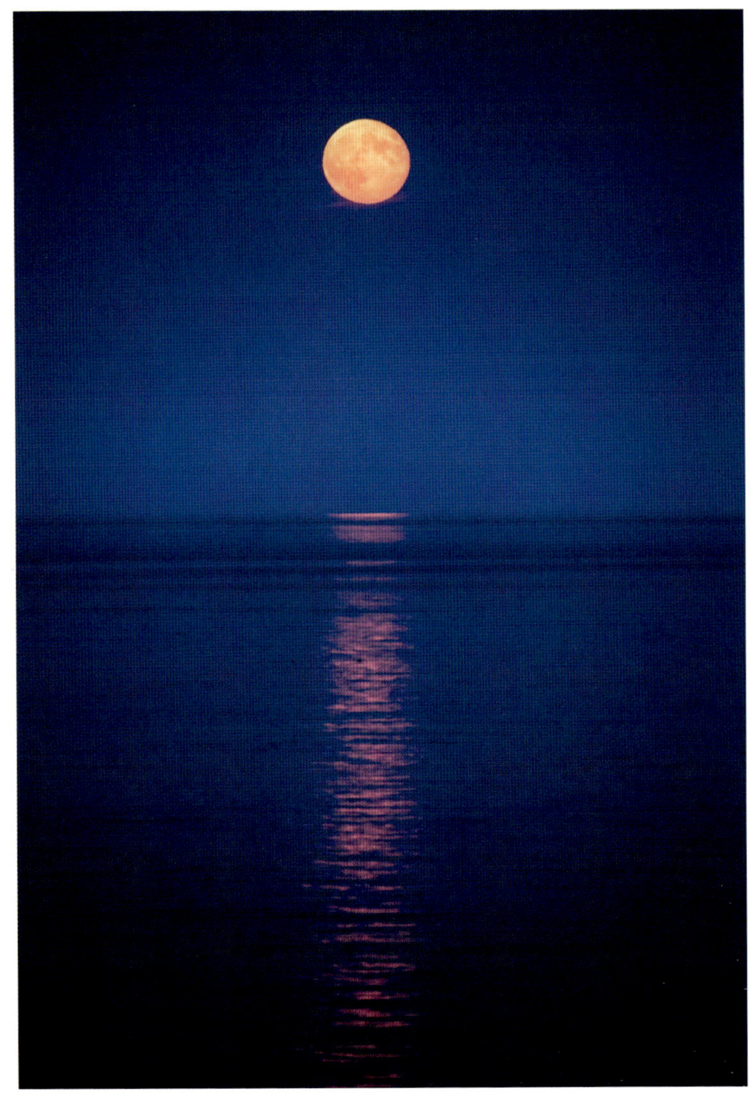

MOONRISE OVER THE GULF OF MAINE NEAR WESTERN POINT

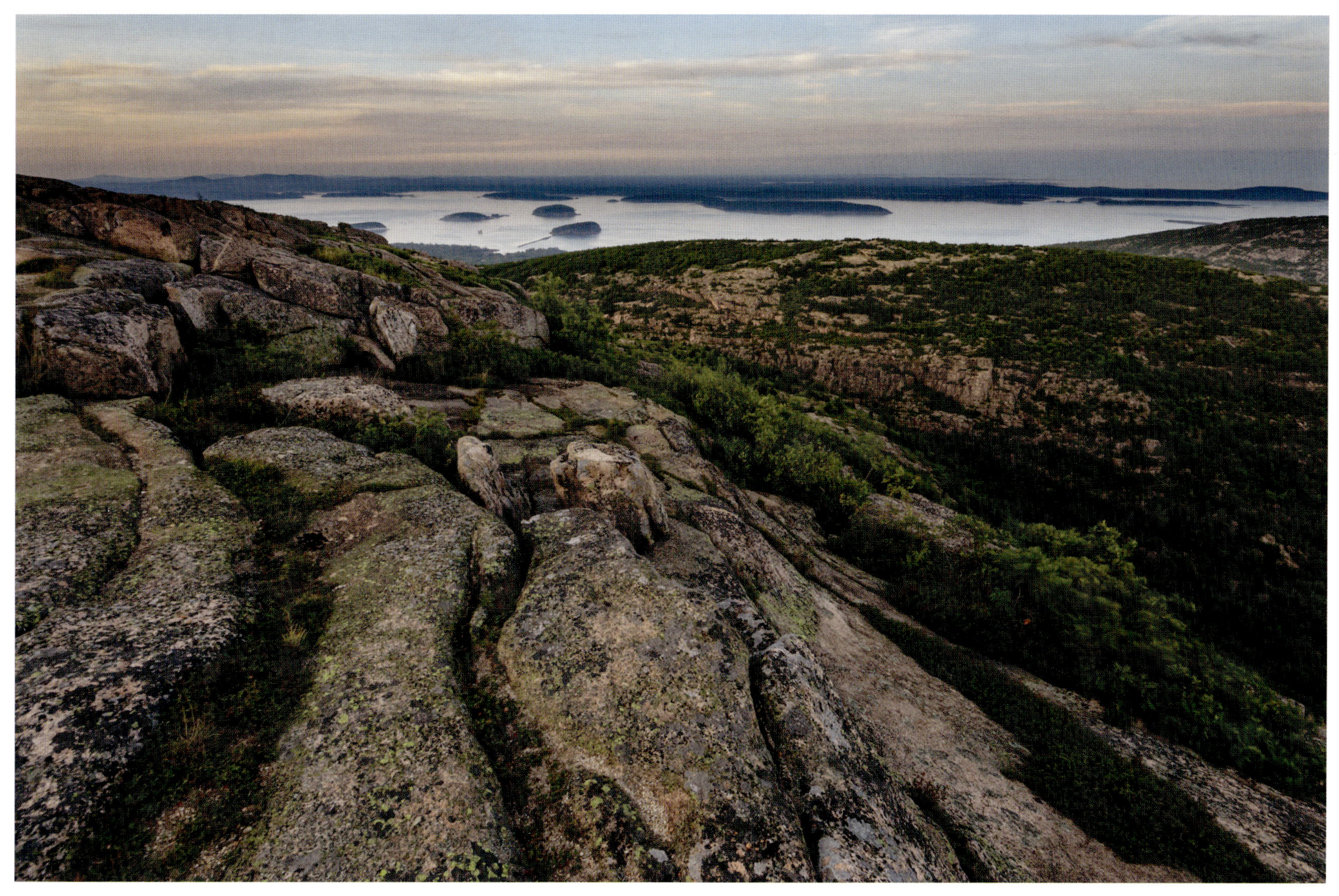

SUNSET FINALE, FRENCHMAN BAY

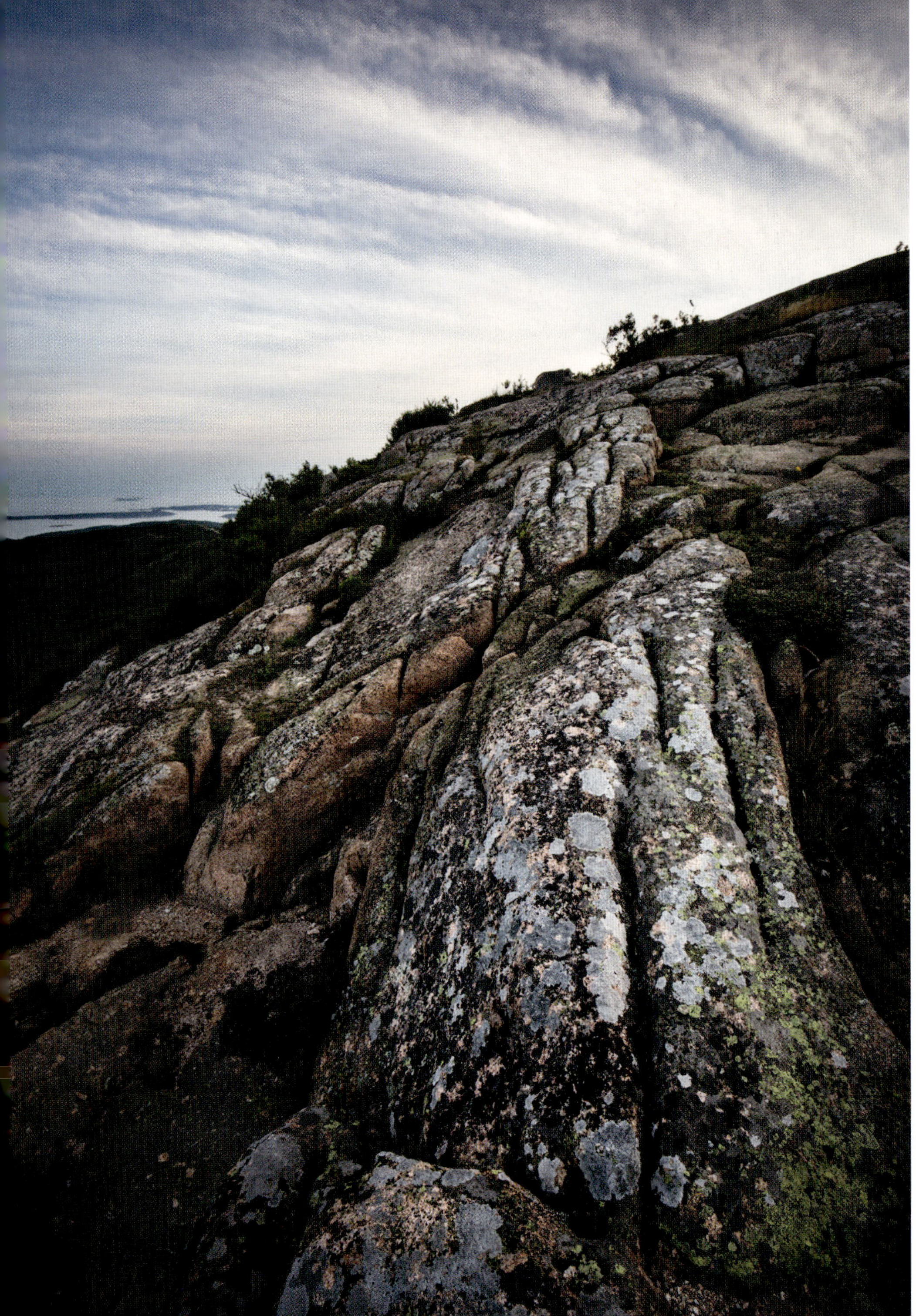

LICHEN AND GRANITE, CADILLAC MOUNTAIN, SUNSET

It had been a pretty clear day, and temperatures were in the low seventies, but clouds were starting to form as the sun began to get lower in the sky. I decided to drive up to the summit of Cadillac Mountain, and maybe I would be lucky enough to get a nice sunset. As many times as I have been on the mountain for sunset, a good image had thus far eluded me, for a variety of reasons. Either the clouds don't cooperate, there are too many people to find a place to park, or there are jet contrails from all the jets coming from or going to Europe. Acadia seems to sit below

CADILLAC MOUNTAIN, GRANITE, LICHEN, AND CLOUDS

the flight path of most airlines going between continents, and that seems to increase during the last hours of daylight.

On this particular night, I couldn't find a place to park at the Blue Hills overlook on the west side of the mountain, so I headed up to the summit to try to get an image of Frenchman Bay and the Porcupine Islands, hoping that there would be some nice light reflected in the sky.

After setting up my gear and composing the image, I sat down on the rocks to wait for the show to begin. I was quite comfortable, it was pretty quiet, and the granite was slowly giving up the heat it had absorbed throughout the day. There was some great color starting to develop in the sky, a little breeze was picking up, and the schooner *Margaret Todd*, with her red sails, was out in the bay. Frequently, the best sunset images are made when looking in the opposite direction from where the sun is setting. This was going to be one of those evenings where we get some magic in the sky, and everything was going to line up like it did two nights ago at Bass Harbor. This was going to be good!

Or so I thought. It was at this moment when every tourist in the parking lot seemed to descend on the rock outcropping that was the foreground of my composition. Many settled in with blankets and cushions and were there for the duration, completely oblivious to us serious (?) photographers. Silently cursing my luck, I packed up my gear and headed around to the south side of the summit to find a more intimate location.

There are a lot of views like this if one takes the time to look. This one is looking toward the southwest, with the Cranberry Islands in the distance. It's the combination of colors that attracted my eye at first, and then I noticed that the folds and crevices in the rocks were repeated by the lines of clouds. The granite is Acadia pink, but all the other colors are from various lichens that have grown on the granite over the years. It's what I've taken to calling "the random chaos of nature" that causes these compositions to form, just waiting for someone to come along and notice. I made only this one image and then moved on to look for other subjects, but by then the wind had picked up and the light was gone out of the sky. It has become one of my favorite images of my year on the island, and a large print of it hangs in my studio.

While preparing for an exhibit of my work in Acadia a few months later, I was struggling with another print for the exhibition that wouldn't cooperate. I saw this print out of the corner of my eye and suddenly wondered, "When did I buy an Eliot Porter poster of this image?," and then realized that no, it was a print I made. It was at that moment that I realized just how much of an impact the American nature photographer Porter has had on me, and how far I've progressed as a photographer and artist. I still didn't get that great sunset image, but I found something of myself that more than made up for it. And it's only taken forty years!

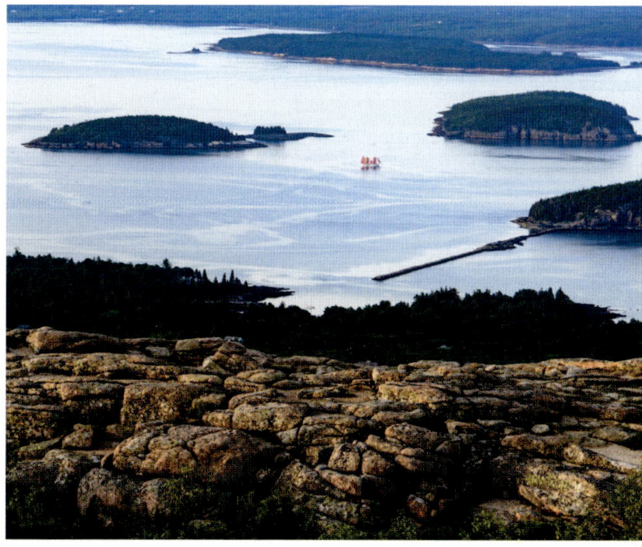

The *Margaret Todd* in Frenchman Bay from Cadillac Mountain

SEA STACKS, EARLY EVENING LIGHT

The Thunder Hole area is one of the more heavily visited areas of the park. However, if you go later in the day, and especially after 5 p.m., the crowds tend to thin out considerably as everyone heads into town for an evening meal. I arrived around 6 p.m.; however, the tide was going out and the ocean was very calm, resulting in very little dramatic wave action. I decided to explore an adjacent area about 50 yards north of the Thunder Hole viewing area. It is an area I had been aware of but not spent any time exploring when I visited the previous year. After working my way down to the rocks from Ocean Path, I scrambled out under a spruce tree and found a granite perch from which to work, about 30 feet above the boulders on the beach. The sea stacks are about 25–30 feet high. I set up the camera on the tripod, selected my 16–35 mm lens, and tried a few different compositions, both horizontal and vertical. I finally settled on the horizontal orientation, since I wanted to include Great Head, Old Soaker, and the Schoodic Peninsula as well as the rock faces on the left.

The sun was setting on the opposite side of the island, but it does shoot between a gap in the mountains so that Great Head receives light until just a few minutes before sunset. Light falling on the sea stacks in the cove was reflected from clouds passing overhead.

With all the artistic and technical decisions made, it was time to observe the wave patterns. Usually it takes about five to ten minutes to get a sense of the rhythm of the sea, and you can begin to anticipate how a particular wave might break or recede. But even this changes as the tide rises or falls, and the point at which a wave breaks can change. When I first arrived, waves were breaking over the lower seaward face of the nearest stack, but by the time I made this image the waves were barely lapping at it. And it is during this time that I began to contemplate the forces that shaped the land. How many millions of waves, tides, and freeze-thaw cycles have occurred to create these granite monuments? Why do these rocks remain while the rock that once surrounded them succumbed? What power must the ocean have to grind mountains into boulders and eventually sand? Another future Sand Beach in the making?

I stayed for about an hour and made several images as the light changed and the tide fell. This one, made about halfway through the session, had the combination of features I was looking for. Shortly after this, the tide receded too far and the clouds dispersed. Even if I had not come away with a good image, it was a perfect evening for sitting in silent contemplation. I packed up my gear and headed back to Thunder Hole to see what else might be waiting for me. I wasn't disappointed.

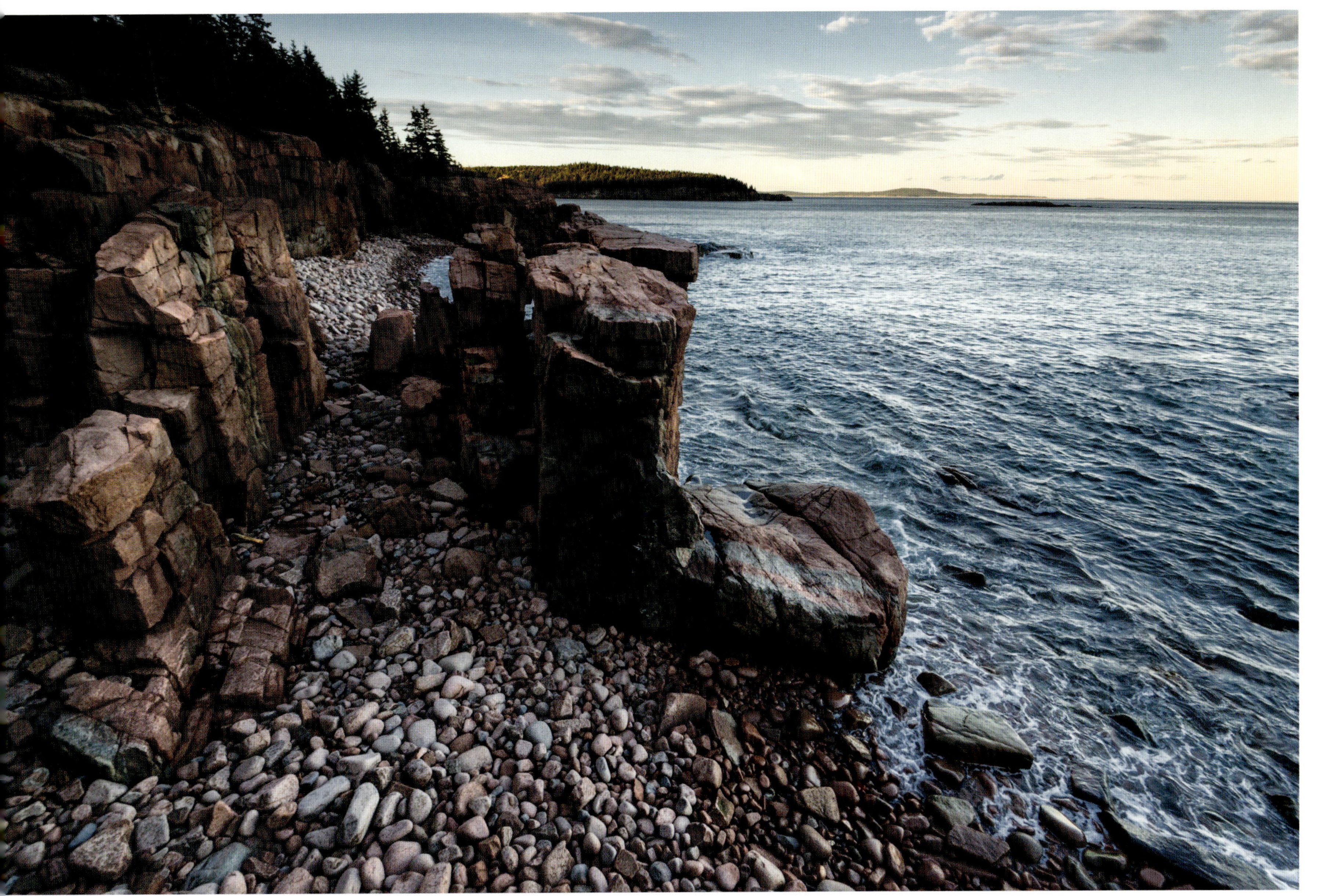

SEA STACKS, EARLY EVENING LIGHT

OTTER CLIFFS AND THE BELT OF VENUS

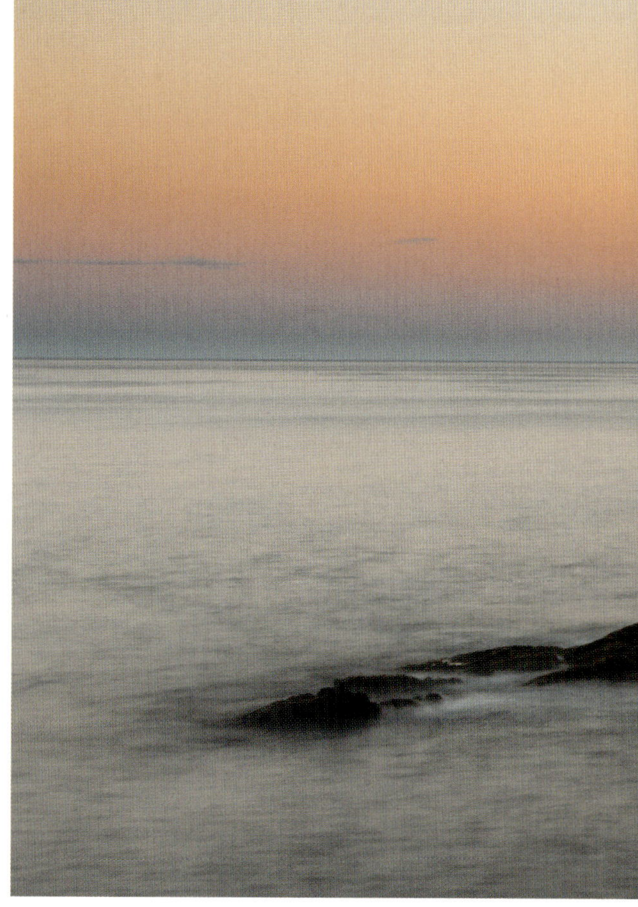

After the sun sets, an interesting phenomenon occurs in the sky in the opposite direction. Looking to the east, the sky takes on a pinkish-orange glow from light being reflected in the atmosphere. Immediately below this is a dark-blue band. The lighter pastel shade of orange-pink color is known as the Belt of Venus; the dark-blue band is the shadow of the earth on the atmosphere. The Belt of Venus is caused by backscattering of reflected light on fine dust particles high in the atmosphere. The color becomes most pronounced 180 degrees from the direction of sunset. It can also be seen in the west shortly before sunrise.

Otter Cliffs rise 40–60 feet above the ocean, and the headland rises to 110 feet. This view is from behind Thunder Hole and was made about forty minutes after the previous image. Probably about 300 feet separate these two spots, and the views are in opposite directions. This area can be reached from the Shore Path, just to the right of the steps leading down to the Thunder Hole viewing area. It's a great place to explore, since the rocks slope down

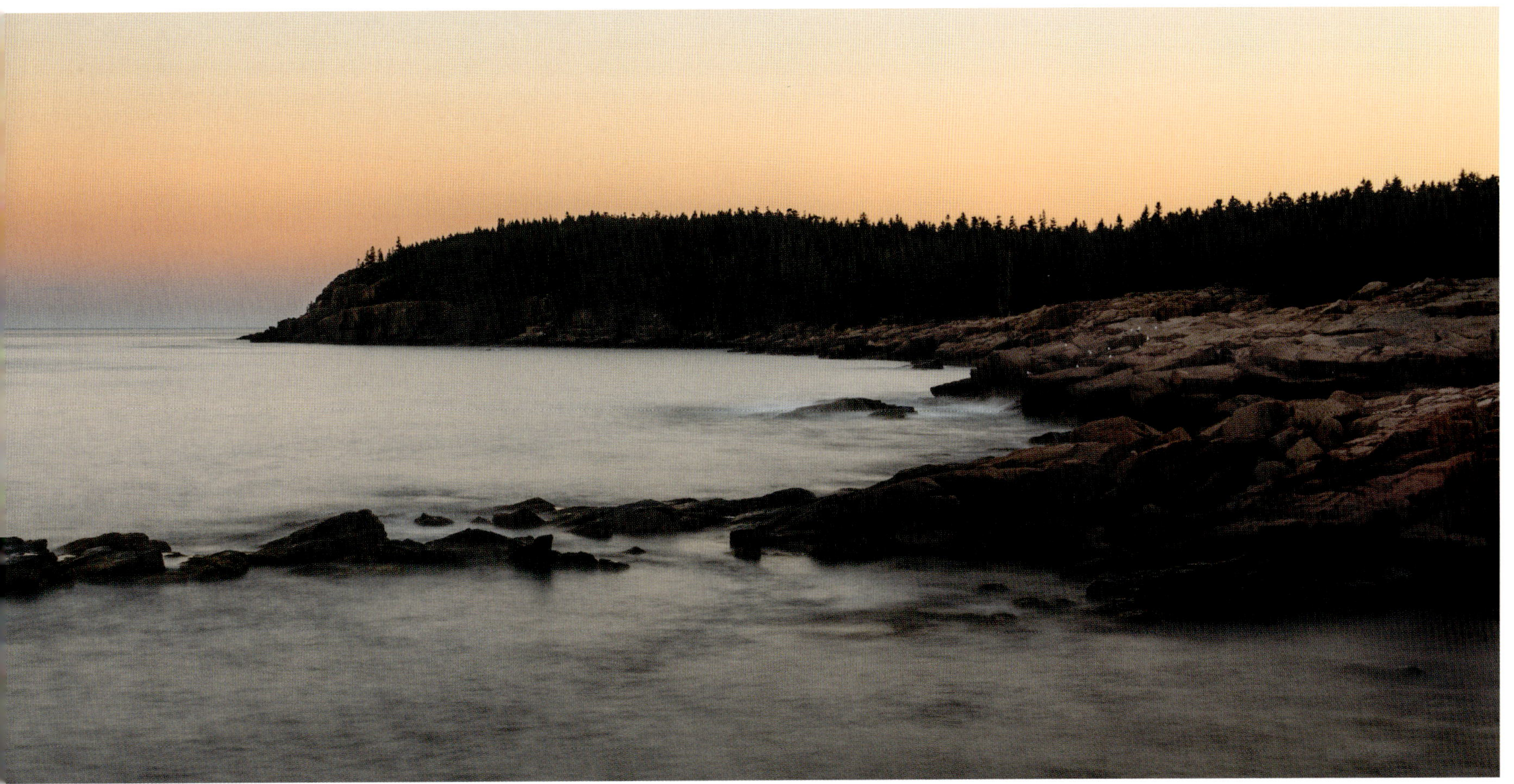

toward the ocean, with lots of fissures, textures, and color variations. I decided to go for a long exposure to obtain a smooth, ethereal look to the ocean. The seas were very calm, and there were no people moving about on the rocks in the middle ground.

By this time of the evening, almost all the visitors had left, and I found myself alone, except for the occasional gull. Only the gentle waves and the buoy bell off the shoals by Otter Cliffs broke the silence. Again, my thoughts turned to ponder the endless cycle of the waves meeting with the granite above, constantly reworking the land. I found a place to sit overlooking the ocean, contemplated what I had been given this evening, and made a few images with which to remember this quiet interlude of sea, sky, and granite.

OTTER CLIFFS AND THE BELT OF VENUS

THE LAST RUGOSA, OTTER COVE

Rugosa can be seen all over the island from May through September. It's pretty hardy considering the pounding they receive during the winter and constant exposure to salt air. The flowers are quite delicate and will tremble in the slightest hint of a breeze. It was mid-August when I came across this last remaining bloom at Otter Cove. Although there are rugosa bushes along the causeway that spans Otter Cove, this was the only remaining bloom to be found on either side of the road. Every other bloom was brown, gone to seed, or tattered by the wind. Most had turned to rose hips already. It was about 6:30 in the evening, and I was hoping for some nice color in the sky as sunset approached. I had been so intent on finding an intact flower that I didn't notice that it was also just about high tide, and the cove was creating a smooth reflecting surface. At low tide the muddy bottom of the cove is all that would be seen. In the background we can see Cadillac Mountain on the left, and Dorr Mountain on the right. This view is looking north, with the sun setting off to the left, as can be seen by the shaft of light painting the right-hand side of the cove. There was almost no wind to ruffle the rugosa bloom or disturb the surface of the cove, except for what was created by the occasional vehicle passing behind where the tripod was set up, since I was standing about 6 feet from the edge of the road.

Compositionally, I wanted the bloom to the left of center, but this would have put it in front of the dark reflections on the left side of the cove, where it wouldn't show up as well, plus I would lose the rose hips on the left, which would enhance the impression that this was the last remaining rugosa bloom of summer. Placing the bloom on the right side preserves this feeling, plus the pink contrasts well with the reflection of the blue sky. The camera was placed low, about 3 feet above the ground, to obscure the mud, rocks, and seaweed on the shore, and again to keep the bloom from intersecting with the reflection of the mountains. I also knew it wouldn't be long before the sky would be filled with contrails from jets heading to and from Europe. I made about fifteen exposures as the clouds moved across the sky, before the wind picked up and about a hundred gulls landed on the cove, breaking the reflections, and the mood.

Otter Cove is one of my favorite places to photograph, with a wide variety of subjects. The constantly changing tide and the foliage on the mountains and surrounding the cove make great subjects. On the opposite side of the causeway, the cove opens out to the ocean, with views of Otter Point on the left, Western Point on the right. Wander the shore at low tide and there are shells, rocks, seaweed, seals, otters, birds, rock formations, and several species of wild flowers.

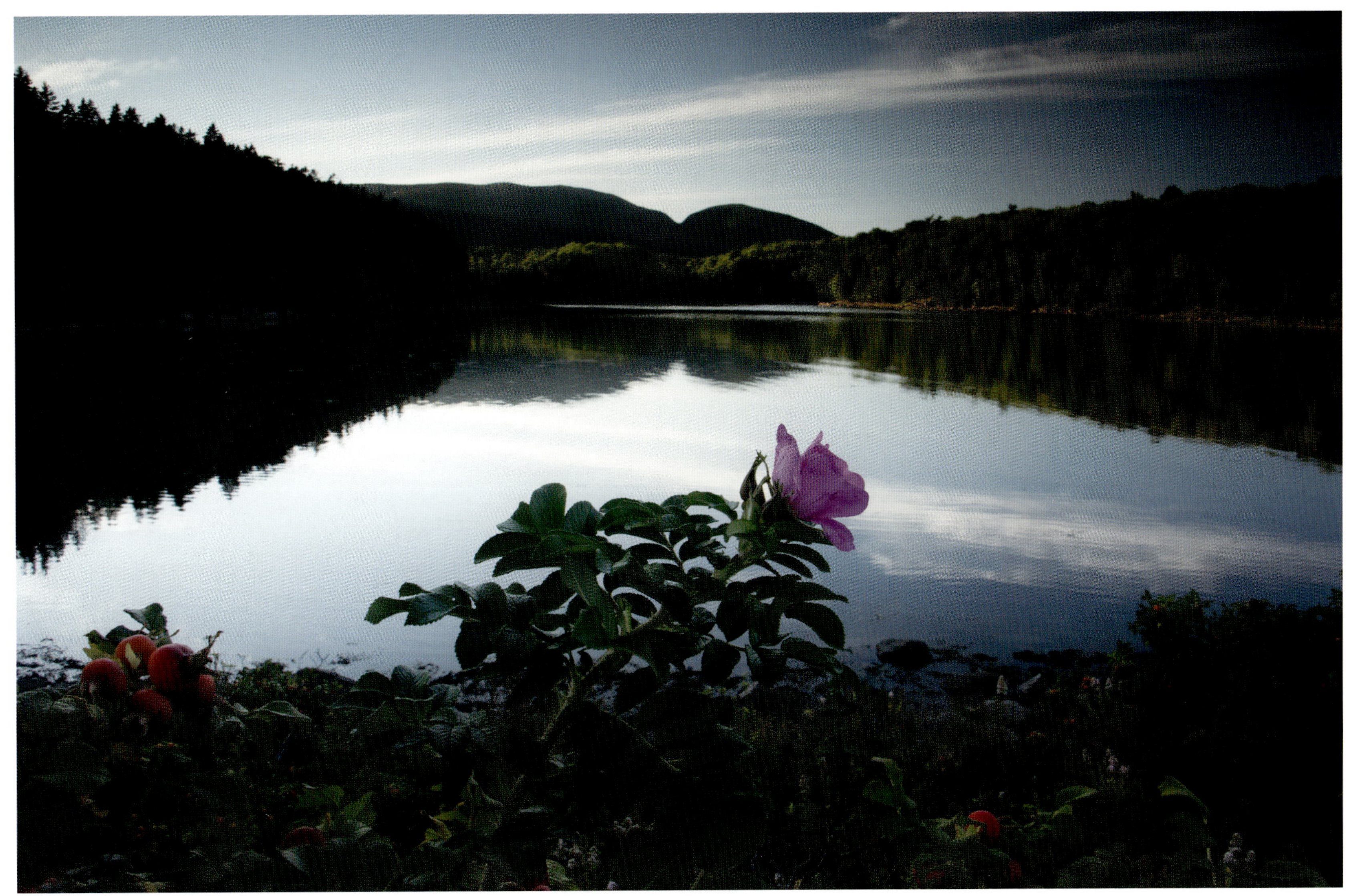

THE LAST RUGOSA

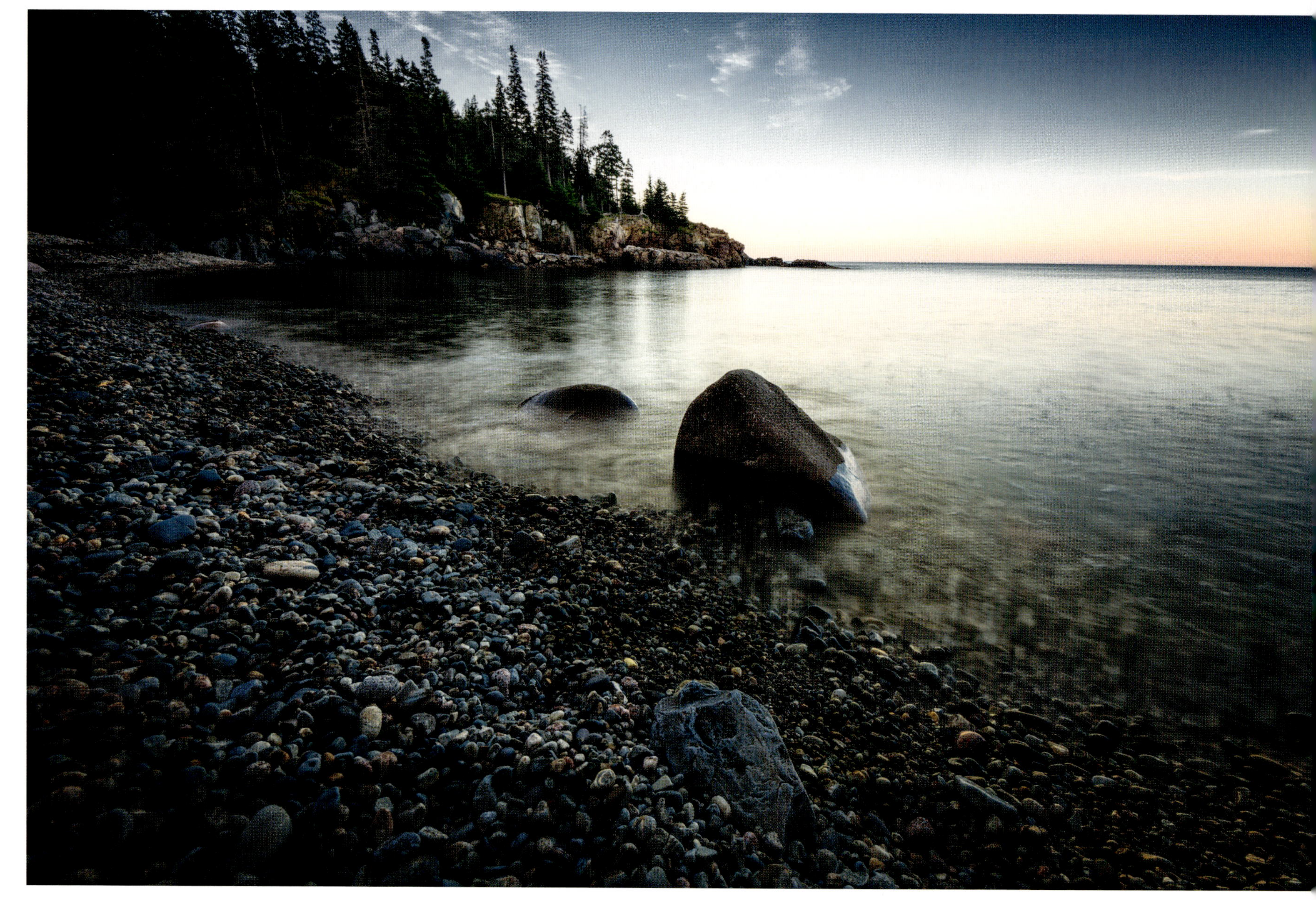

TWILIGHT, LITTLE HUNTERS BEACH

TWILIGHT, LITTLE HUNTERS BEACH

It's easy to drive right past Little Hunters Beach. There are no signs, and you can't see the beach from the road. It's about 2 miles beyond the bridge at Otter Cove—look for a bridge and a few parking spots on the right-hand side. A wooden stairway on the left will take you down to the beach, where the stream disappears into the rocks. There is also a trail to the left of the stairs that leads out to the rocks. It is rarely busy here, even in the middle of tourist season. A good place to escape to when Thunder Hole and Otter Cliffs become too crowded.

Little Hunters Beach is essentially a large, deep rock pile, with only air occupying the spaces between the stones and cobbles. As you walk across the beach, the stones will shift slightly and unexpectedly. The sound of the rocks grinding against one another can be quite pleasant, especially close to the water's edge. Drop a rock and you'll get a rather hollow "thunk" in response. Sit on the rocks, wiggle around to get a comfortable seat, and relax. Listen to the waves as they move the rocks and cobbles about. Breathe in the salt-tinged air as it mixes with the aroma of the spruce and pines that surround the beach.

The beach faces to the southeast, so it doesn't receive direct light at sunrise, even during the winter. One would have to be on the extreme right side to observe it. Also, the Park Loop Road is closed between November and April, so the only way to reach this area is by foot, snowshoe, cross-country skis, or snow mobile. Sunsets occur on the other side of the island, but this is a nice place to go to see the afterglow, the Belt of Venus, and stars, especially the Milky Way and Andromeda galaxies during the summer. There is almost no light pollution as you are looking directly out to sea, and the rock faces on the right side of the beach block what little light comes from the few houses on the Cranberry Islands.

On this particular evening the ocean was calm, with almost no wind. I arrived just a few minutes before sunset, wandered around to find a pleasing composition near the water's edge, and made myself comfortable on the rocks to wait and see what would transpire. I liked the juxtaposition of the large boulders and the smaller stones and cobbles. The stones also had a great variety in color and texture that I liked. Finally, the backscatter sunset light in the sky, reflecting in the water, made the entire scene very transcendent. Once again, I had the entire area to myself for several hours, as I stayed to watch the stars make their nightly trek across the sky.

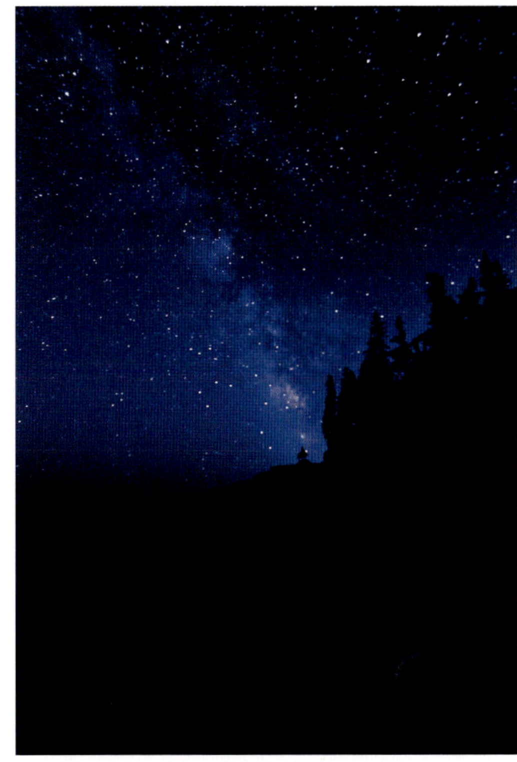

MILKY WAY FROM LITTLE HUNTERS BEACH

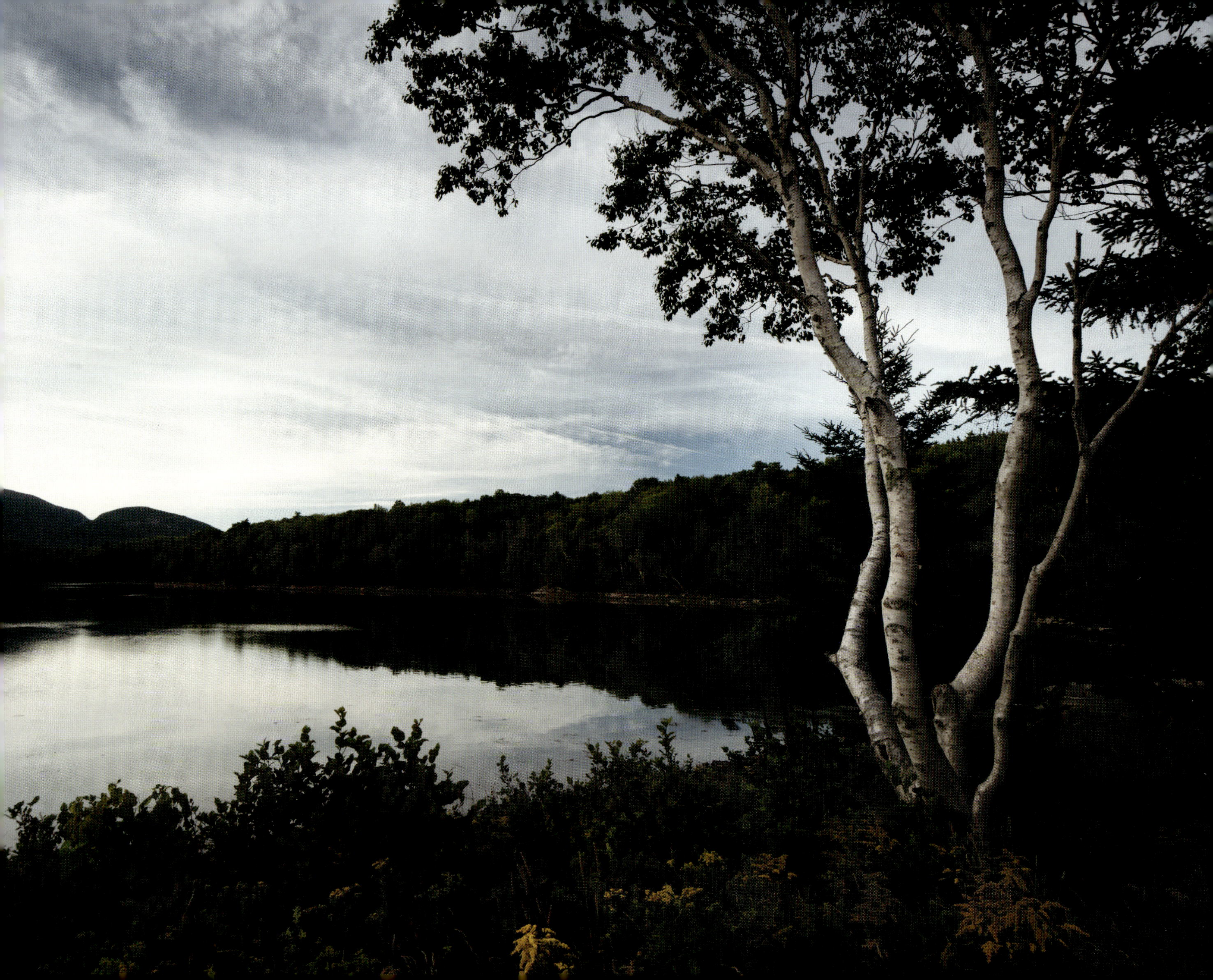

BIRCH QUARTET, OTTER COVE

Along the causeway that crosses Otter Cove, there are several birch trees, and I am particularly drawn to this grouping. They have a rather sinuous, twisted form, and it takes a bit of moving about to line up the trunks in a way that minimizes them from overlapping each other. I have tried several different angles, but I find this one most pleasing to me. They are right along the side of the road; I had to set up my tripod in the right-hand lane to make this image. Since parking is allowed in the right-hand lane in this area, it's not as if I was creating a traffic hazard. Simply stop and park about 10 feet before you get to these beauties, set up your gear, and make your images. At this time of the evening, most people are in town eating, or heading up to Cadillac for sunset. There are only a few folks around and most don't stay very long.

It was high tide. I was anticipating some color on the clouds over Cadillac and Dorr, and I liked the way the light was softened by the clouds. Goldenrod in the foreground provides a contrast to all the green. After making this exposure, I started chatting with a woman from Otter Creek Village, a small community hidden behind the trees at the far end of the cove, who was out for an evening stroll. She had lived here her entire life, over eighty years, and she never grew tired of island life. I asked her what season she liked best. "Winter," she replied, "It's beautiful and still in the

BIRCH QUARTET AND GOLDENROD, OTTER COVE

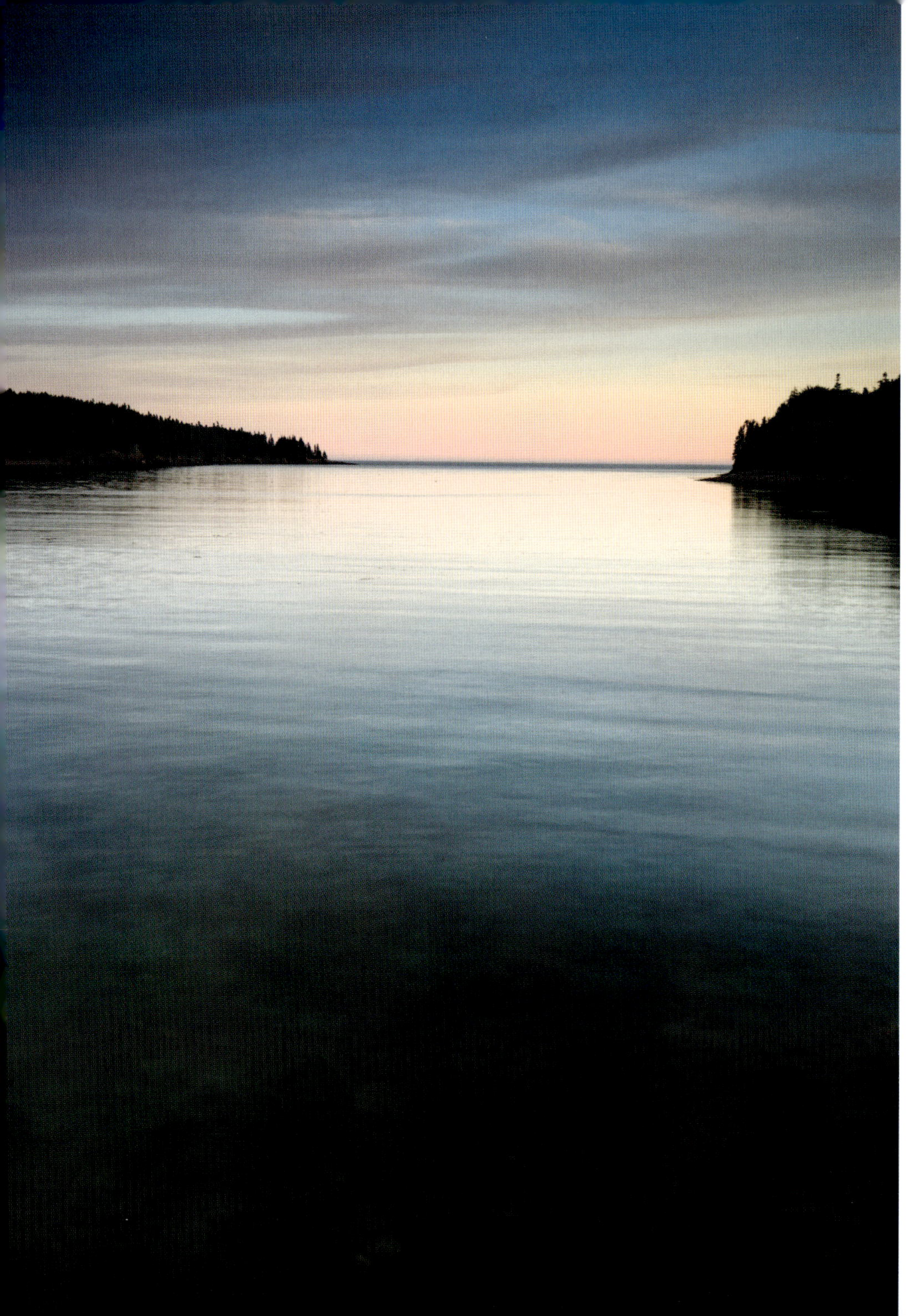

The Belt of Venus reflects on the quiet surface of Otter Cove at high tide, just after sunset.

winter. You have to return in the winter." And she headed off, wandering toward the woods on the right, wanting to get home before it got too dark.

All the while during our conversation I was keeping an eye on the sky, which grew darker but never picked up any color. Instead, what I at first thought was fog started forming about the cove, but it soon became evident that it wasn't fog, but wood smoke from campfires at the nearby Blackwoods Campground. Within ten minutes, the smoke was so thick that the view was obscured, and this was the only image I made that evening, but I didn't mind, I had shared a few moments with a kindred soul, and I fondly look back on that evening every time I see this image. And yes, I did find the winter to be still and beautiful.

It was my intention to photograph this tree in all four seasons, and in the course of putting together this book, I discovered that I did not have a winter image. This part of the Park Loop Road is closed in winter, so to get here one must park in the Fabbri picnic area and walk a half mile on a snow-covered road to get to the causeway. In the late winter of 2017, I had an opportunity to drive up to Acadia and make the winter image. After driving all night to arrive just before sunrise, I hiked out to the causeway and found that the smallest of the four trunks, the dead one, had succumbed to the heavy snowfall from the previous day and broken off. I still made the image, and now quartet is a "treeo" (pun intended).

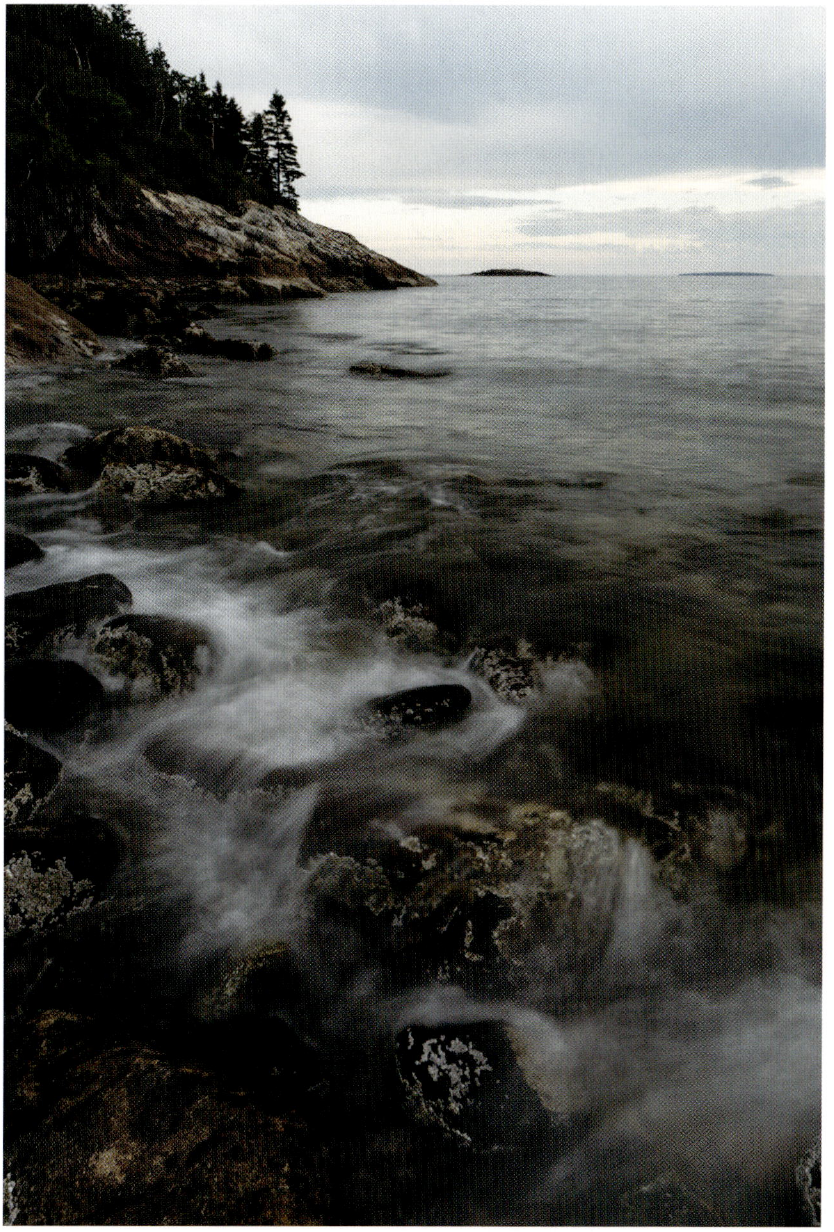

SAND BEACH, BOULDERS AND COBBLES, HIGH TIDE

A QUARTER PAST SUNSET

The sea appears flat tonight, with small swells, tiny wavelets, and minimal surf action. It's a few minutes after sunset; the light has gone from Schoodic and Great Head, and only the high clouds beyond the island's shadow have any illumination. Farther from shore, a darkness descends on the distant sea and slowly moves toward the land. It will not last much longer. A few gulls swoop by, looking for what the sea has to offer. The tide is rising, slowly replenishing nearby tide pools. There is a subtle beauty here, for those who take the time to observe. Slow down, take in the light, and inhale the salt air; the surging and receding waves will provide the soundtrack. My breathing has slowed, matching the rhythm of the waves.

Now, just there! Look again, see the tide pool over there, see that the clouds overhead are mirrored in the surface as the pool drains, before the next wave rushes forward to refill it. The wavelets, ever moving, ever changing, reflect the hue and luminance from above, and then before we can fix our eyes upon it, the sea changes the angles, returns to the ocean colors, and comes back again, never showing itself in quite the same way. A submerged ledge smooths and momentarily flattens the water, a pastel rose and turquoise appears briefly, and in an instant, it is no more. As soon as we comprehend what we have just witnessed, it is no more. Opalescent, the sea mimics the sky's colors and for a few moments we are mesmerized. All our concentration is focused on catching that all-too-brief moment of wonder, of fascination—each special, each unique. All the cares of the day wash out on the tide, and our minds become still; the pulse slows. Can a day end any better?

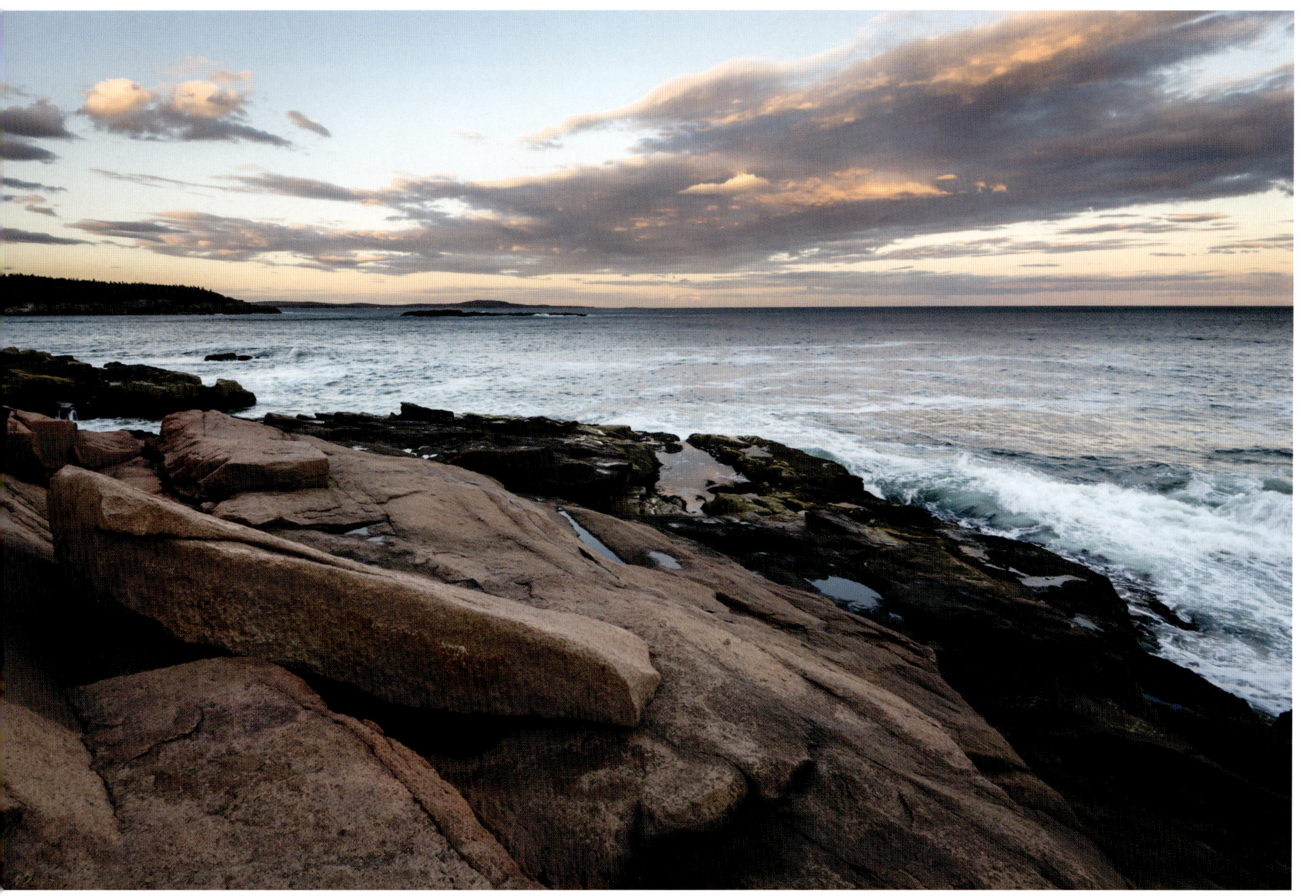

A QUARTER PAST SUNSET, NEAR THUNDER HOLE

CLEARING STORM AT SUNRISE, THUNDER HOLE

It was almost 5 a.m., and I was trying to decide whether or not to sleep in this morning; the sky seemed to be overcast. Dawn had started around 4 a.m., but sunrise was not until 5:53. It did not look promising. It was 29 August 2014, a Friday, and I would be heading home later in the day, a 320-mile drive in heavy tourist traffic. Just as I decided to sleep in, my wife called me to tell me that the news station in Boston was announcing a high-surf advisory for Down East Maine. That was all I needed to hear. I jumped out of bed; threw on some clothes; tossed batteries, flash cards, a protein shake, and granola bars into my bag; and was out the door. She really knows how to get me going in the morning. I knew exactly where I wanted to be. Twenty minutes later, I was

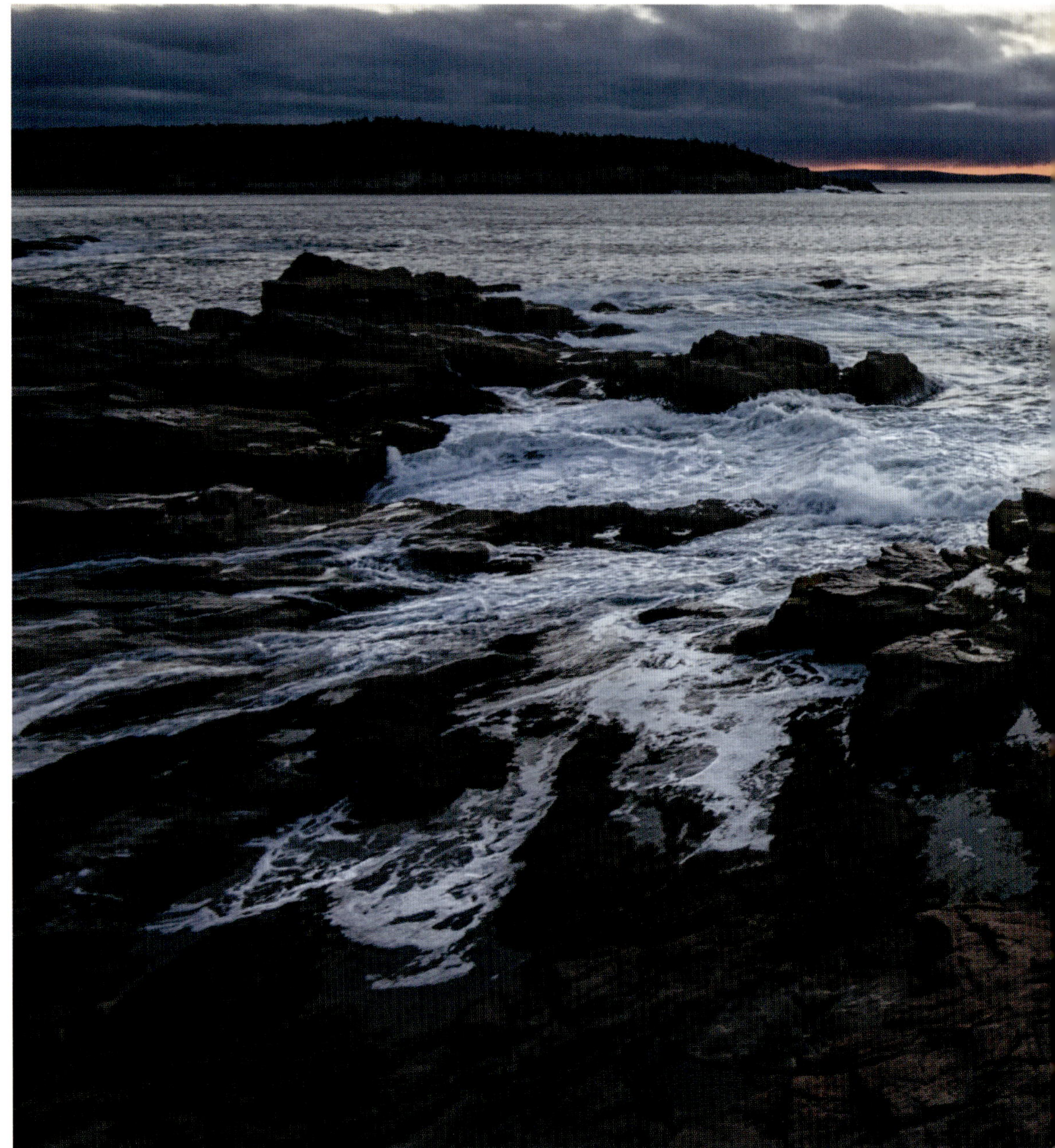

SUNRISE AT THE STORM'S EDGE, NEAR THUNDER HOLE

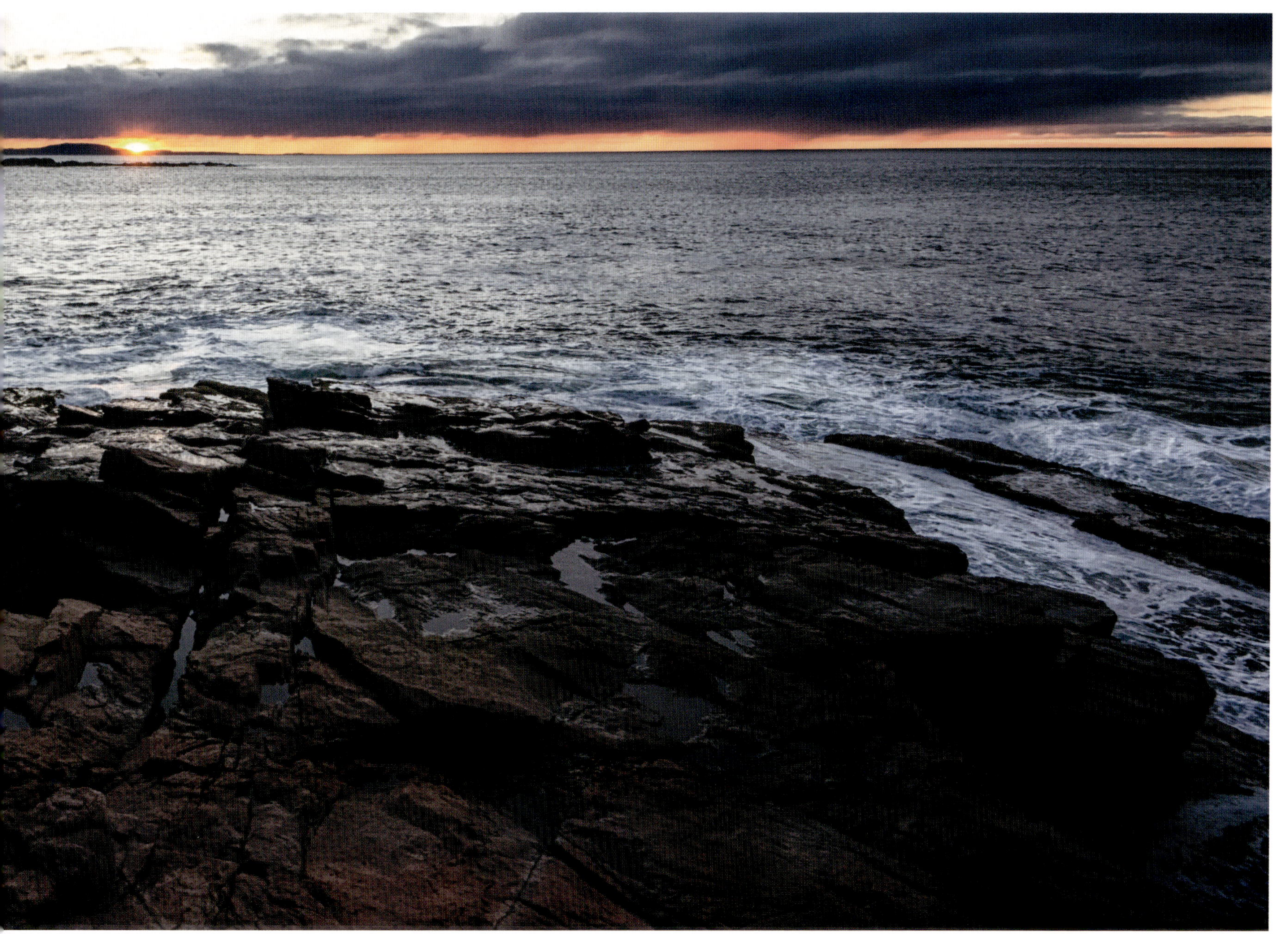

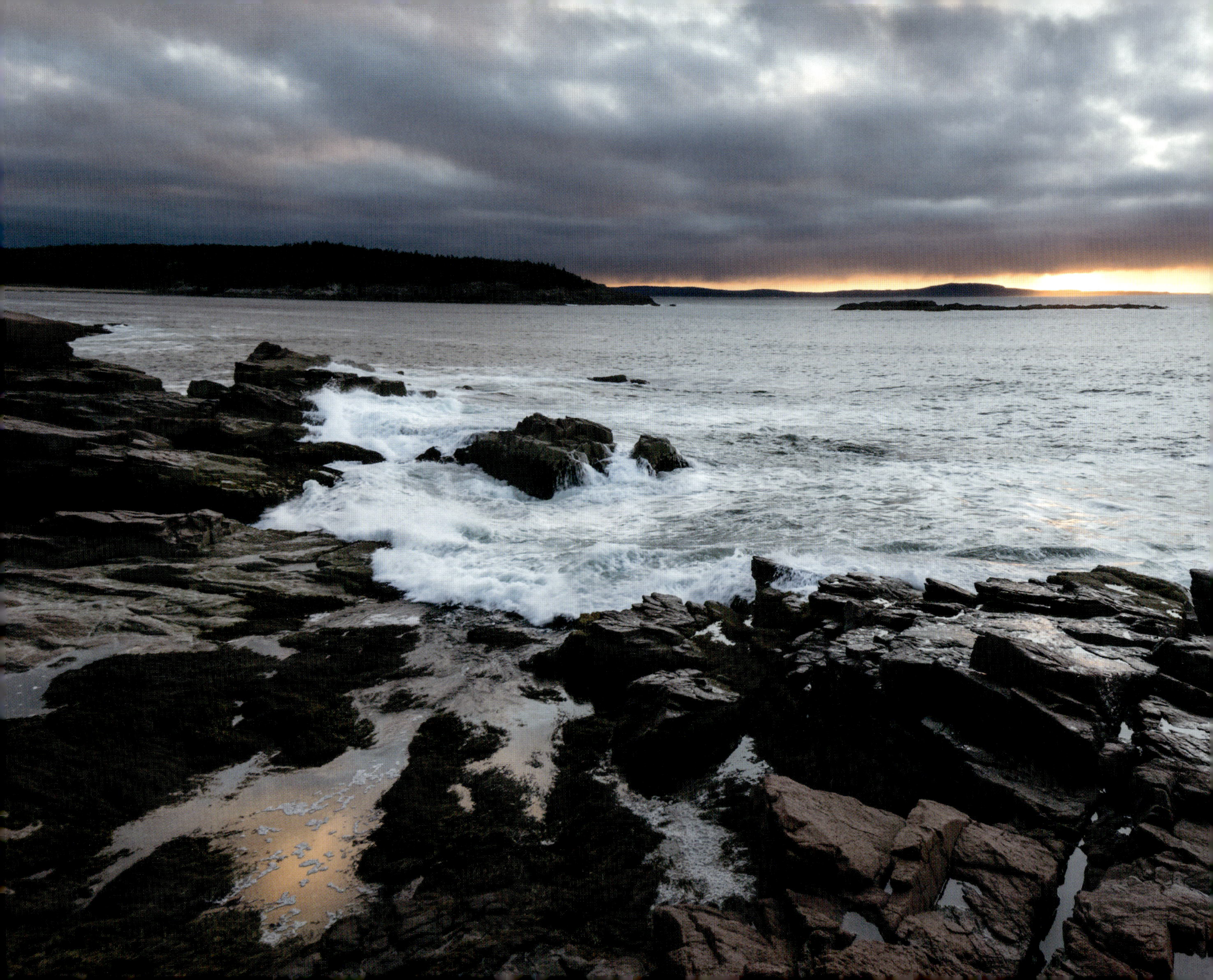

at Thunder Hole, setting up as close to the surf as I could safely get. A light, warm breeze was blowing and the temperature was about 65 degrees. Out to sea some several hundred miles, Hurricane Cristobal was tracking up the East Coast, and its effects were being felt at Acadia.

Once in place, I observed a bit of color to the northeast, just over Schoodic Peninsula, with just a small sliver of clear sky between the clouds and the horizon. I was in luck: the clouds were moving easterly, so there was a good chance this window would remain open.

I made several images, checking exposure and composition, tried different shutter speeds to gauge the amount of blur and detail in the waves, made several sequential images as waves rushed onshore and receded, and chatted with a few other park visitors who were out and about, all the while adjusting and fine-tuning the exposures. And then the magic happened.

There was just enough of a gap between the clouds and the horizon to reveal the sun ascending above Schoodic, but not enough to illuminate the bottoms of the clouds. The foreground rocks, wet from the surf action of the last few hours, shimmered with reflected light, as did the sea. I waited for the next large swell to approach the gap in the rocks, and tripped the shutter, snapping off several continuous frames to capture the action. I repeated this several times as the sun rose higher in the sky, hoping for "the big wave," but it never occurred. I kept shooting until the sun disappeared behind the clouds.

In the meantime, I was concentrating so much on this image that I hadn't noticed that the sky directly above my position had cleared completely, and it looked like there would not be much color once the sun rose above the clouds. Looking to the northwest, though, I saw another large group of clouds were moving to fill the sky above my position. Now the race was on: Would these new clouds be in place before the sun completely disappeared behind the clouds over the horizon? Once again, my luck held.

As the sun was beginning to move behind the clouds, it was now also high enough in the sky that water was reflecting the pink and orange hues. Small gaps in the cloud cover were allowing just a bit of color to accent the bottoms of the clouds. And those colors were reflecting in the tide pools as each wave receded and the pool became momentarily still.

An intricate dance evolved as I moved my tripod and camera—left, right, forward, back, raised it, lowered it, switched to vertical, back to horizontal, repeat. For some twenty minutes we performed (much to the amusement of a couple from New Jersey), the sea, sun, clouds, and surf—my partners in this ballet—never repeating the same move, always showing something just a bit different, unique. Finally the clouds grew too heavy and ended our dance, our moment of exhilaration. It had been an exciting start to the day, and I had lots to show for it. Over 550 images in about forty minutes, and I couldn't wait to get home to start processing. But first, back to the hotel for a shower and some fresh clothes, and then a stop at Jordan's Restaurant for some Maine blueberry pancakes.

CLEARING STORM AND SUNRISE REFLECTIONS, NEAR THUNDER HOLE

BASS HARBOR MOONRISE, EASTERN APPROACHES, AND BASS HARBOR AFTERGLOW, SEPTEMBER 2014

I had planned to go to Bass Harbor after work to photograph the full moon and the sunset glow on the rocks, looking in the opposite direction from Bass Harbor Light. Bass Harbor is on the other side of the island from Bar Harbor, and to reach it I had to drive through Southwest Harbor, where there was major construction on Route 3, reducing travel to one lane. Instead of the usual thirty-minute trip, it took over an hour. I was getting anxious that I would miss both the moonrise and sunset. However, I made it with about twenty minutes to spare. Once there, I grabbed my gear and headed for the stairs that lead down to the viewing area and the rocky shore.

It was early September and there were still a lot of visitors to the park, so the rocks at the lighthouse-viewing area were swarming with people, but this was not a problem, since I was planning to shoot in the other direction, looking east. This view of the lighthouse is looking northwest.

The moon rose on schedule and began to reveal itself; I made several images before it slipped behind the clouds. Since the moon was no longer visible, I looked to my right and saw these beautiful, wispy cloud formations over the eastern approaches to Blue Hill Bay. Always a good idea to keep your head moving, since you never know what unexpected opportunities will present themselves. I had wanted to make an image of a grand cloudscape for a long time, and here it was. Generally, in New England, there are few places to make this type of image, since there always seem to be man-made intrusions into the visualized image. I had not considered the sea as a possibility for foreground. It was about this time that I realized it had become very quiet, with just the waves and the buoy bell to accentuate the silence.

I turned and looked back toward the lighthouse, and, amazingly, there was not one person remaining on the rocks. The sun had set, the tourists had departed, and I found myself alone with the lighthouse and this amazing afterglow in the sky. Realizing I had only a few minutes at most, I furiously set about making as many exposures as I could, since the clouds were moving rapidly away and the light was fading fast. I came away with several satisfactory images, but best of all was the incredible experience that I now have to share along with these three images.

Ansel Adams once said, "Chance favors the prepared mind." It may be that someone else said it before him, but I read about it first from Adams. Now, I was at a place and in conditions where all my preparations over the last several years were being put to the test. Had I been less prepared, maybe I would have still made acceptable images, but being prepared, I knew instinctively how to respond and take advantage of the view unfolding around me. Only the things I had no control over were left to chance.

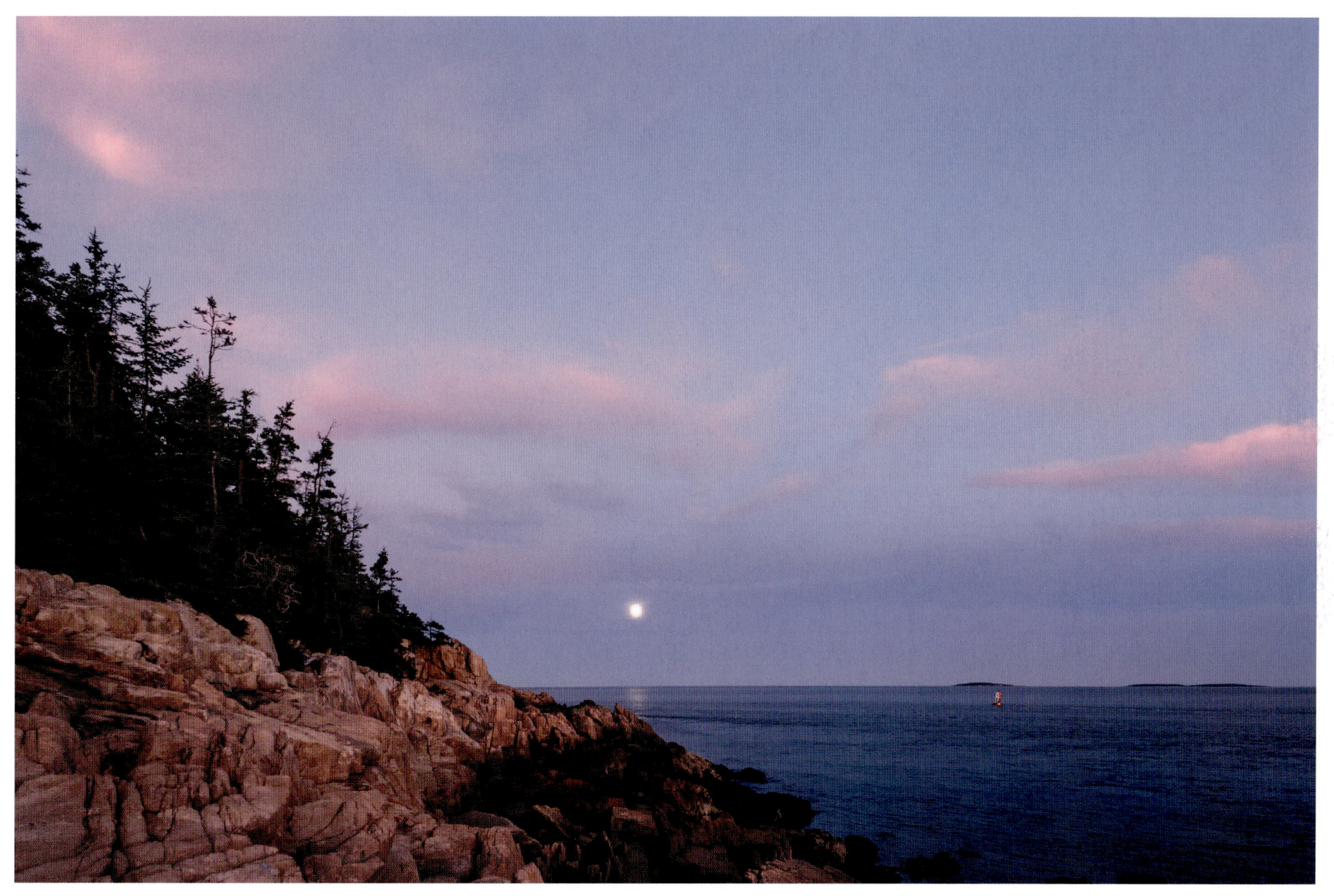

MOONRISE AT SUNSET, BASS HARBOR LEDGES

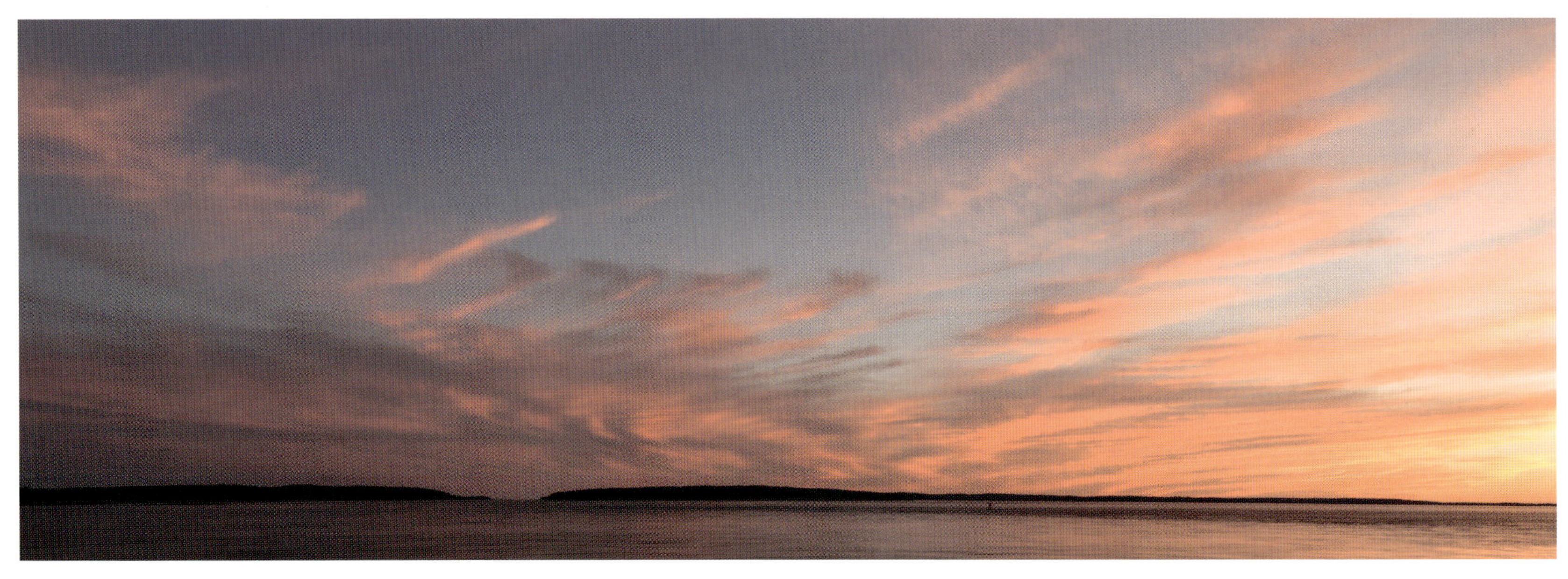

CLOUDSCAPE, EASTERN APPROACHES, BLUE HILL BAY

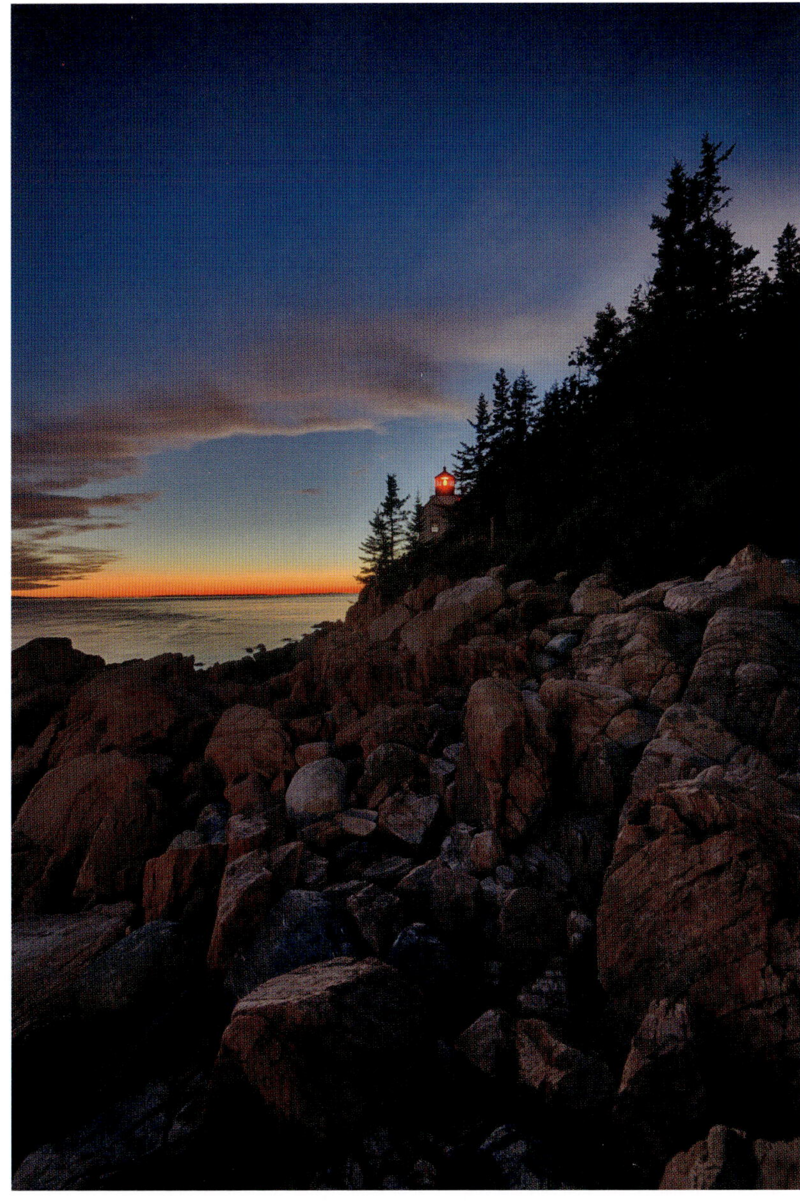

BASS HARBOR AFTERGLOW

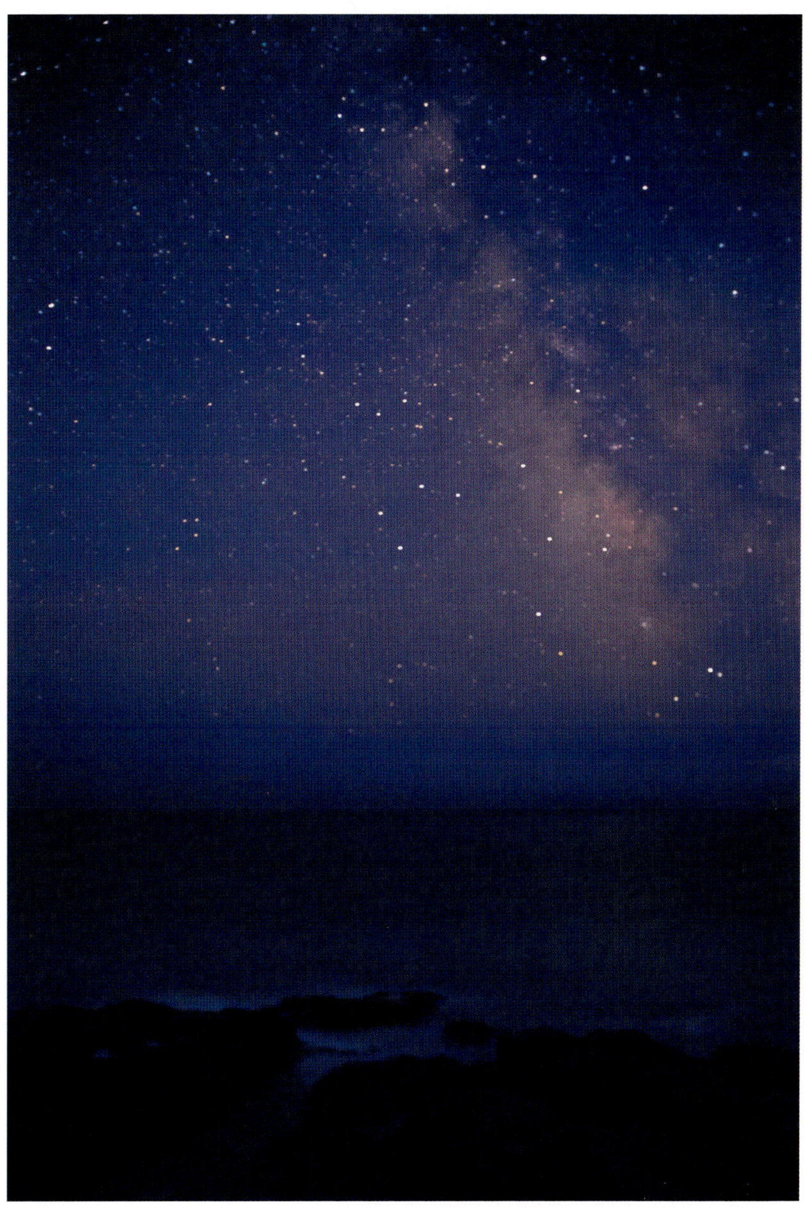

NEAR LITTLE HUNTERS BEACH: HIGH TIDE AND THE MILKY WAY

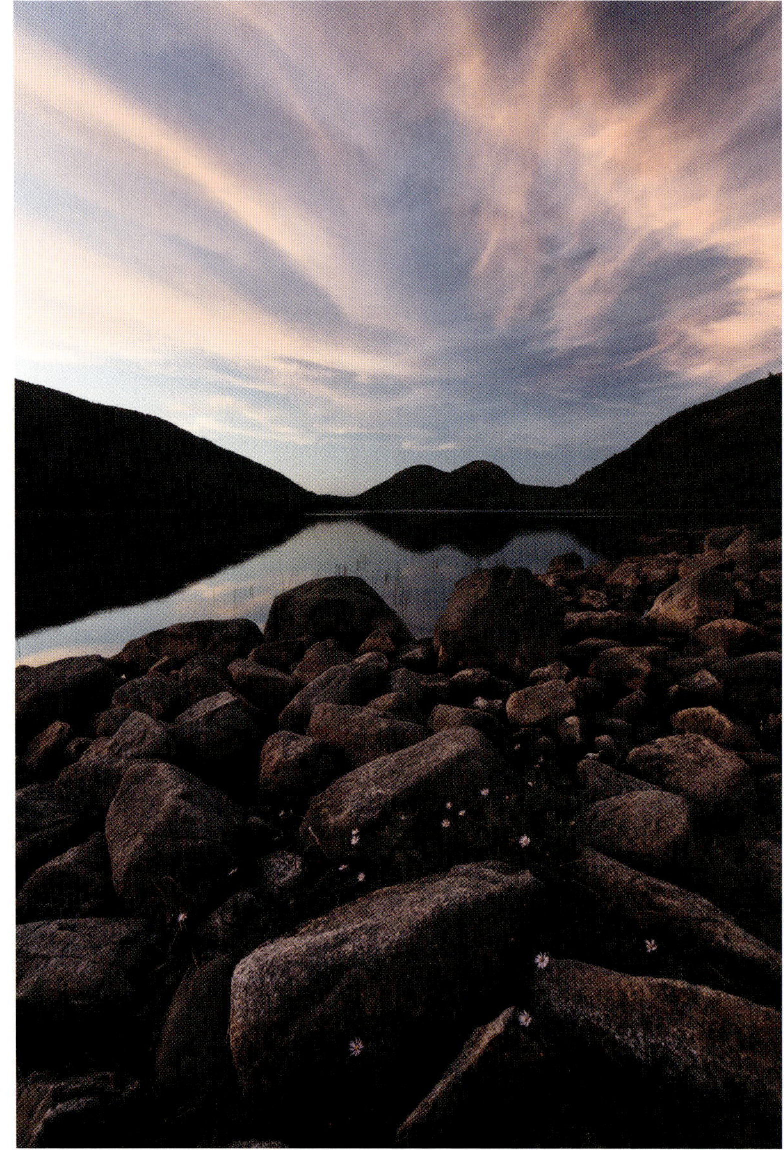

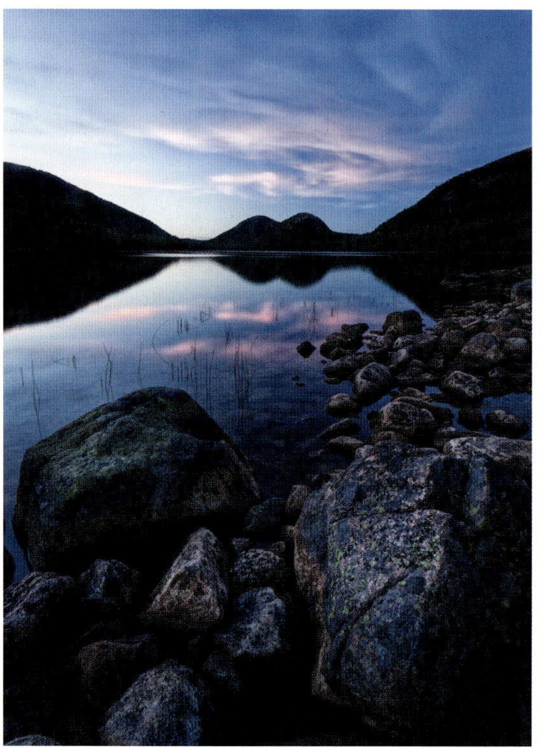

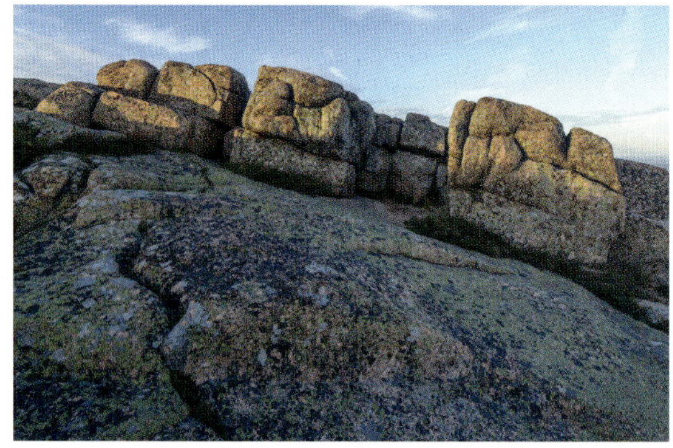

BOULDERS AND ASTERS, JORDAN POND AT SUNSET

SUNSET AFTERGLOW, JORDAN POND AND THE BUBBLES

CADILLAC MOUNTAIN GRANITE, SUNSET

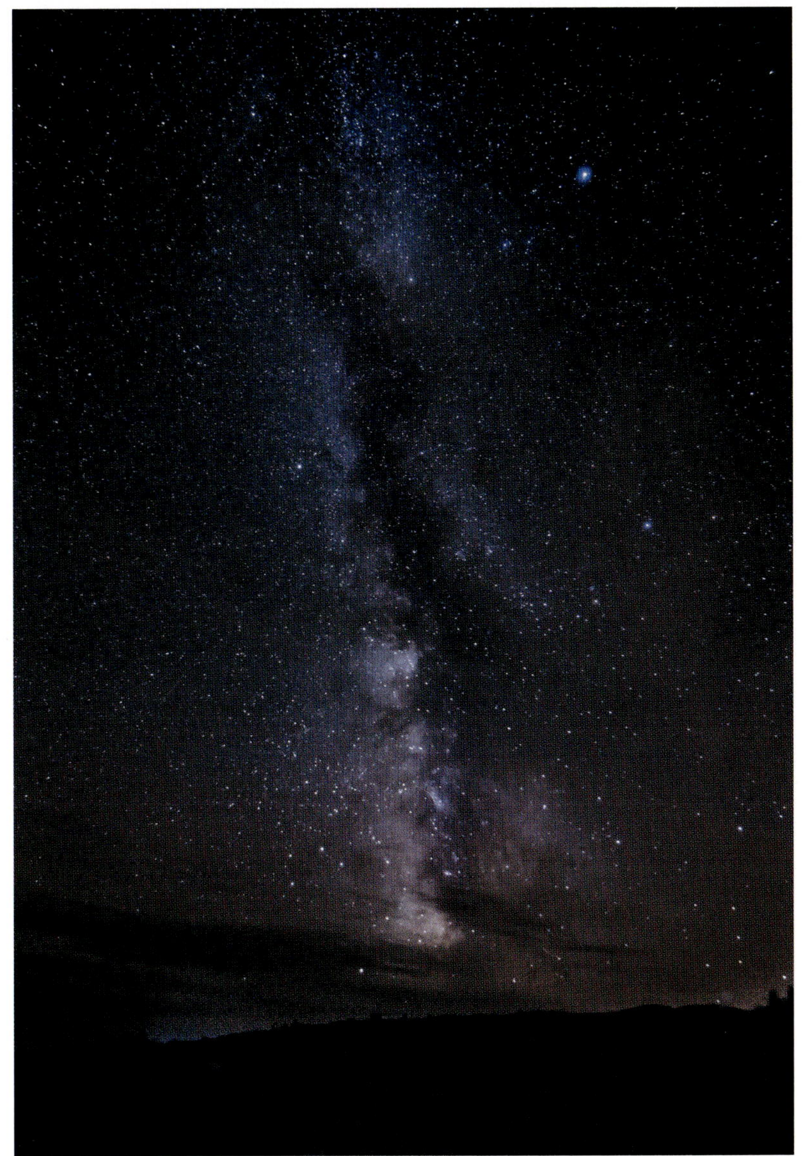

The Milky Way from Cadillac Mountain as a storm moves in

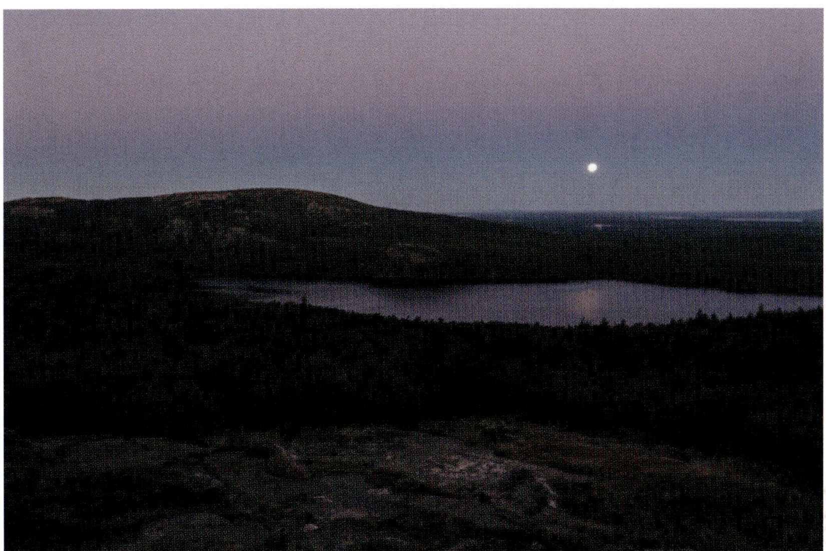

PRE-DAWN MOONSET, EAGLE LAKE OVERLOOK

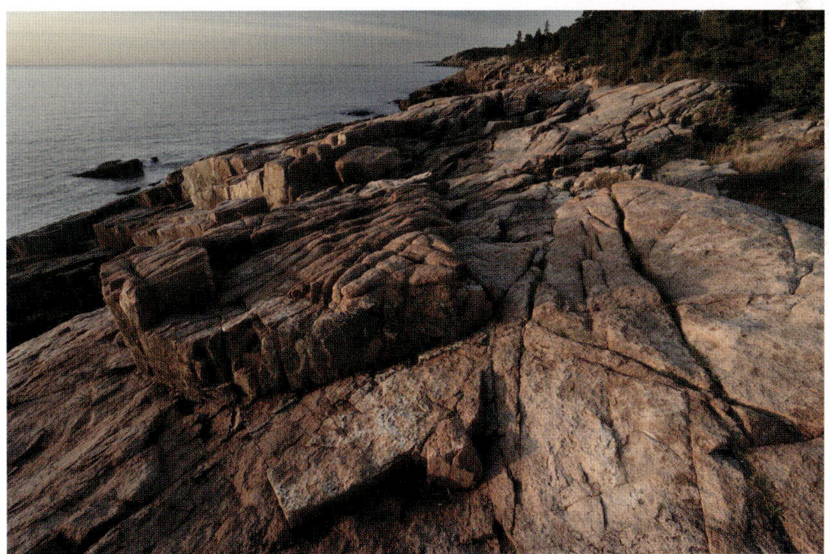

SUNRISE ON A HAZY MORNING ALONG OCEAN PATH

Autumn

At first it starts almost imperceptibly; then, here and there, a leaf, a branch, one tree standing out just a bit more from its neighbors. A bright splash of yellow or orange seen from the corner of the eye, against the deeper evergreens. A maple here; over there an aspen. Rugosa blooms turn to rose hips and even the poison ivy begins to go from green to red.

High on the ridges and shoulders of hills, sometimes glimpsed as one rounds a curve, they begin to show themselves. We are the messengers: summer is fading and it is time to go dormant, but before we do, we will put on such a show! But summer does not relinquish its hold easily. Still the days are warm, and the goldenrod and asters continue to push forth their blooms.

Autumn is Acadia at its most boisterous, colorful, loud, exuberant.

In late August it begins; never mind that the calendar tells us that it's still four weeks until "Fall Begins."

If we are fortunate, we get the right amount of rain and enough cool nights, and the winds behave themselves, then the color is spectacular. If we are not so fortunate, it's still pretty darn nice.

Once the momentum builds, toward the end of September, the color seems to spread farther and faster, filling in the gaps that were left untouched earlier in the season. On cloudy, stormy days, the colors are intense and saturated. On bright, sun-filled days the colors are bright and bold.

By the week before Columbus Day, autumn finally ignites with its full passion, displaying the most-brilliant hues of reds, yellow, and oranges against a background of granite, dark spruce, and pine, and that amazing blue-green ocean. Everything is illuminated by a sun that is not quite as high, lengthening the available golden hours, even as the days grow shorter. As the days grow shorter, the light seems less strong, shadows just a bit longer.

Color is at its zenith on Columbus Day weekend and hangs on for a few days more, maybe, but within a week it begins to fade as strong winds, rain, and the occasional hurricane bring the season's glorious show to an end. They bring their own variations and embellishments to the season, though, and create another experience of time on the island. Winter is coming, but not quite yet.

Autumn is also the time that the park begins to slow down, vacations are over, families have returned to start new school years, the summer help has gone back to college, and snowbirds head back south. And parking is much easier in town. Everything in the stores is on sale. The roads are less crowded, except for the days there are cruise ships in the harbor. But even then, if you plan well, you can still find your moments of isolation for quiet contemplation.

And while the calendar may tell you it's autumn, you are far enough north and the weather is fickle enough that by November, snow and ice can factor into your time at Acadia. Autumn is the best season to be in Acadia.

EARLY TRANSITION, BEAVER POND

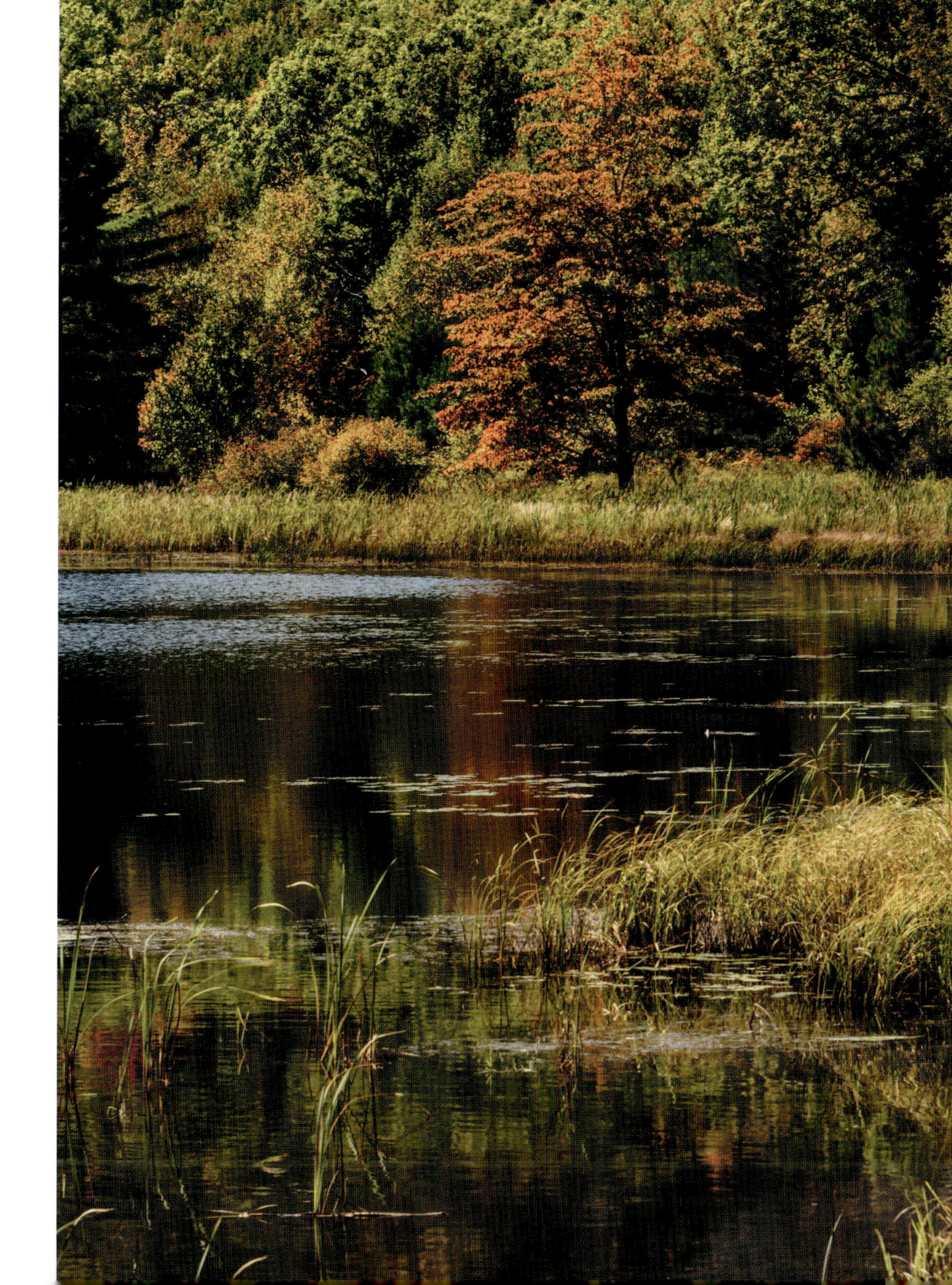

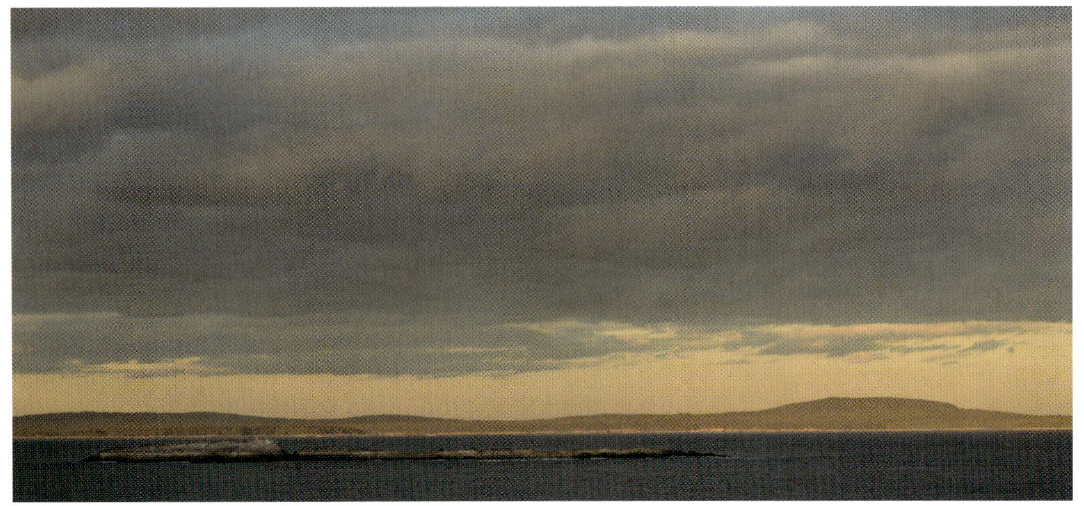

SCHOODIC HEAD AND THE OLD SOAKER

•

Another evening when the light was reminiscent of a Frederic Church painting

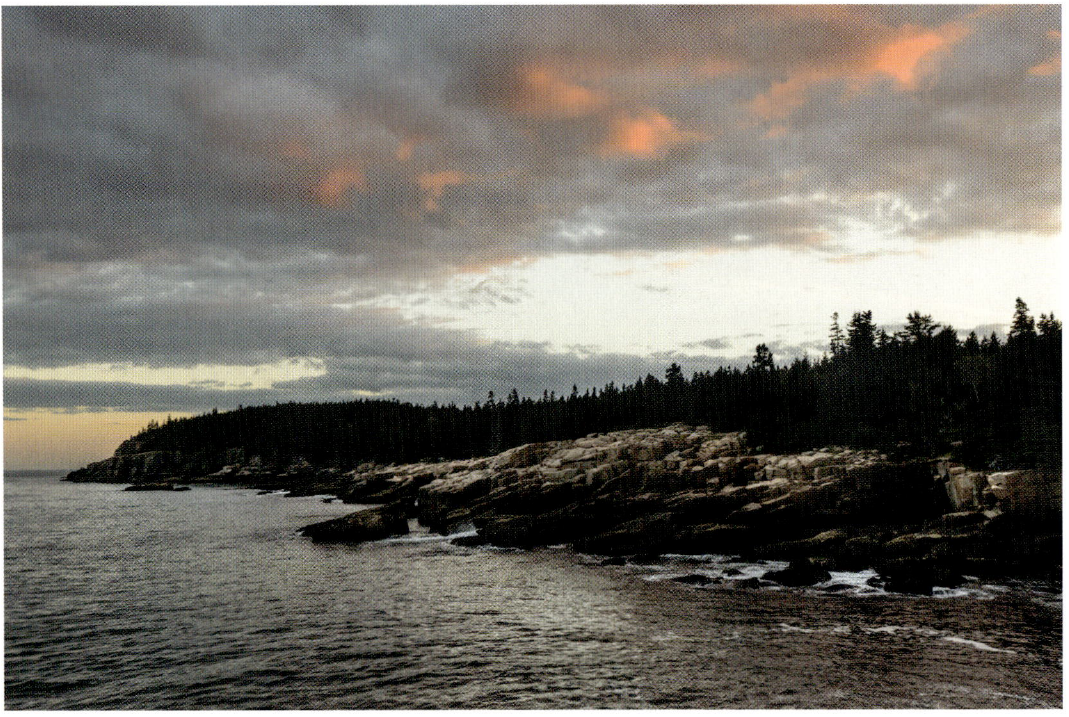

MONUMENT COVE AND OTTER CLIFFS AT SUNSET

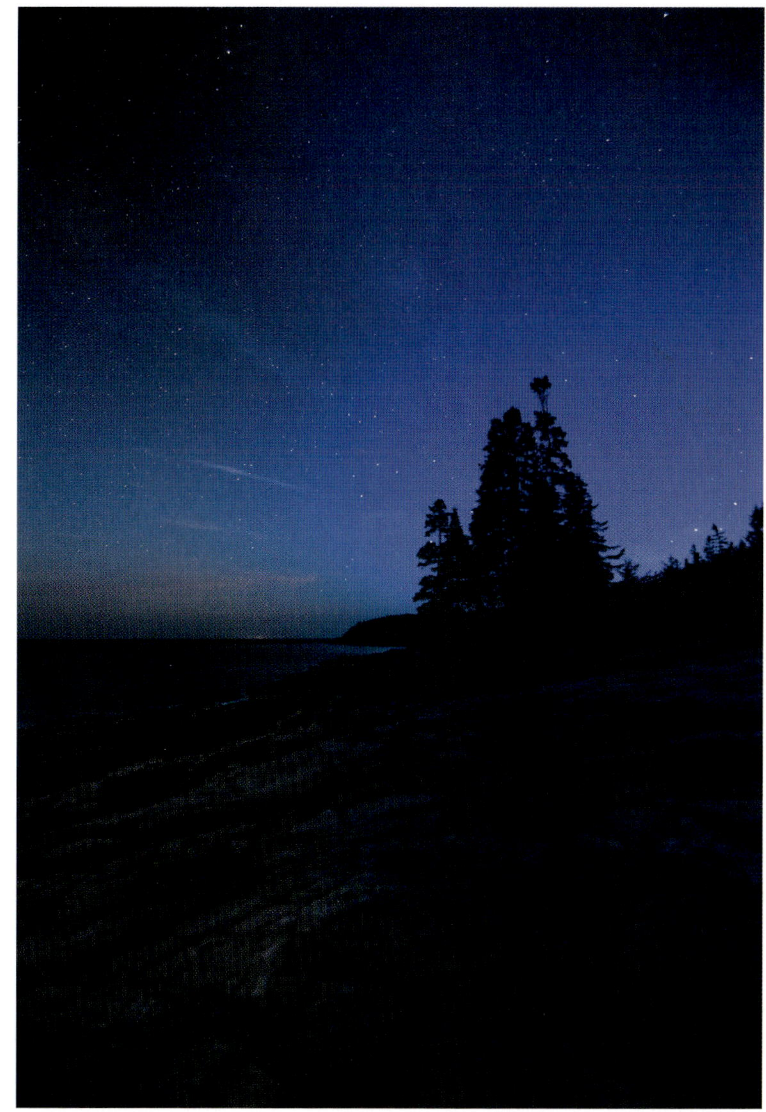

. . . and the stars smiled down

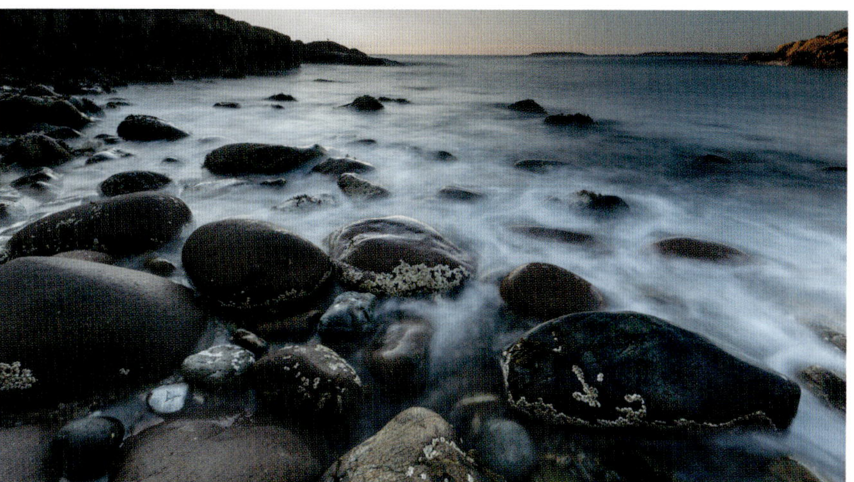

COBBLES AND PEBBLES, LITTLE HUNTERS BEACH, SUNRISE

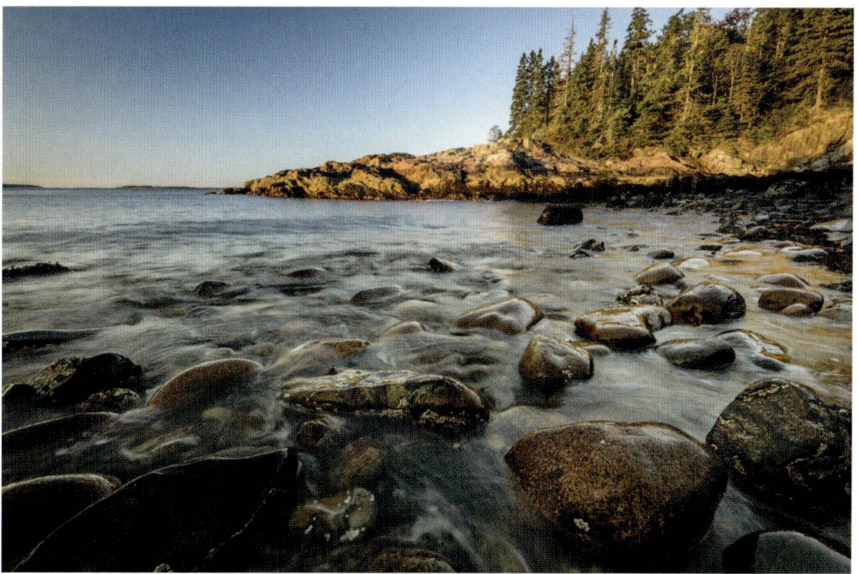

COBBLES AND SURF, SUNRISE, LITTLE HUNTERS BEACH

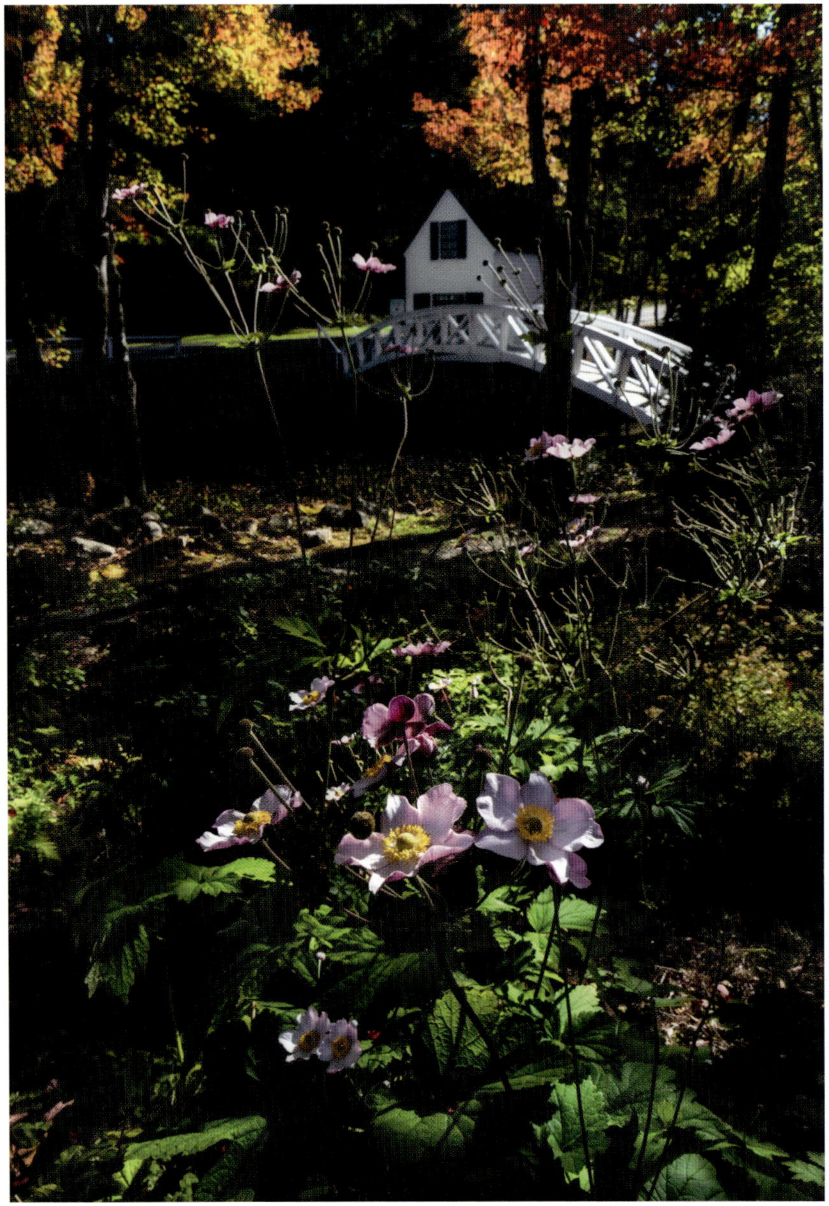

AUTUMN COSMOS AT SOMESVILLE

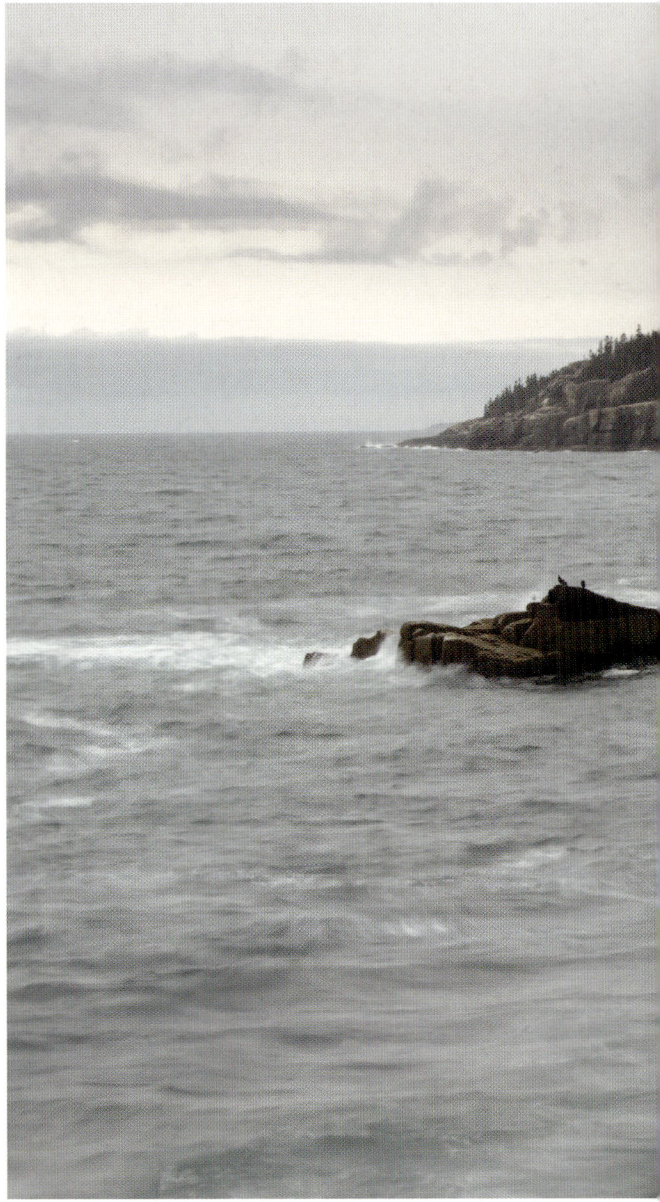

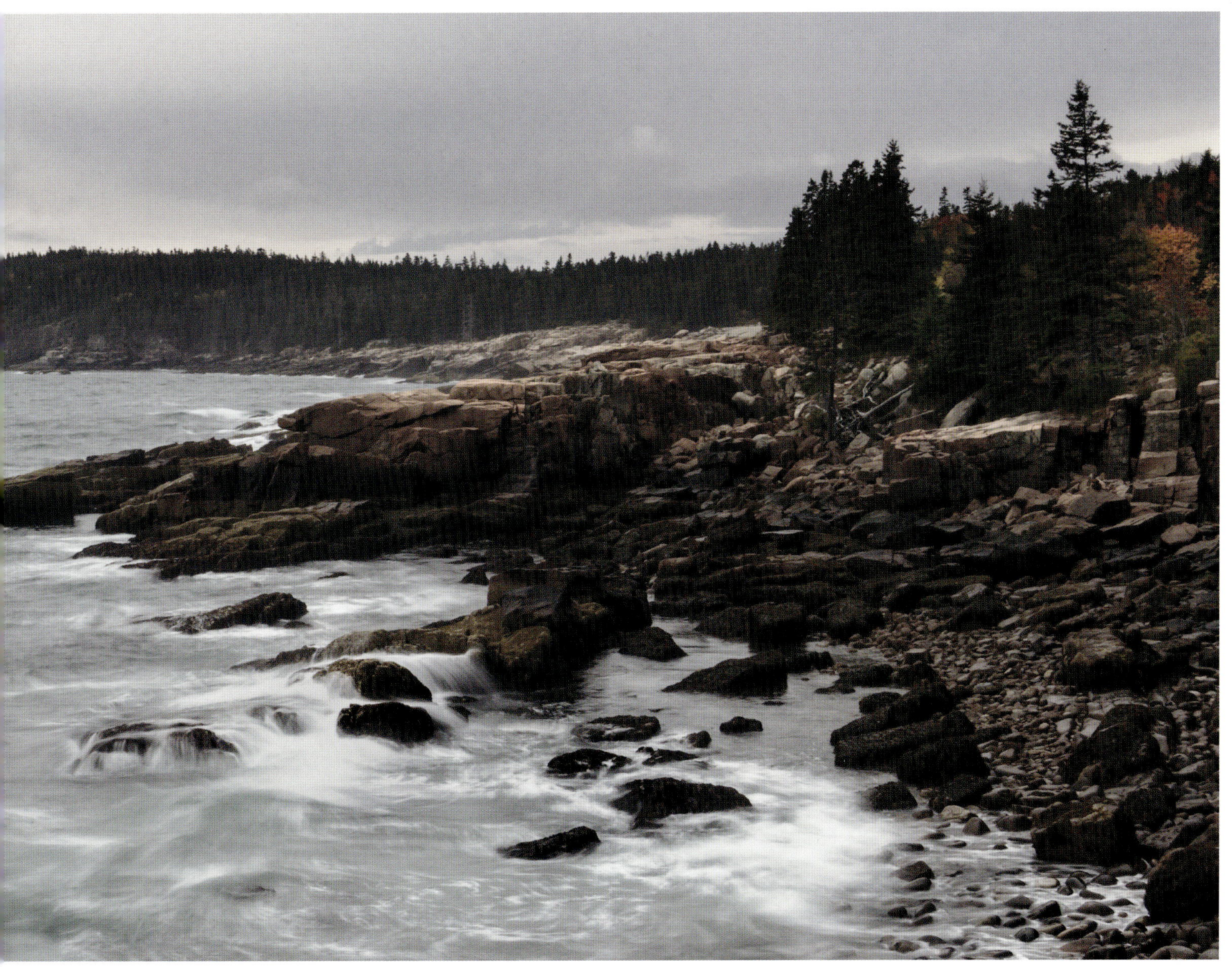

STORM, MONUMENT COVE AND OTTER CLIFFS

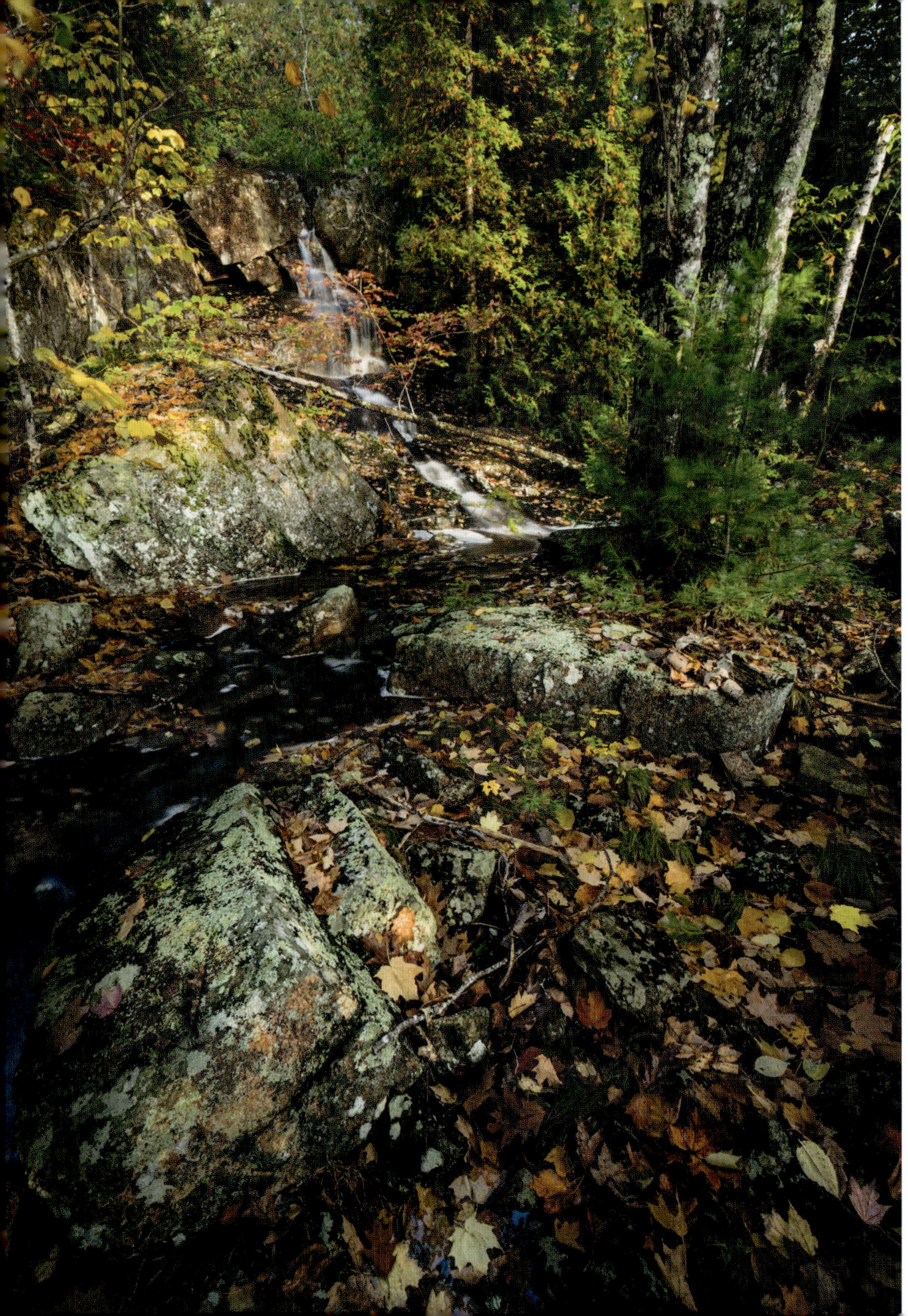

HIDDEN

CASCADE

AUTUMN

SPLENDOR

HIDDEN CASCADE, AUTUMN

I can't tell you where this is; I'd have to show you. It's not a secret, but it's not very evident, unless it's raining, usually for several hours and coming down very hard. Or in the spring, when the meltwaters from Cadillac search for a way to Eagle Lake. It's quite well hidden, even though it's only 20 feet from the edge of the road. Most times it's dry, with just some trees and some rocks and ledges—nothing remarkable. Unless it's raining.

I first discovered this location (well, I'm sure someone else found it before me!) in the spring of 2010. My wife and I had been camping on the island, it had been raining intermittently for several days, and we had been subjected to several hours of torrential downpours on the day we found this spot, quite by accident. Driving along the road between Jordan Pond and Cadillac Mountain after the rain had stopped, we had opened our windows as we drove along, when I heard the sound of falling water. I told my wife, Judy, to stop; there was no one behind us on the road. Once I had located the source, I told her to either park nearby or come back in an hour. I unloaded my gear and began shooting. I knew I had found a special place.

Now, almost four years had passed, I had been on the island for two months, and we hadn't had any appreciable rain. I had driven by several times, only to see dry ground. I knew that if we could just have a rainstorm, there would be a great possibility for an image with excellent autumn colors, accented by moss, lichens, tree trunks, and granite. A magnificent carpet of fallen leaves completed the scene.

Finally it happened, but not quite what I expected. It was October 8, just before Columbus Day weekend, and we had rain all day. I anticipated heading for this spot as soon as I got out of work. As luck would have it, the clouds began to clear to the west, and the sun was shining through sporadically. Due to the rain during the day, the air was exceptionally clear, as an area of high pressure was moving in behind the storm, giving the atmosphere a special quality. I quickly got into position and began composing images, then waited for the sun to briefly pop behind the clouds before making the exposure. Because there are several trees between the stream and the road, lighting was very uneven when the sun was not behind the clouds, creating several bright, overexposed areas and deep shadows. When the sun was behind the clouds, lighting was more even. I stayed here for about an hour, until the sun dropped down below intervening mountains. I came away with several nice images, some of which best expressed what it was I saw and felt that splendid afternoon.

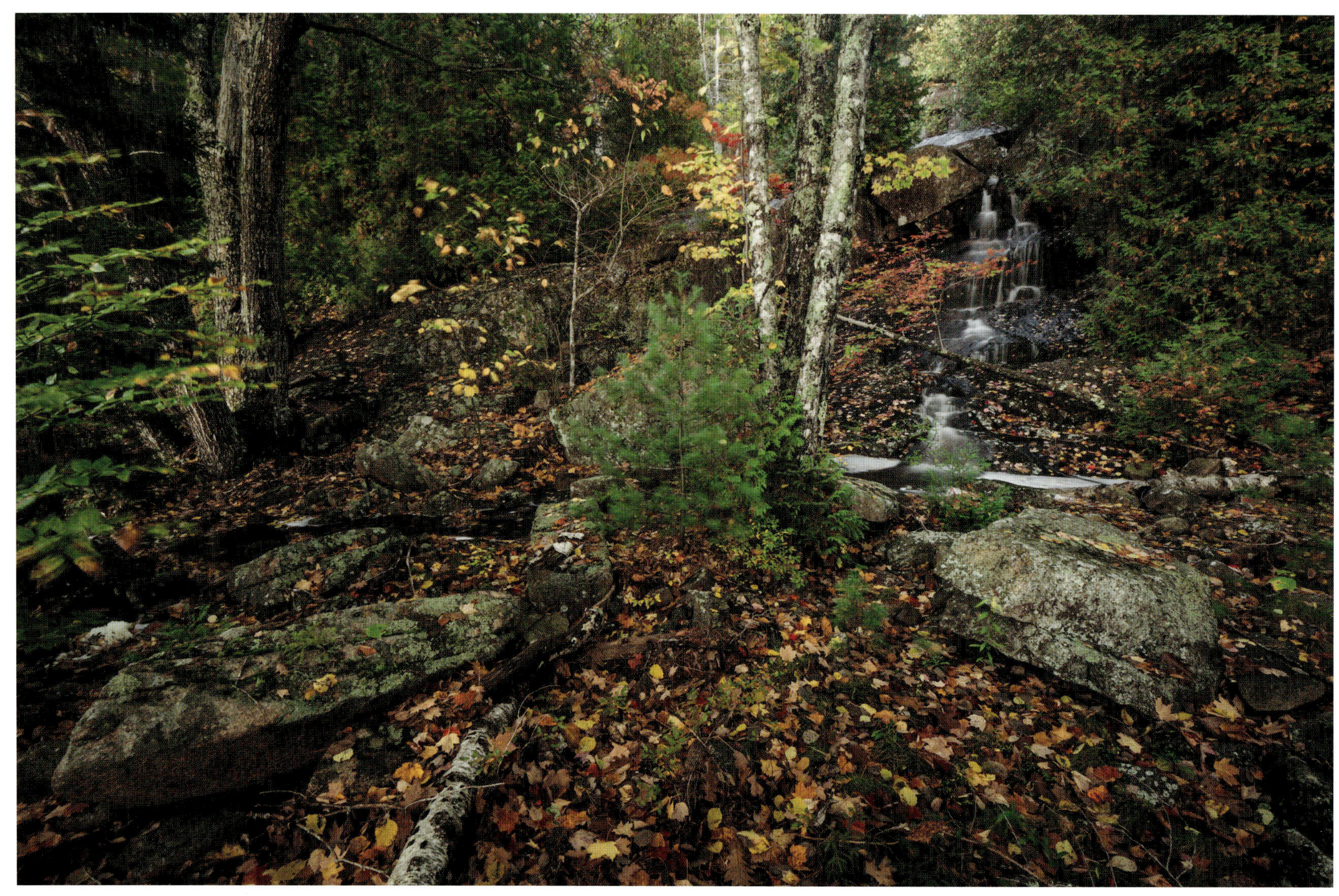

AFTER THE AUTUMN RAIN

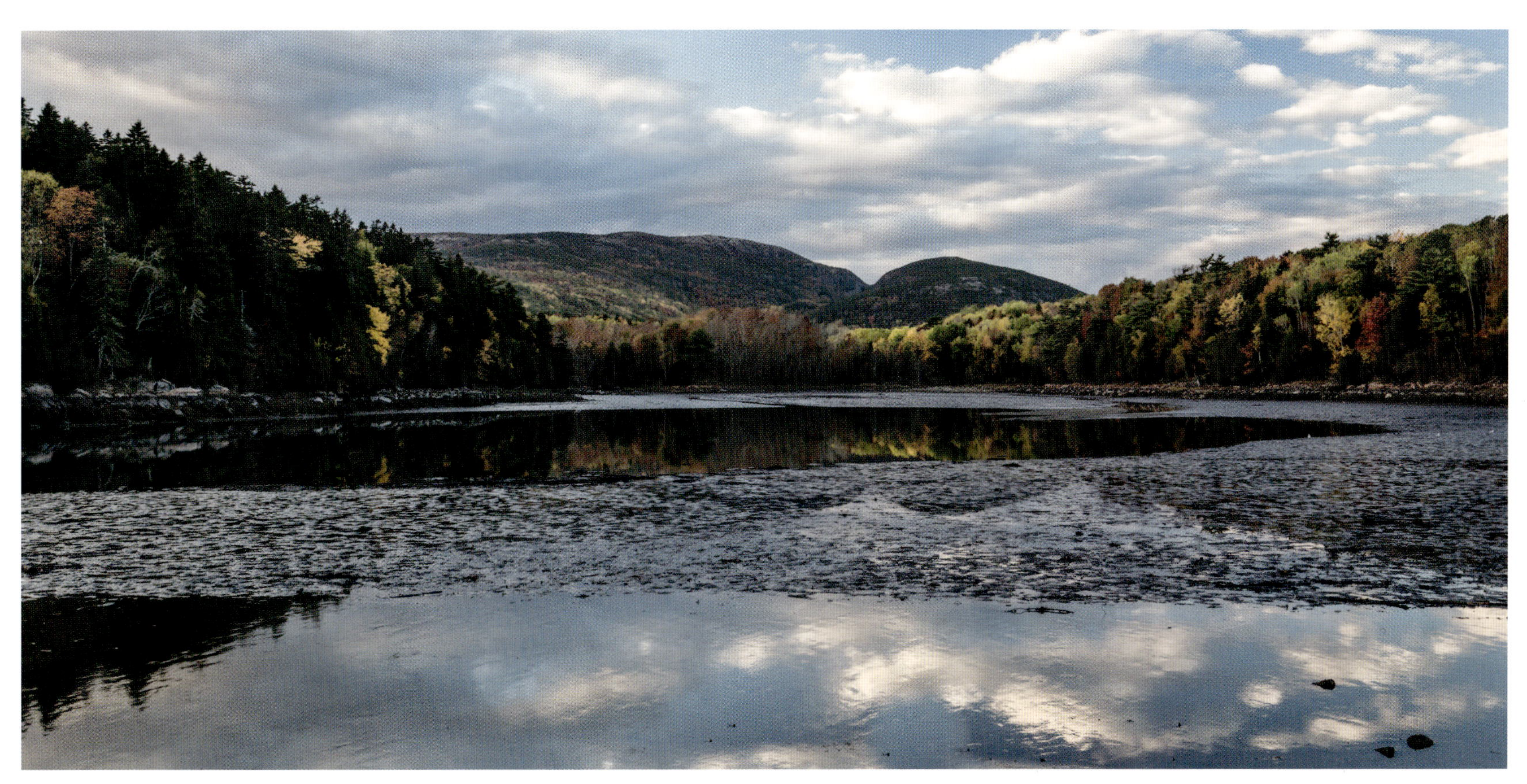

OTTER COVE, REFLECTIONS AT LOW TIDE

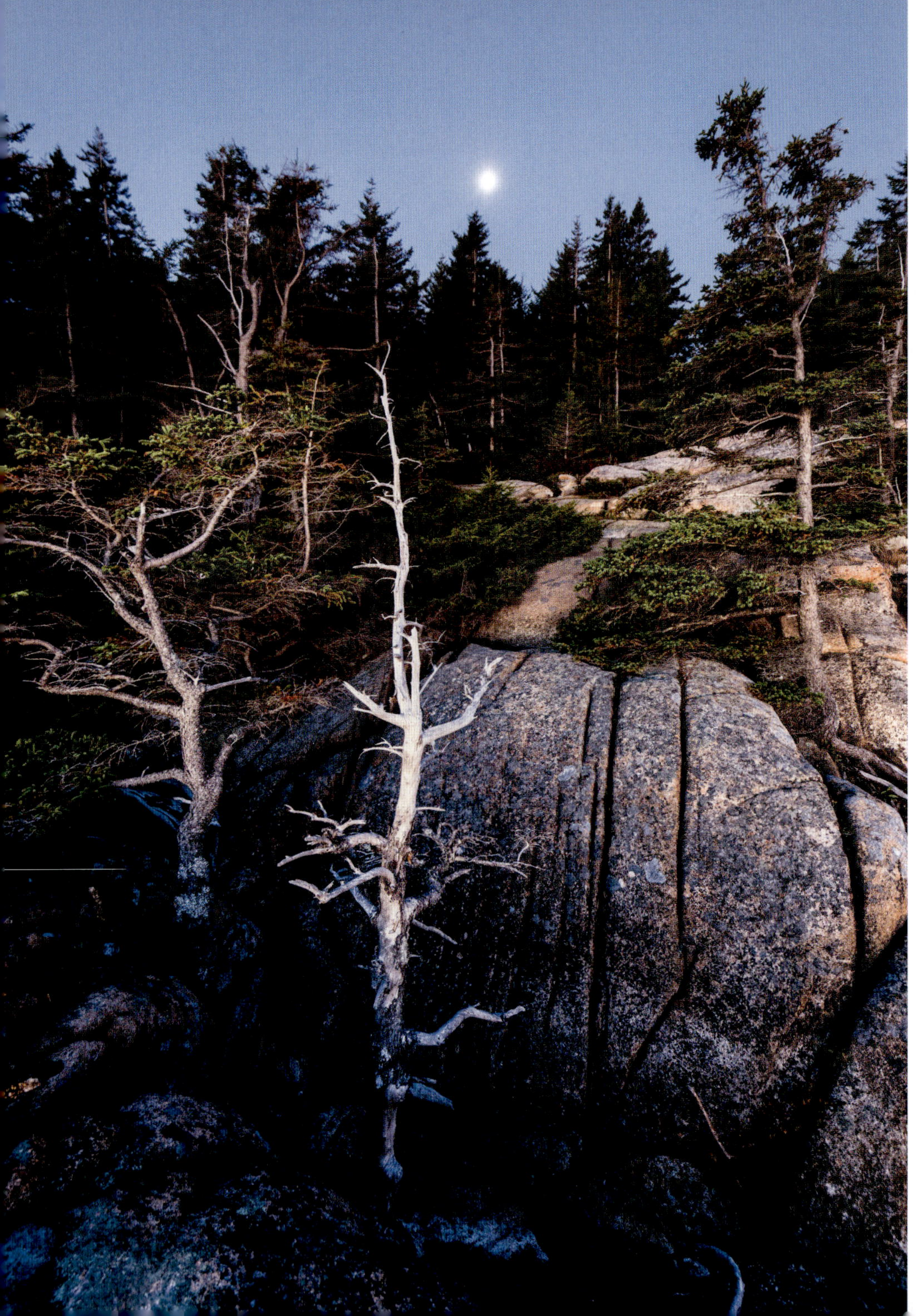

MOONSET AT SUNRISE, OTTER CLIFFS

FIRST LIGHT AND A SETTING MOON, OTTER CLIFFS

It was Columbus Day weekend, and the park was filling up again. Since Labor Day, the volume of visitors had steadily declined as families returned home to get the kids back in school, and summer help returned to college. The number of cruise ships visiting Bar Harbor increased to three or four a day, but mostly these folks stayed in town or went on bus tours of the park. Since the cruise ships left in the early evening, the park was pretty quiet after about 4 p.m. My wife, Judy, was driving up from our home in Massachusetts for the long three-day weekend; this was to be our first time to see the fall colors in Acadia. I had been scheduled to work on the island that week, so I had a five-day head start on the autumn spectacular.

My routine of going out early in the morning continued all week. Judy, not being much of an early riser, would wait for me to return from a morning shooting session, then we would head over to Jordan's Restaurant for a breakfast of eggs and blueberry pancakes. Then into town and out in the park for more shooting, sightseeing, dining, and general touristy stuff.

All my morning sessions during the weekend were at Otter Cliffs. Mostly I had the area to myself, arriving around 5 a.m., scouting a location, and then settling down to watch the morning arrive. Every day was a bit different, and I was glad I had two cameras since there often was interesting light and color occurring in opposite directions, usually at the same time.

While scouting for a good location to observe the morning light on the mountains towering over the cliffs along Ocean Drive, I found a dead tree wedged among the rocks above Otter Cliffs, still standing proud. The rocks and nearby trees were beginning to pick up a faint pinkish glow, although the sun was still below the horizon. Overhead, the setting moon was visible through some very thin clouds. I set up my tripod and began framing the composition and realized that even with a 16 mm lens, I was too close to include all the elements I wanted. Behind me was the edge of the cliff, about 3 feet away from a 70-foot drop, followed by two bounces and a short roll into the ocean. I didn't have a wider lens, the color was changing, the moon was setting, and I didn't want to forgo the image. Lowering my tripod to about 18 inches high, I sat down on the rock surface and slowly eased myself backward toward the cliff. With about 10 inches to spare, I was able to frame the image. I made about five images before the moon disappeared behind the trees. By that time the sun was just starting to reach the tops of Gorham and Champlain Mountains and their autumnal splendor, so I moved on to capture those views.

I didn't get a chance to return to this spot and the trees until the following spring, but the harsh winter of 2014–15 had finally been too much for the dead tree. I found it broken among the rocks. I don't know how long that tree had stayed upright, but I'm glad to have seen it at least once.

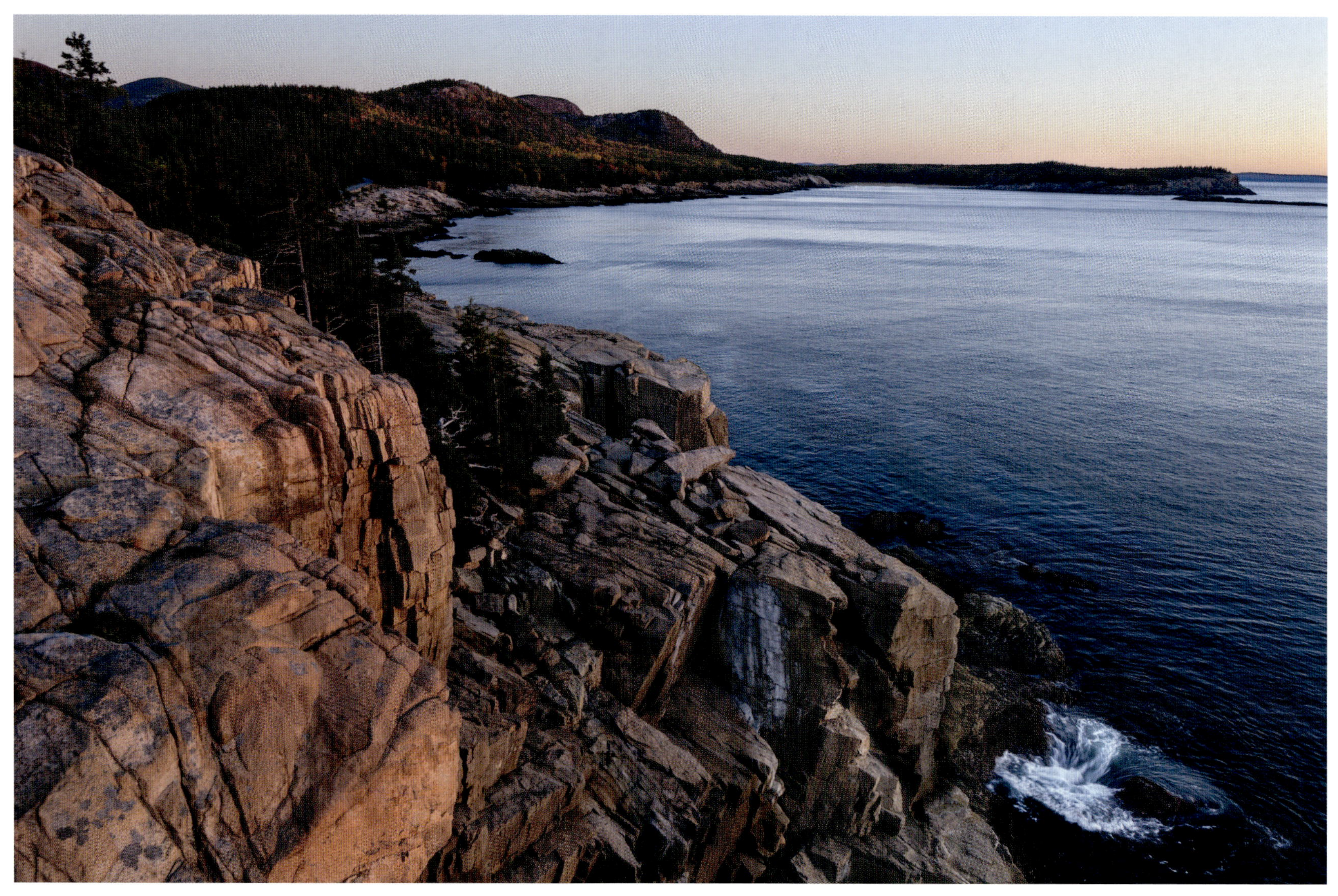

OTTER CLIFFS, PREDAWN LIGHT

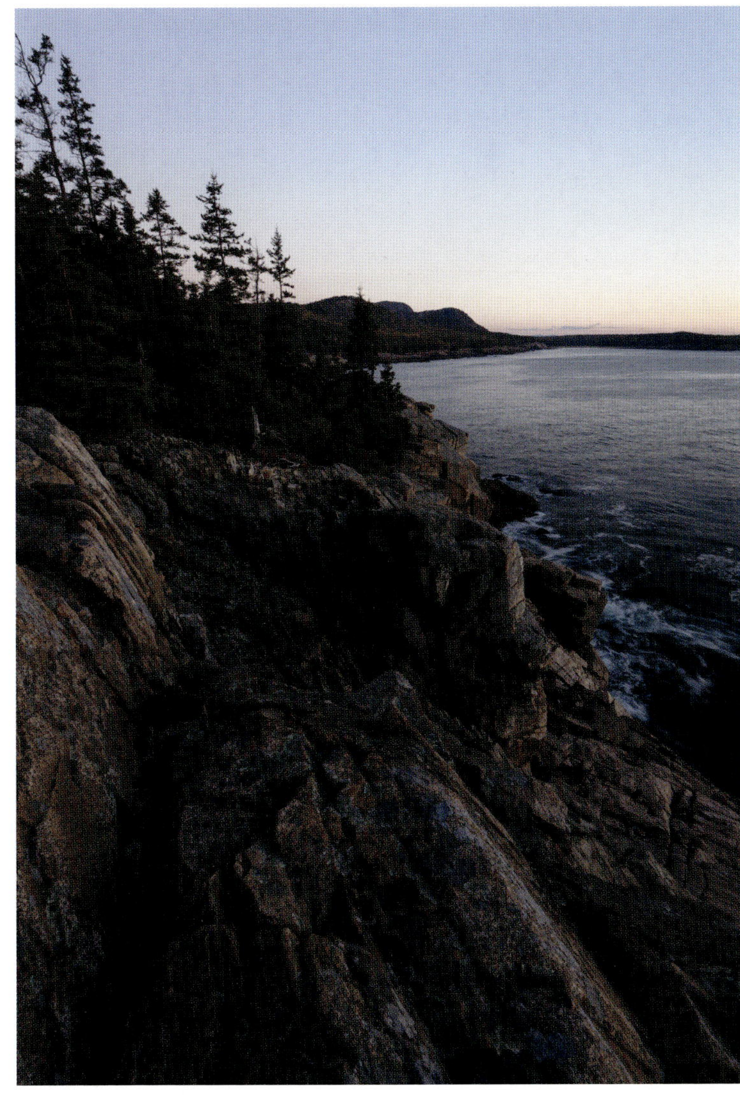

AUTUMN BLUE HOUR, OTTER CLIFFS

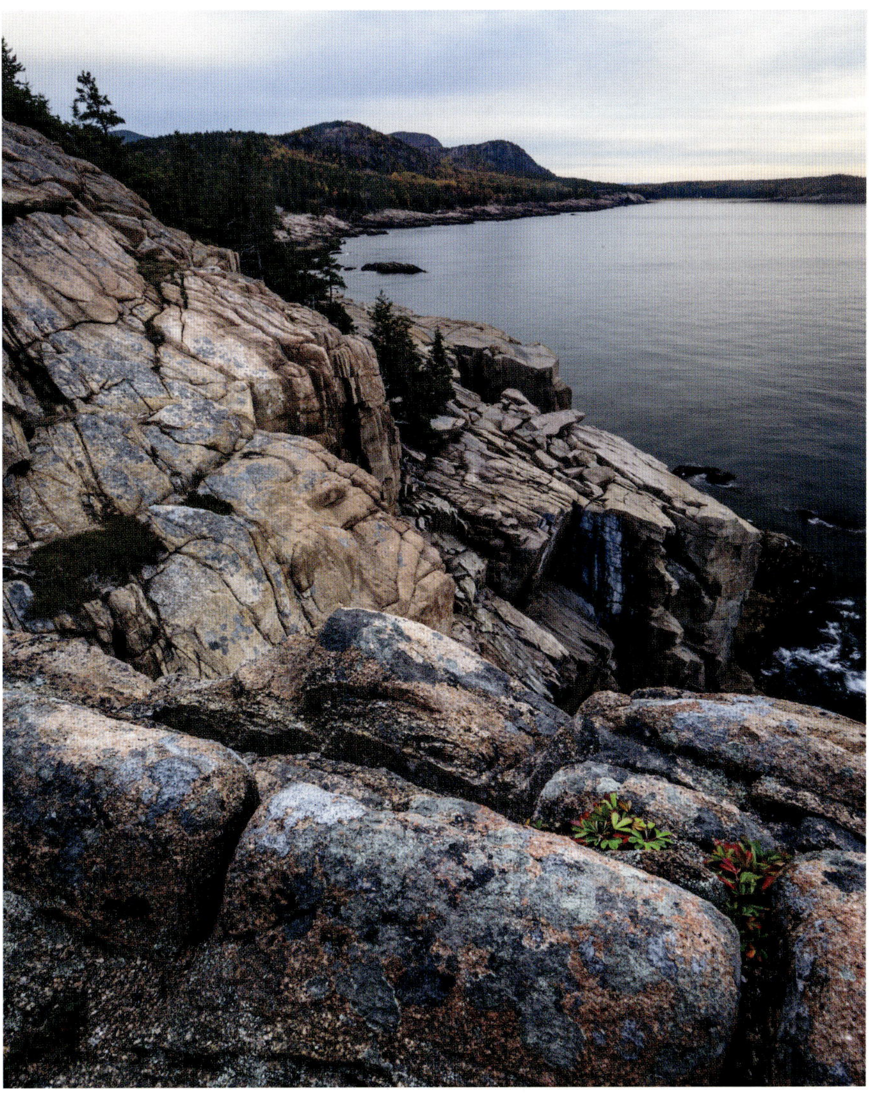

OTTER CLIFFS AND LICHEN BEFORE SUNRISE

MAPLE GLORY AT LITTLE LONG POND

I discovered Little Long Pond by accident. We were on the island for Columbus Day weekend and looking for a place to stretch our legs when we happened upon Little Long Pond, and as luck would have it a parking spot opened up. It is usually pretty busy, and we had not been able to stop before, either due to time, other commitments, or lack of parking. Many people use the area to take a stroll, walk dogs, or ride horses, and it's a pretty easy walk.

Initially, I spent some time at the south end of the pond, photographing lily pads and taking some distant shots of this tree from across the pond. From this side it appears that there is just one tree, with the branch extending out over the pond in full red color. However, it is actually two trees, one with just the solitary branch. The other one is a bit farther up the bank. It is the only remaining branch of what once was a large maple tree right on the edge of the pond. Judging from the size of the trunk, it had to be at least forty years old. From this side of the pond, in late-afternoon light on a cloudy day, the color was nice, and I played with the reflections a bit.

Eventually, we started exploring the area and trail around the pond, and that's when I realized that there were two maples. I made a few images and then continued around the pond.

About an hour later it started to get dark and the clouds began to thicken up, so we headed back to the car and dinner. As we passed by this tree with a single branch, the colors appeared much more saturated, but there was enough light in the sky that I still could make an image. There was almost no wind, and all the dogs had stopped jumping in the pond, so the water was still. The shadows were deep blue, and a bit of fog was starting to form. I knew I would need a long exposure, so I set up the tripod, framed up the shot to isolate the branch, and made two exposures before the wind picked up and the light faded. It was a quick Zen moment, it seemed, and I would have liked to spend a few more minutes in contemplation.

It was several months before I was able to get around to processing the photo, and as it happened, this may be a one-of-a-kind image. I made this image in October 2014, and I shot it again in July 2015. I wasn't able to return again until September 2016, but the tree with a lone branch was no more. Only the stump remained; the branch appears to have finally succumbed to a hard winter snowfall in 2015–16, since I found it lying in the bottom of the pond. This has happened many times: I have seen a subject I've wanted to photograph but put it off, only to return later to find the tree destroyed by storms, vandalism, or development. My advice is to shoot it when you see it, since you may get only one opportunity. Make the most of it. I'm disappointed that this tree no longer remains, waiting for someone else to admire its beauty, yet another reminder that the time allowed each of us is all too brief.

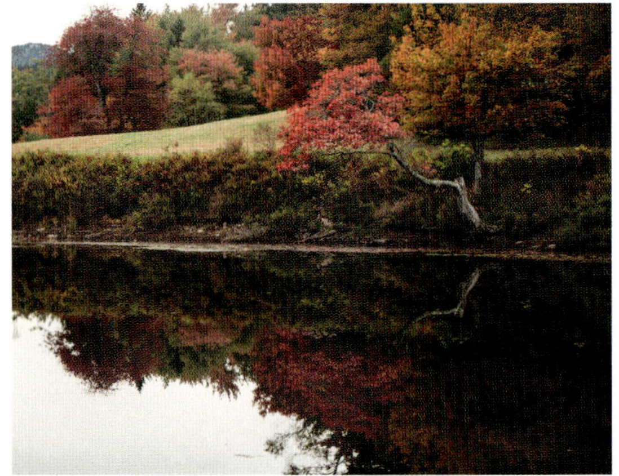

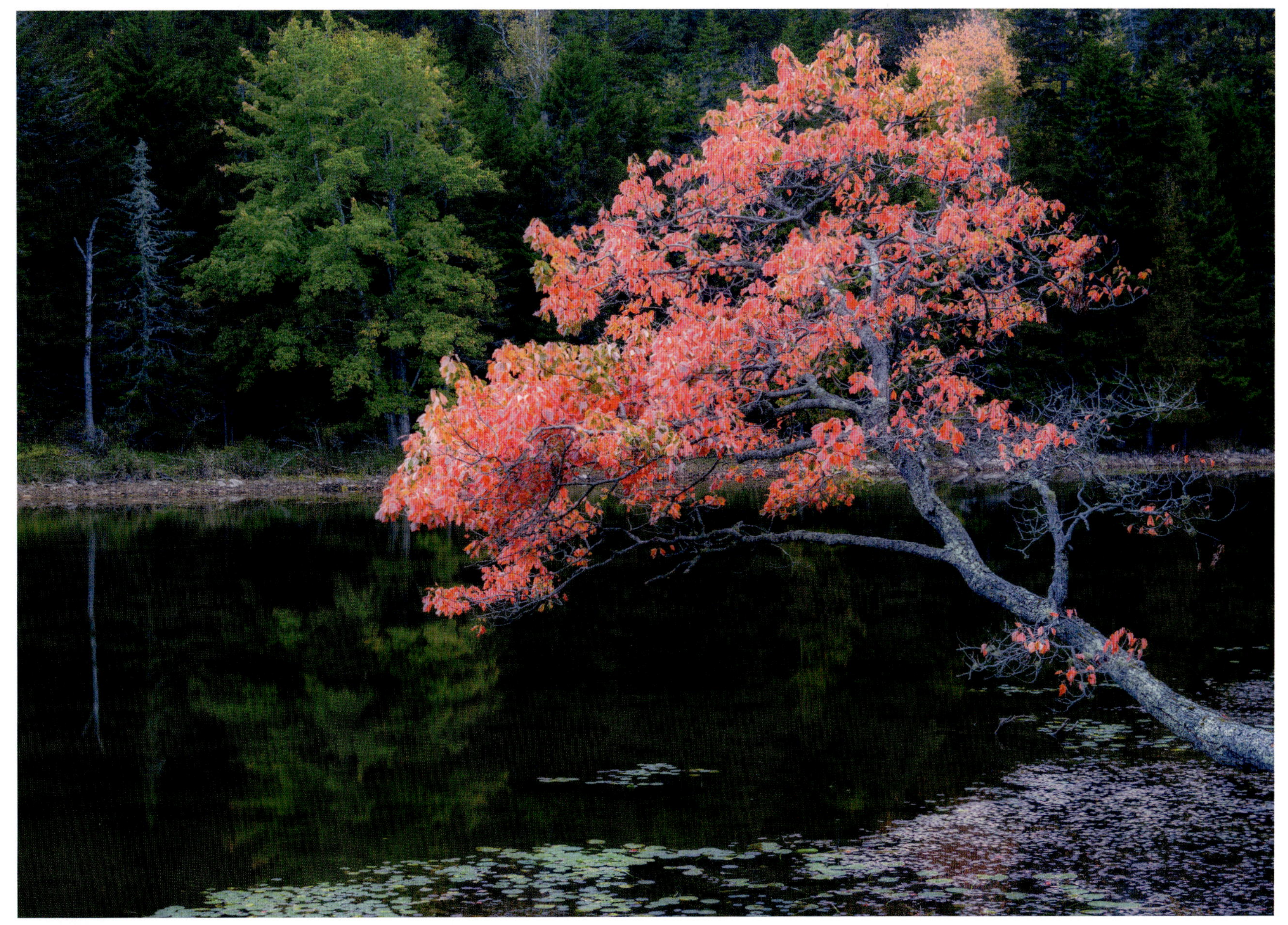

MAPLE GLORY AT LITTLE LONG POND

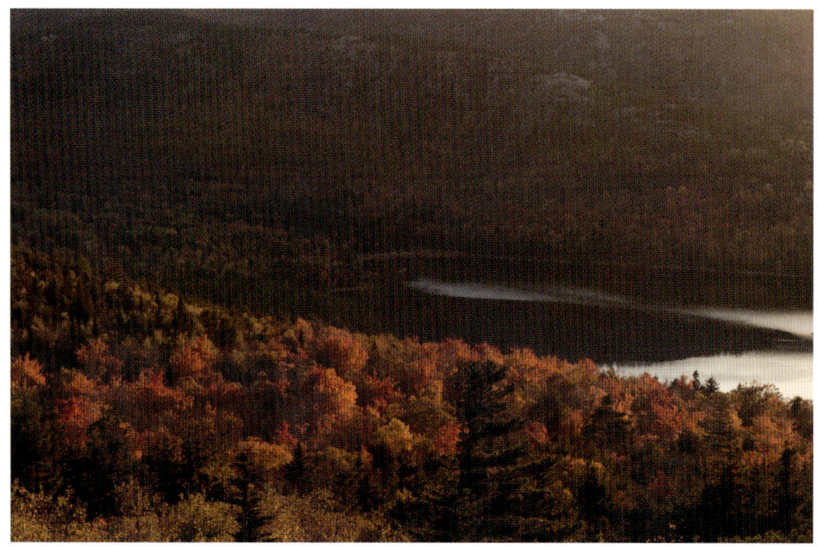

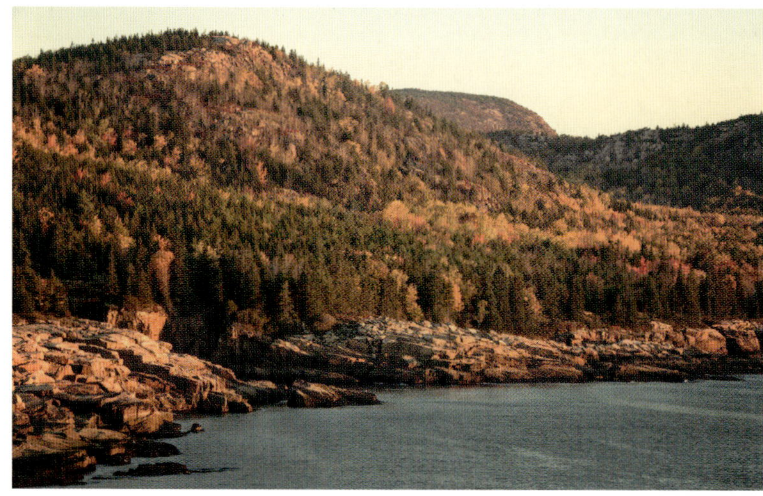

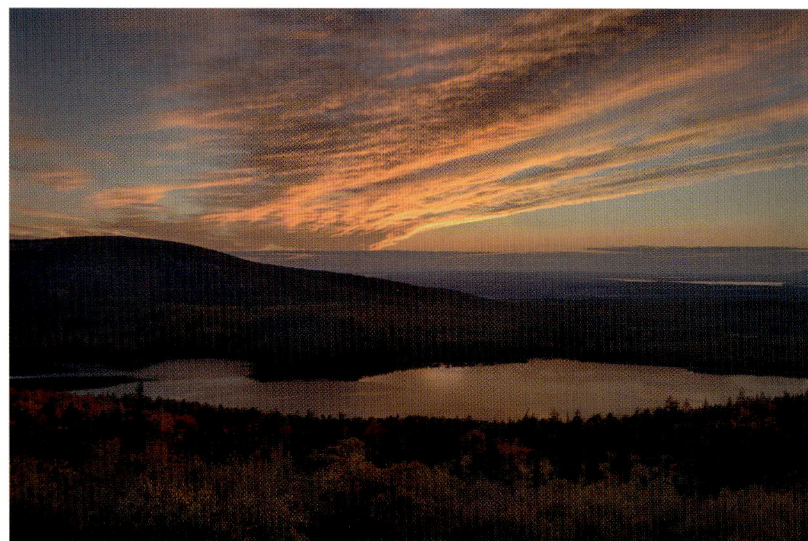

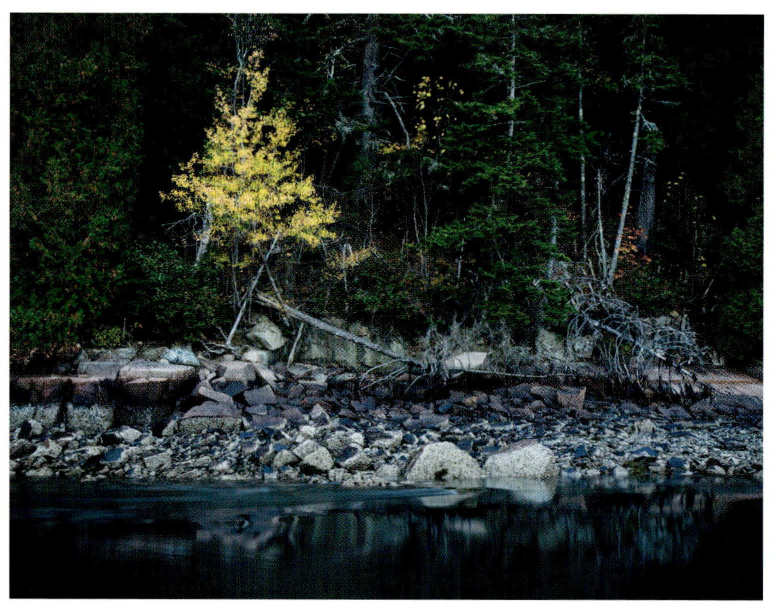

EAGLE LAKE AND THE NORTH BUBBLE, SUNSET

EAGLE LAKE FROM CADILLAC MOUNTAIN

GORHAM MOUNTAIN AND MONUMENT COVE, SUNRISE

FLAMING BIRCH, OTTER COVE, TWILIGHT

LINGERING COLOR ON THE SOUTH BUBBLE

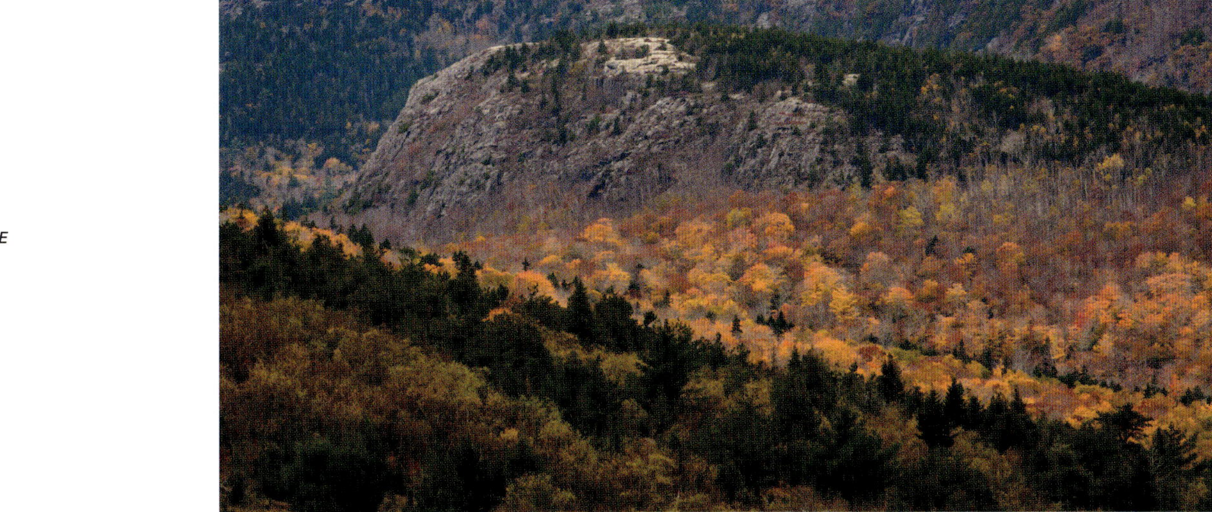

BUBBLE POND, QUIET SUNSET

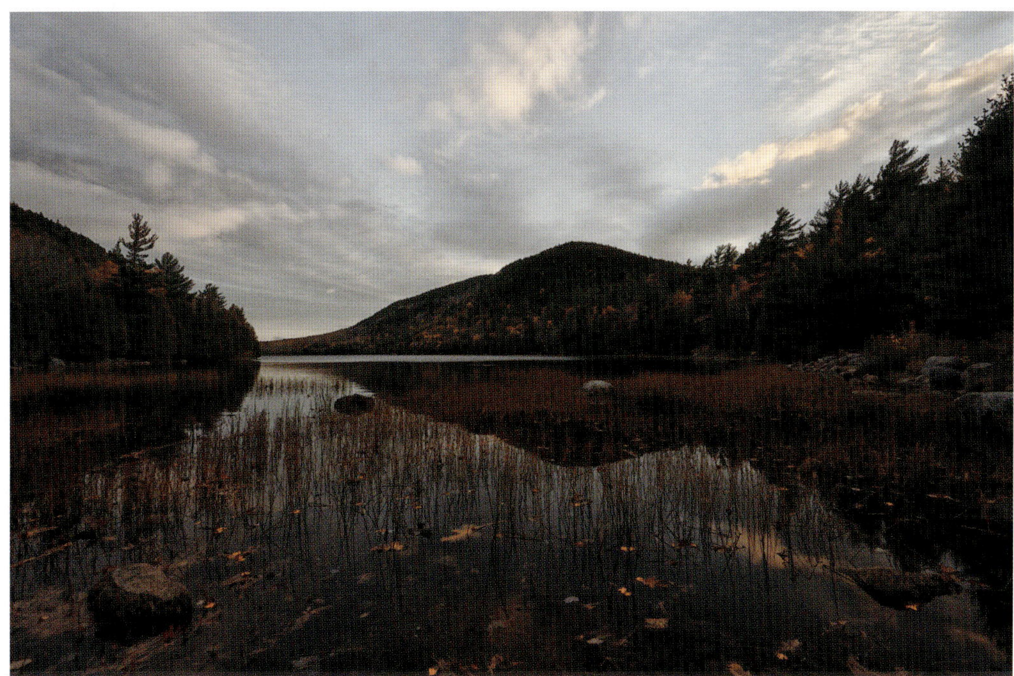

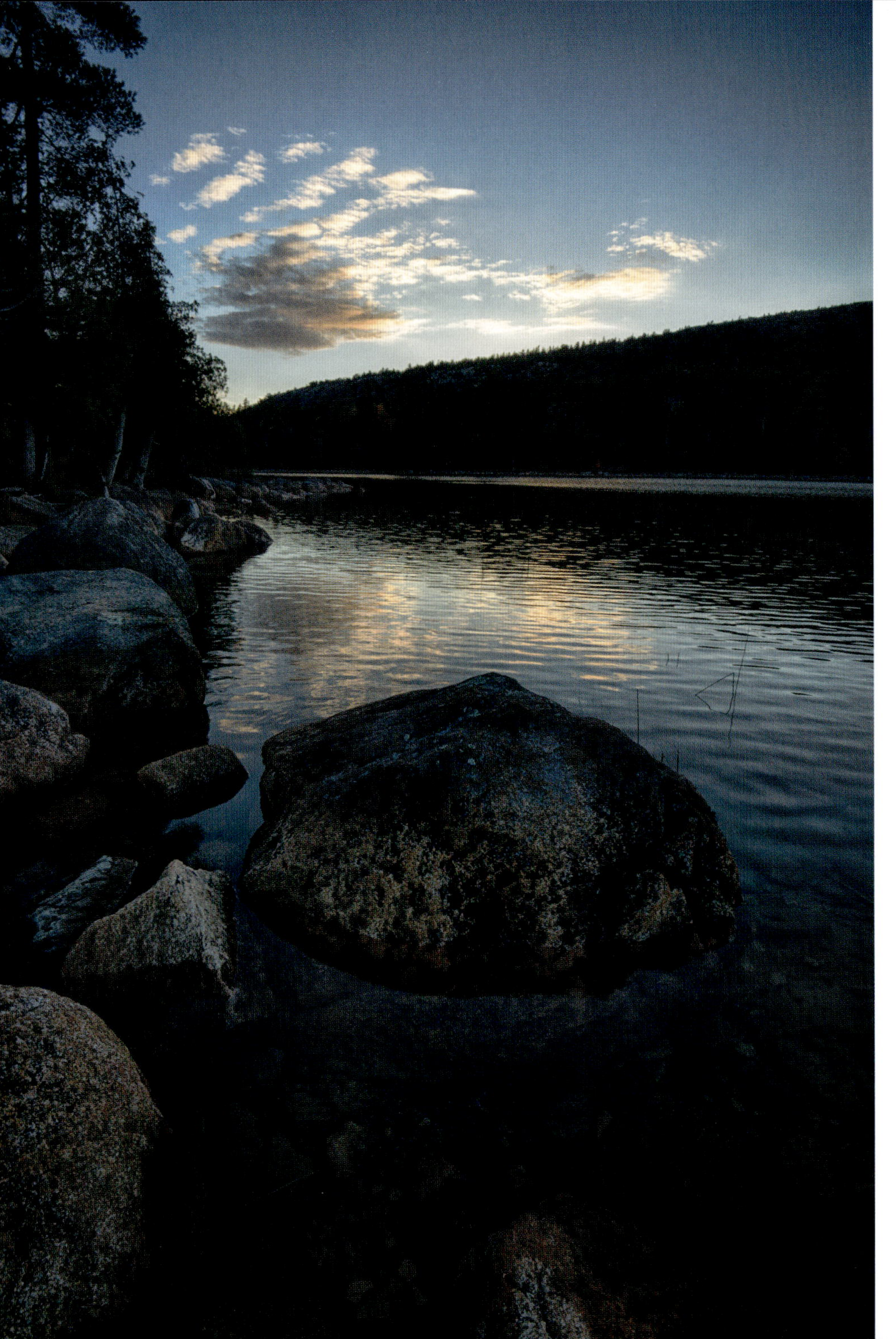

SUNSET RIPPLES, JORDAN POND

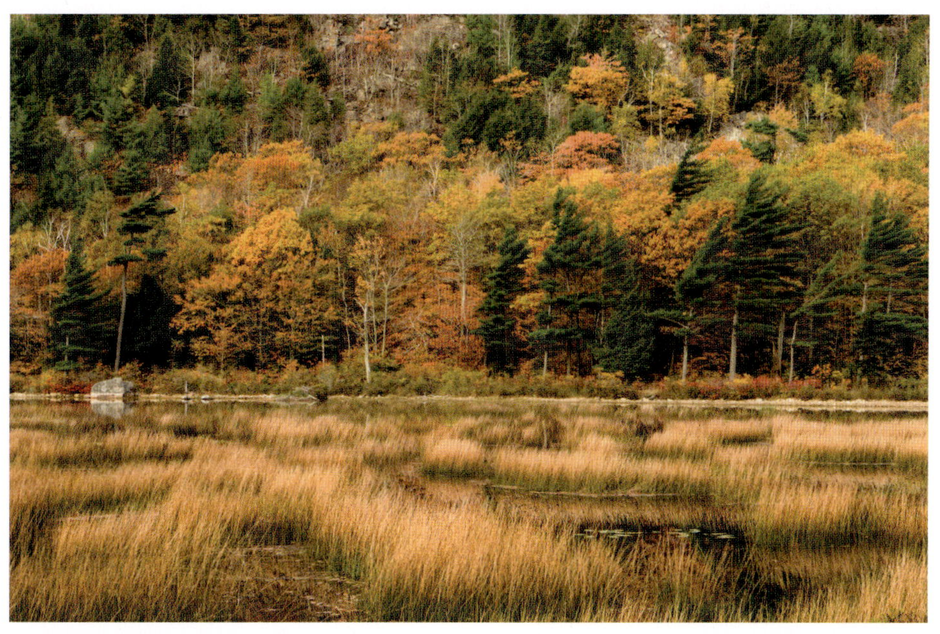

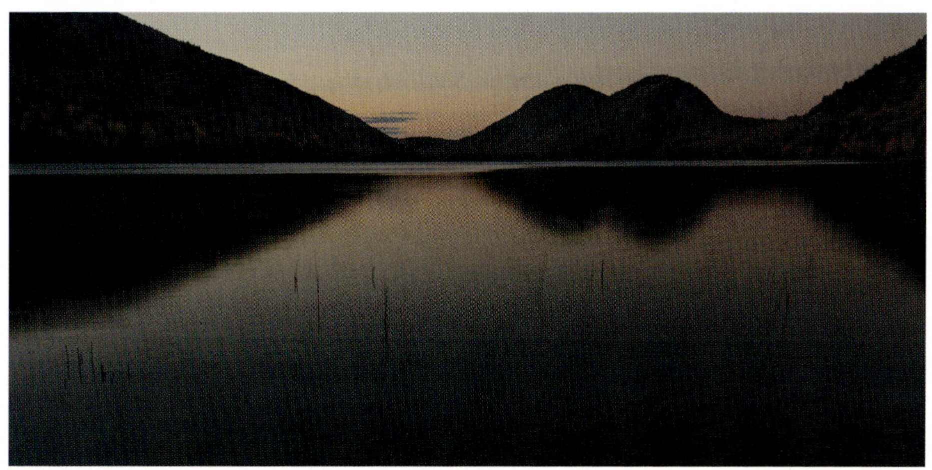

THE TARN IN AUTUMN COLORS

LAST LIGHT ON JORDAN POND

STURM UND DRANG

The German words "Sturm und Drang" (Storm and Stress) were running through my mind, although they bore no relation to Beethoven's Piano Sonata no. 9, which bears the same title. It was a wild day, and my life's soundtrack (which only I can hear) was fluctuating wildly. One moment it's the fourth movement for Beethoven's Pastoral Symphony no. 6, and then an abrupt transition to a few lines of Bob Dylan's "All Along the Watchtower" with Jimi Hendrix's guitar solo for accompaniment seemed appropriate:

> *"Outside in the cold distance*
>
> *A wildcat did growl*
>
> *Two riders were approaching*
>
> *And the wind began to howl."*

After all, I was standing just above Monument Rock, which could be considered a watchtower of sorts. And the wind really was howling. Being completely soaked and waterlogged left me chilled but fully alive.

At times some of the dramatic themes from Smetana's "Moldau" and "Má Vlast" played thunderously to the crescendo of the waves.

It was a day of wild weather, howling winds, rain in the face, chills, and exhilaration. Many people were out and about, reveling in the ferocity of the storm. Waves pounded into the rocks and cliff faces relentlessly, tossing spray 20, 30 feet into the air, where the wind grabbed it and carried it farther inland. Trees bent with the stress of the wind's force but held fast, and we watched in fascination, wondering if the next gust would bring down a weakened spruce. Within an hour, we were all thoroughly soaked, rain gear notwithstanding. Numerous times I cleared the lens and camera equipment during brief periods of relative calm, only to have the image ruined by a sudden blast of wind-driven rain and spray. Still I persisted; my companions danced on the edges of the cliffs, daring the waves to reach up for them, oblivious to the danger of being dragged out into the tumultuous ocean.

I wanted to stay longer, but I had a six-hour drive ahead of me and it was getting late, and I was thoroughly soaked. I found a place to change clothes, grabbed a cup of coffee, and headed for home, full of anticipation, looking forward to working on images the next day. Well, the storm extended quite far inland, and it took me six hours just to reach Portland due to heavy wind, rain, and poor visibility. Home was still over two hours away, and after a brief stop for dinner, I arrived home around midnight. By 6:00 the next morning I was processing images. It had been a most exhilarating day. The three images that follow are a testament to the power of the weather that day.

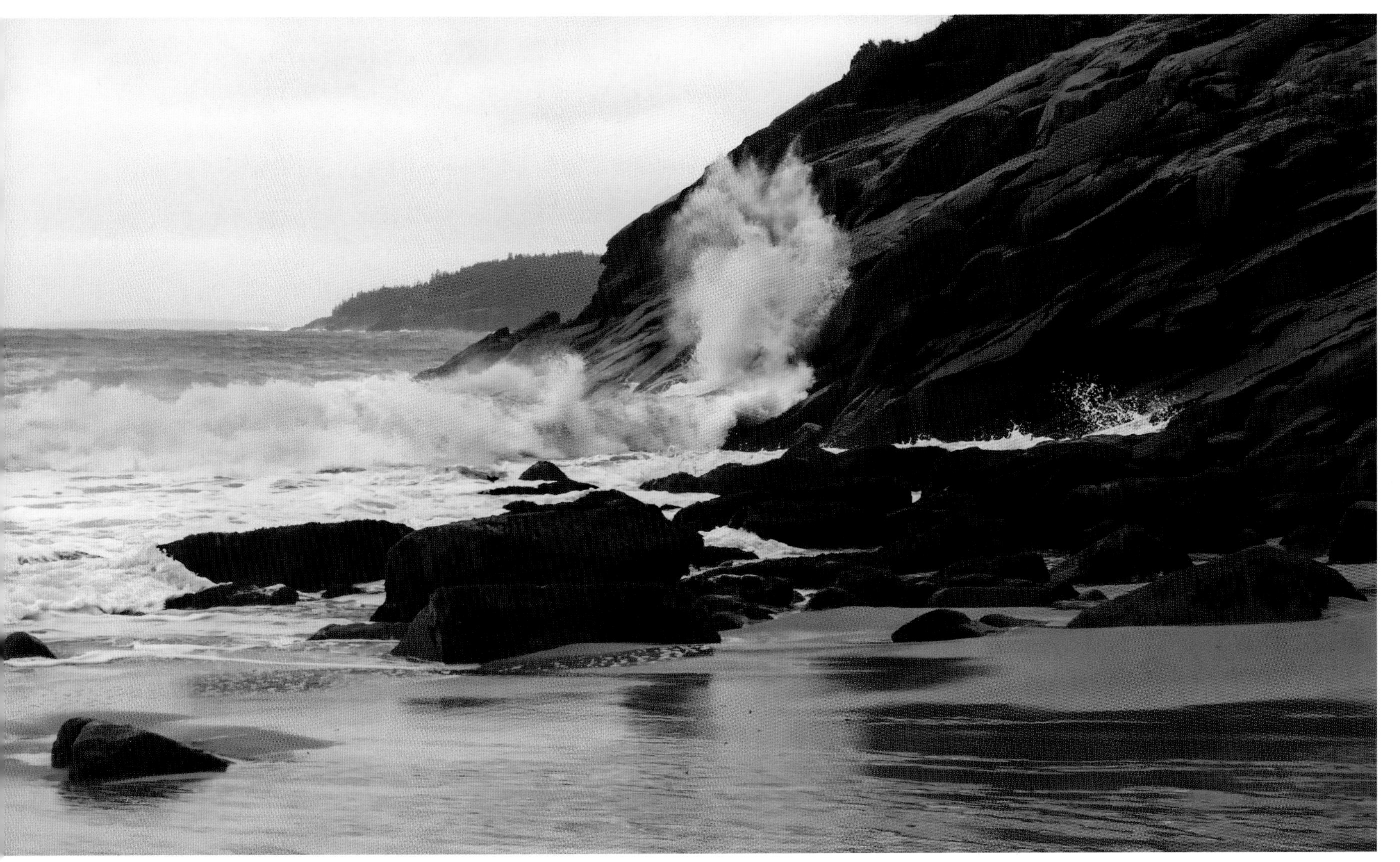

SAND BEACH, OCTOBER STORM

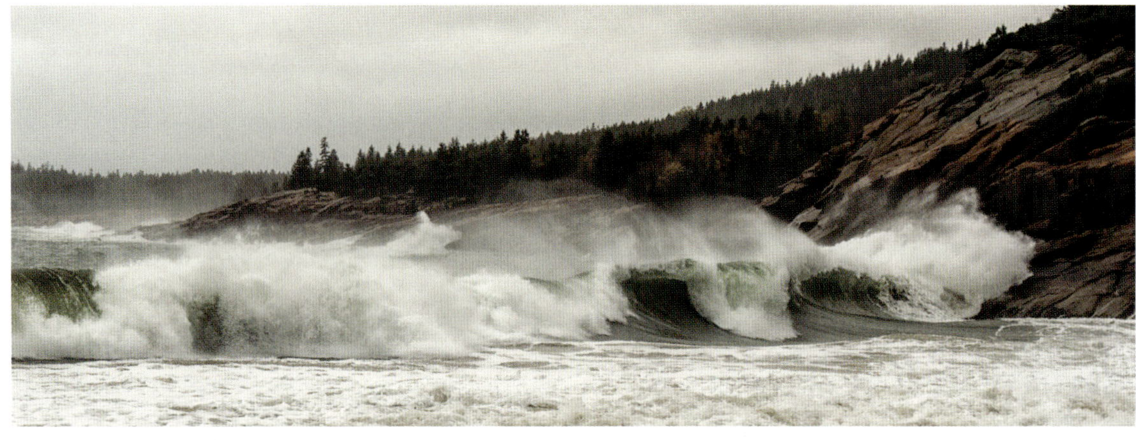

OCTOBER STORM SURF, SAND BEACH

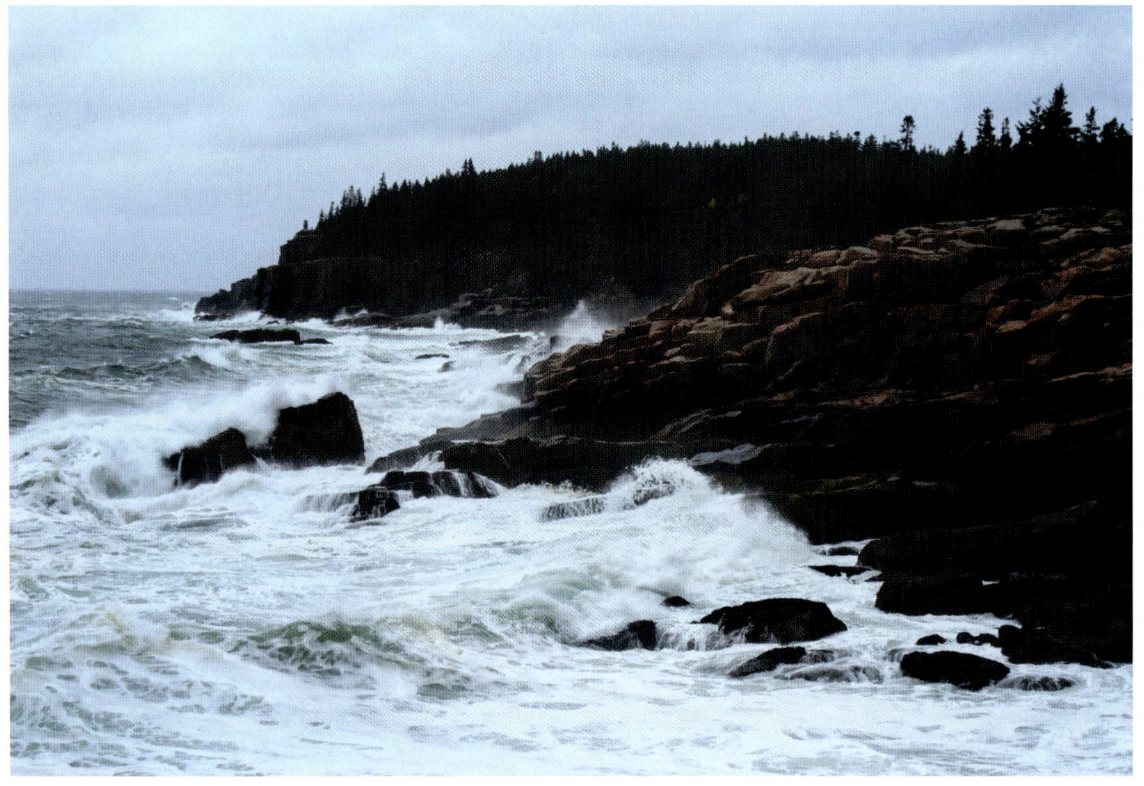

HURRICANE SURF, MONUMENT COVE AND OTTER CLIFFS

•

"I don't fear the sea, but I do respect her some."
—Retired lobsterman

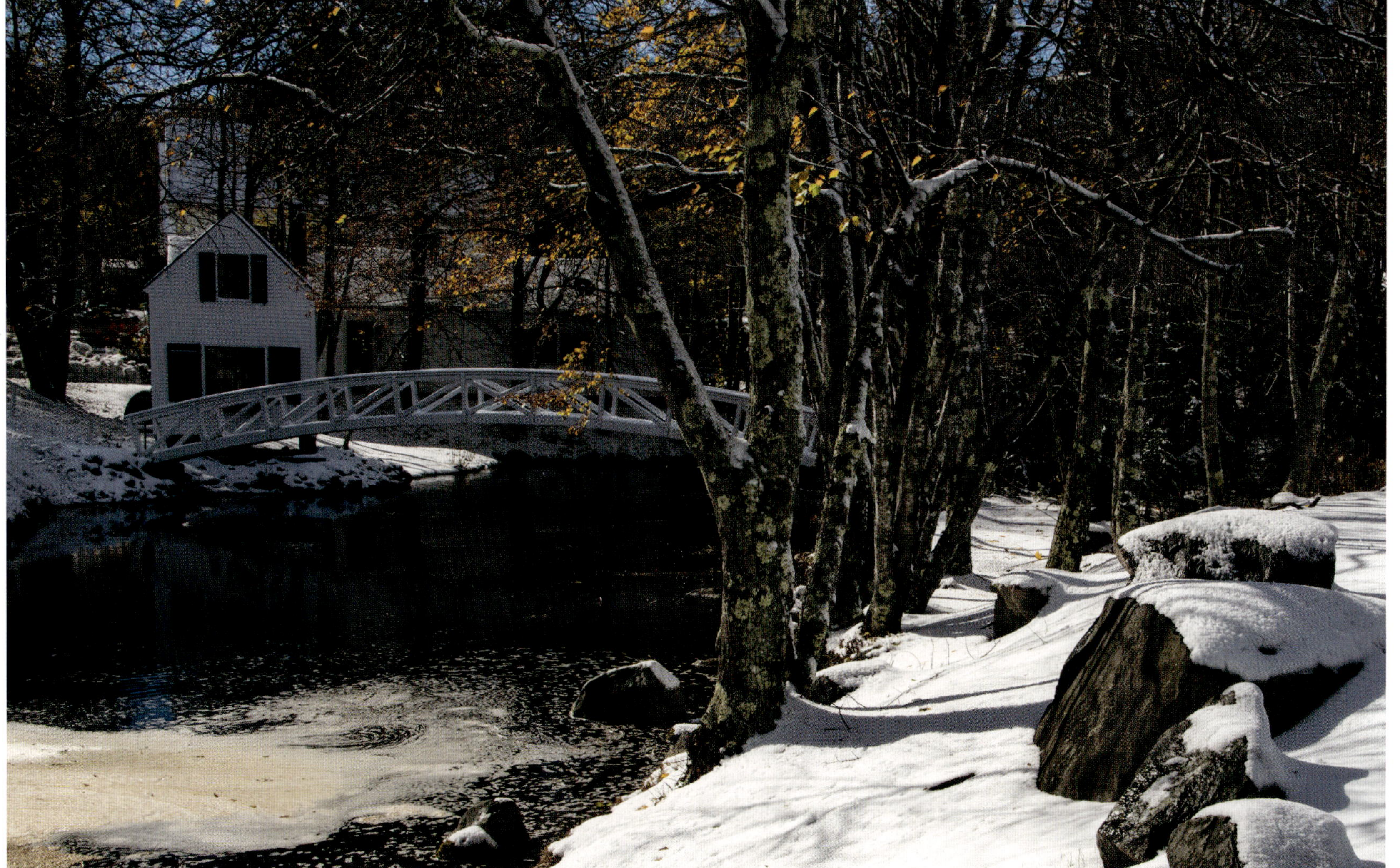

FIRST SNOW, SOMESVILLE, NOVEMBER 3RD

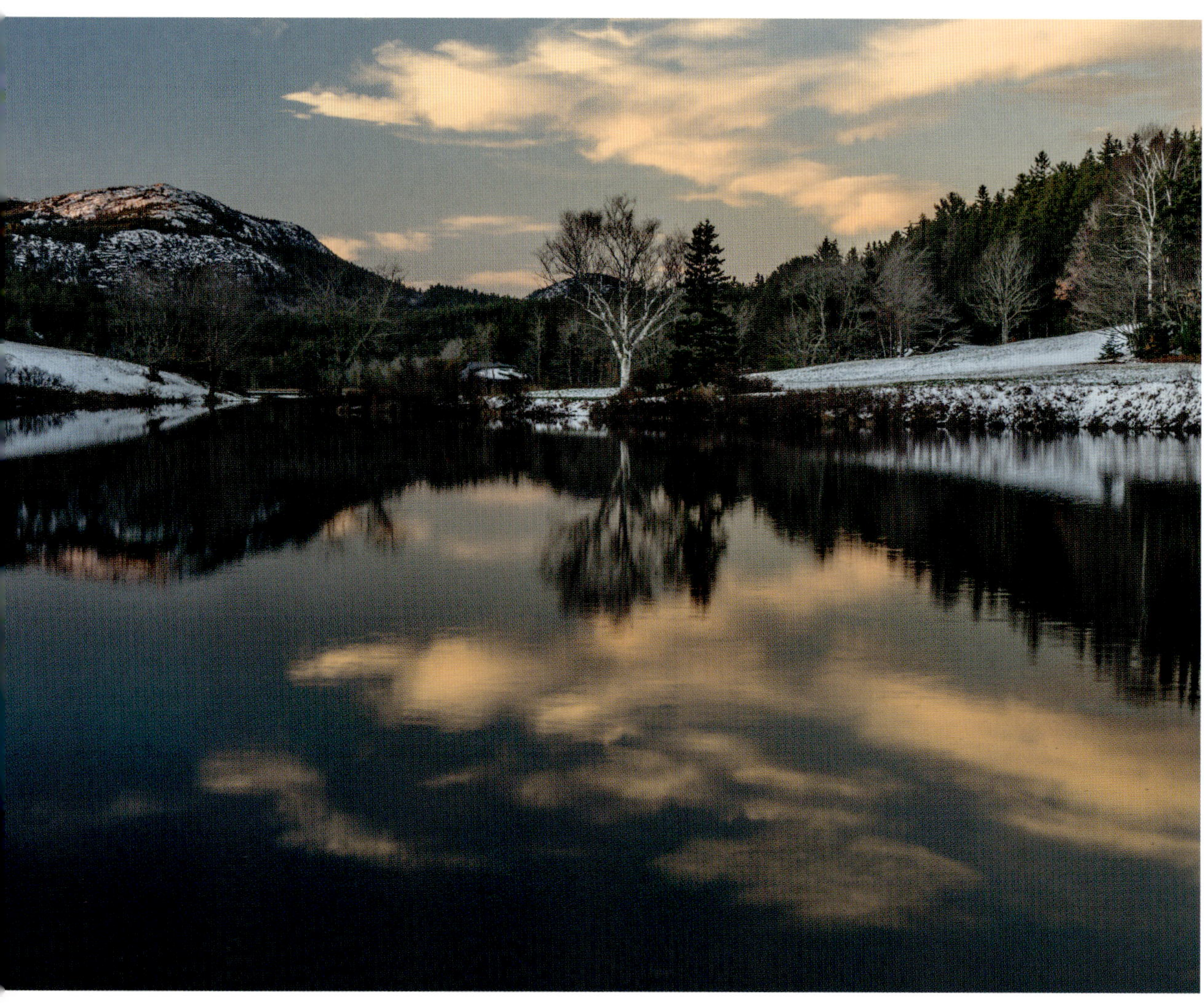

EARLY NOVEMBER SUNSET, LITTLE LONG POND

•

As the days grew shorter, I found that I would have only about an hour at most to photograph in the afternoon. That severely limited my location choices. By mid-December, it was dark by 4 p.m.

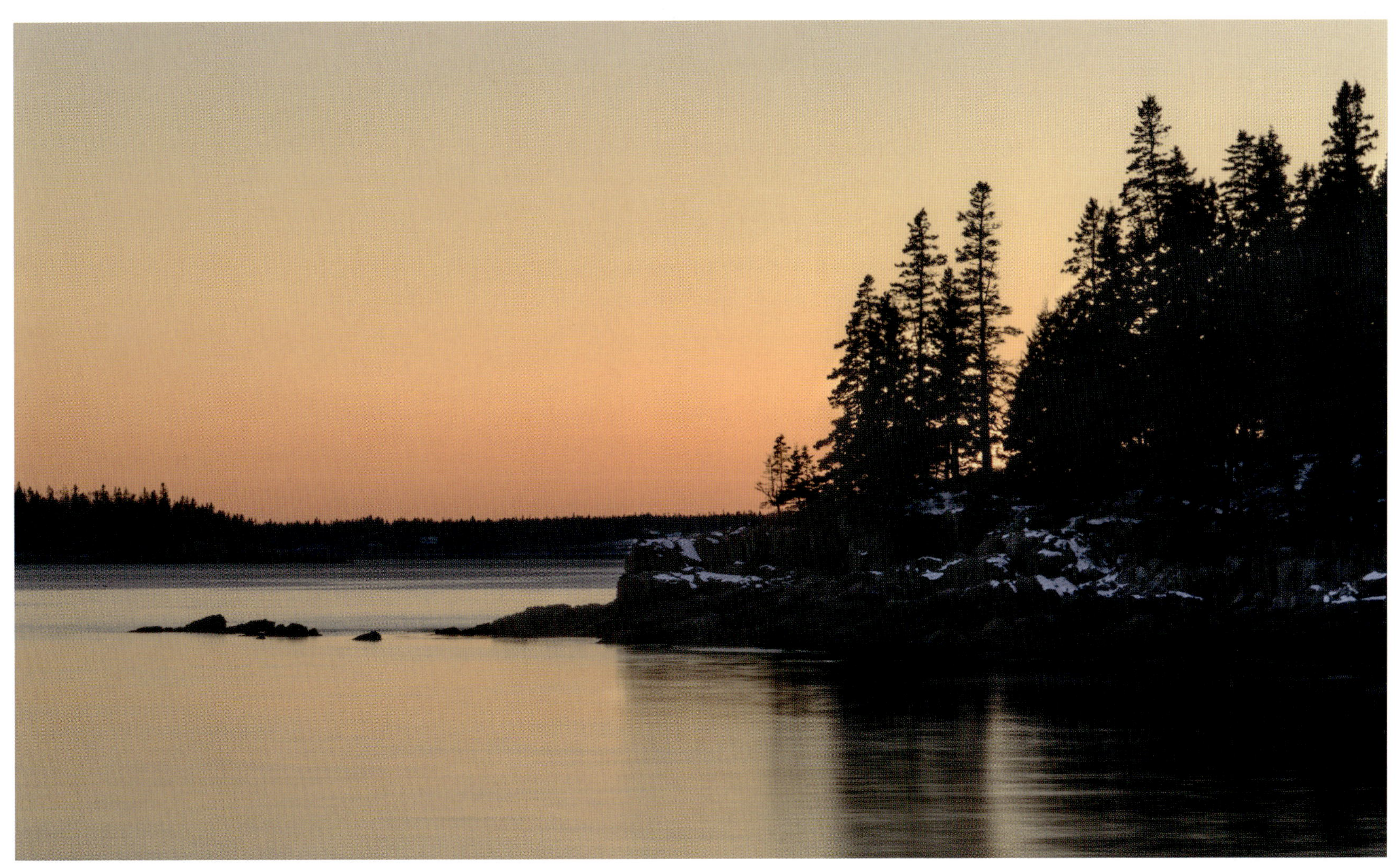

BRACY COVE, TWILIGHT SILHOUETTE

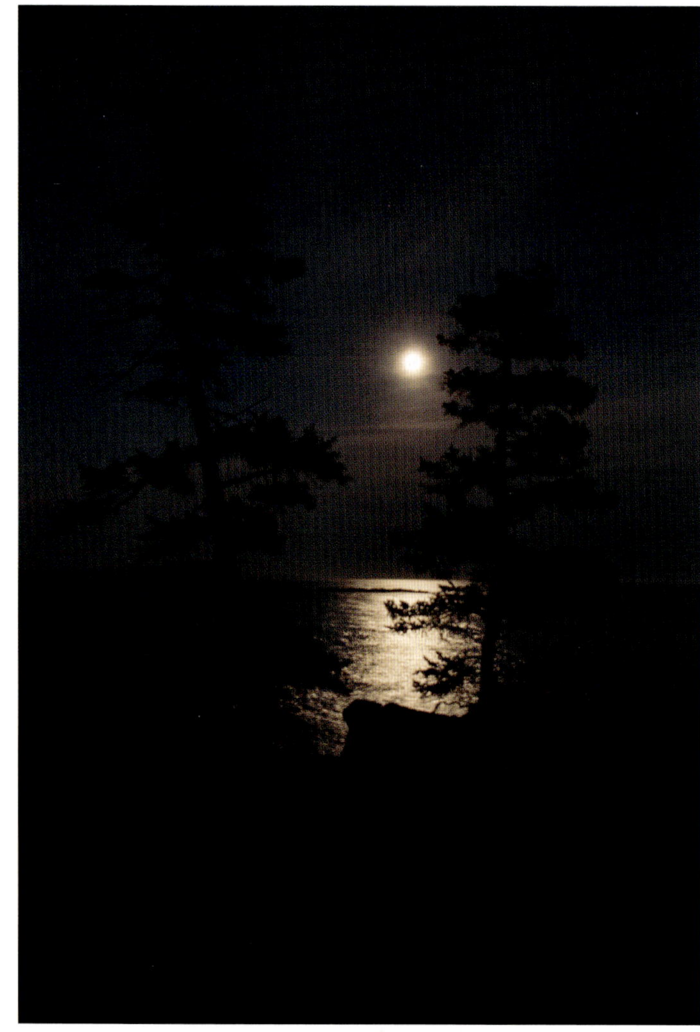

NOVEMBER MOONRISE NEAR THUNDER HOLE

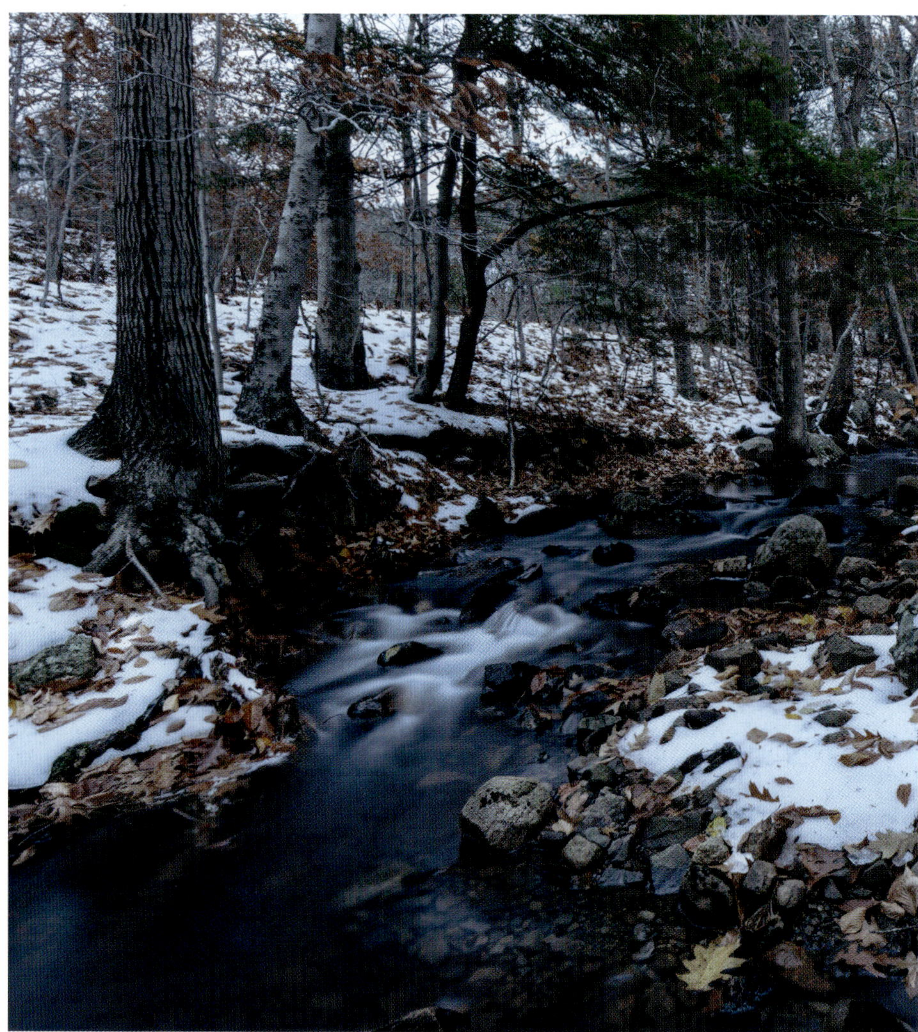

CROMWELL BROOK, EVENING TWILIGHT

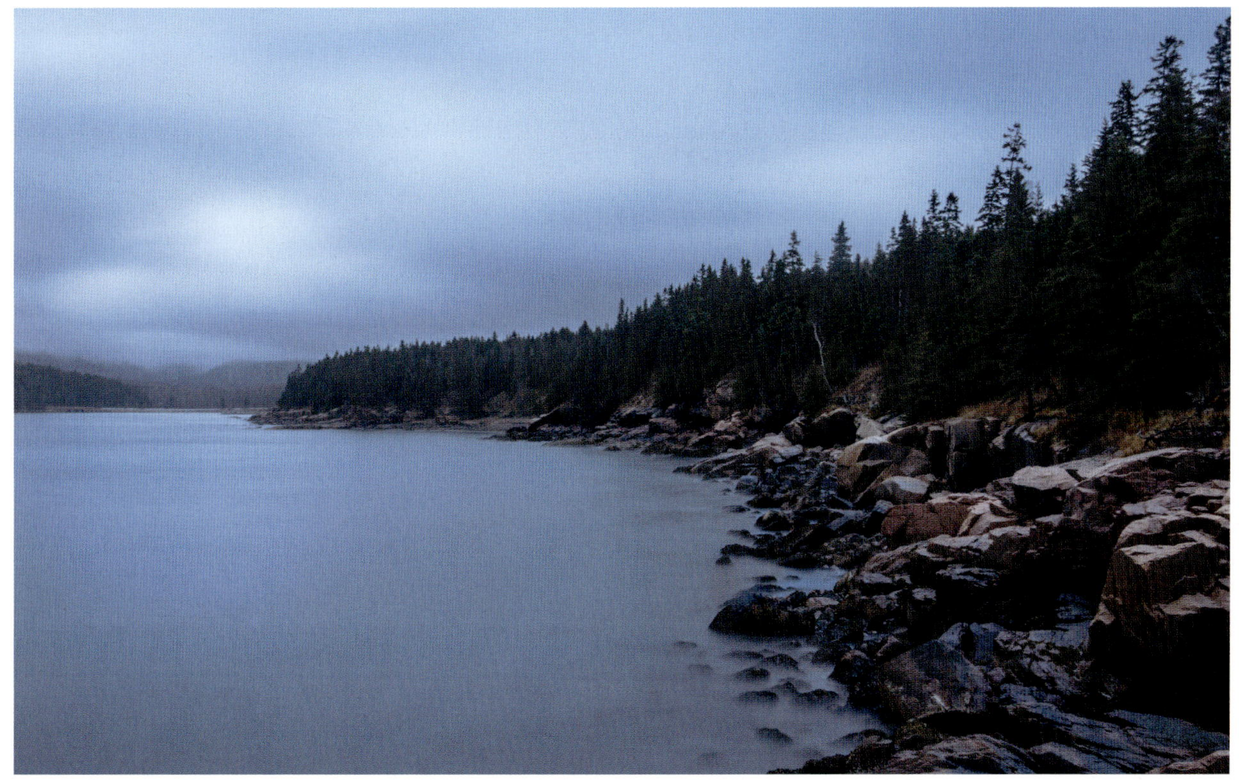

OTTER COVE, NOVEMBER RAIN, BLUE HOUR

•

Shot from Otter Point after a damp walk from Fabbri picnic area in the cold drizzle. The loop road is closed for the season at Otter Cliffs, so the only access is on foot. A long exposure seemed appropriate since the water was very calm. The walk back in the dark and damp was quite a surreal experience, when one considers just how busy the road was just a few weeks earlier.

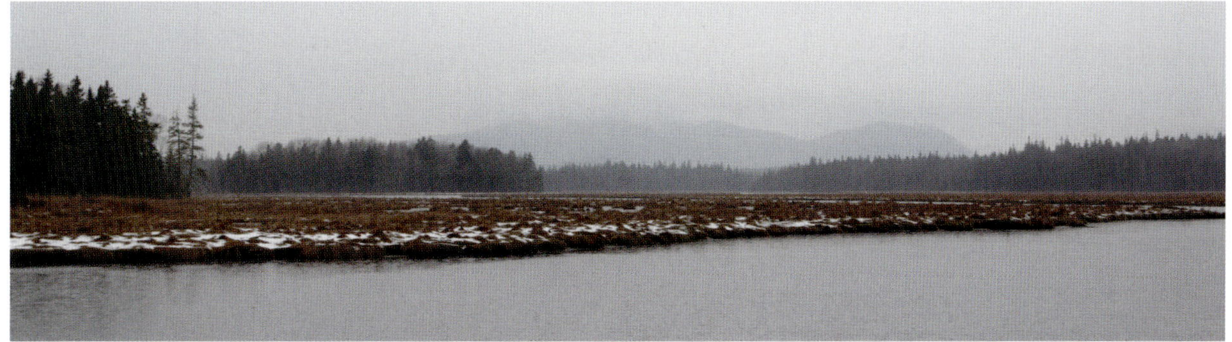

BASS HARBOR MARSH, NOVEMBER FOG

CHAMPLAIN MOUNTAIN

Between mid-April and mid-November, one enters the park on Park Loop Road and drives past the Precipice Trail area. However, during the rest of the year, Park Loop Road is closed between the Hulls Cove visitor center and Sand Beach. I knew the Ocean Drive area between Sand Beach and Otter Cliffs was open year-round, but how to get there was the mystery. That's when a coworker, a resident of the island who knew of my photographic interests, told me the secret. Just turn right going out of the parking lot, and you're there in about three minutes. I was surprised it was that easy. However, the bigger surprise was what I found once I drove down Schooner Head Road.

The road is lined with aspen and birch trees for about a mile, until you come to a marsh area. To the left the land rises, blocking views of the ocean; to the right there are trees and marshes. Then the trees open up to reveal an unobstructed view of Champlain Mountain and the cliffs of the Precipice Trail, a view that can't be seen from Park Loop Road, since there are so many intervening trees. Here also is a small pond, reflecting the mountain perfectly. For years, I had speculated that there had to be a good place to photograph the cliffs, but I was never able to find a suitable spot along the loop road. Now, not only had I found the spot, it turned out to be more than I had hoped for. This soon became a favorite spot to go to, since I could even get here on my lunch hour, make a few images if there was anything interesting happening weather-wise, and be back to work in less than 10 minutes. After a while it became my habit to drive by here every morning before work, and again at the end of the day.

It was about a week before Thanksgiving, a cold November morning, and we were having intermittent snow squalls, with the sun popping in and out of the clouds. As I drove down the road, I could see the light pouring through a large break in the clouds, and fresh snow on Champlain, and I reasoned that I might get a good image if the clouds stayed open. I arrived at the pond, quickly set up, and made a few images before the clouds moved on and I was hit by another squall. But I knew that I had something good. It lasted only a few minutes, but I was thankful for being there to see it.

What I love about this image is the golden light, the dark-blue and gray clouds filled with snow, and this immense rock facade. To add to the magic, the tips of the birches and aspen branches add the maroon bit of contrast. A cloud's shadow drifts over the mountain, adding some depth. At the base of the aspens and birch trees on the left, you can just make out the loop road. The pond, partially frozen, reflects the golden light and makes an abstraction of the face of the cliff. It was a majestic morning.

I returned here often and, most times, was rewarded with something special. Several of those images are in this book, but this is the first time I captured this view. For me, this is just as majestic as anything I've seen in Yosemite, Zion, McKinley, or Glacier National Parks, but more special, 'cause it's Maine.

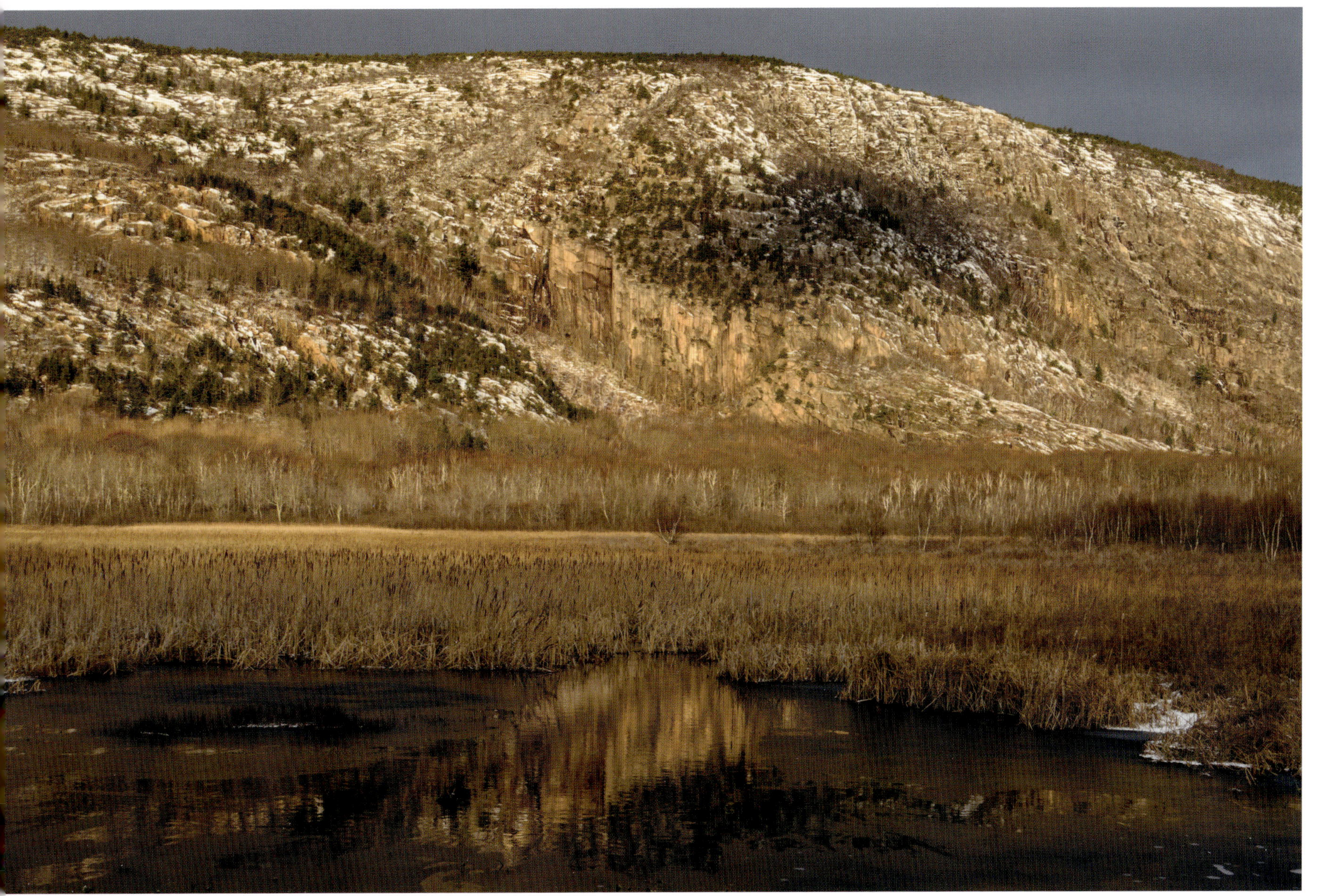

CHAMPLAIN SUNRISE

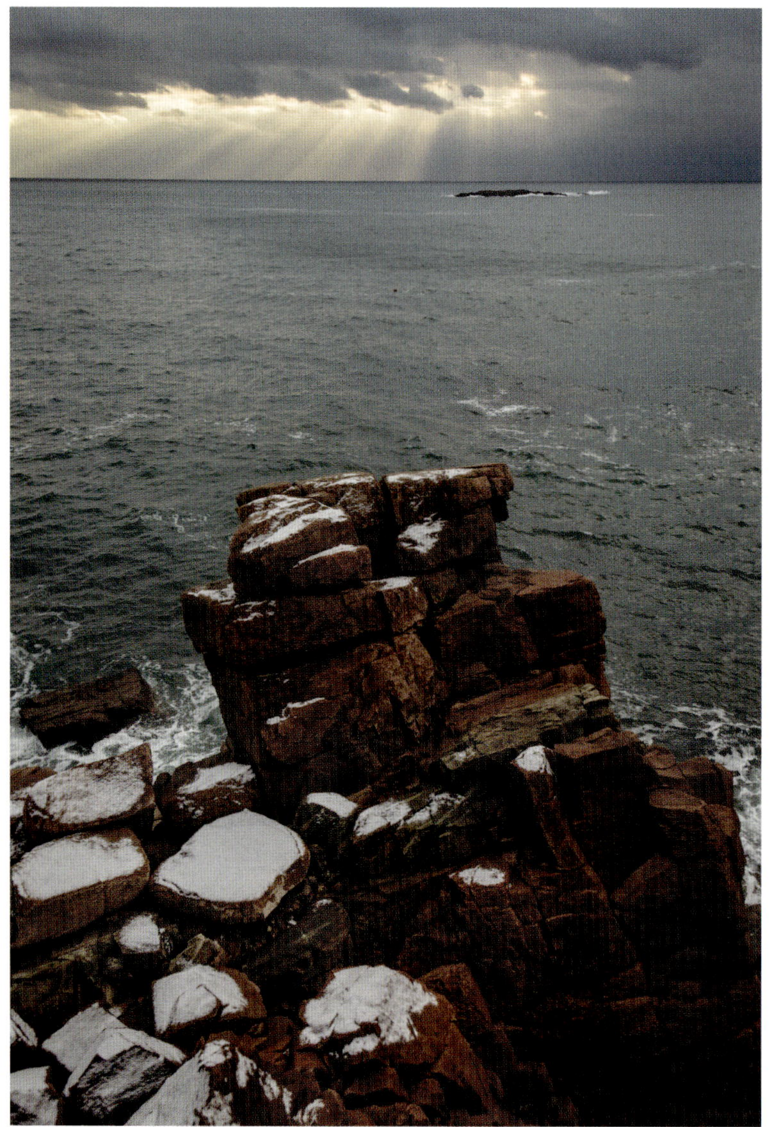

SEA STACKS, SNOW SQUALLS, AND CREPUSCULAR RAYS

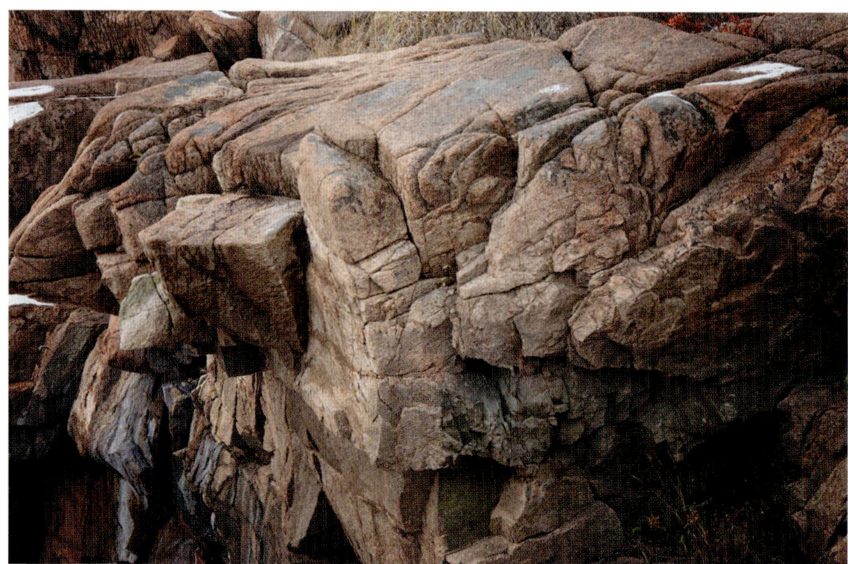

SUNRISE GRANITE COLOR

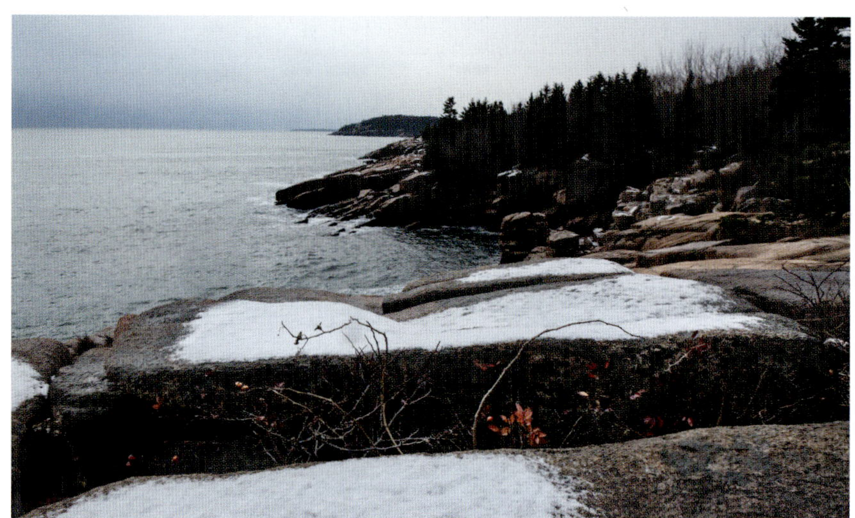

RUGOSA LEAVES AND CORN SNOW

NOVEMBER MORNING, INCOMING TIDE

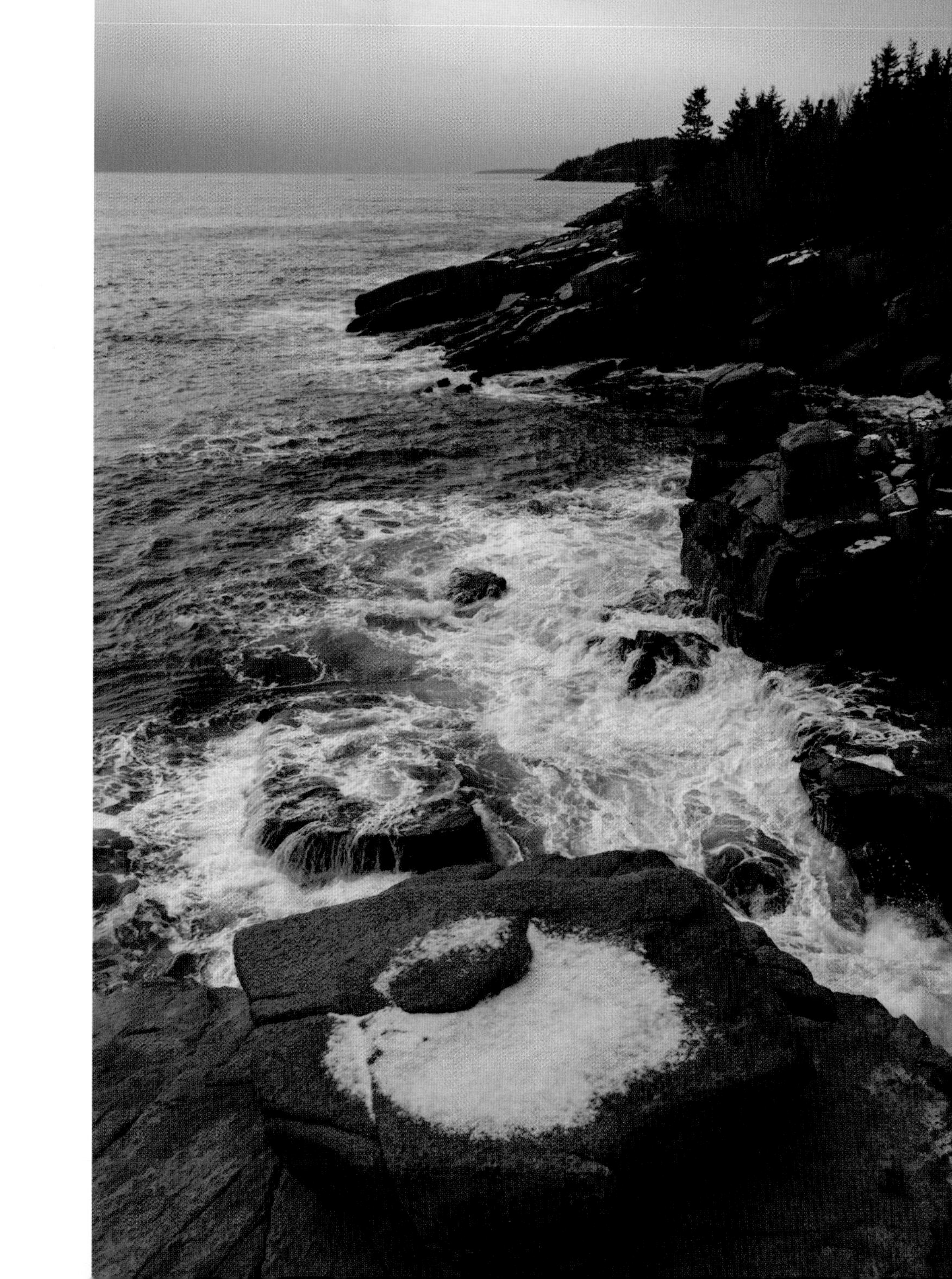

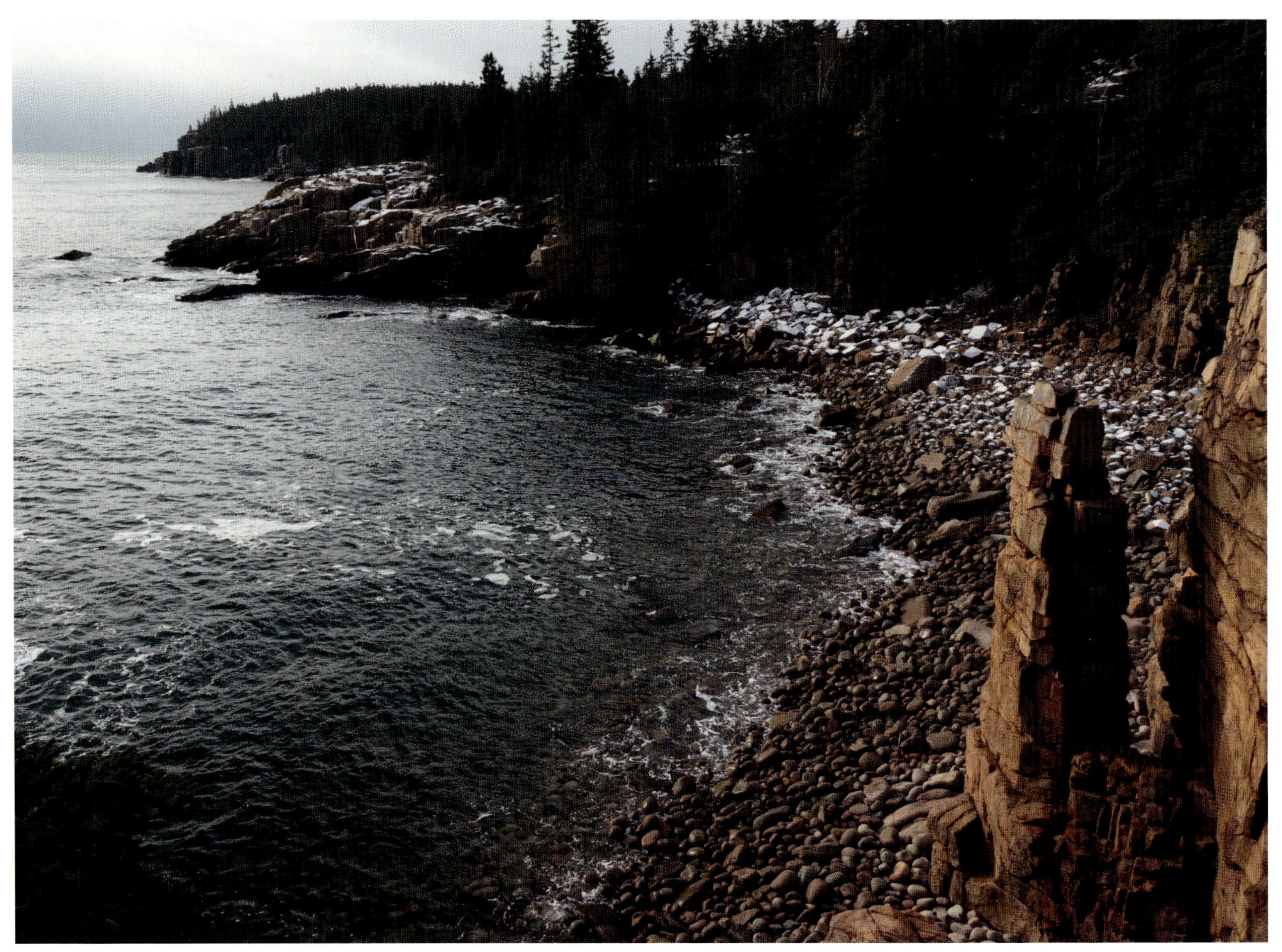

MONUMENT ROCK, SUNRISE, FRESH SNOW

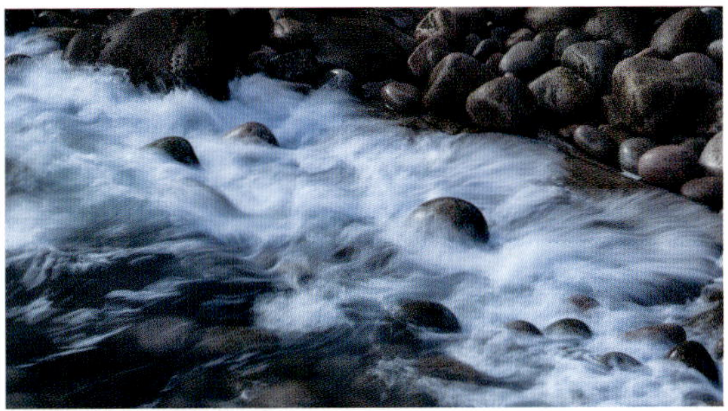

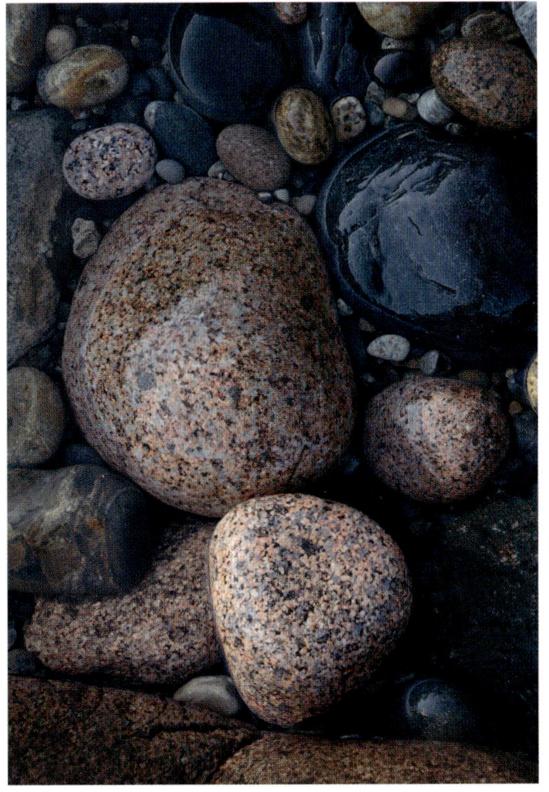

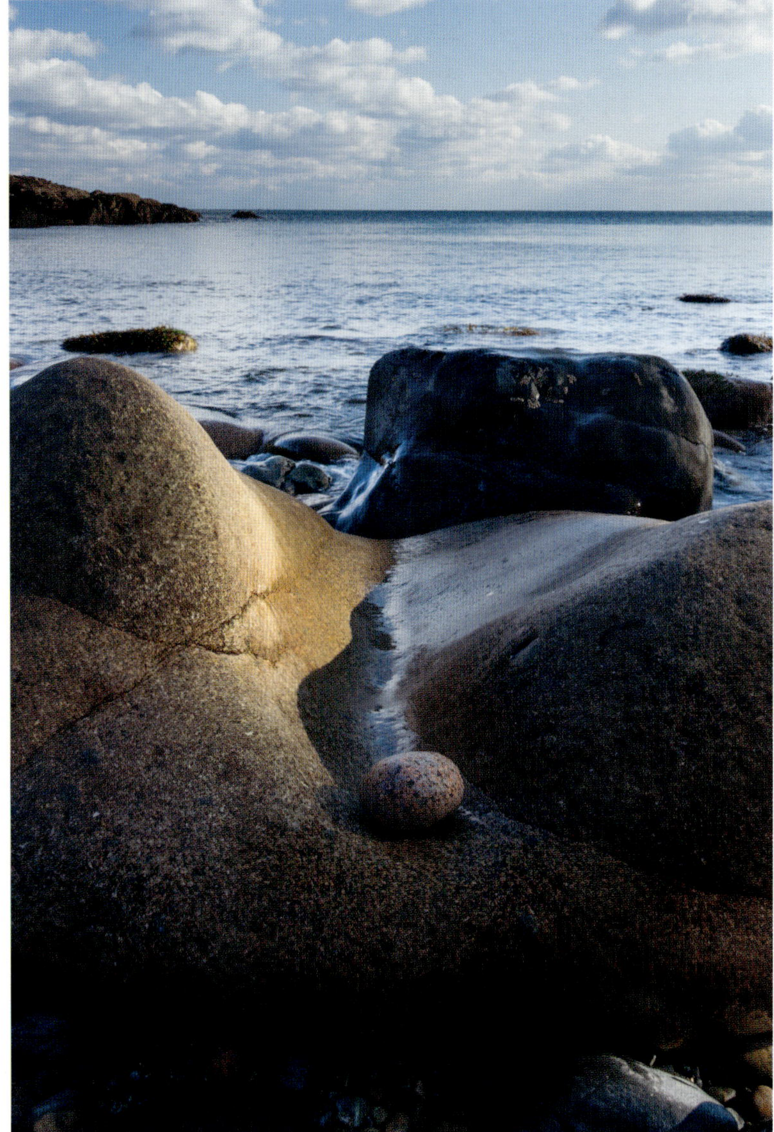

COBBLES AND SURF, MONUMENT COVE

LITTLE HUNTERS BEACH COBBLES

BOULDERS AND COBBLES AND CLOUDS, LITTLE HUNTERS BEACH

NOVEMBER LIGHT

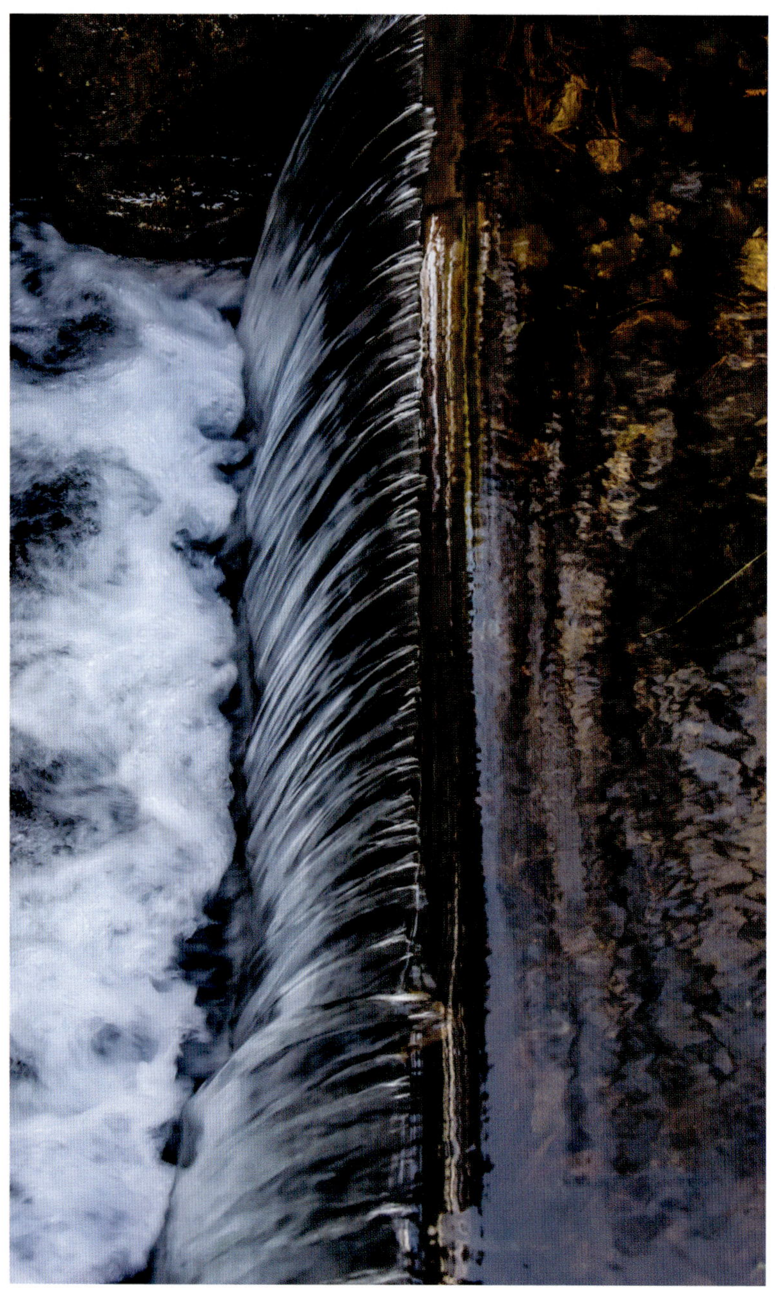

SPILLWAY AT BUBBLE POND

•

A silly thought popped into my head at the time; I kept wondering why the reflection of the trees never slipped over the edge.

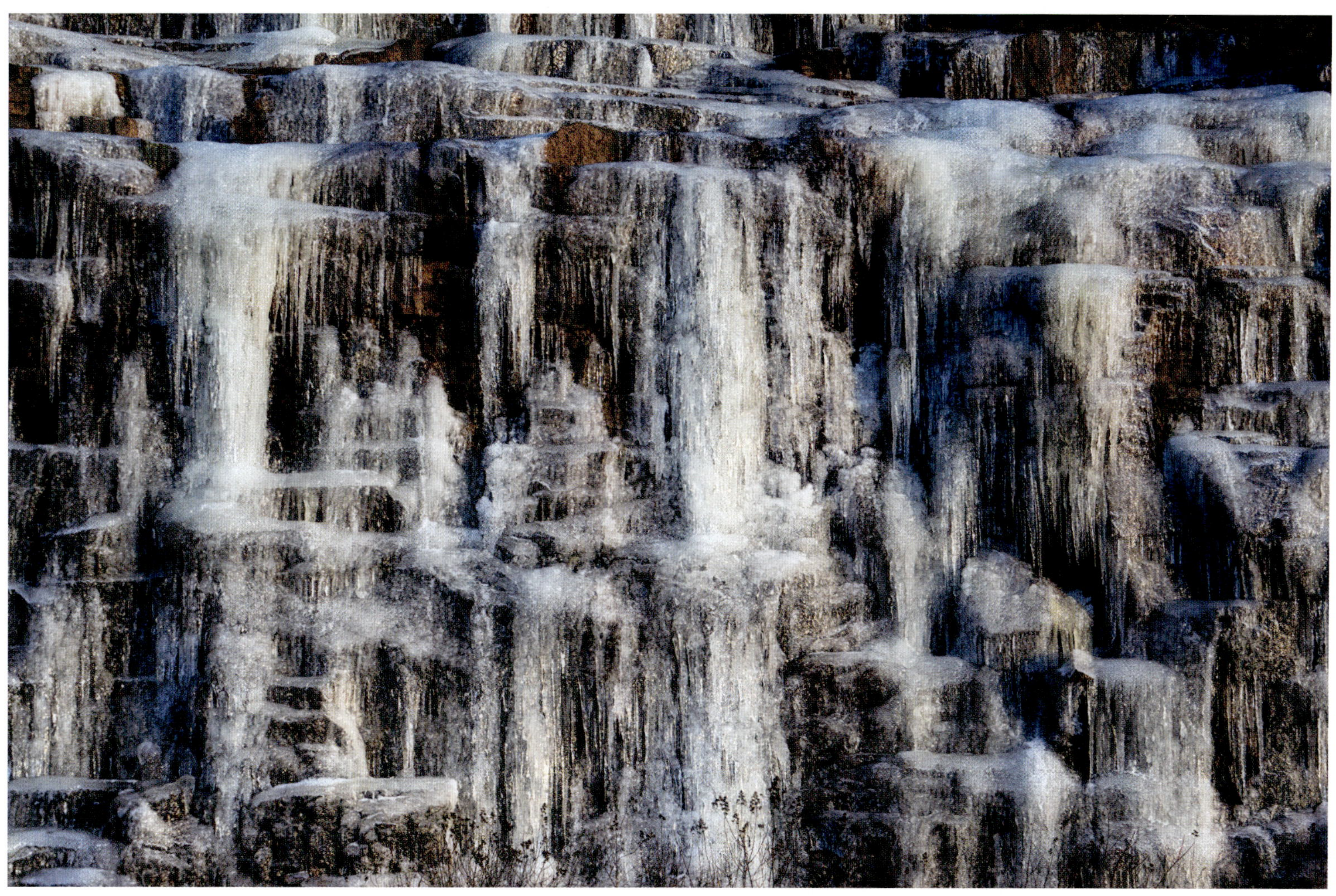

ICE FALL, CADILLAC MOUNTAIN

•

Normally, the Cadillac Mountain road is closed in the winter, but a warm spell created an opportunity for the National Park Service to open the road for a few extra days. Snowmelt from earlier in the week created a frozen cascade along the road near the summit.

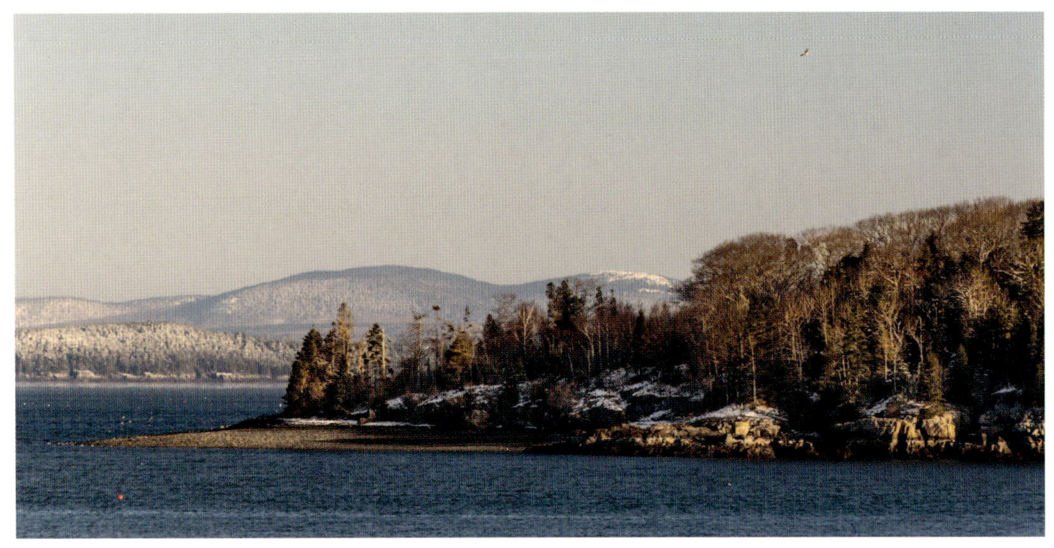

RETURNING TO THE NEST

•

An eagle (*upper right*) returns to the nest at just after sunrise on an early December morning. Winter is still twenty days away, although fresh snow covers the Schoodic on the far side of Frenchman Bay.

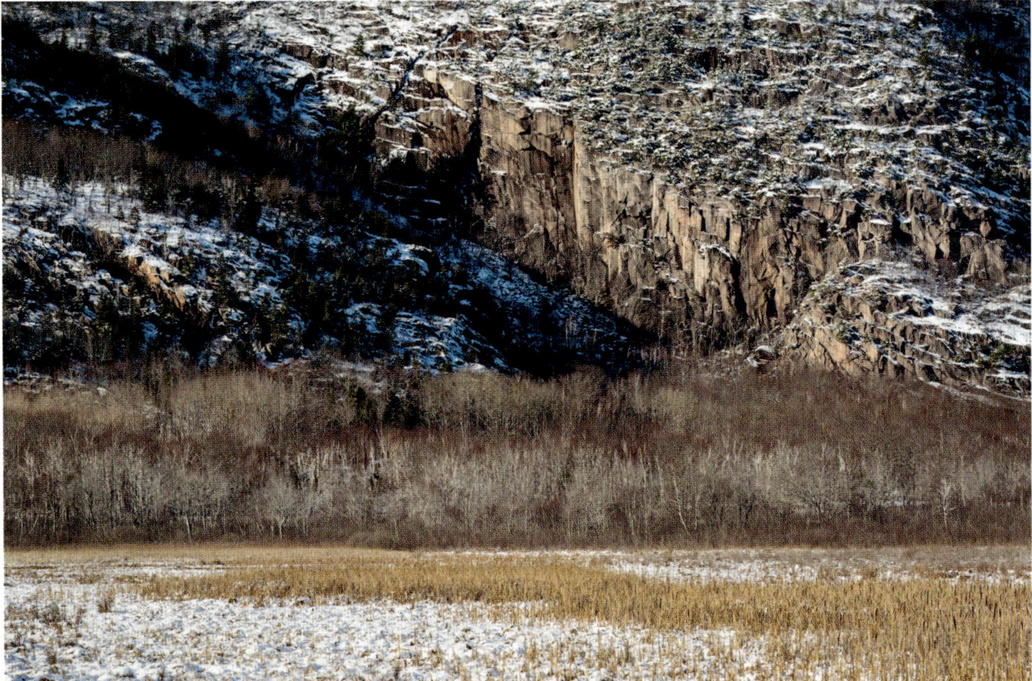

FRESH SNOW ON CHAMPLAIN MOUNTAIN

MIDMORNING AT OTTER CLIFFS, EARLY DECEMBER

SAND BEACH LAGOON AND THE BEEHIVE, THE SHORT, STEEP MOUNTAIN WHICH LOOKS LIKE A BEEHIVE FROM SOME VIEWING ANGLES

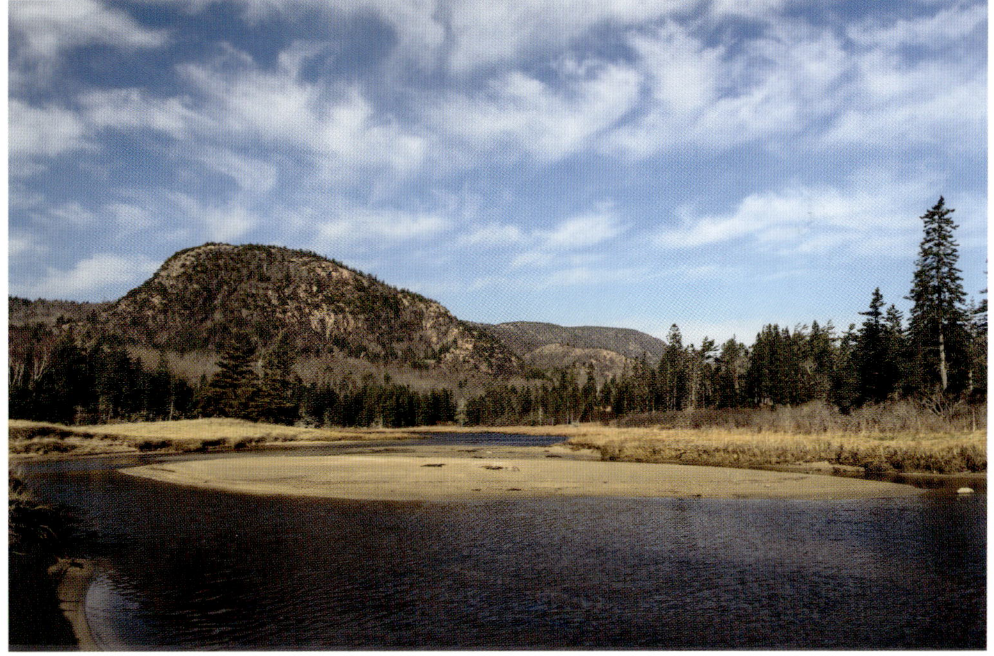

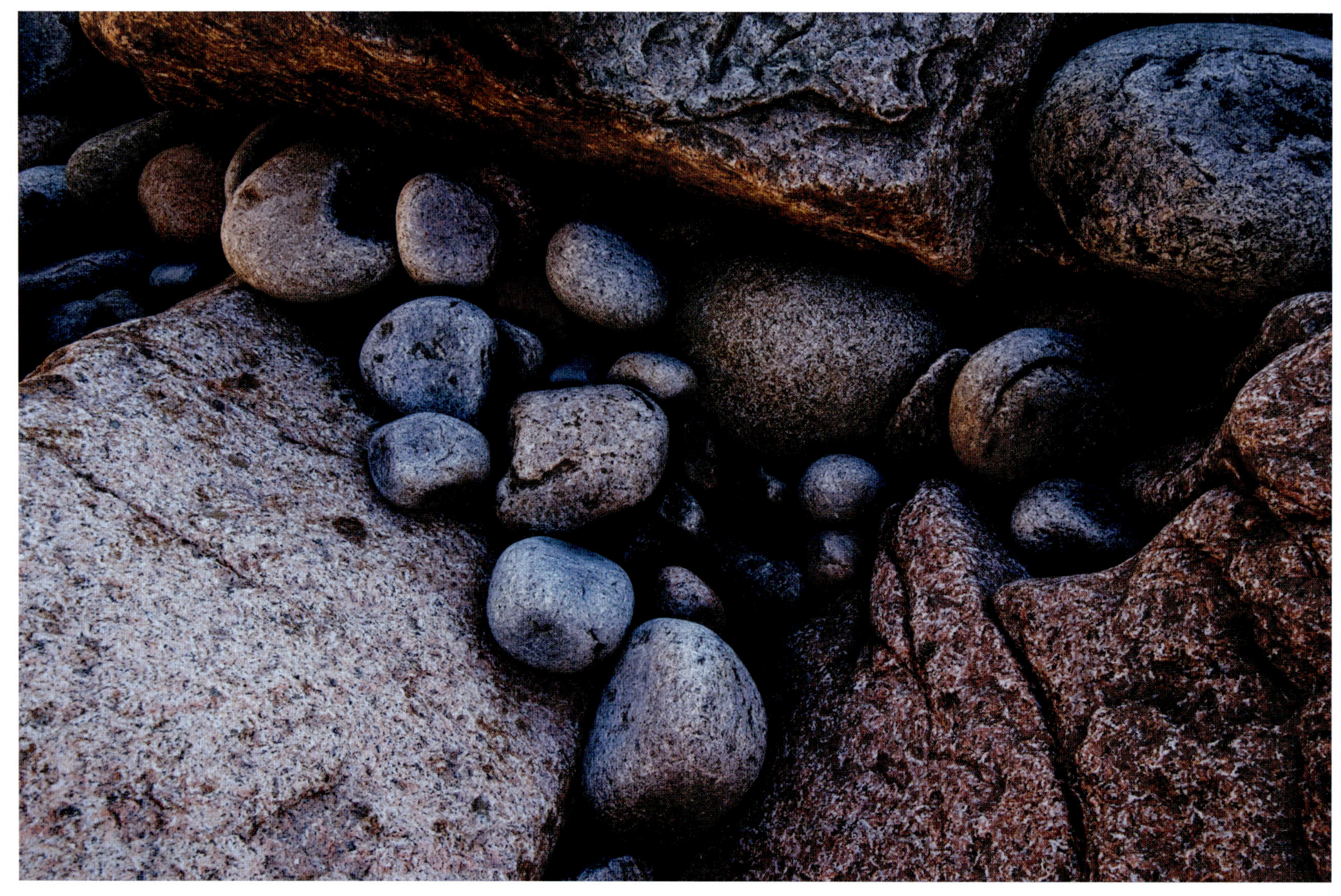

SUNRISE LIGHT AT BOULDER BEACH

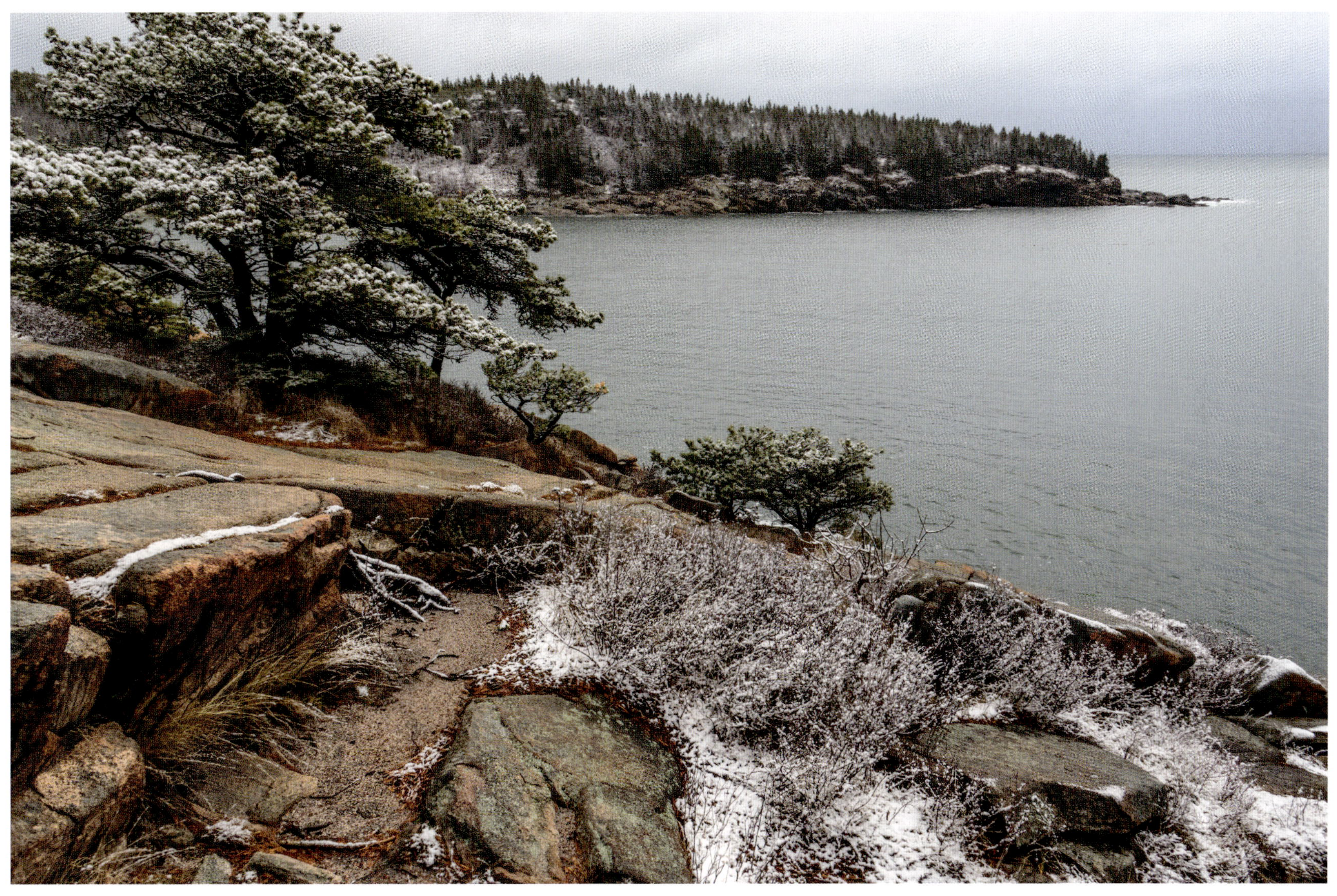

GREAT HEAD WITH FRESH SNOW

•

Fresh snow seemed like a daily occurrence.

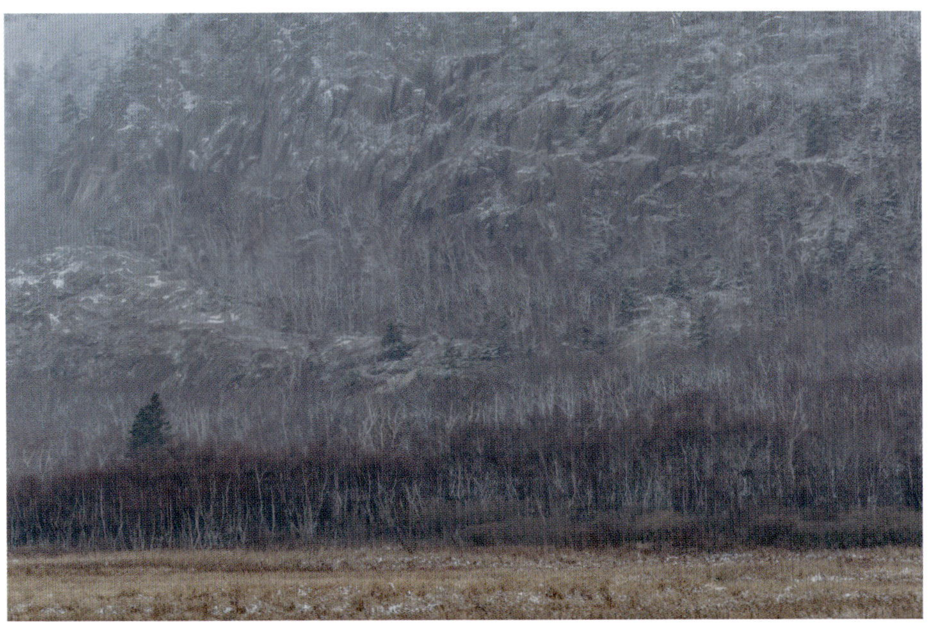

BIRCHES AND ASPENS ENDURE A SNOW SQUALL BELOW THE PRECIPICE TRAIL ON CHAMPLAIN MOUNTAIN

•

I love snow squalls, brief moments where much is obscured and mysterious, quickly followed by a moment of clarity, repeated over and over, always changing.

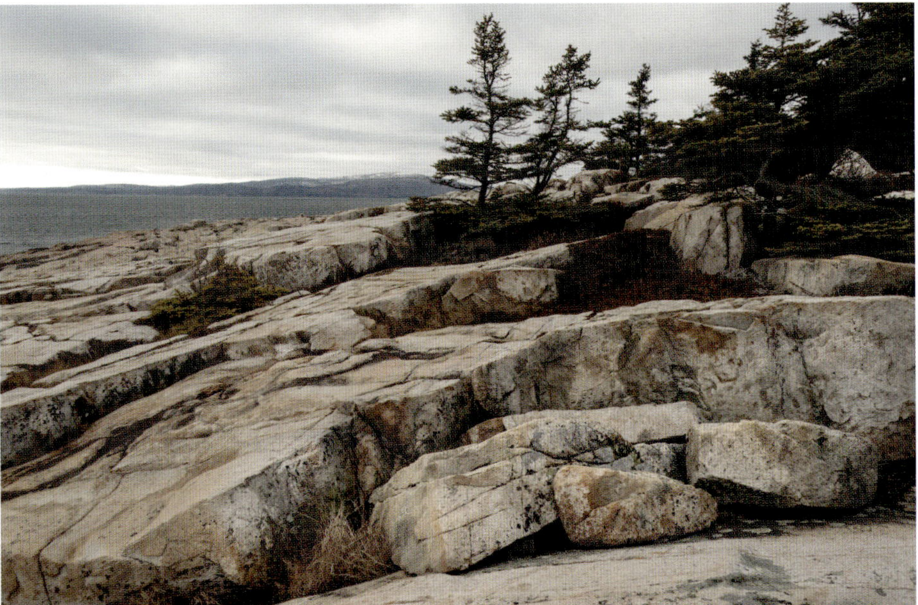

A DAY WITHOUT COLOR, SCHOODIC PENINSULA

•

Without bright light and deep shadow areas, my eyes were drawn to the sublimity of the textures, forms, and what muted colors are present. The sky suggests impending snow.

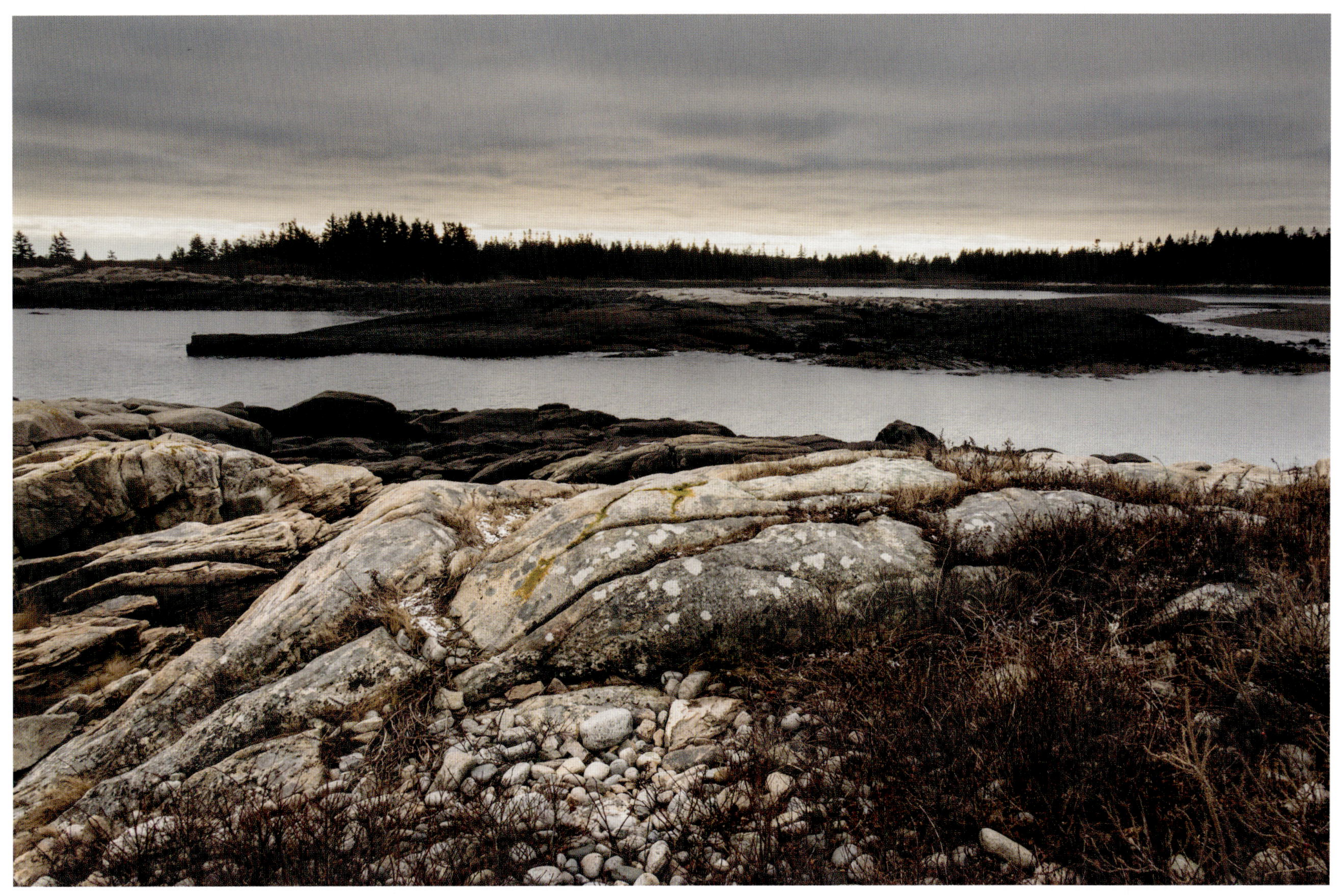

LATE AFTERNOON, SCHOODIC PENINSULA

WINTER

It's the first day of winter, but it feels like it's been here for a month. My first image with snow was made on November 3, more than seven weeks ago. Earlier in the summer I had encountered an elderly year-round resident who told me how wonderful it was on the island in winter. She had wandered out of the woods near Otter Cove, we chatted for a few minutes, and she spoke of how she loved the silence, the solitude, of the winter. It was August, but I was looking forward to seeing the park with a mantle of white. I wanted to experience that solitude for myself. The opportunity to make more-contemplative photographs was appealing. I just wasn't quite prepared for just how much solitude and silence was in store for me.

During the summer, there can be 250,000 people on the island, but in the winter, there are fewer than 10,000 permanent residents. All but three hotels are closed, and only six restaurants/bars remain open during the quiet months, and even they seem to rotate which weeks they will be open. Some weeks I don't think I saw more than fifty people all week.

The Park Loop Road closed down in mid-November, opened up briefly once during a November thaw, but then closed down a few days later. The only way into the park is to take Schooner Head Road, which will get you access to the area between Sand Beach and Otter Cliffs. At Otter Cliffs, Otter Cliffs Road will take you back to Route 3. You can also get to Jordan Pond by taking Jordan Pond Road in Seal Harbor. All the other roads are closed, unless you snowshoe, cross-country ski, hike, or have a snowmobile. Eagle Lake is open for these activities as well.

It was a particularly hard winter, and one evening in late February, I was having supper at the Thirsty Whale. I struck up a conversation with the guy sitting next to me at the bar, talking about—what else—the weather. "Do you know that since January 1st, we ain't had but two hours where the temperature was above freezing?" he told me. As luck would have it, I was home in Massachusetts and missed it. That night the wind gusted to 50 mph, and the next morning the wind chill was −19 degrees—Fahrenheit. It was the first time I had even seen sea smoke.

Winter days are very short, with sunset occurring shortly before 4 p.m. and sunrise around 7 a.m. With limited access, short days, and uncertain weather conditions, there were very few opportunities to shoot. However, the sun is low in the sky all day, making for some great light, and with a little bit of planning and effort, some fine images were there to be had. It is also a great time to make star photographs, and you don't have to stay out late to do it. I had a great time one night on Sand Beach around 7 p.m., photographing on a relatively calm evening.

But mostly, I like the solitude and the chance to slow down and make more-contemplative images, as long as my fingers can still work the camera controls.

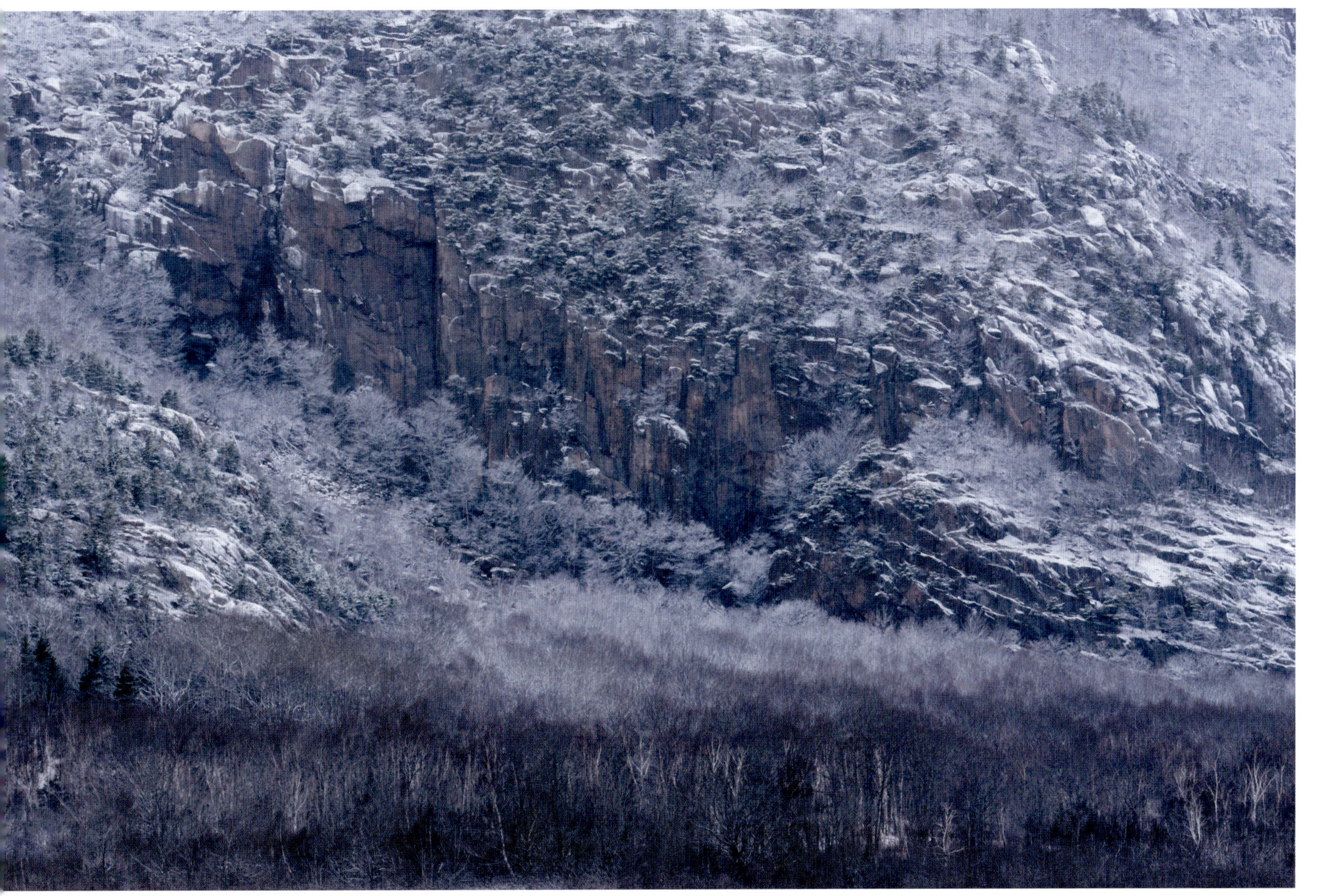

NEW DUSTING ON CHAMPLAIN MOUNTAIN

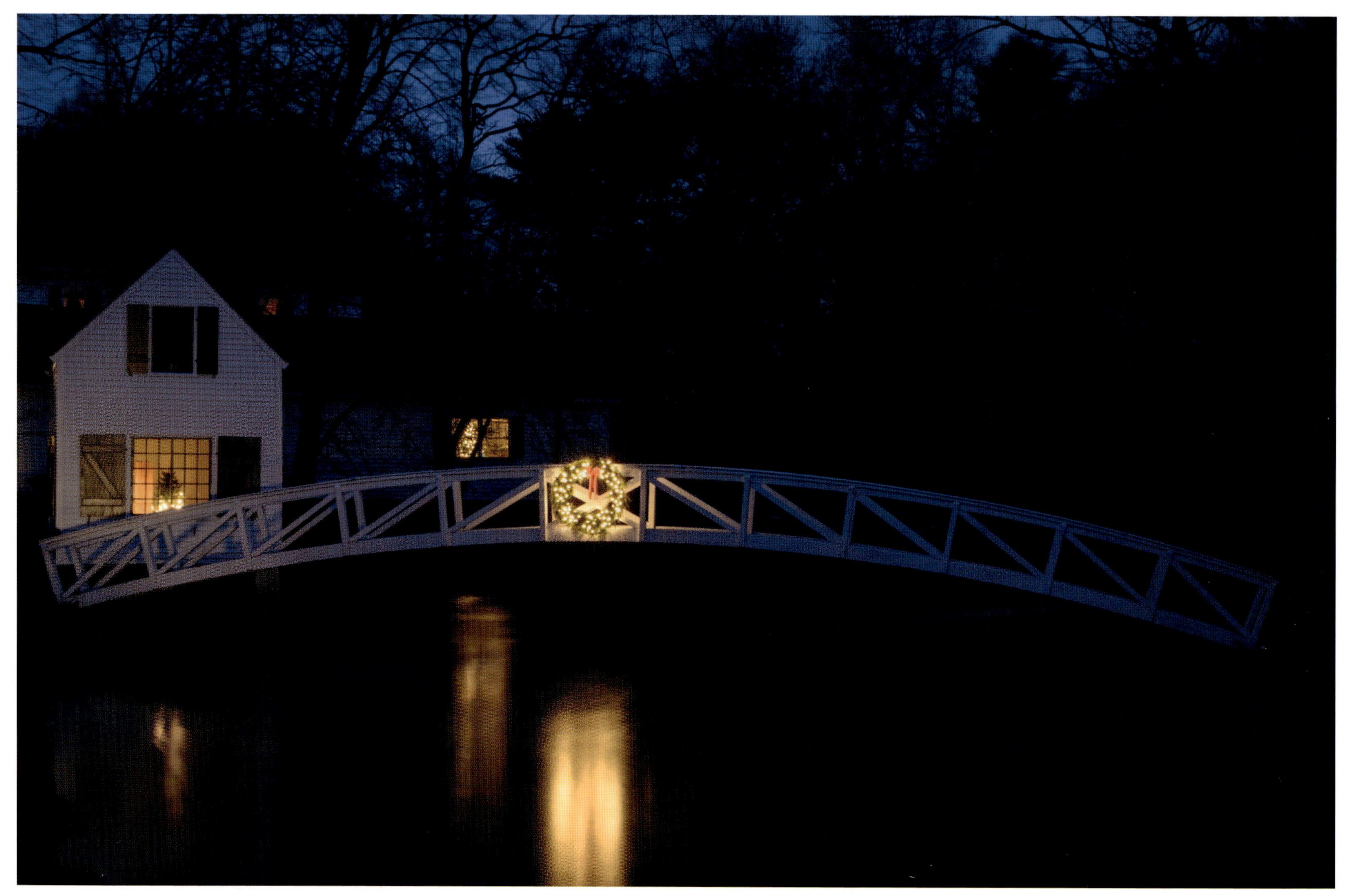

SOMESVILLE, CHRISTMAS

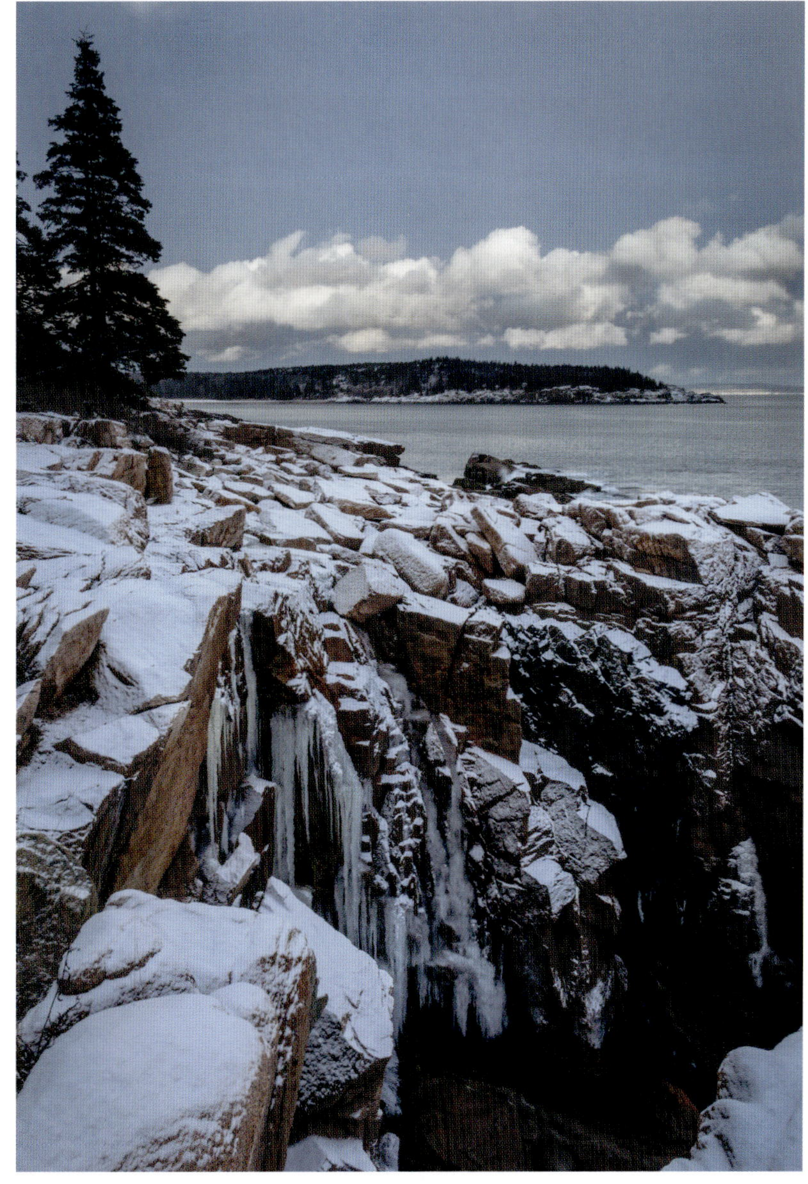

ICE, GRANITE, AND EVENING CLOUDS

SEA SMOKE

It was a long, somewhat sleepless night; the wind was howling all night, gusting to 50 mph, and it just seemed to find a way into a small gap in the window of my fourth-floor hotel room. I had a balcony that faced out toward Frenchman Bay.

I had gone to bed the previous evening with the plan of going out to Ocean Drive for sunrise, and I had my clothes laid out, batteries charged, and a quick breakfast ready to go. I finally gave up trying to sleep around 4:30 a.m. and, with dawn still almost two hours away, decided to get up and try getting some documentation done for my job. Besides, it looked pretty cloudy outside; I couldn't see any stars, so maybe it might not be a good morning. I checked the outside temperature. It was −19 degrees F and the wind was gusting to 40 mph, so I didn't even bother to look at the wind chill. Sunrise could wait.

As I continued to prepare a presentation for a meeting later that day, the sky got lighter, and I noticed movement over the surface of the water. That's when I recognized that the bay was obscured by sea smoke, a phenomenon that occurs when the air is significantly colder than the water below it. Grabbing my camera, I opened the balcony door and stepped outside. After about thirty seconds, I was back inside, way too cold to be out there in just gym shorts and a T-shirt. I went back inside, put on all my cold-weather gear, grabbed the tripod, and stepped out onto the balcony; all thoughts of workflow diagrams had vanished. I had something very special happening outside, and I was going to make the most of it. After making a few exposures, I was once again forced back inside since I could hardly feel the tips of my fingers. After a few minutes inside, I went back out on the balcony and shot some more. Each time I did, I was able to stay only a few minutes before I needed to return inside. I continued this process for the next ninety minutes.

As the sun approached the horizon, and color began to appear in the sky, the smoke began to take on the hues of the dawn. The low mountains on the far side of the bay were touched by and bathed in the sun's pinkish glow, while the sea smoke in the bay remained in blue shadows. The wind tore at the sea smoke, swirling it and twisting it as it rose in the air, forming small clouds that were then blown eastward, out of the bay. Bar Island popped into and out of the smoke, alternately hiding and revealing itself. Sheep and Burnt Porcupine Islands also appeared and vanished in the mist. The sea smoke shredded itself in the trees of the islands, creating a mysterious mood and isolating small patches of the island.

Had I gone out as I planned, I would have come away with completely different images. I've since found out that sea smoke rises up to 130 feet high and makes visibility at sea or ground level difficult. Since my balcony was on the top floor of the hotel, and the hotel was another 40 feet above the ocean surface, I was in a very good position. By 8 a.m., the light was too harsh and the sea smoke dissipated, and it was time to go thaw out in a nice, hot shower before heading to work, feeling very fortunate to have had the experience. Although I made several good images, this image is the best expression of what it was like on that very frosty morning, and it remains my favorite.

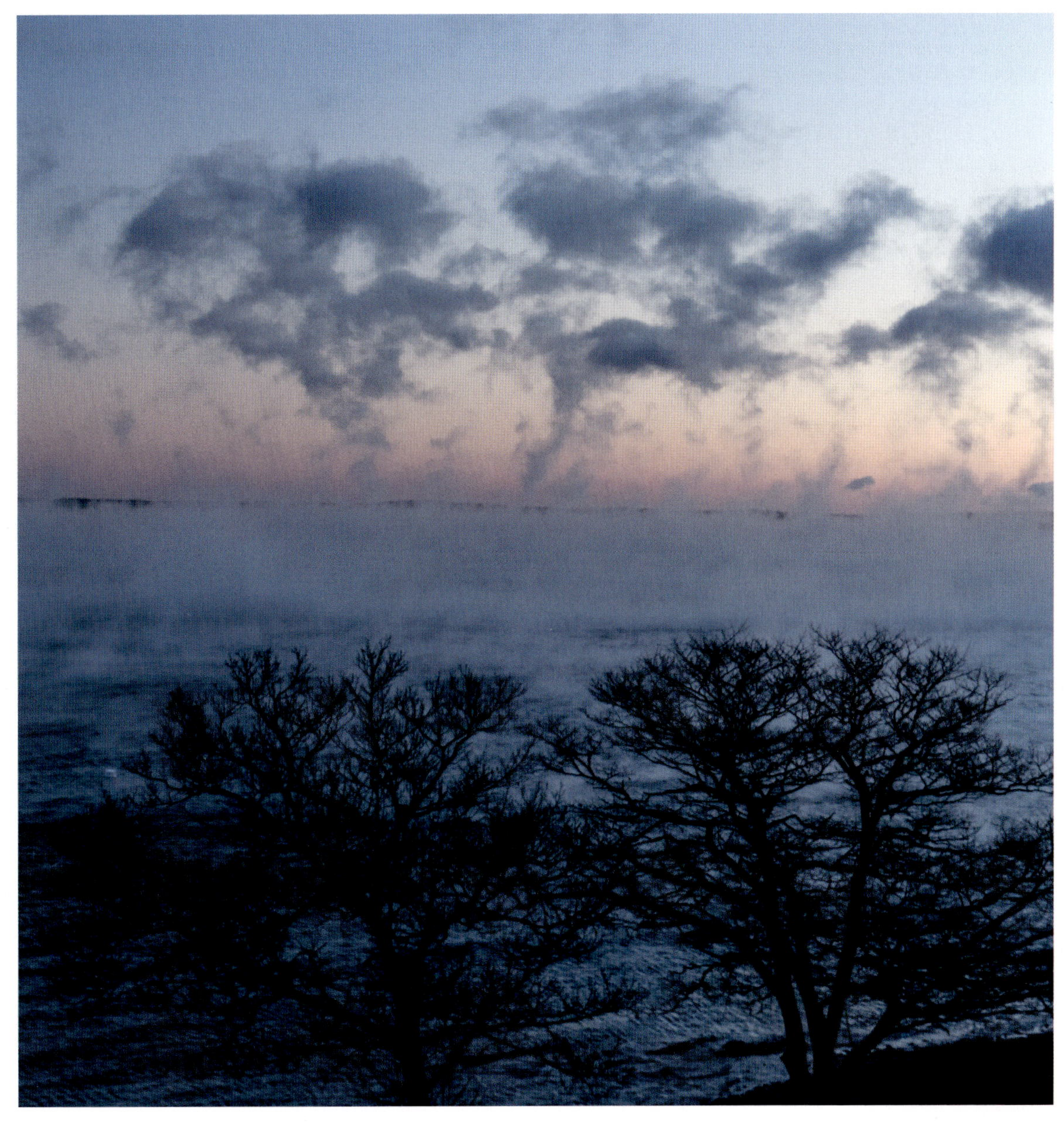

SUNRISE SEA SMOKE, FRENCHMAN BAY AT 19 DEGREES BELOW

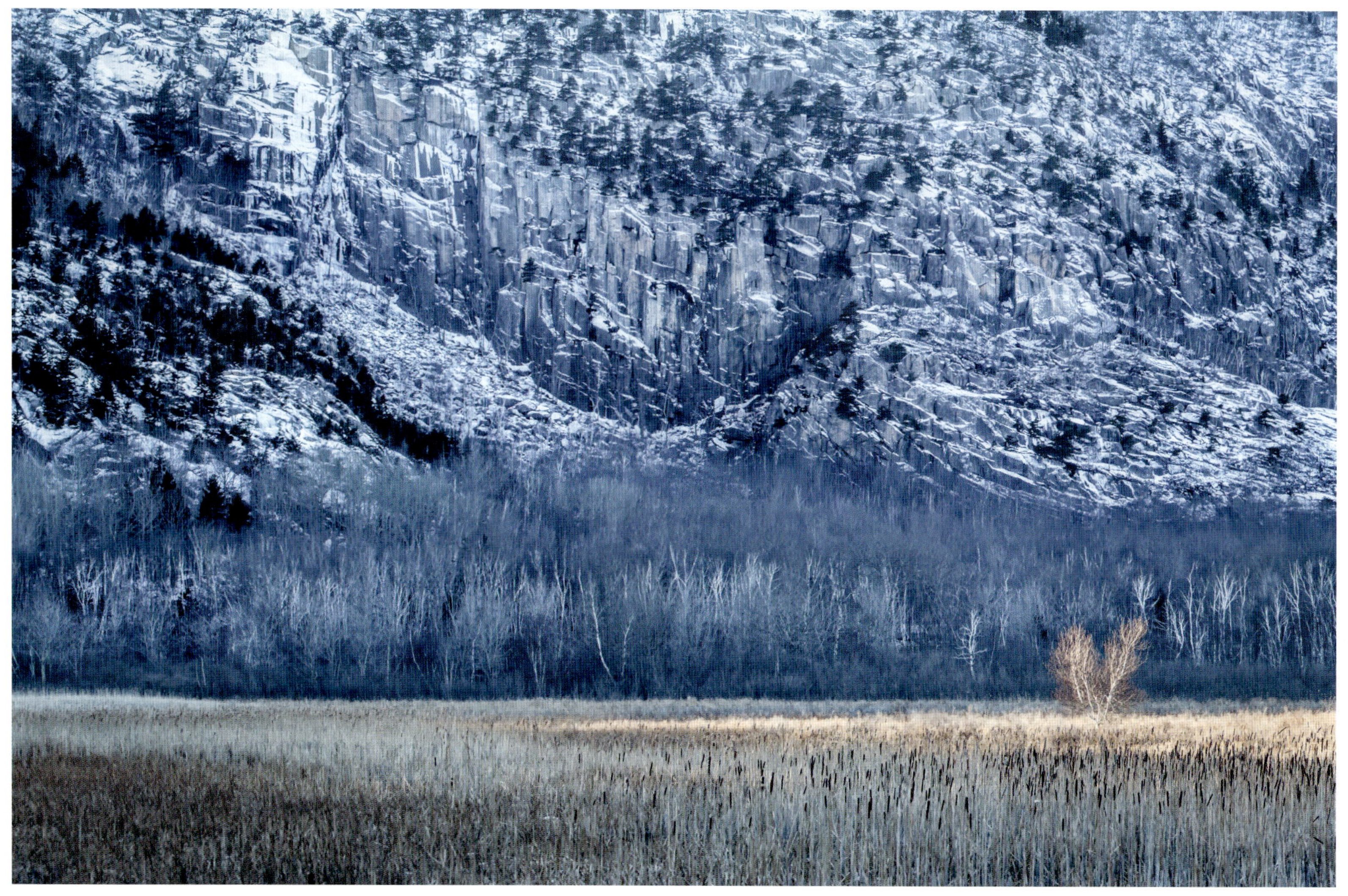

ONE SHINING MOMENT

•

The clouds parted briefly to spotlight this lone birch tree.
Champlain Mountain provides the backdrop.

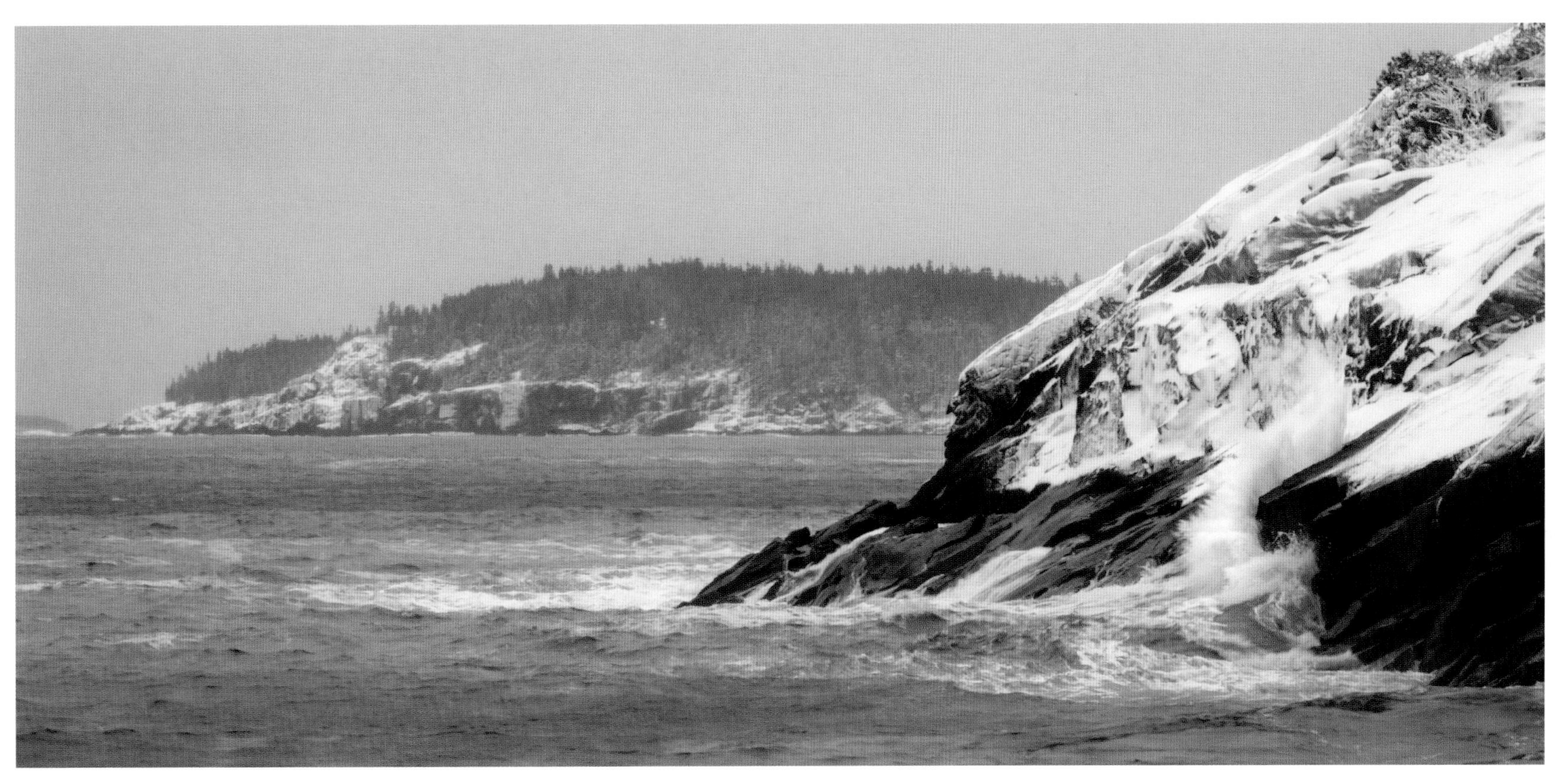

An early January blizzard turns Sand Beach into
Blizzard Beach.

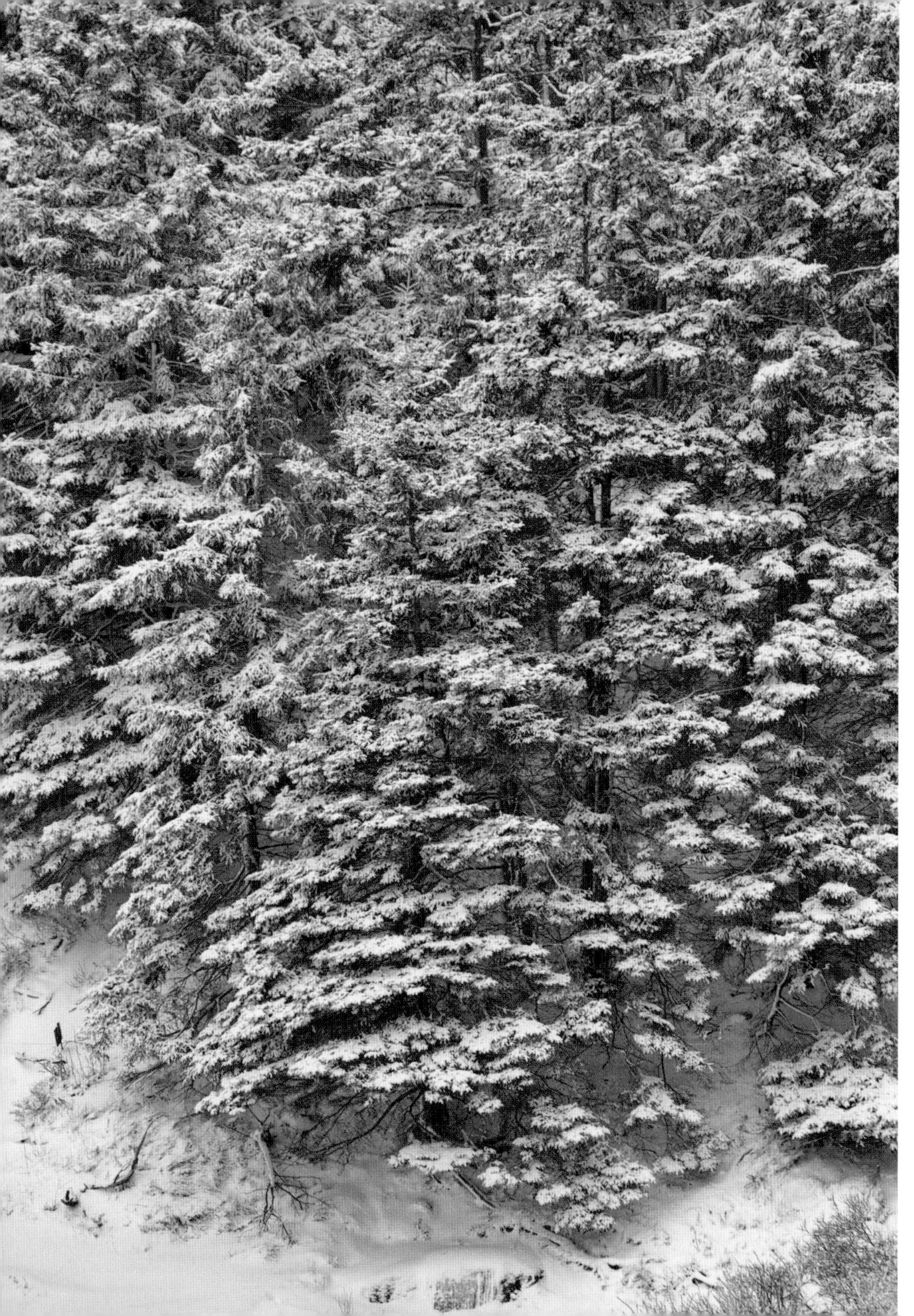

Spruce trees encrusted with snow and sea spray at the edge of Sand Beach, creating an abstract image

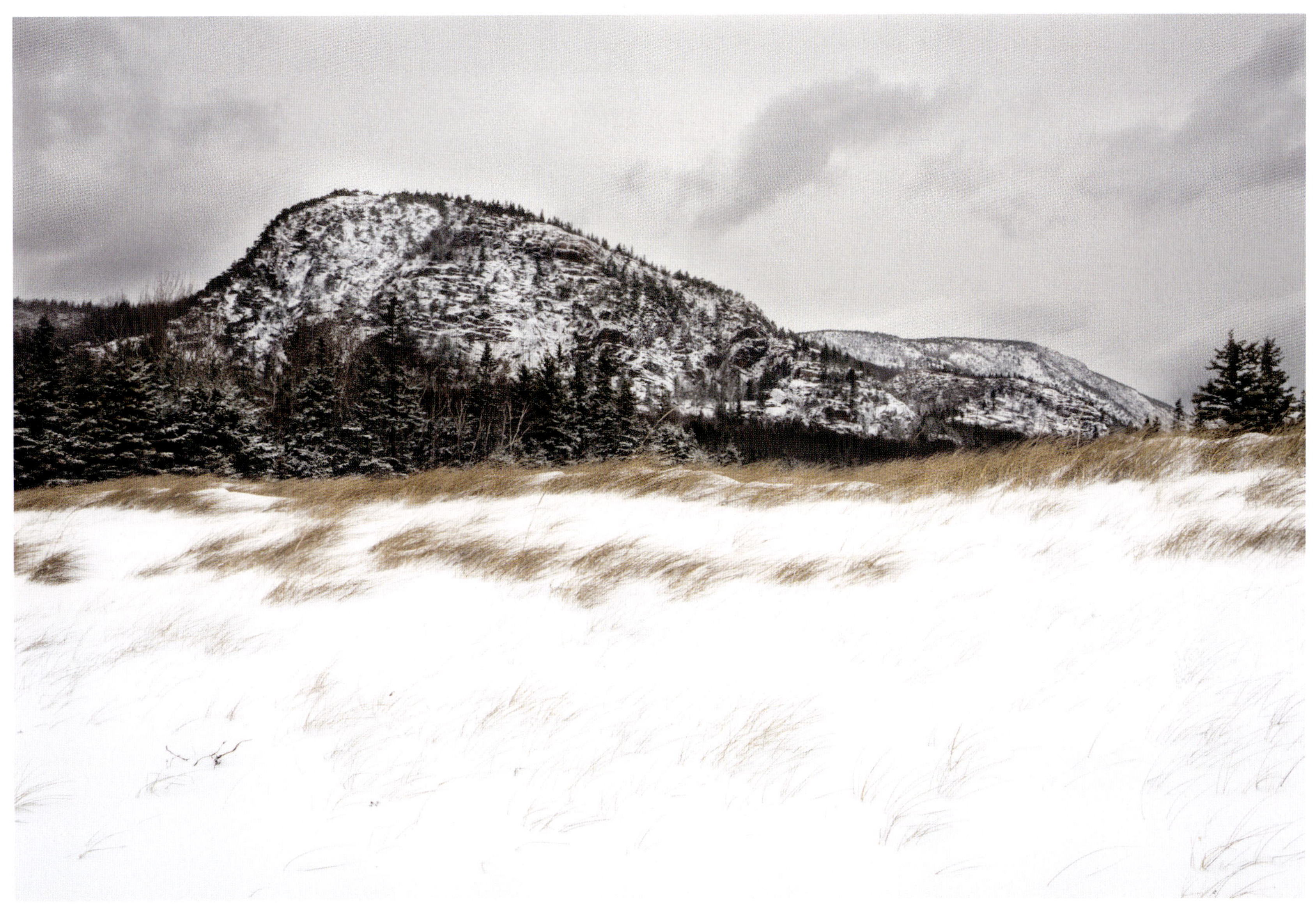

Snow covers the sand dune at Sand Beach as a blizzard winds down. The Beehive watches silently.

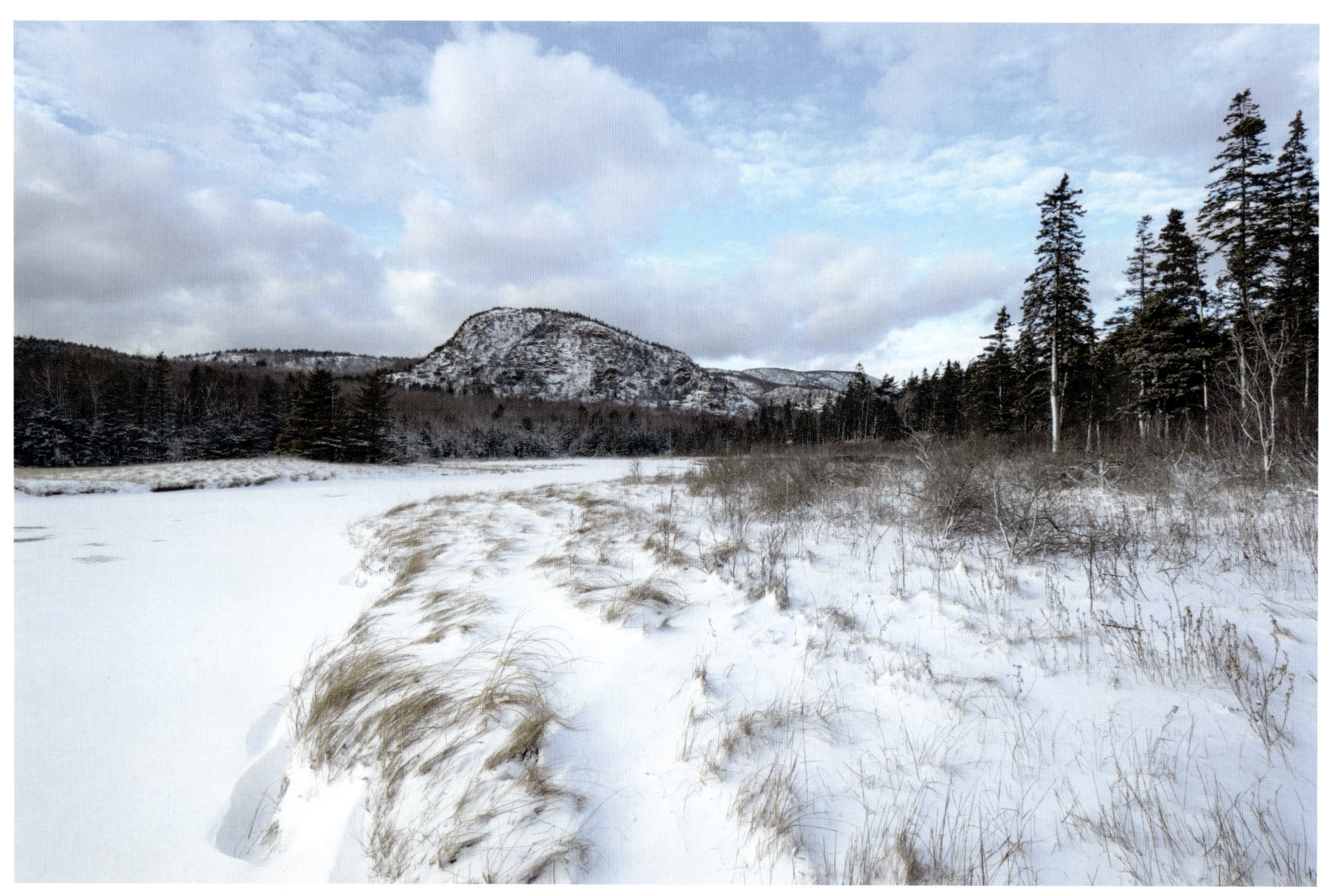

SAND BEACH LAGOON AND THE BEEHIVE, CLEARING STORM

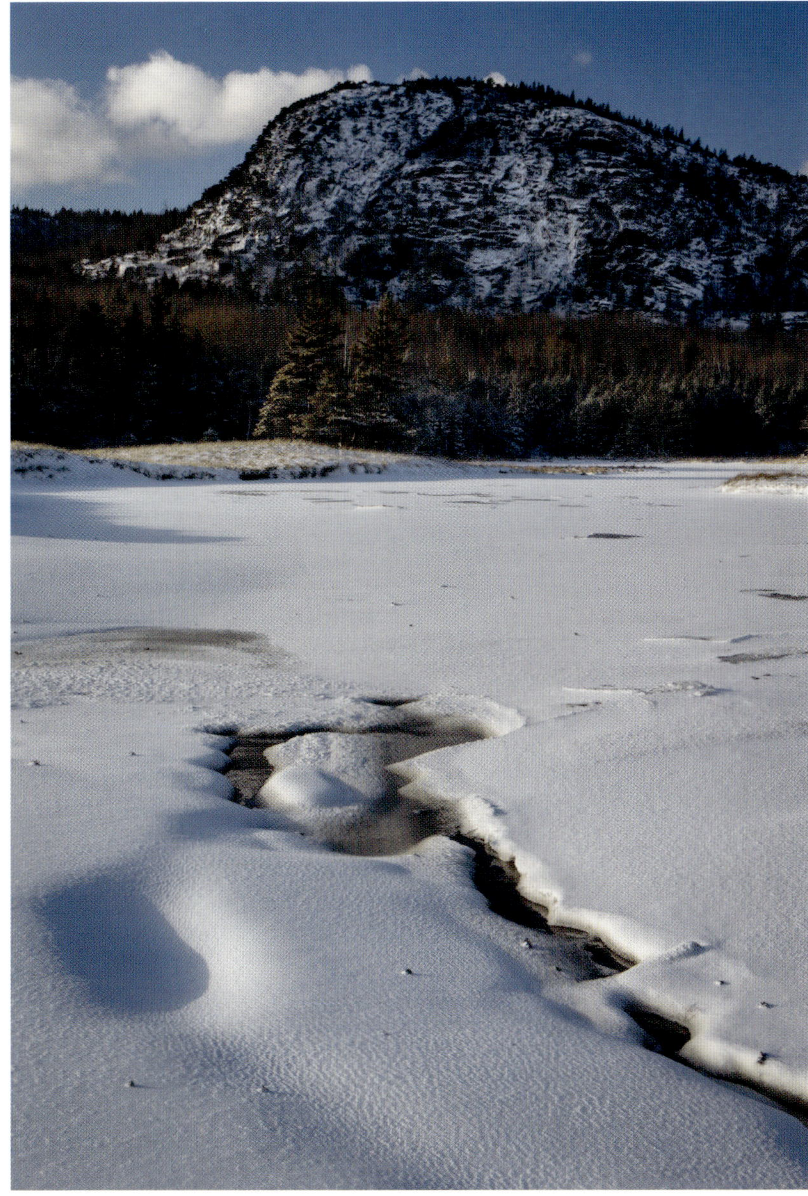

THE BEEHIVE AND SAND BEACH LAGOON, POST BLIZZARD

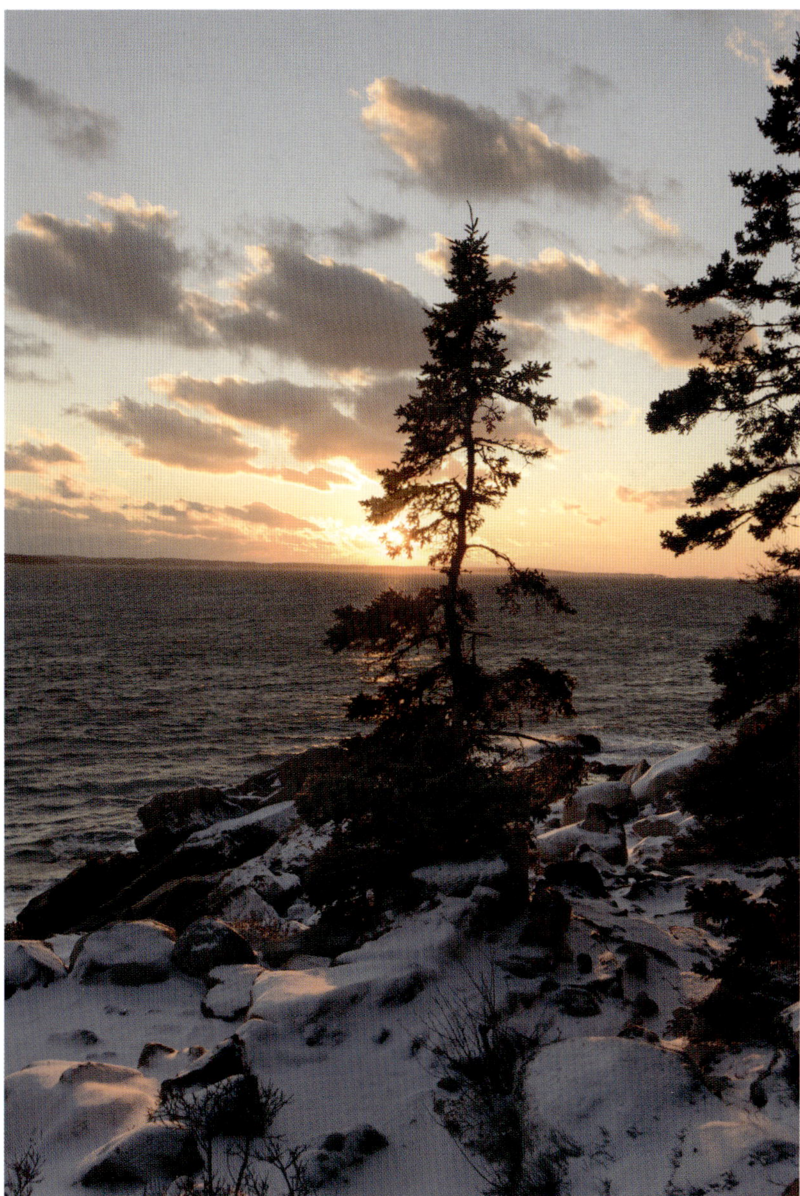

DAY'S END, BLUE HILL BAY

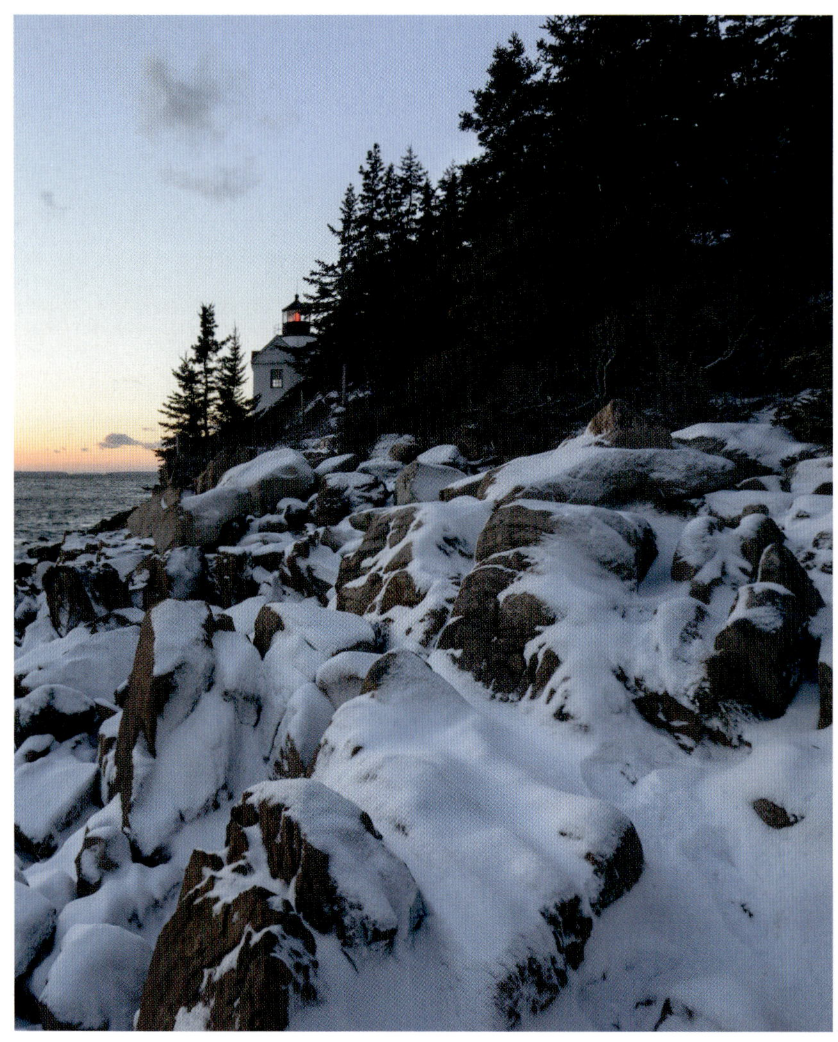

BASS HARBOR LIGHT, WINTER SUNSET

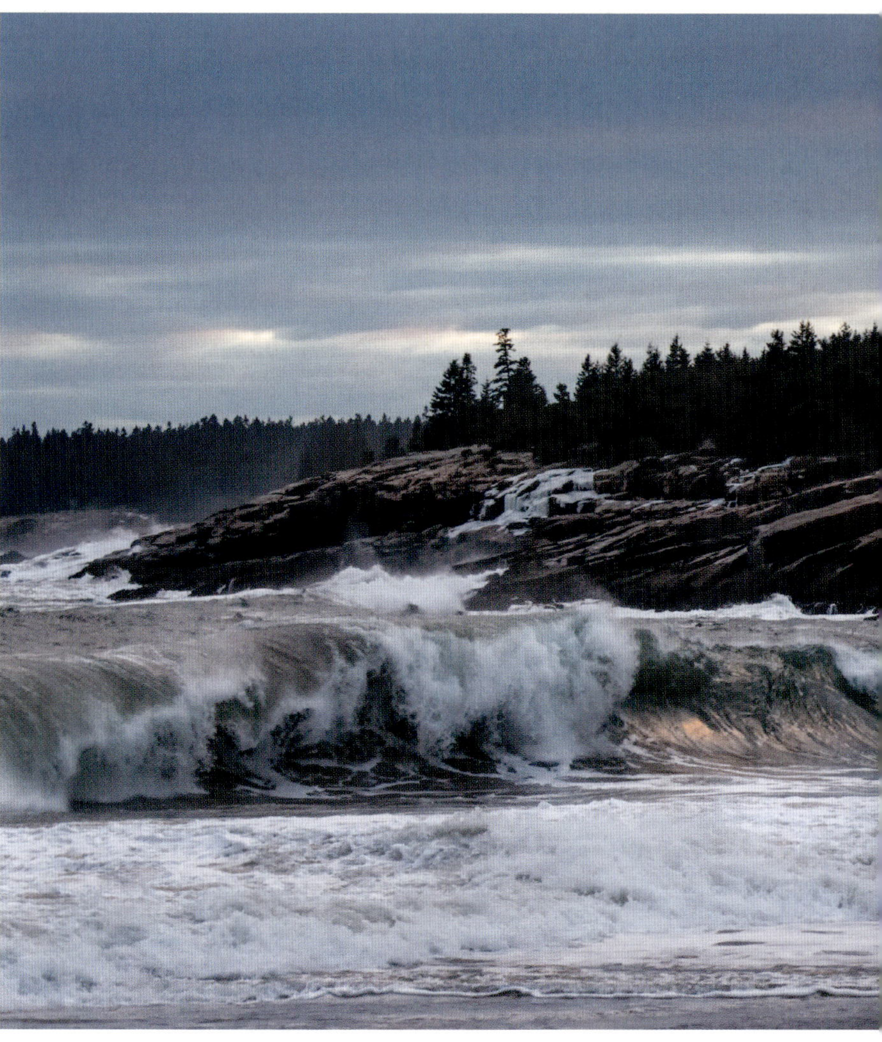

Sunset color from overhead clouds is reflected in the surf on a winter's day on Sand Beach.

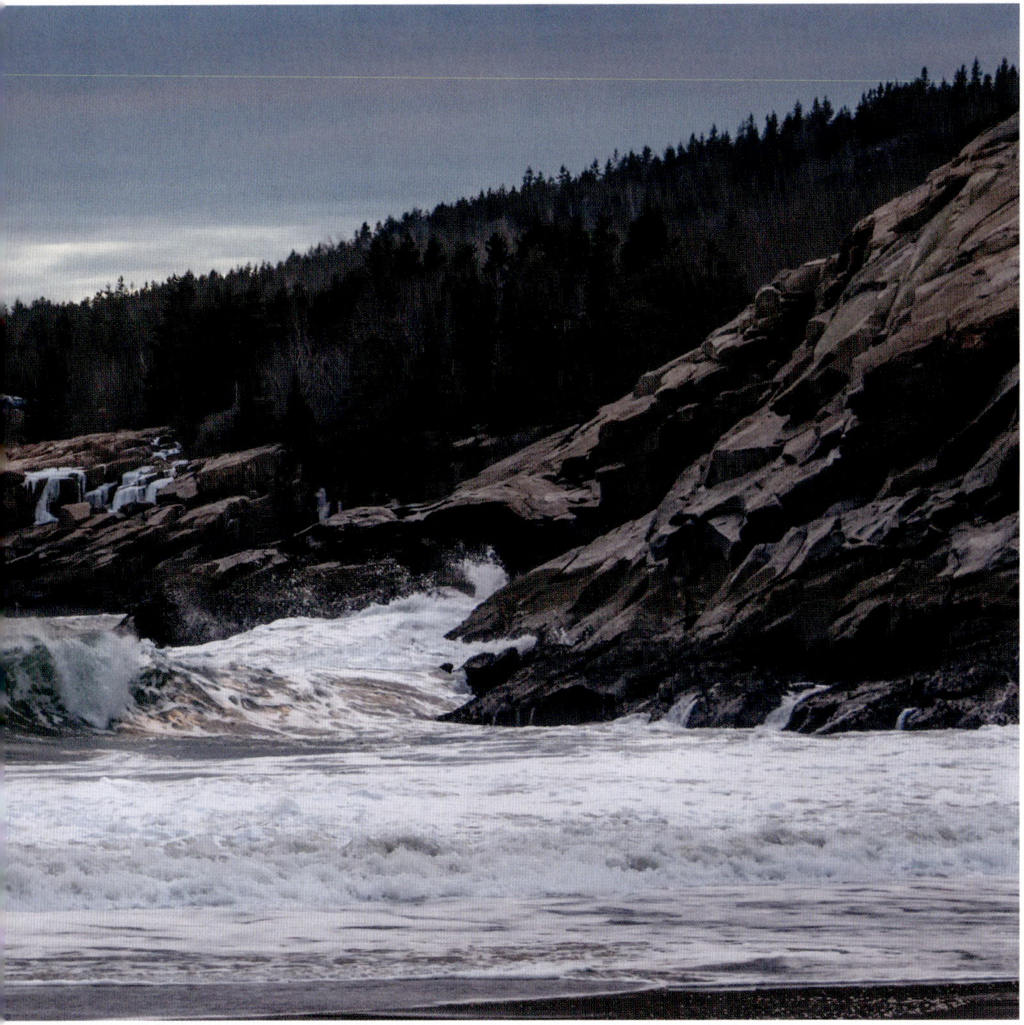

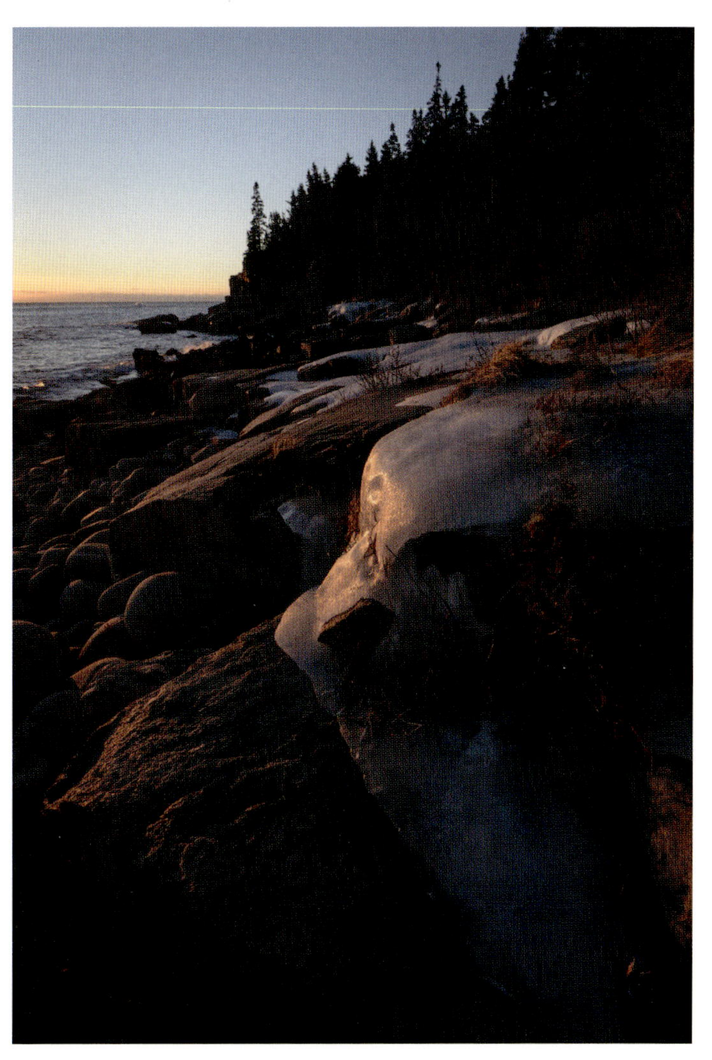

WINTER SUNRISE FROM BOULDER BEACH

OTTER POINT SOLITUDE

With most of the roads closed, as mentioned earlier, getting to some destinations is possible if you don't mind walking a bit. I decided to try photographing a winter sunset from Otter Point. I drove to the Fabbri picnic area, parked, and then walked up Park Loop Road to Otter Point. During the summer tourist season, this would be difficult, but since the road is closed at Otter Cliffs, it is a unique experience. It is about a half-mile walk, there wasn't much snow on the road, and it was about 30 degrees with very little wind. I headed up toward the point with my gear and tripod on my shoulder.

Since Otter Point is on the south side of the island, it tends to be more exposed to the sun, so the snow was only a few inches deep and somewhat mushy, so not too difficult to walk through. I stayed in the middle of the road, thinking that this would be impossible to do in August. I had more than enough time to make it to the point before sunset, spend an hour, then head back to the car by starlight.

The spruce trees that lined either side of the road made it somewhat eerie, but along the way I had glimpses of the shore that you just can't see from a car: steep, almost vertical bluffs that rose from the granite shore. I was amazed at the amount of deadfall that had occurred, thinking it would be quite treacherous to pick my way through that to get clear of the trees to see the cove. I decided to keep going toward the point as I originally planned. Twenty minutes of walking put me at the point in plenty of time. There was very little snow on the rocks, just some ice here and there, remnants of the constant freeze-thaw cycles.

What I hadn't planned for was a milky, heavy overcast that seemed to draw all the color out of the world, to the point of being almost monochromatic. However, I was determined to work with the light I had, so after a few minutes of observation, I found a grouping of boulders and ice that seemed to reflect the austere Maine winter we were experiencing. Everything seemed to be devoid of color. The rocks, the sky, and even the ocean were somber. There wasn't much contrast either. Without the deep shadows or bright highlights, it seemed all the objects were getting equal attention. The blue-gray sky gave its hue to the ice and snow, and rock faces revealed their textures and colors that would not be so evident on a brighter day. The ocean almost seems to merge with the sky in the distance. It felt as if I had been drawn into a Wyeth painting.

After about forty minutes, I was packing up my gear and getting ready for the walk back in the darkness when the clouds broke, and the day ended in a bit of pink and orange. I quickly pulled out my gear, found a new vantage point, and came away with a few images before the sun dipped below the horizon. It lasted all of five to ten minutes. Packing up my gear again, I headed back to my car in the gathering darkness. Halfway back, I was startled by a very large buck with a good-sized set of antlers emerging from the woods. I stopped where I was, not wanting to spook him, and waited for him to cross the road back into the woods on the other side. He stopped about halfway across and noticed me. We stayed there like that for about two minutes, as it got darker. Finally, I moved back away and gave him some space, and he continued into the woods for the night. I arrived at my car about ten minutes later, exhilarated both from the encounter with the buck and the images I had made. It was a good day.

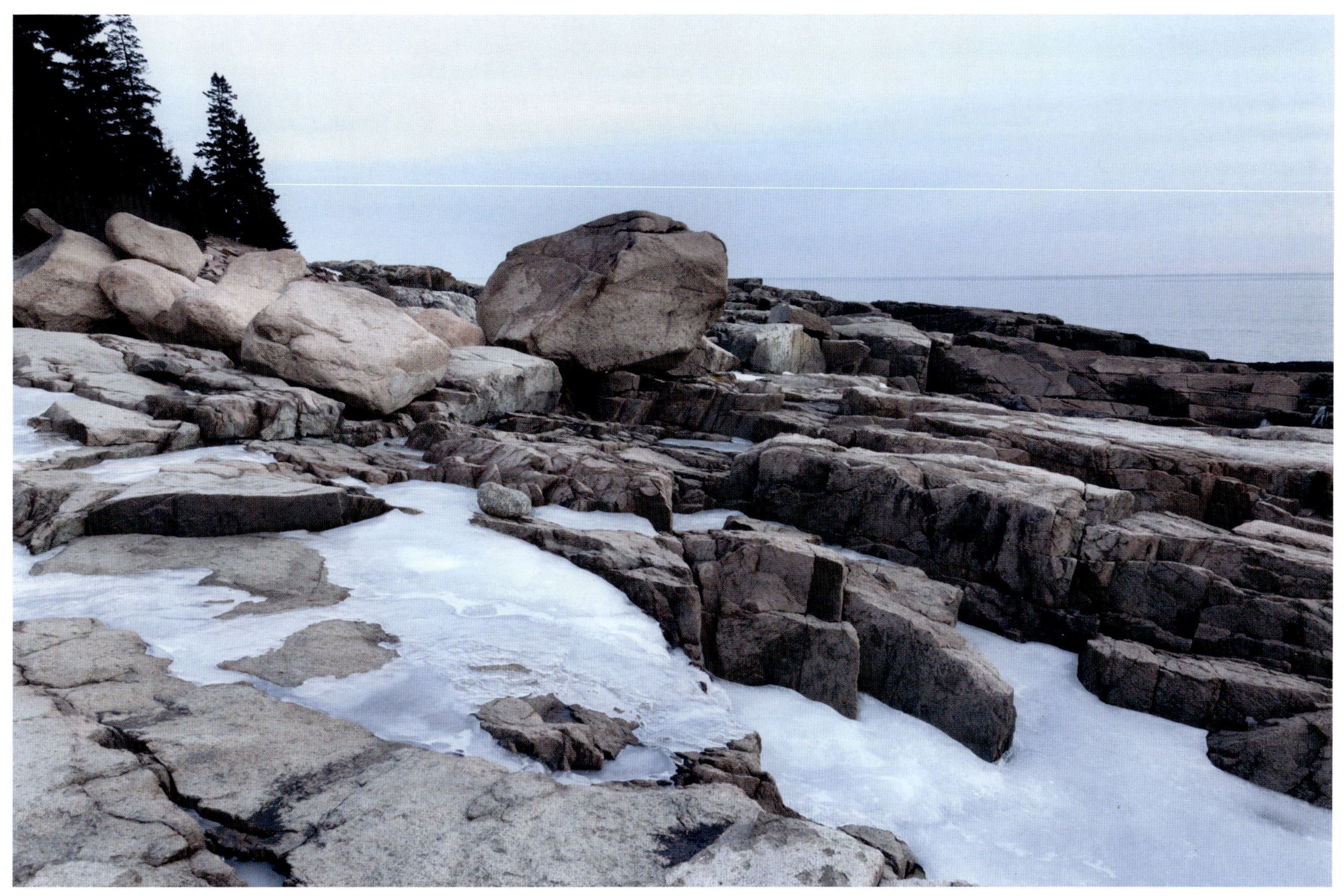

ICE AND PINK GRANITE JUST BEFORE SUNSET, OTTER POINT

•

After a half-mile hike from the Fabbri parking lot, I tried to make the most of the rather dull, flat light. It was going to be a long, unfulfilling walk back in the dark, or so I thought.

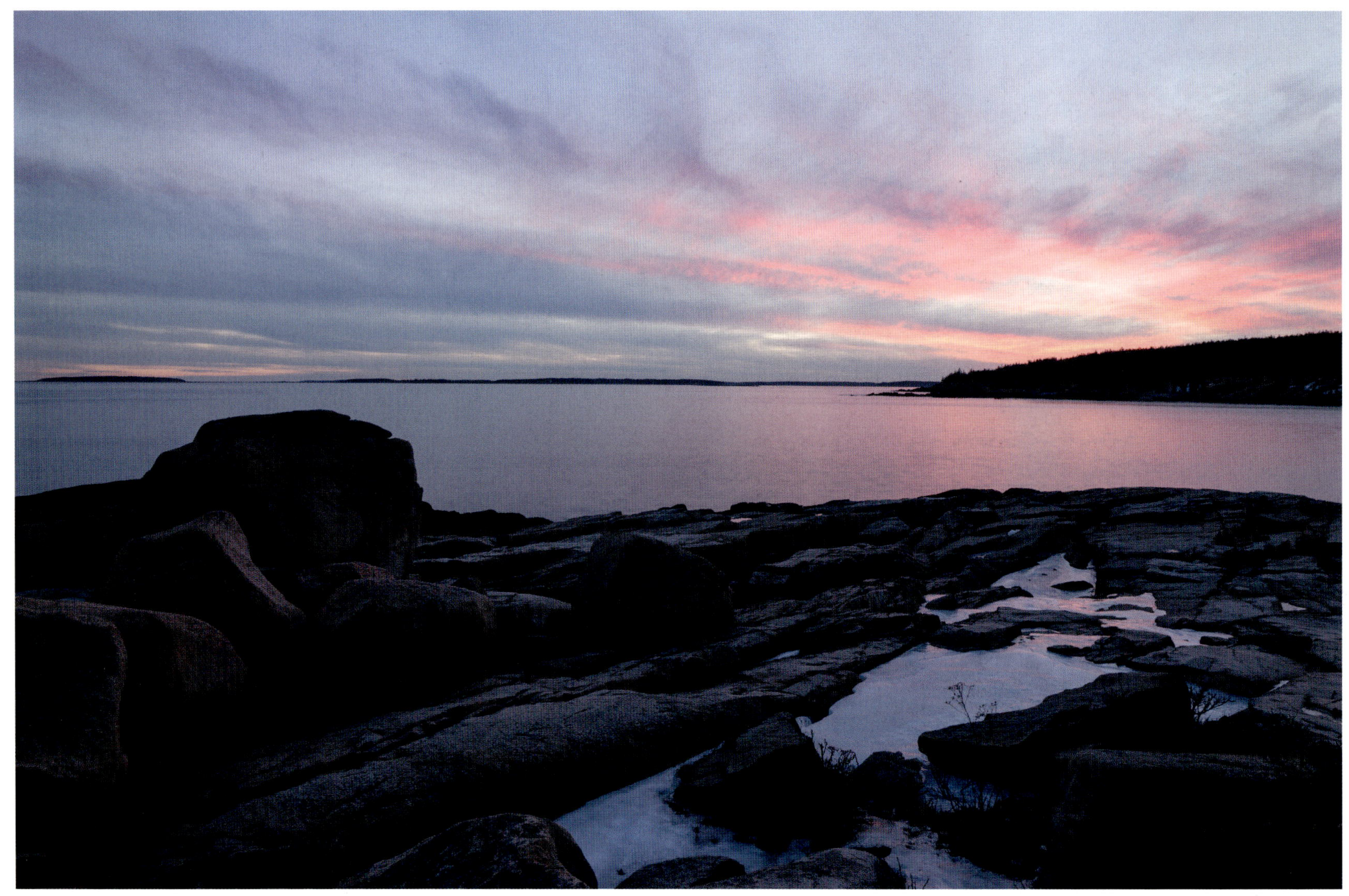

OTTER POINT, WINTER SUNSET

•

A few minutes later, the clouds thinned enough to grace the sky, sea, and ice with color.

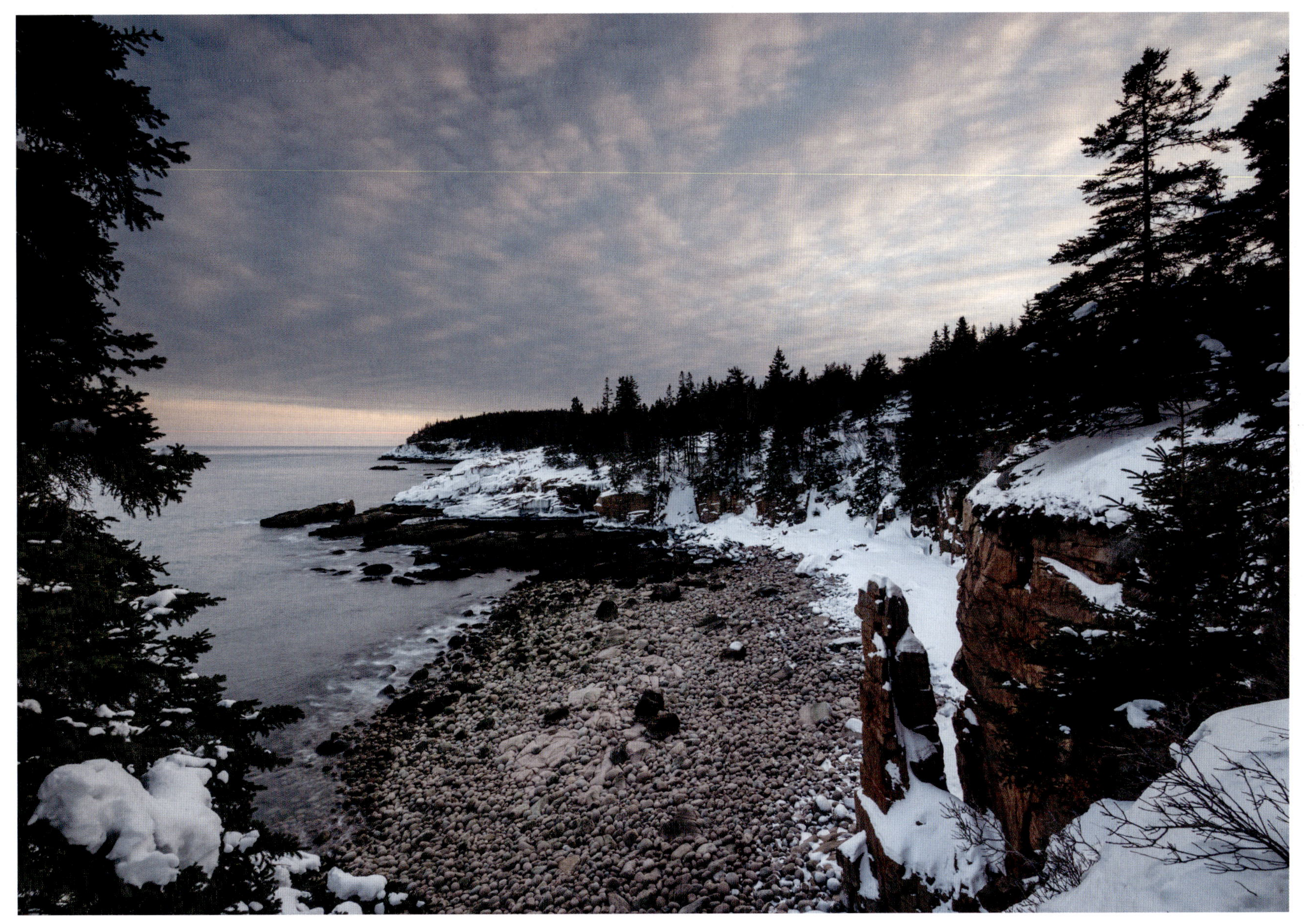

WINTER EVENING LIGHT, MONUMENT COVE

JORDAN POND AND THE BIG DIPPER

A friend had invited me out to eat one night in the town of Ellsworth, about 15 miles from Bar Harbor. On my way back, it was still light enough to shoot, so I decided to go and explore the Jordan Pond area. The only access to the pond is on Jordan Pond Road through the village of Seal Harbor. Once I arrived at the Jordan Pond parking lot, I realized I had left all my cold-weather clothes back at the hotel. No sweaters, no thermal underwear, no earmuffs. Just my chinos, a shirt, a winter jacket, gloves, and a ball cap. Well, it's not windy and it's about 20 degrees, and I'm going to be here only a few minutes; sunset doesn't look too promising with the clear sky, and this is just a scouting survey, nothing serious. I'll grab my tripod, though, just in case. Having justified my actions (at least in my mind, and besides I'm from Maine anyway; I lived in Alaska too, I continued to reason), I headed down to the pond, getting several quizzical glances from a few well-equipped hikers (yeah, well, I survived the Blizzard of '78, too!). Once I got down to the pond, I noticed there was a bit of wind blowing across the pond.

I made several images of ice-bound boulders, and as expected, the sunset was completely unremarkable. However, the sky was exceptionally clear; the wind had died down once the sun set. I continued to explore along the shore, looking for a particular grouping of boulders I had found last summer; there was still some light in the sky, maybe enough for just one or two more shots.

And then I realized just how really clear the sky was, and here was an opportunity to get some star shots. As it grew darker (and colder) and the stars began to reveal themselves, I found the boulders I was looking for. I quickly set up my camera, framed the shot, and waited. In the cold silence, I could hear the ice creaking and groaning and echoing off the granite of the nearby Penobscot and Pemetic Mountains, which surround the pond. Just a bit of pink light remained in the sky. Overhead, a few meteors streaked through the sky. It was quite an ethereal moment.

The Big Dipper started to rise above the Bubbles, just to the right of South Bubble, sliding up over Pemetic Mountain. It took about twenty minutes before everything was lined up for the image I wanted. In the meantime, the temperature kept dropping, but I hung in there until I got the shot I wanted. Packing up my gear, I headed back to my car and a warm hotel. I had been out there less than an hour, but those last few minutes seemed to go on forever. Had I been properly dressed, I would have stayed longer.

It was an unforgettable experience that I can't find the words for, but I hope these pictures convey the excitement I felt that night.

By the time I got back to my car, the temperature gauge was reading 10 degrees F. Adjusting my plans for the night, I ended up at the Thirsty Whale for a bowl of clam chowder and an Atlantic Real Ale before heading back to my hotel.

JORDAN POND, THE BUBBLES AND THE BIG DIPPER ON A FRIGID JANUARY NIGHT

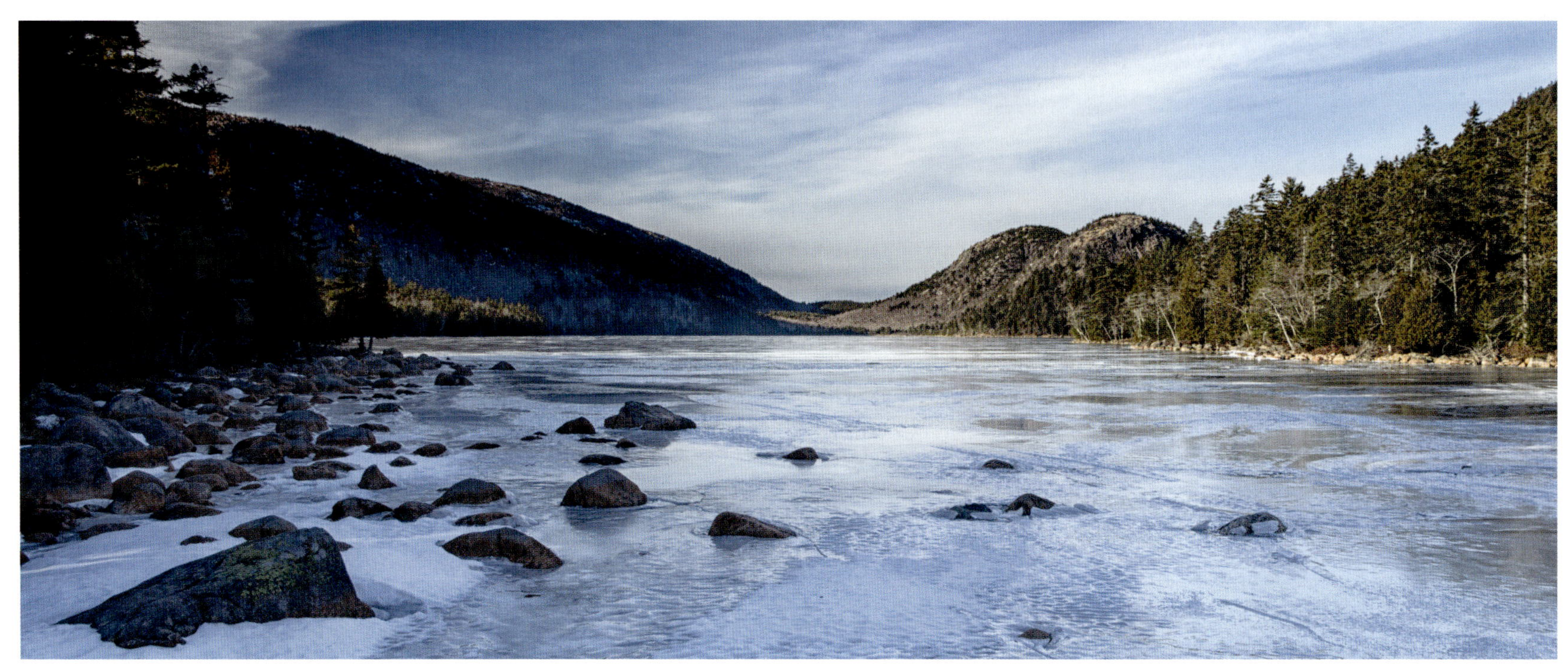

ICE BOUND BOULDERS AT JORDAN POND

•

I returned to Jordan Pond in midafternoon a few days later for a different view. A well-maintained trail makes it possible to circumnavigate the pond all year, but it can be icy.

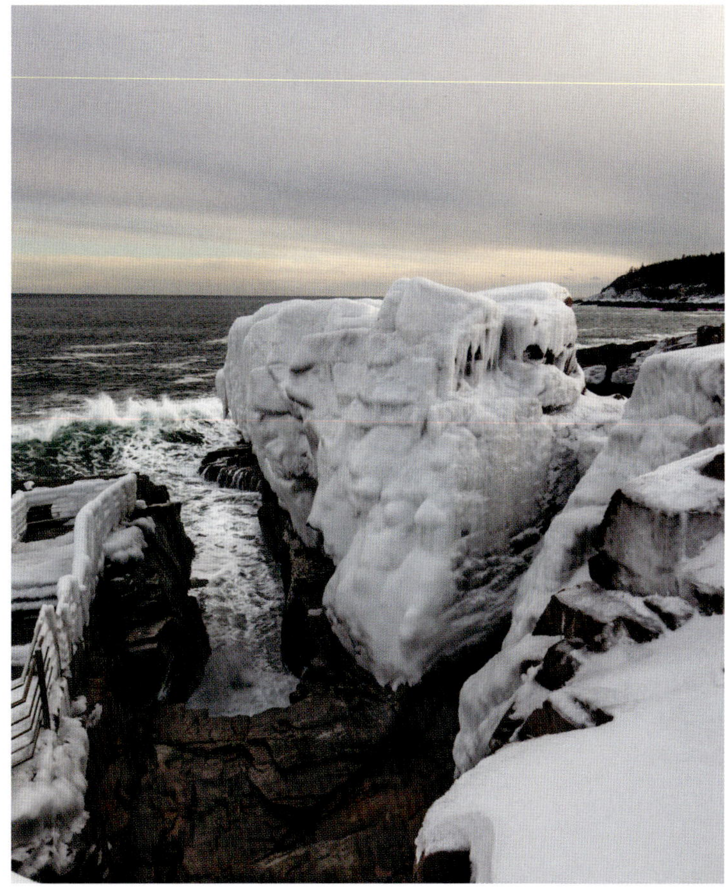

ICE COATED THUNDER HOLE JUST BEFORE SUNSET

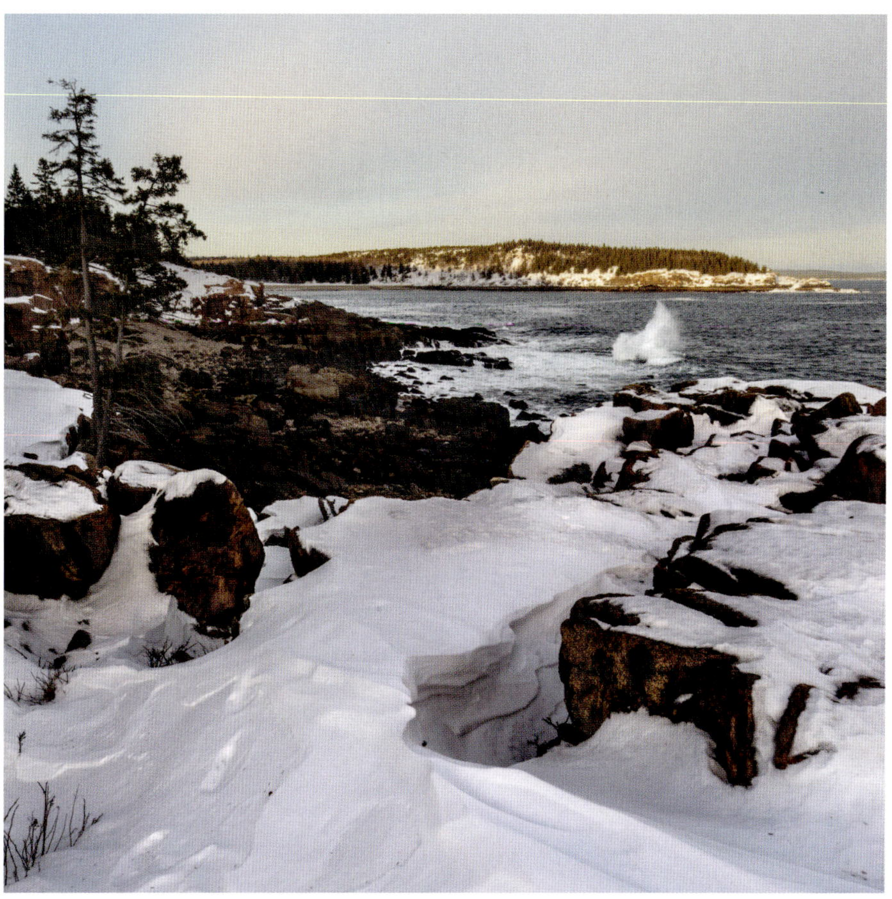

WIND SCULPTURED SNOW DRIFTS NEAR THUNDER HOLE

RANDOM THOUGHTS DURING A TWENTY-SECOND EXPOSURE

January 22, 2015 07:43:08 PM;

44.3292°N 68.1820°W

SAND BEACH, GREAT HEAD, AND JUPITER RISING

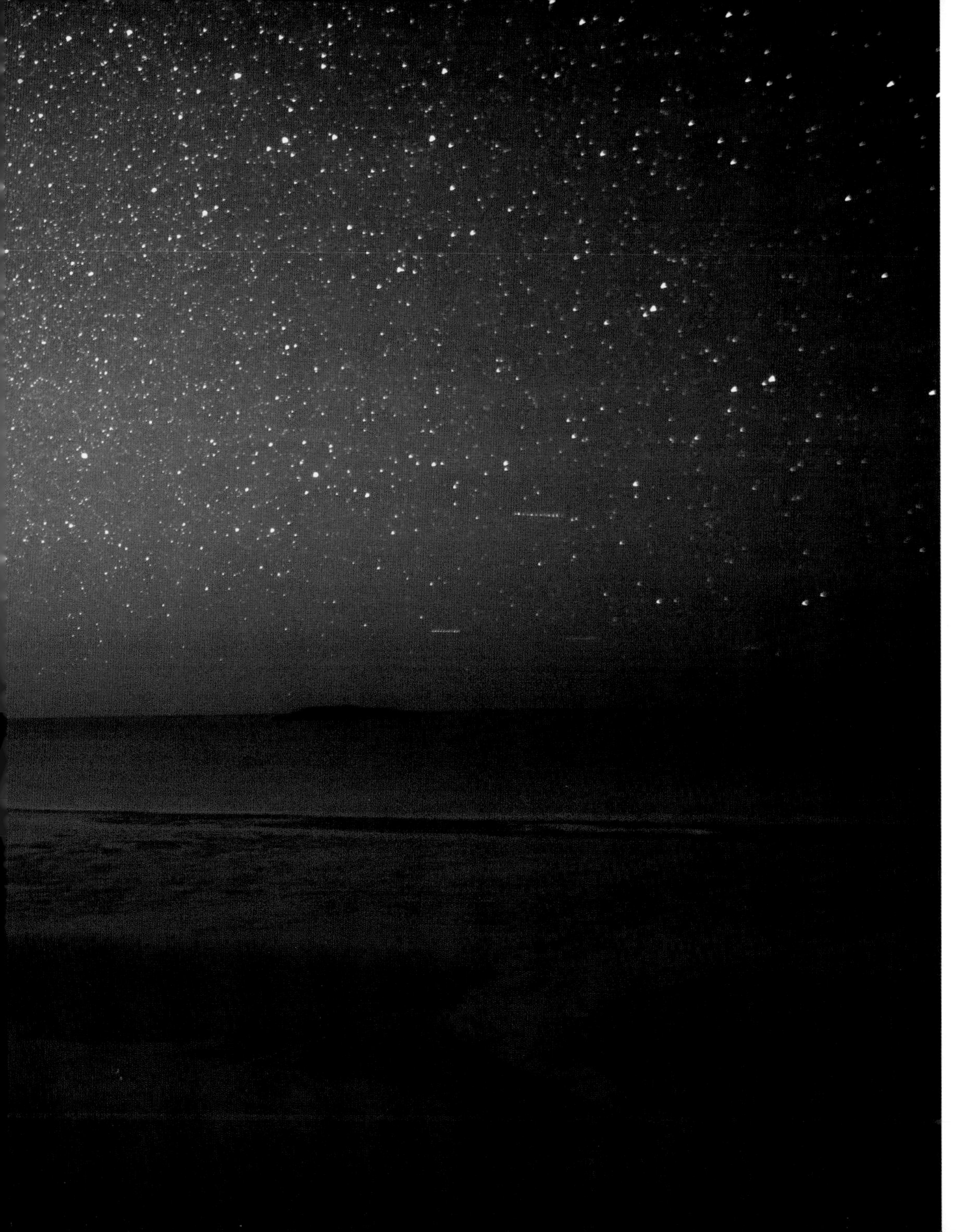

On a beach.

In Maine.

In January.

At night.

Looking at Jupiter.

In below-freezing, single-digit weather.

Contemplating the grains of sand,

the number of stars,

the flakes of snow,

the light reflected off Jupiter that left the sun
90 minutes before the shutter opened,

the uncountable waves,

the unknown tidal cycles,

and yet very little has changed since the first
human saw this view.

Just reflecting, to keep things in perspective
while traveling on the third rock from the sun.

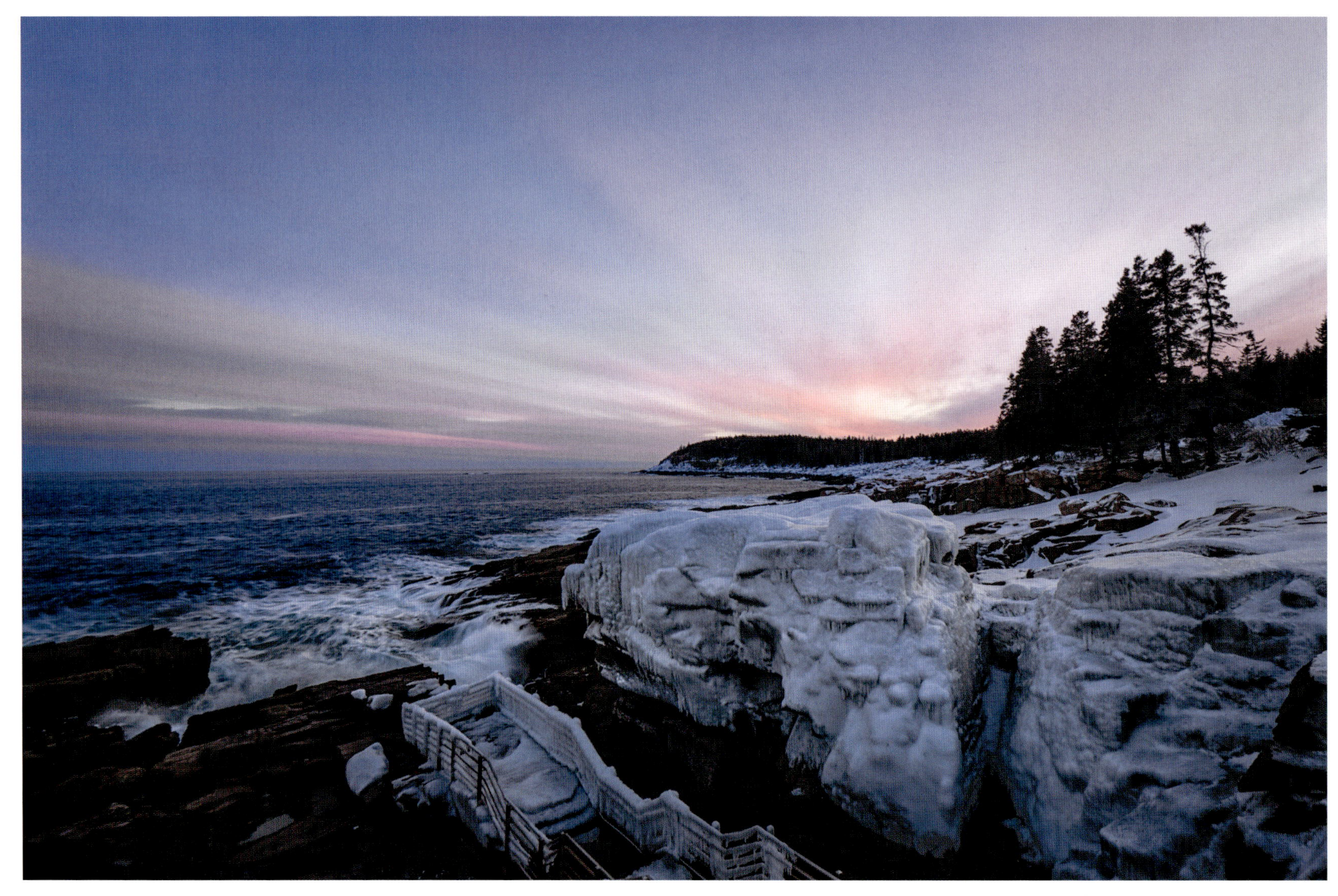

WINTER SUNSET AT THUNDER HOLE

ALONG OCEAN PATH ON A WINTER'S AFTERNOON

•

Brilliant sunshine on fresh snow and a shimmering sea

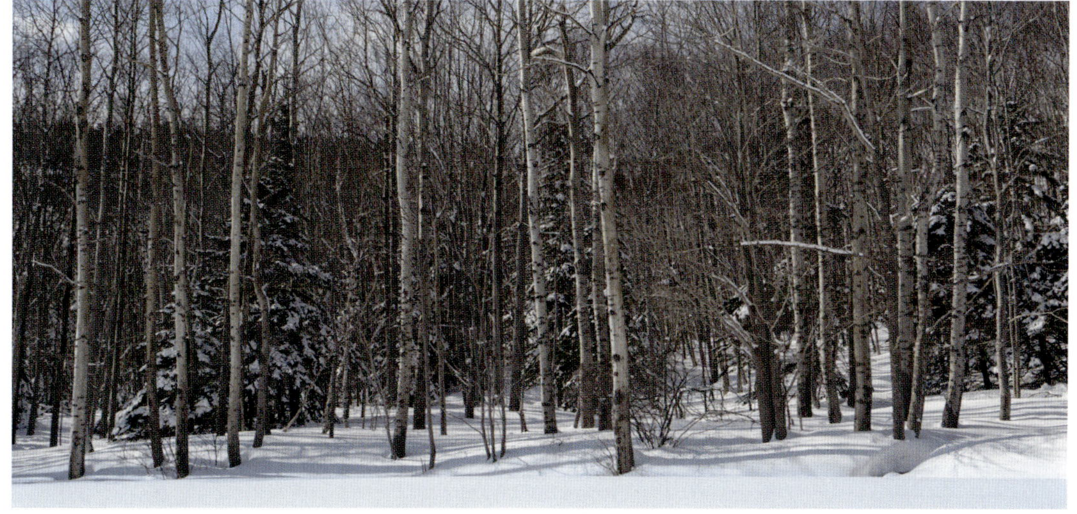

ASPENS AND BIRCHES IN FRESH SNOW

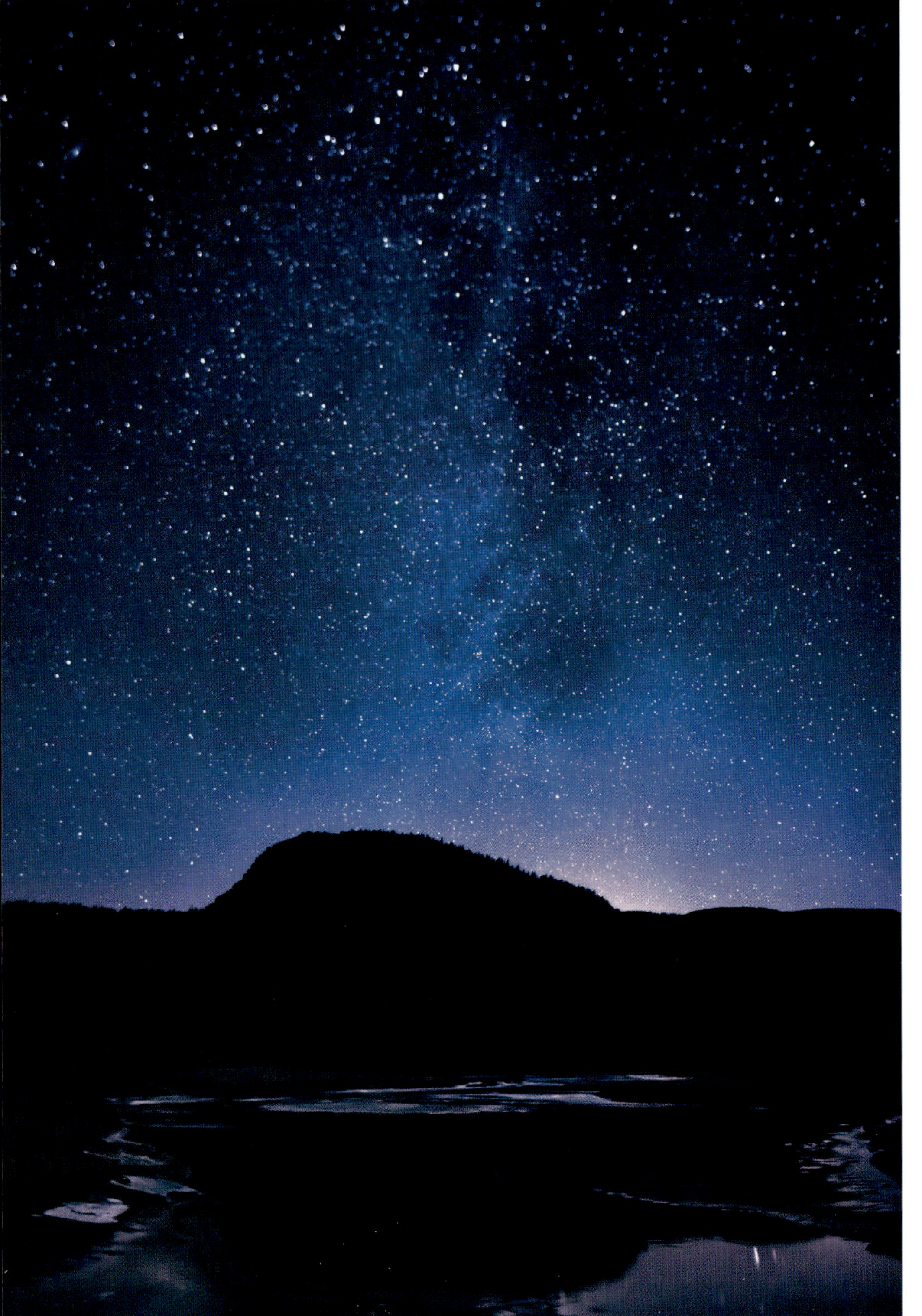

THE BEEHIVE, SAND BEACH LAGOON, AND THE WINTER MILKY WAY

•

The bright glow to the right of the Beehive is Bar Harbor.

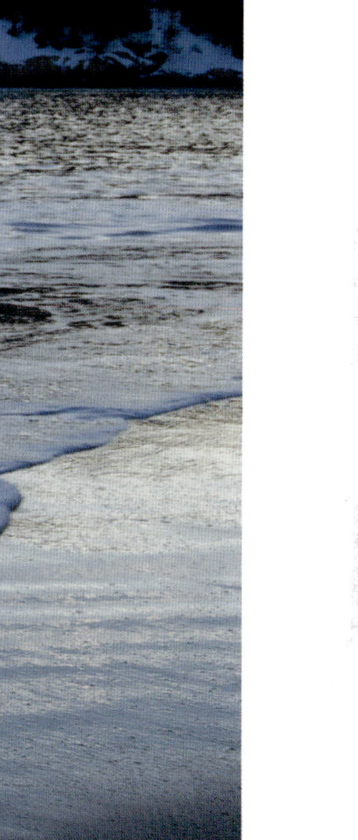

SAND BEACH EARLY EVENING

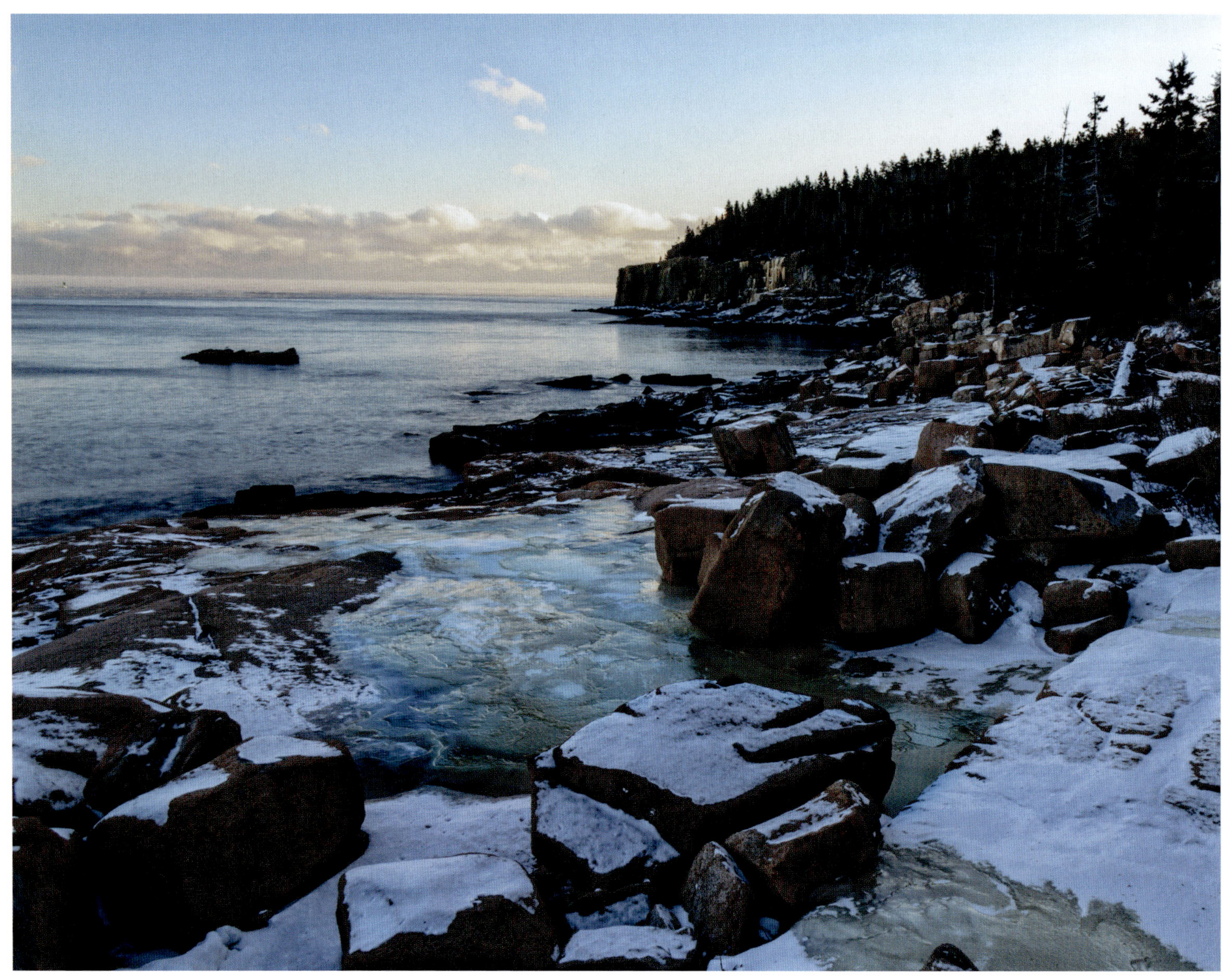

ICE AND BOULDERS NEAR OTTER CLIFFS AT SUNSET

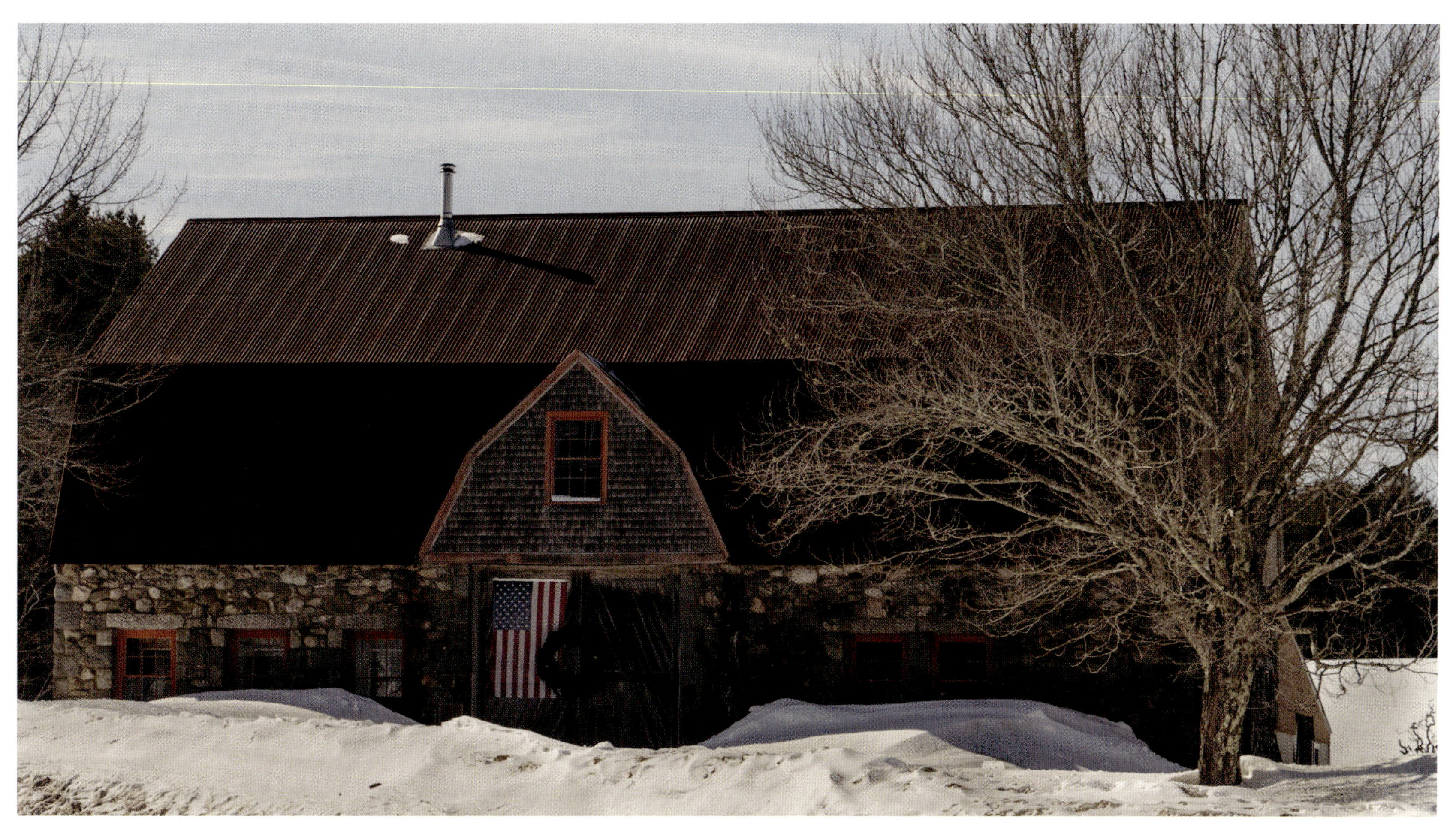

THE OLD STONE BARN IN LATE WINTER

Spring

Winter gives way to spring grudgingly. Not only had winter encroached on autumn by almost eight weeks, it now overstayed its visit to the island by another month. While autumn boldly arrives in flaming yellows, reds, and oranges, spring makes its arrival in a burst of fluorescent greens of the birches and aspens and the return of birds, seals, and newborn wildlife. Later come the water lilies in yellow and white, the pink rugosa, and the vibrant violet, red, and blue lupine.

Streams fill with the snowmelt, creating cascades and temporary waterfalls that had been dormant over the long winter. This excess moisture brings to life the grasses and ferns in Great Meadow, which complement the greens of the birches overhead.

The roads are opened slowly, and each announcement of progress is greeted by island residents as an event to be celebrated. First the park loop is opened from Hulls Cove to Otter Point, then to Jordan Pond, and next the section between Jordan Pond and Cadillac Mountain. Finally, the road up Cadillac is opened.

It's light outside when folks go to work in the morning; the lengthening of each day is perceptible, and each week there is more to the day. Business owners begin to return to prepare for the coming tourist season. It was exciting for me to return to the island every other week to see the changes both in the park and in Bar Harbor. And the restaurants were opening again.

While I had anticipated the return of the waterbirds, I was completely taken by surprise by how many bald eagles were returning to the island. On more than one occasion I was "buzzed" by these low-flying raptors while out walking, sometimes while crossing a parking lot in town. Only during my time in Alaska have I seen so many of these magnificent birds.

Activity on the water also increases, as the lobstermen are back on the water, setting their traps and staking out territory as the waters of the Gulf of Maine begin to warm (hey, it's all relative; 60 is warmer than 45, right?).

Days are warmer; maybe you need only a light jacket, if at all, but still it cools off quickly at night. The bright center of the Milky Way also returns to the sky, making for memorable evenings along south-facing shores of the islands.

By late May and early June, the lupine begin the blooming season, spreading a profusion of color all over the island. Bunchberry also begins to bloom at this time. By Memorial Day weekend, all seems ready for the tourist season, but it remains still, quiet for a few more weeks until it finally morphs into summer.

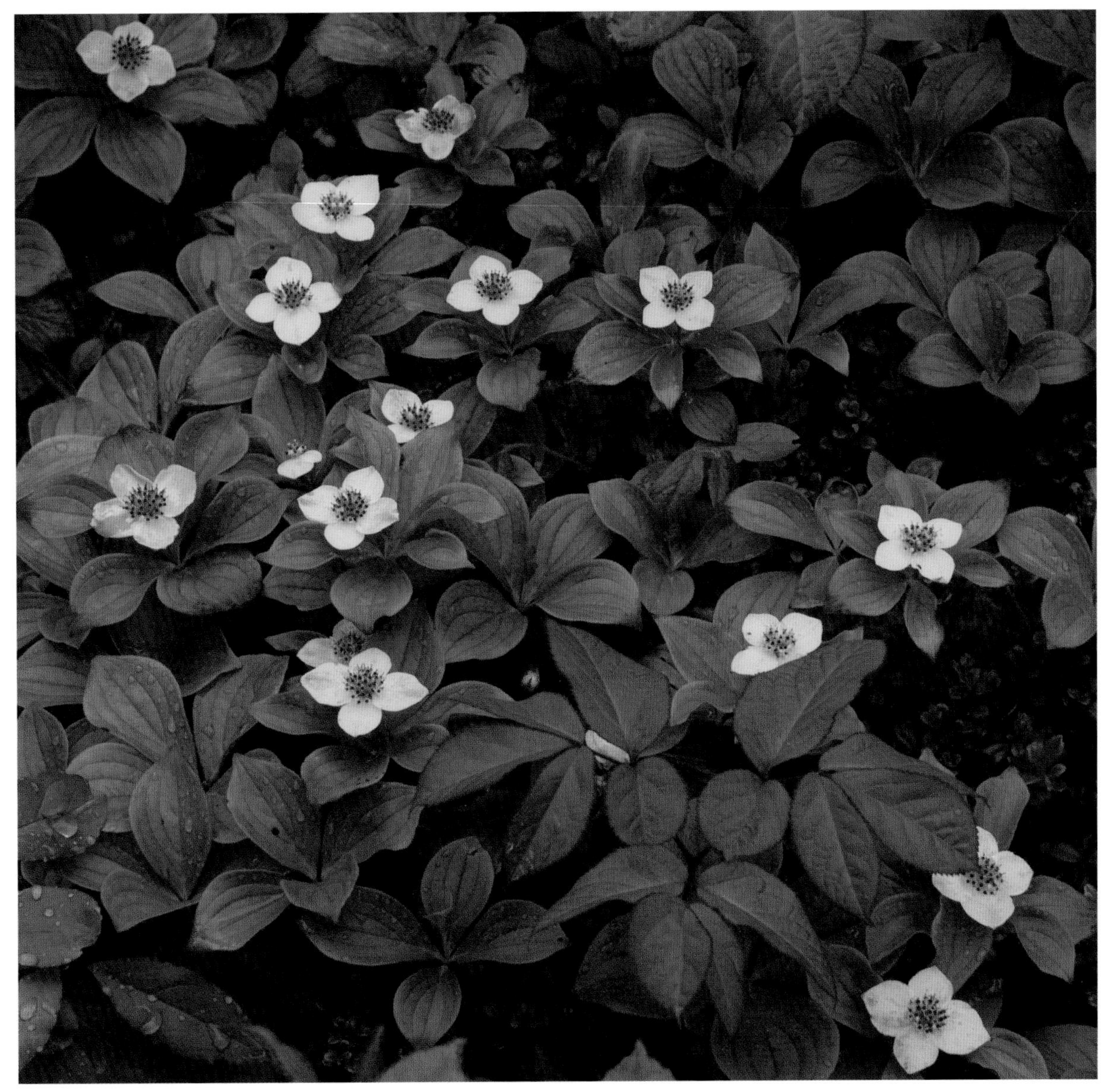

BUNCHBERRY NEAR BASS HARBOR

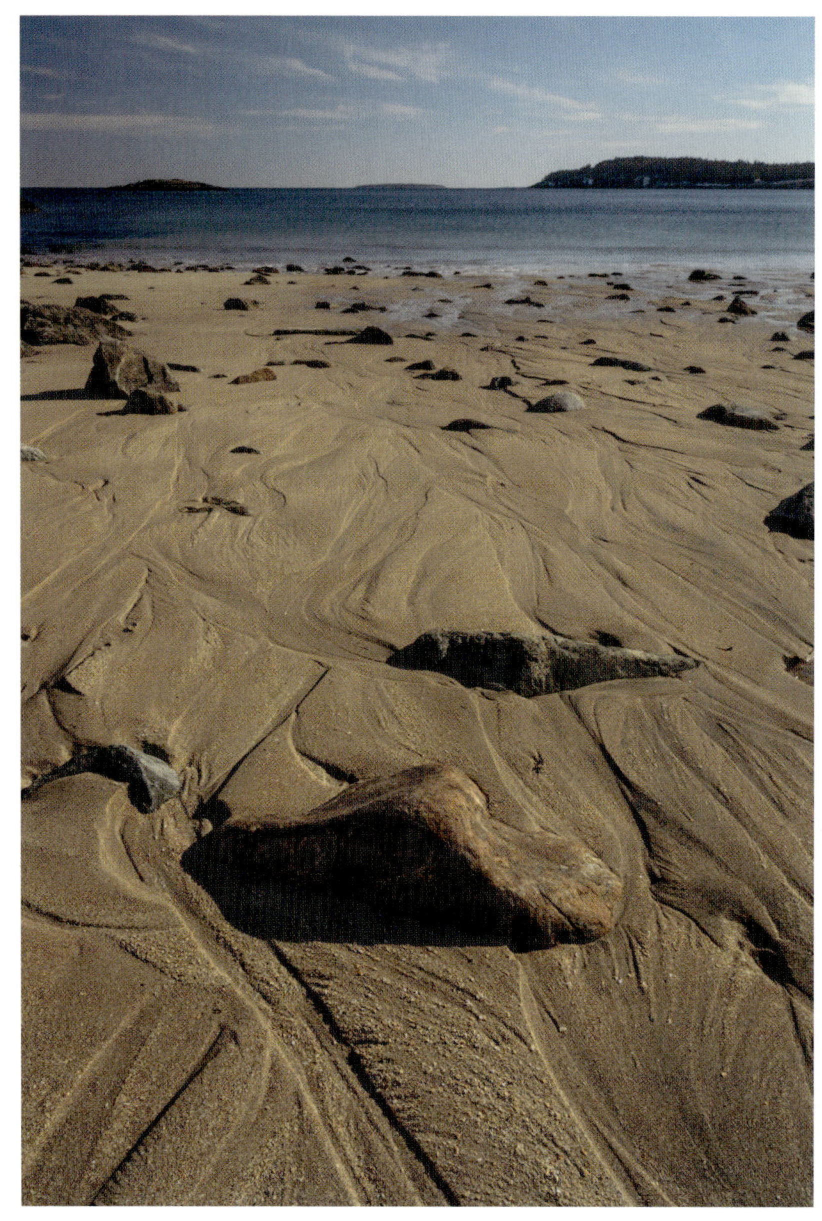

FROZEN IN PLACE, SAND BEACH

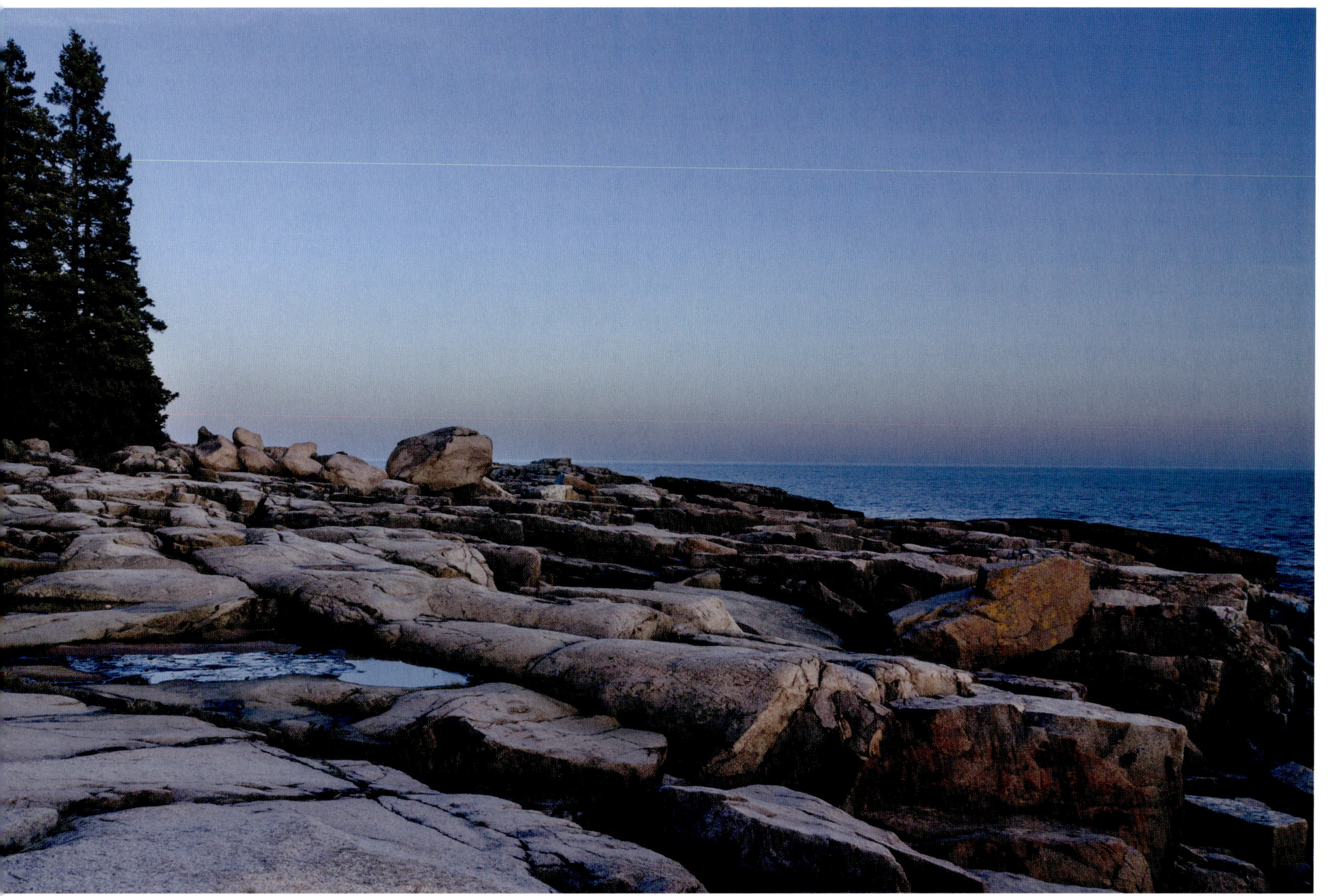

OTTER POINT, EARLY SPRING AFTERGLOW

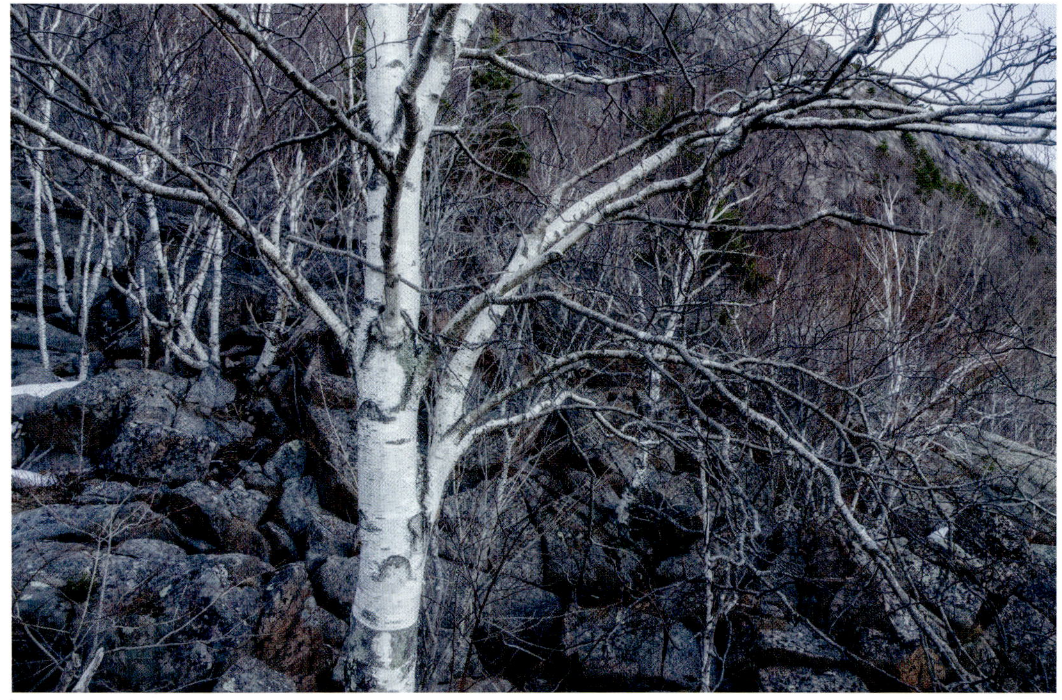

SPRING COLOR ALONG PRECIPICE TRAIL

•

The trail was closed and I could hear ice falling from the rock faces above.

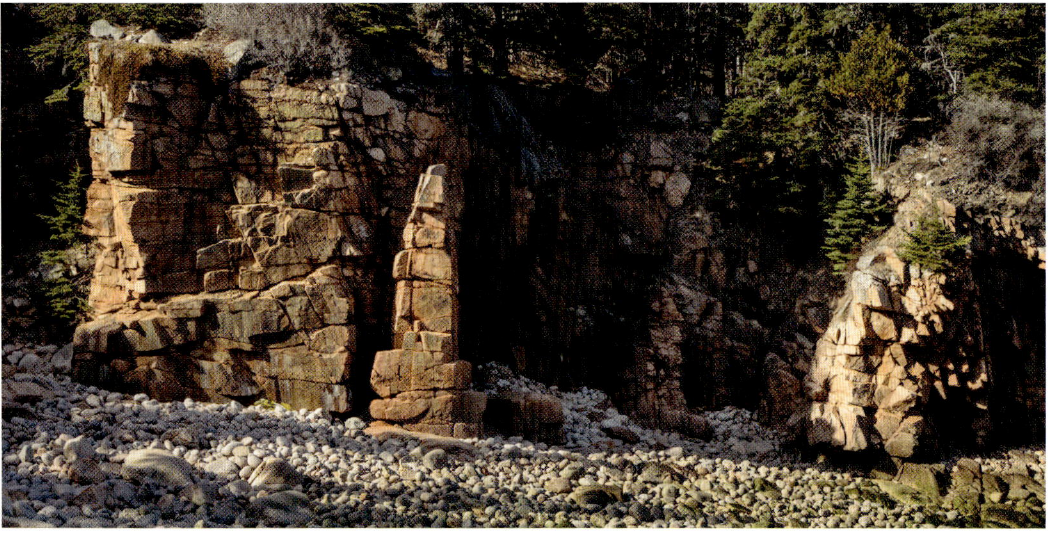

LATE AFTERNOON, SPRING, MONUMENT ROCK

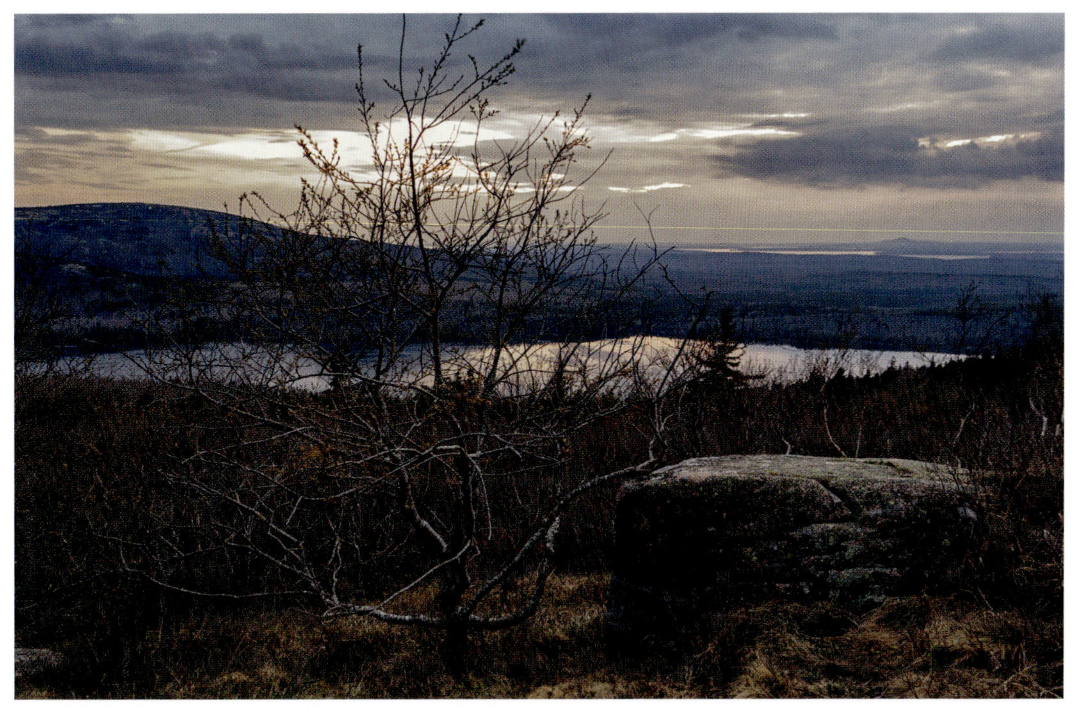

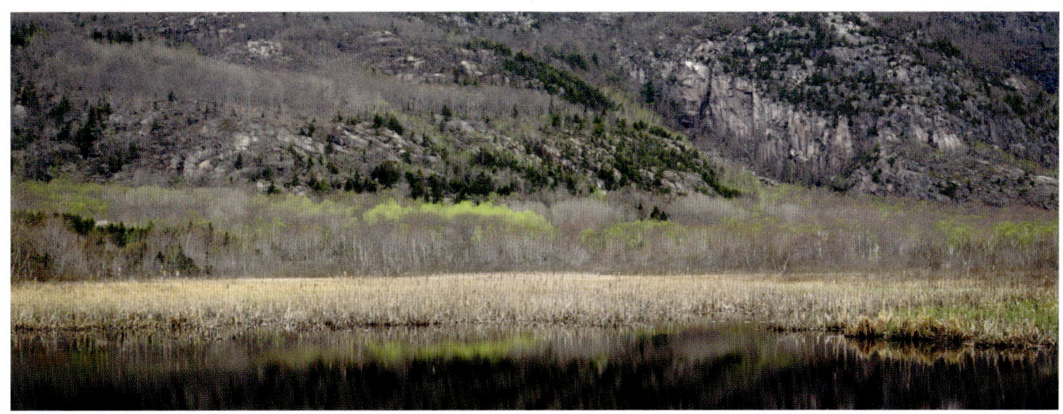

APPROACHING STORM OVER EAGLE LAKE AT SUNSET

SPRING AWAKENING, CHAMPLAIN MOUNTAIN

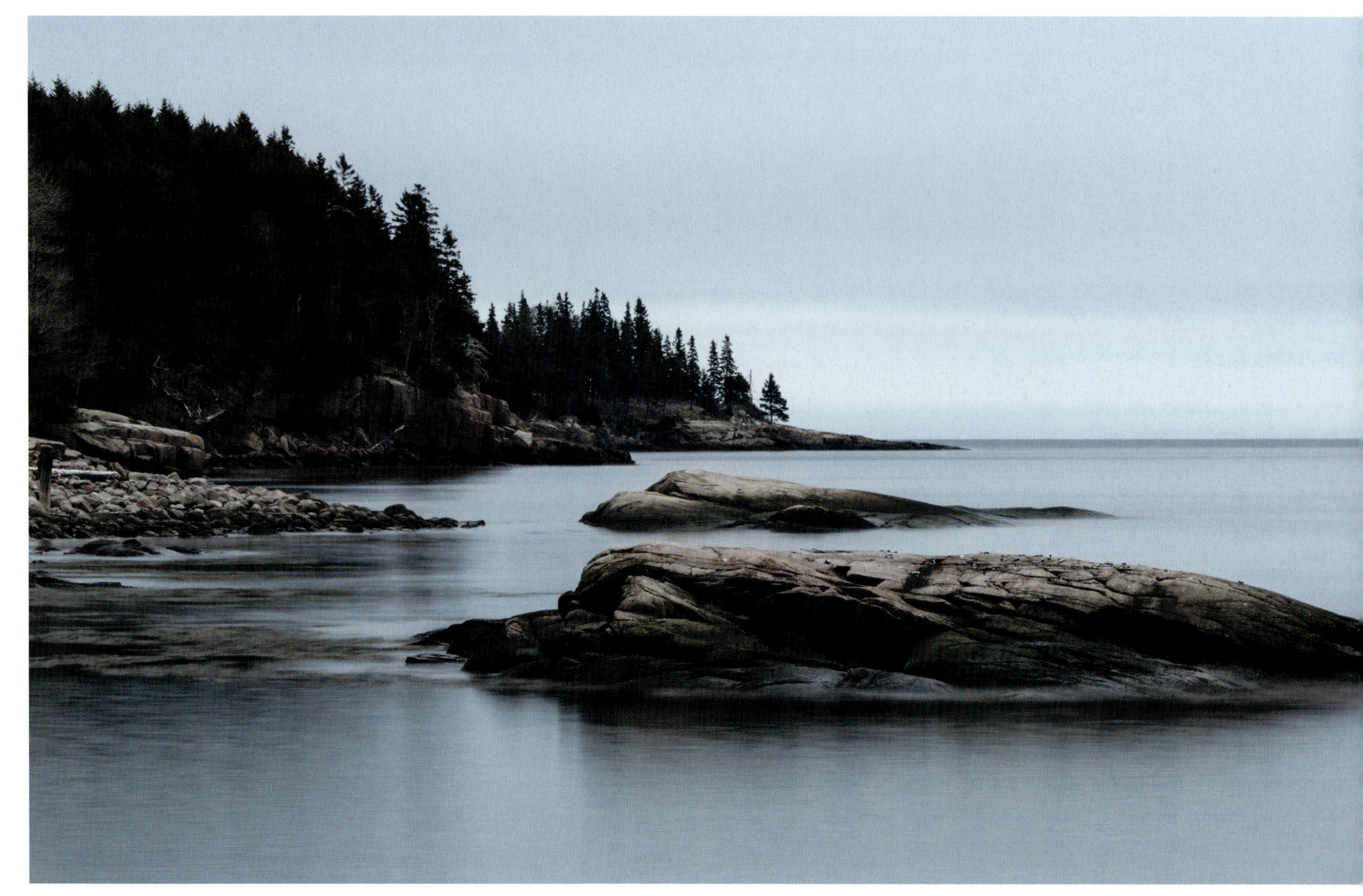

OTTER COVE AT HIGH TIDE ON A STILL EVENING

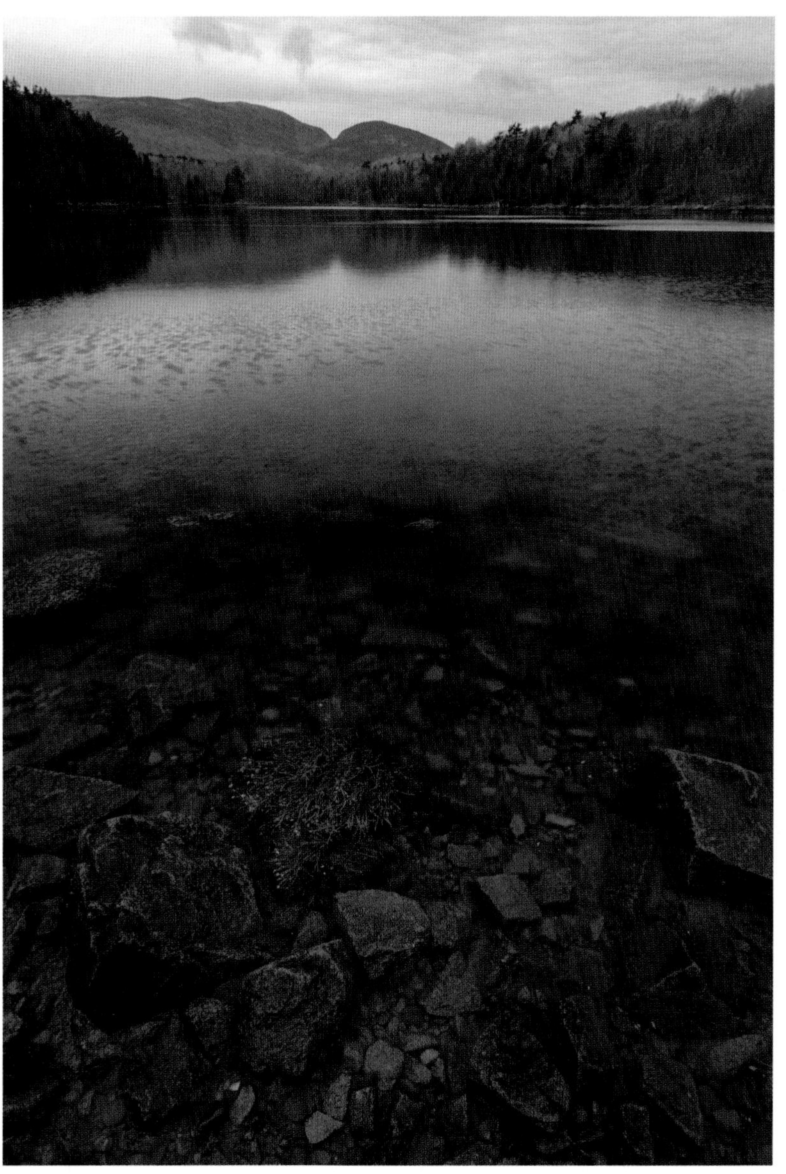

ROCKWEED AND BOULDERS, HIGH TIDE, OTTER COVE

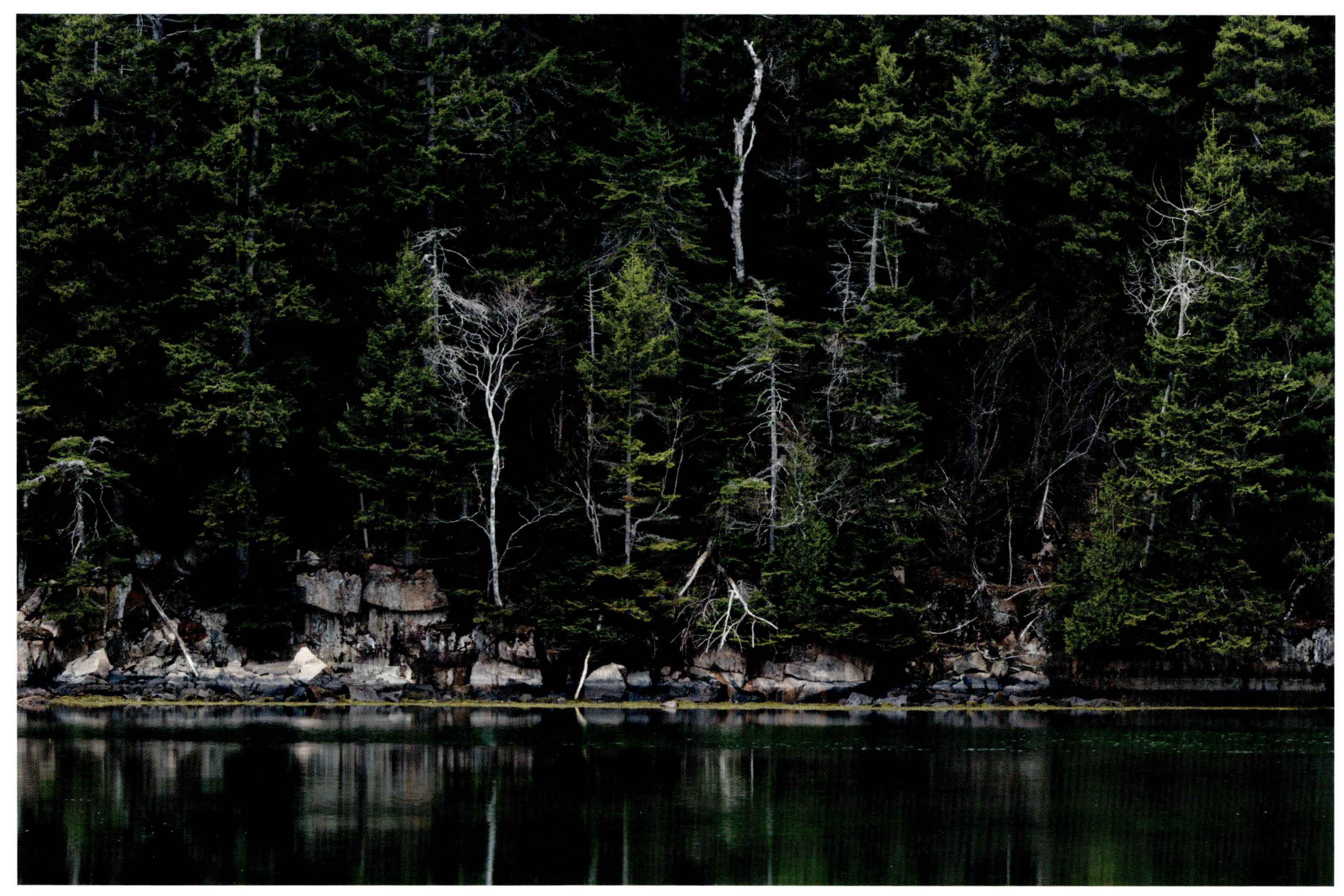

NEW SPRING GROWTH ON EVERGREENS ALONG OTTER COVE

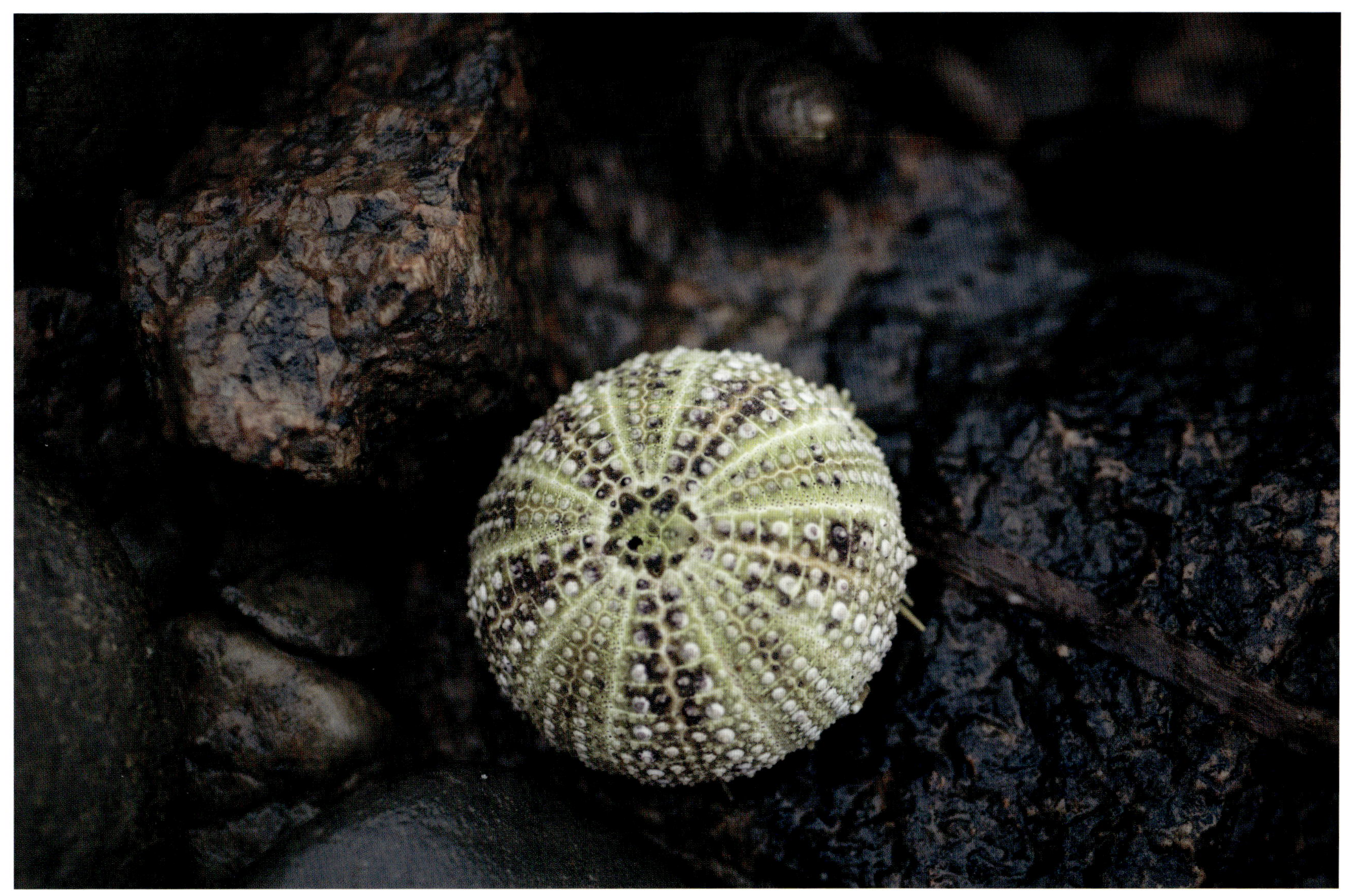

SEA URCHIN

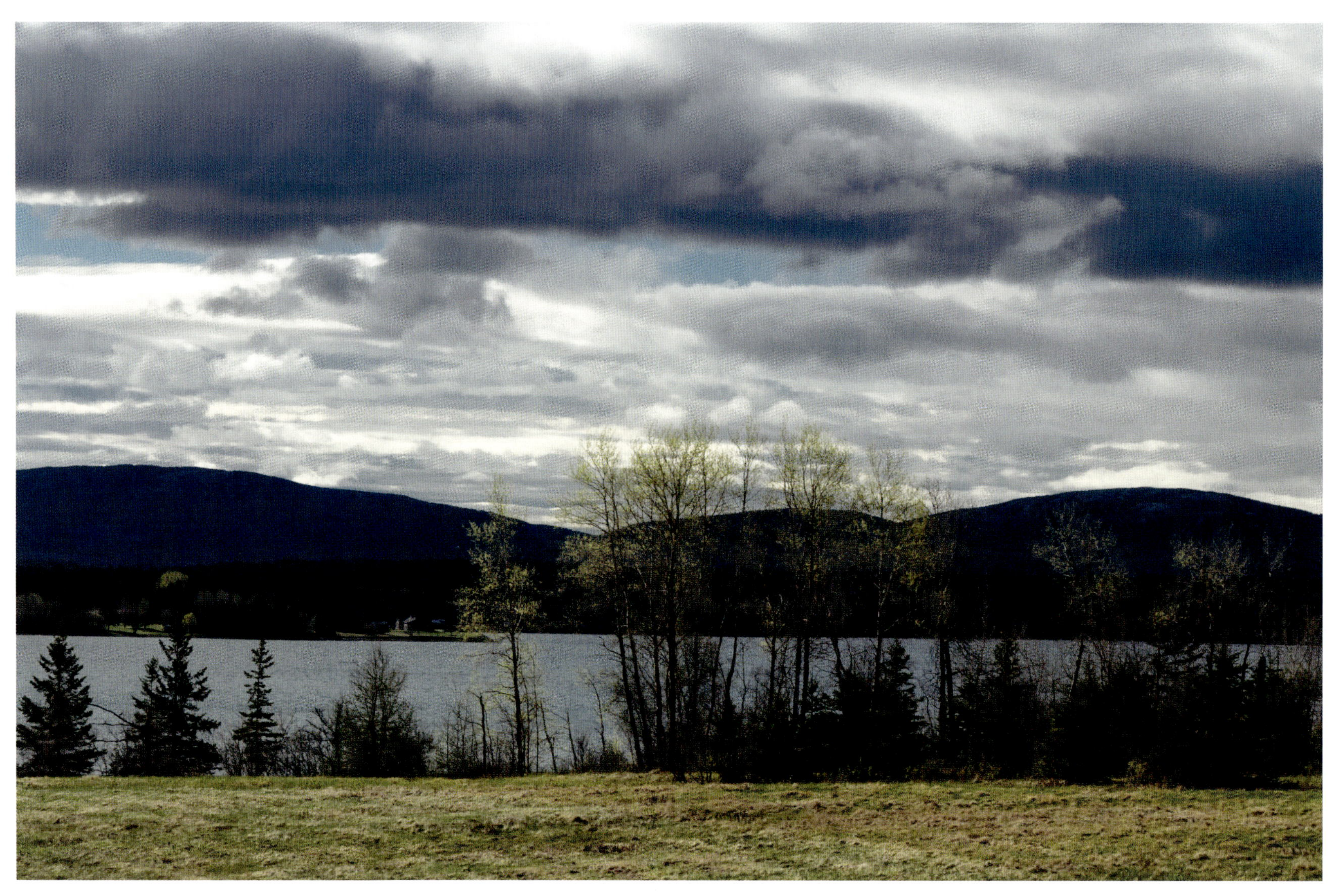

MOUNT DESERT ISLAND AND THE NARROWS FROM THE MAINLAND

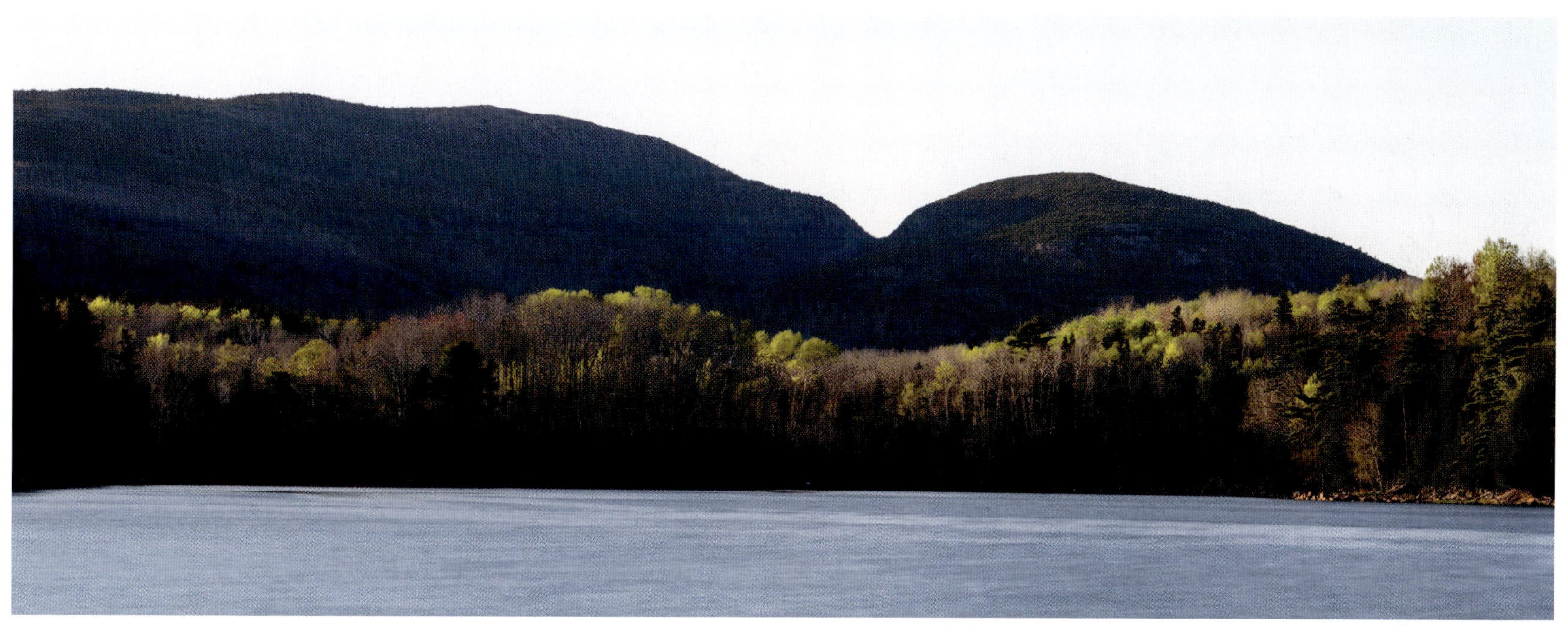

CADILLAC AND DORR MOUNTAINS FROM OTTER COVE

•

Just before slipping behind the summits, the sun's last long rays highlight new spring growth.

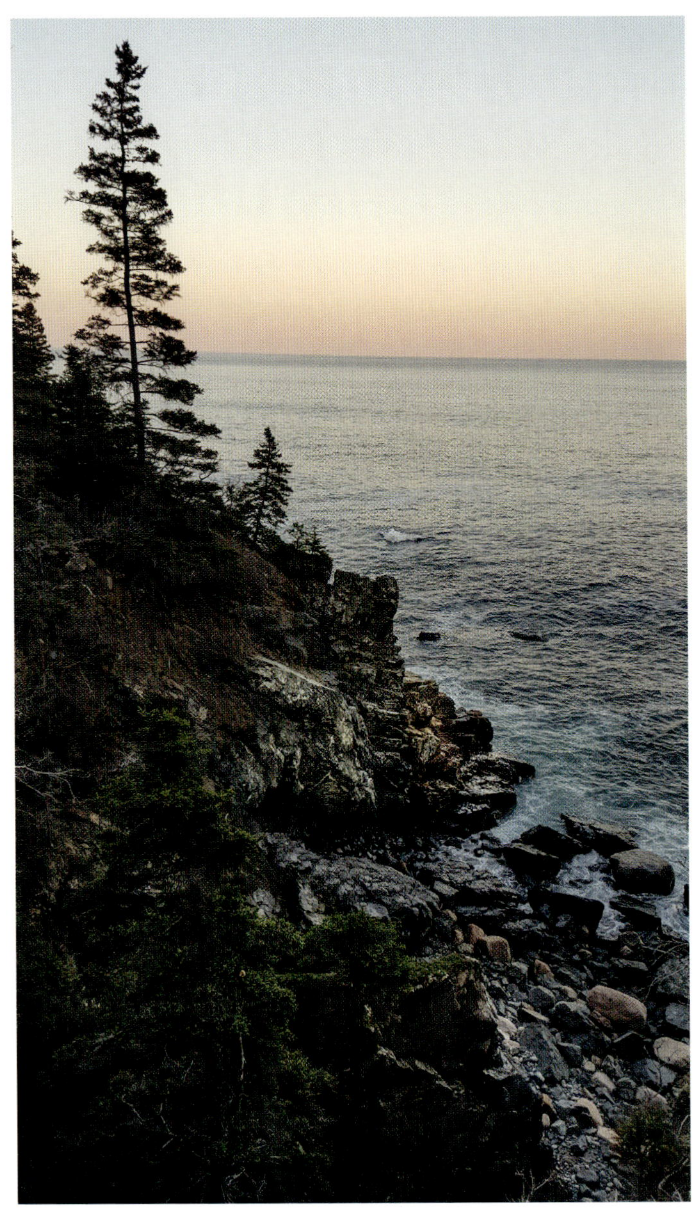

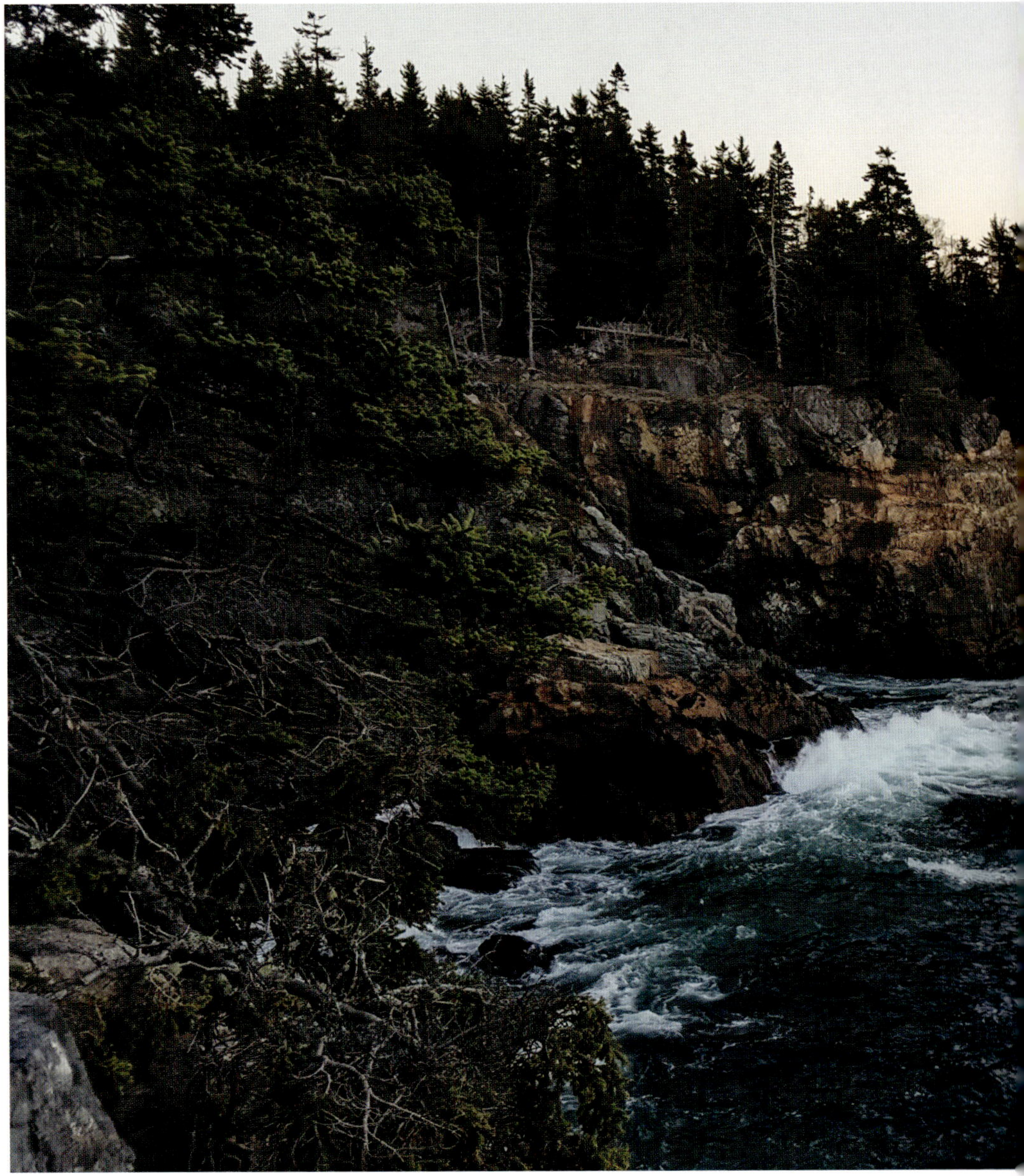

WESTERN POINT TWILIGHT

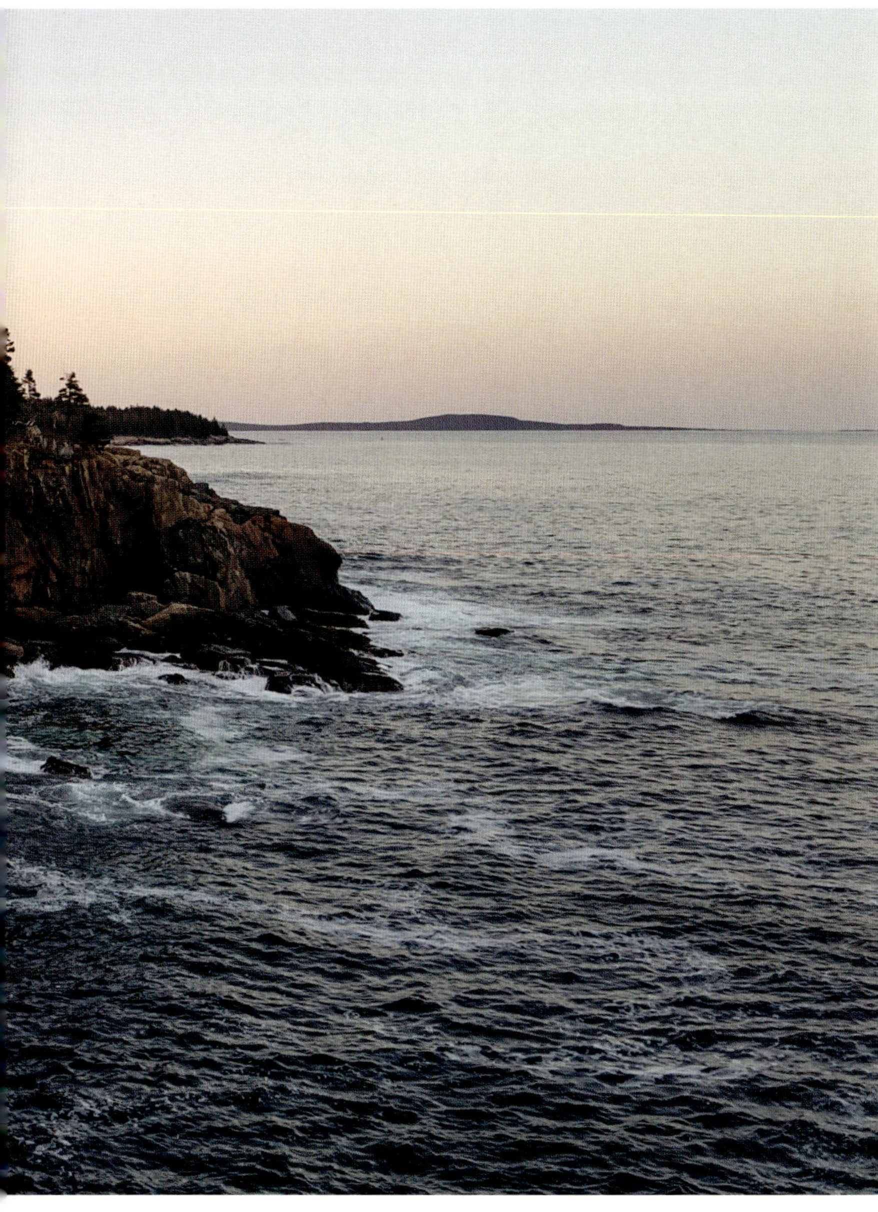

Opalescent light tints the sky and sea between
Western Point and Little Hunters Beach.
Schoodic Peninsula is on the horizon.

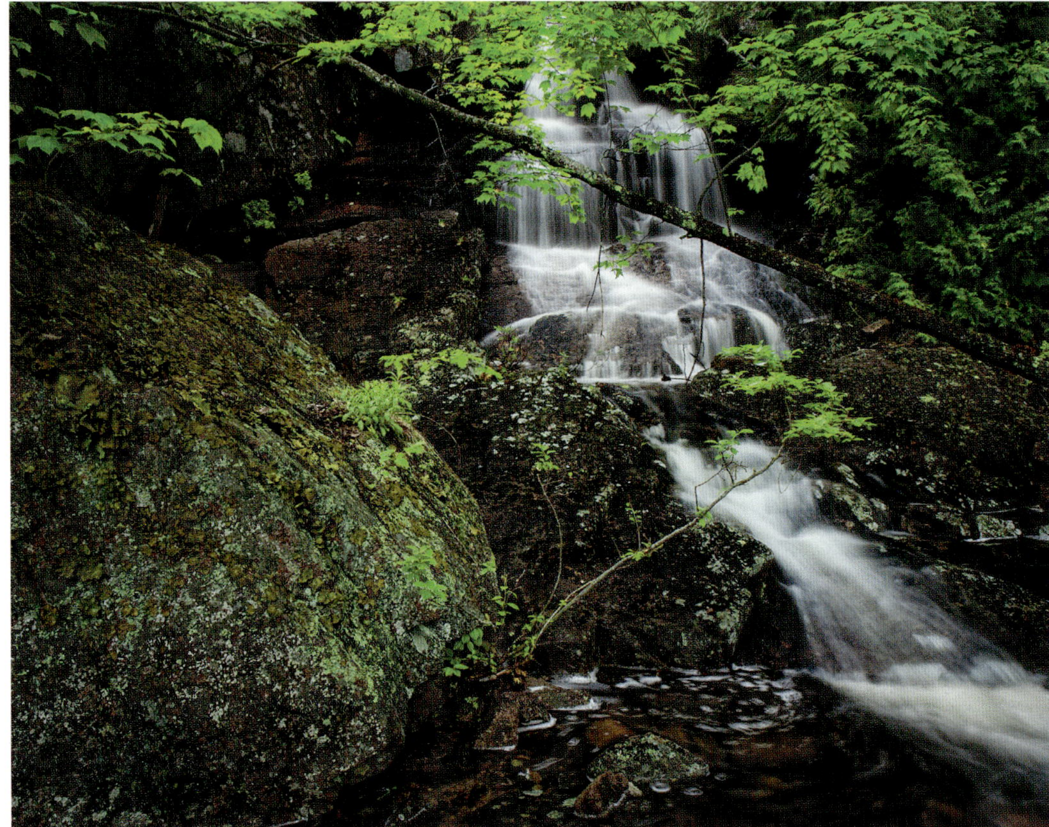

HIDDEN CASCADE IN SPRING COLORS

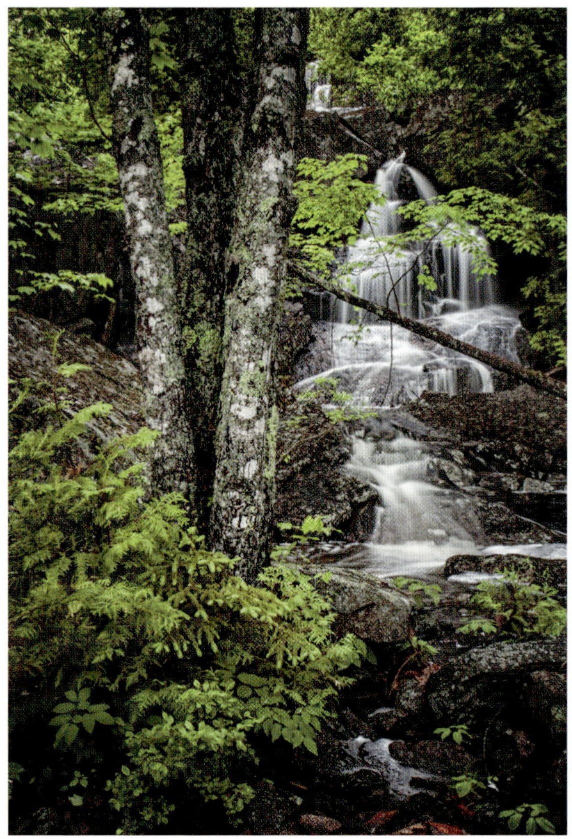

Lichen-covered maples and a hidden cascade after several hours of heavy rain

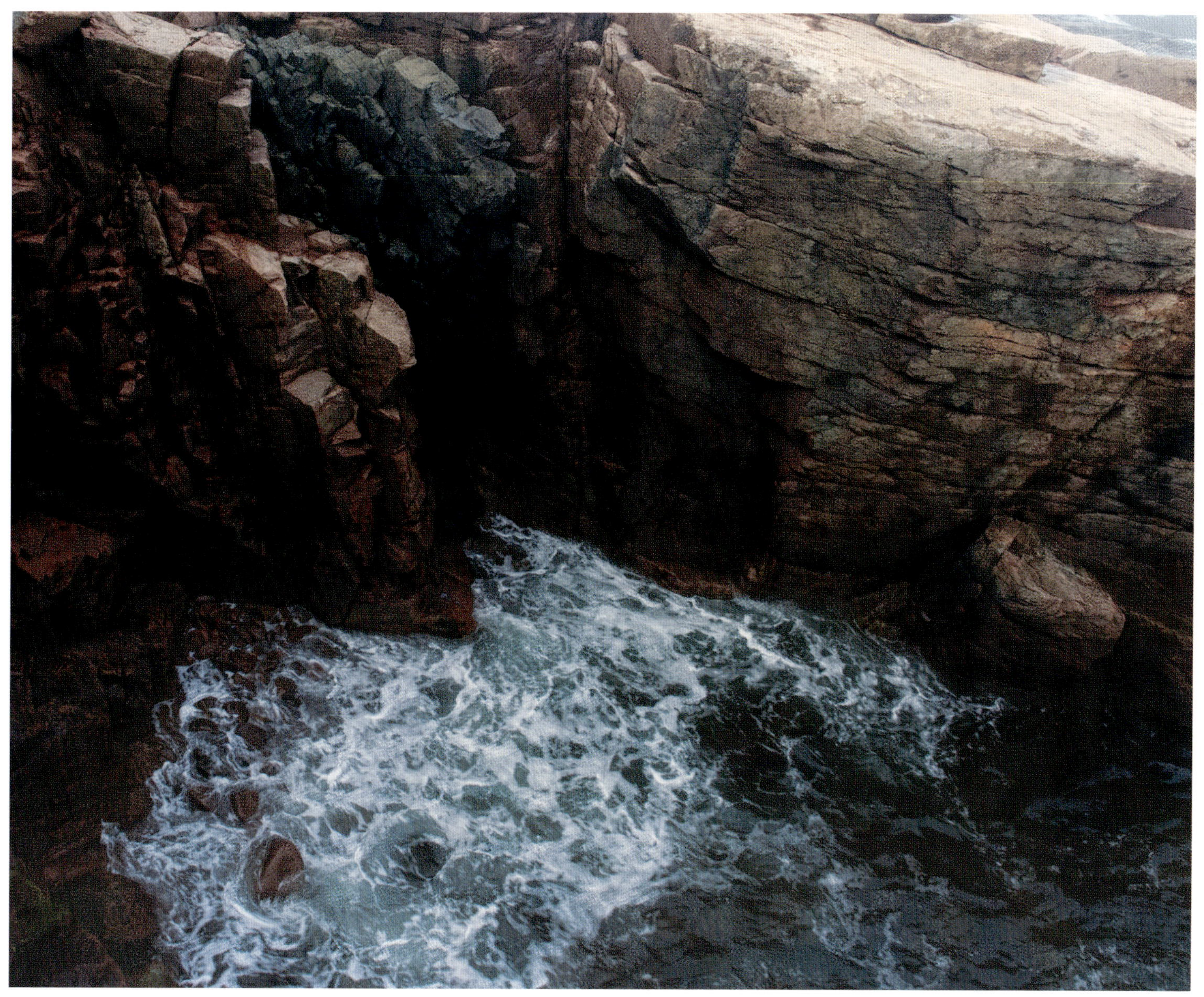

Fog and rock faces near Thunder Hole on a stormy day

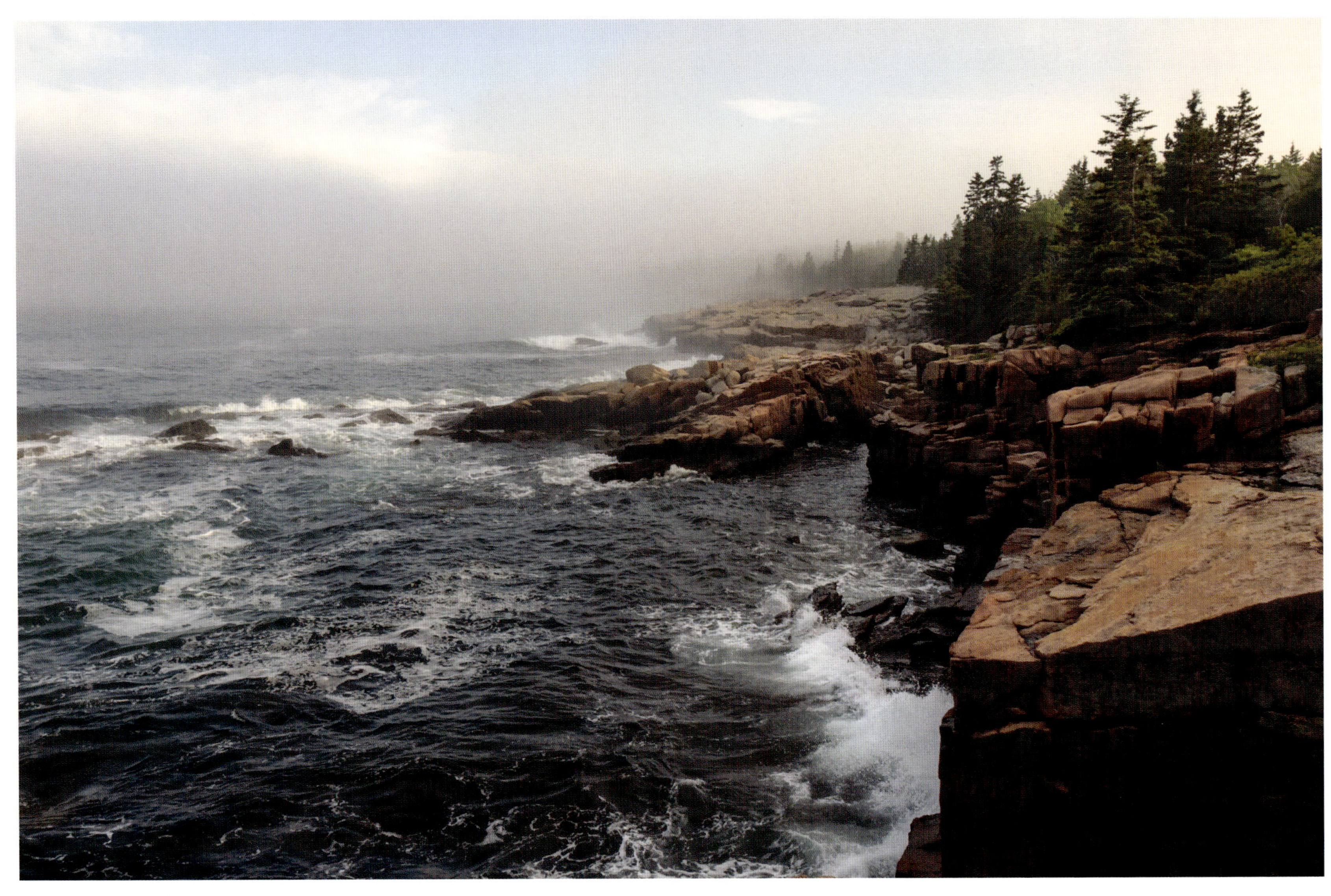

Sunset adds a subtle tint to the evening fog at high tide along Ocean Path.

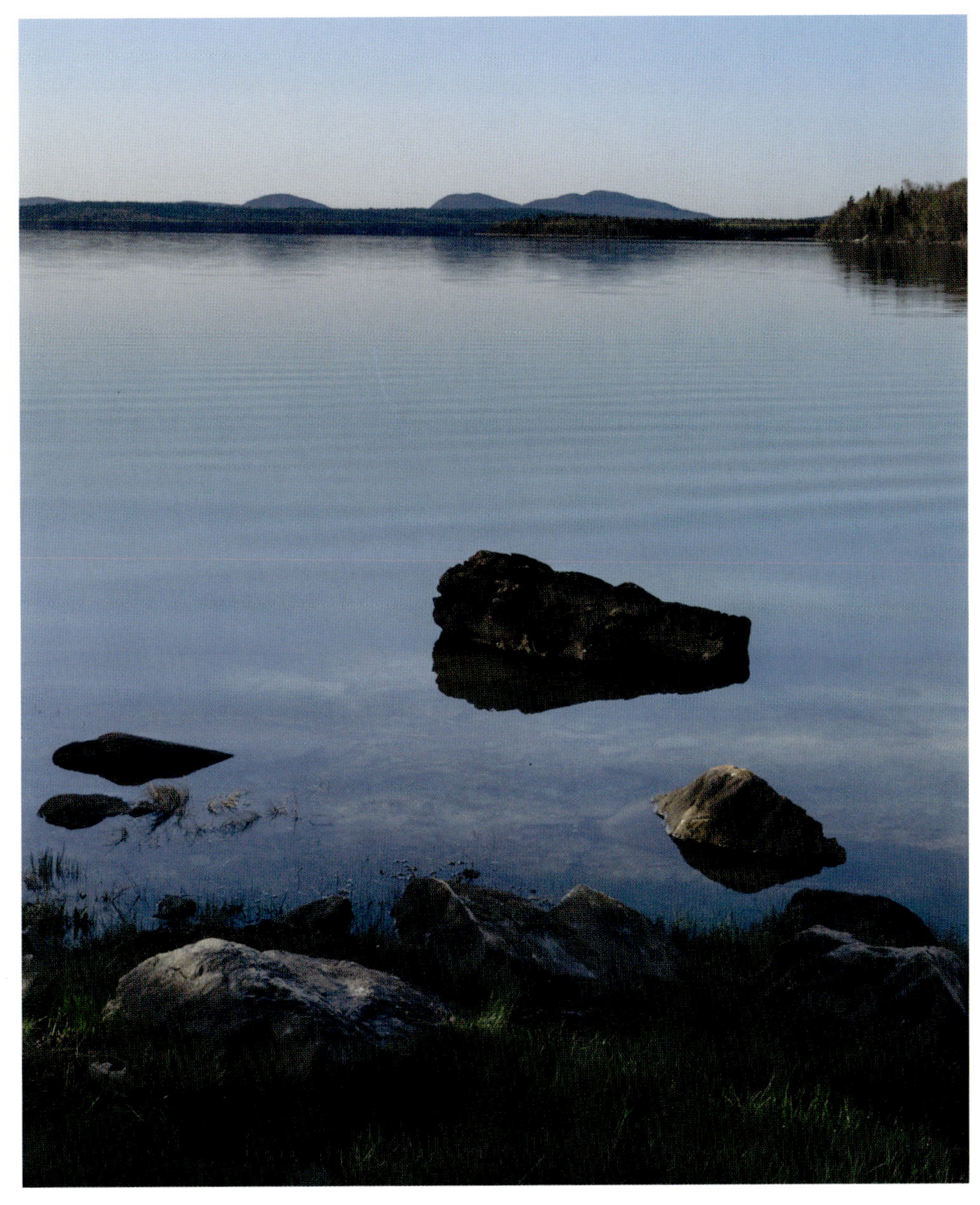

MOUNT DESERT ISLAND FROM GOOSE COVE ON THE MAINLAND

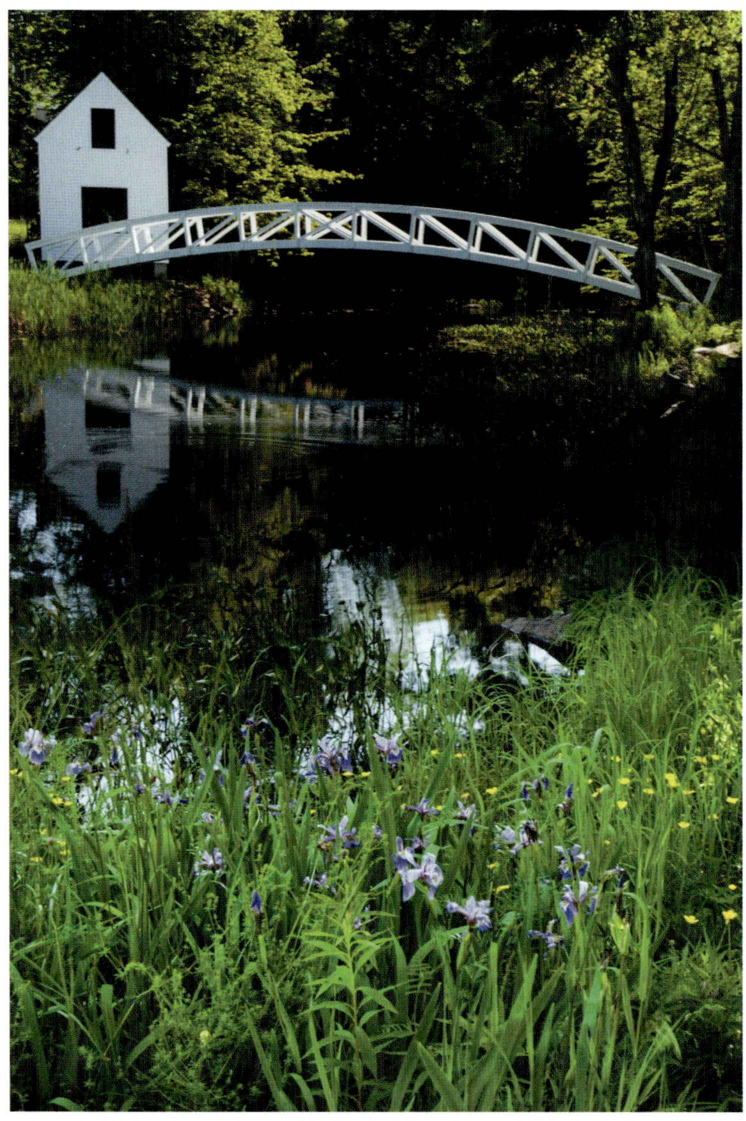

SOMESVILLE, SPRING IRISES

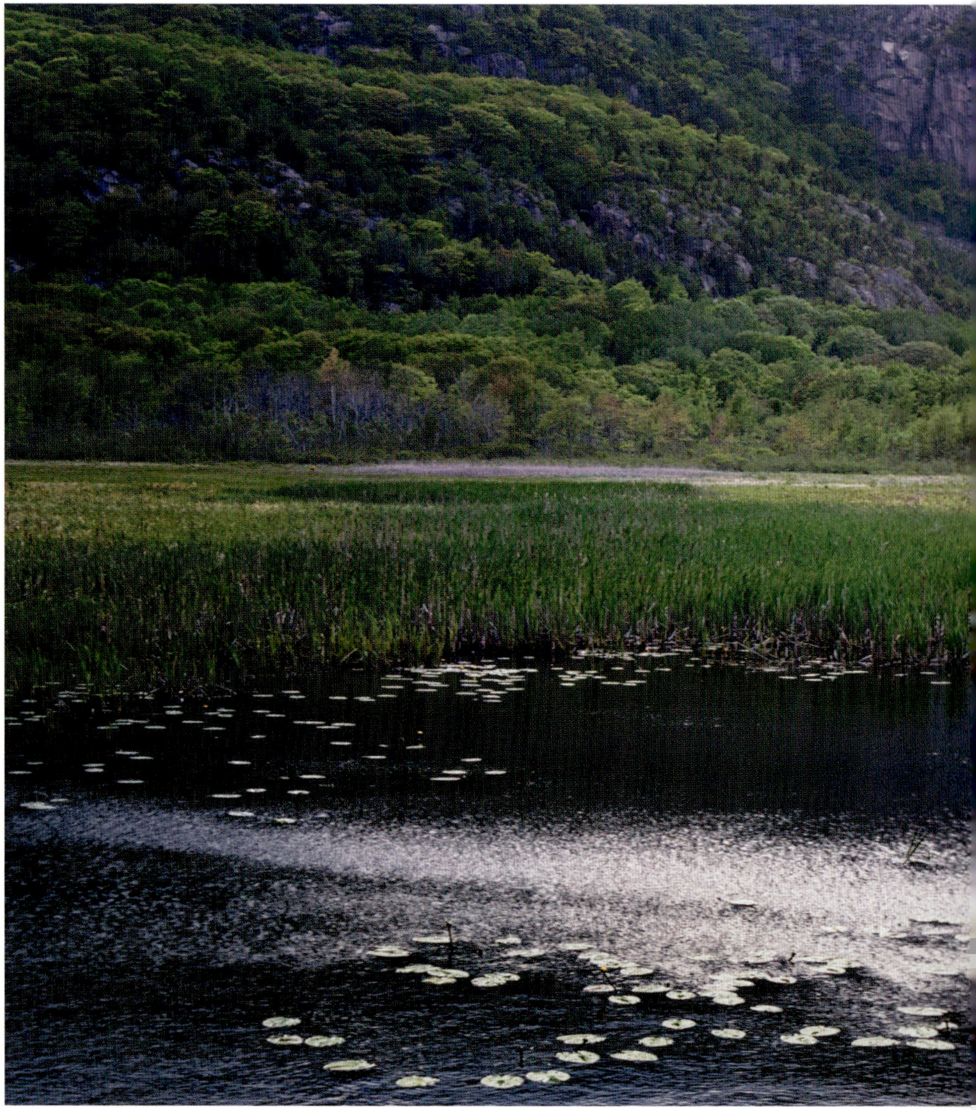

A slight breeze ripples the surface of the pond near Champlain Mountain, causing a shimmering of the light.

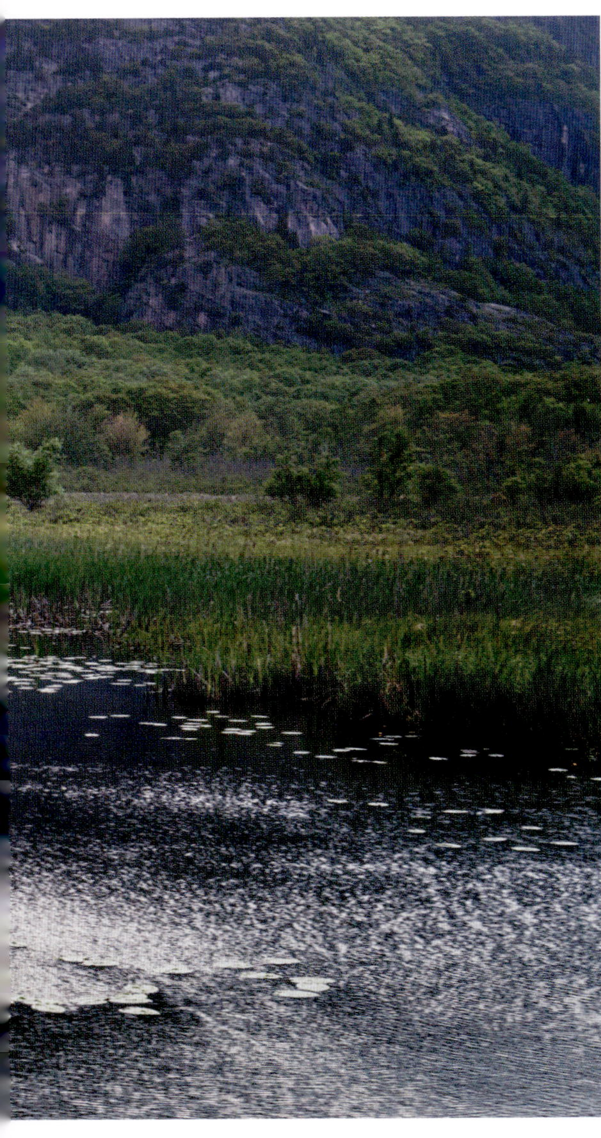

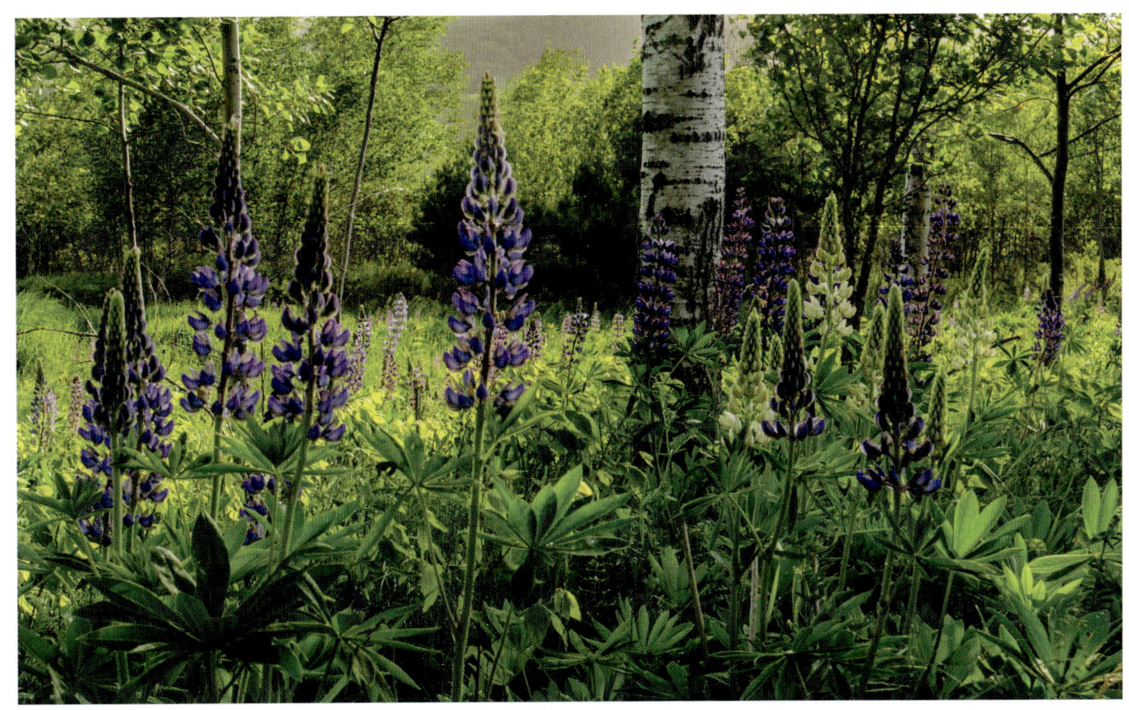

LUPINE GLORY AT SUNSET NEAR GREAT MEADOW

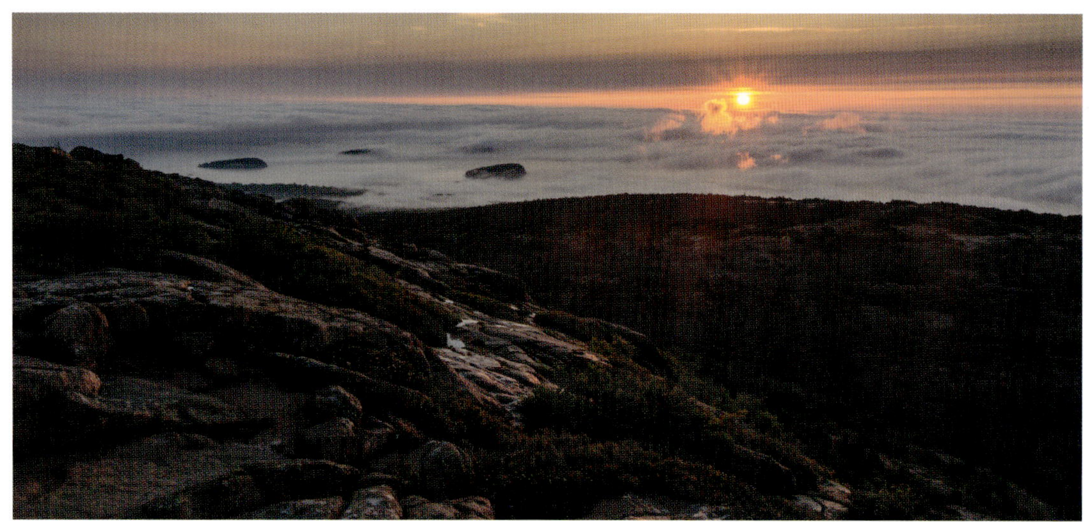

A heavy fog blankets Frenchman Bay and the Porcupine Islands at sunrise. One of the rewards of rising early (around 3 a.m.) to view the day's beginning from Cadillac Mountain.

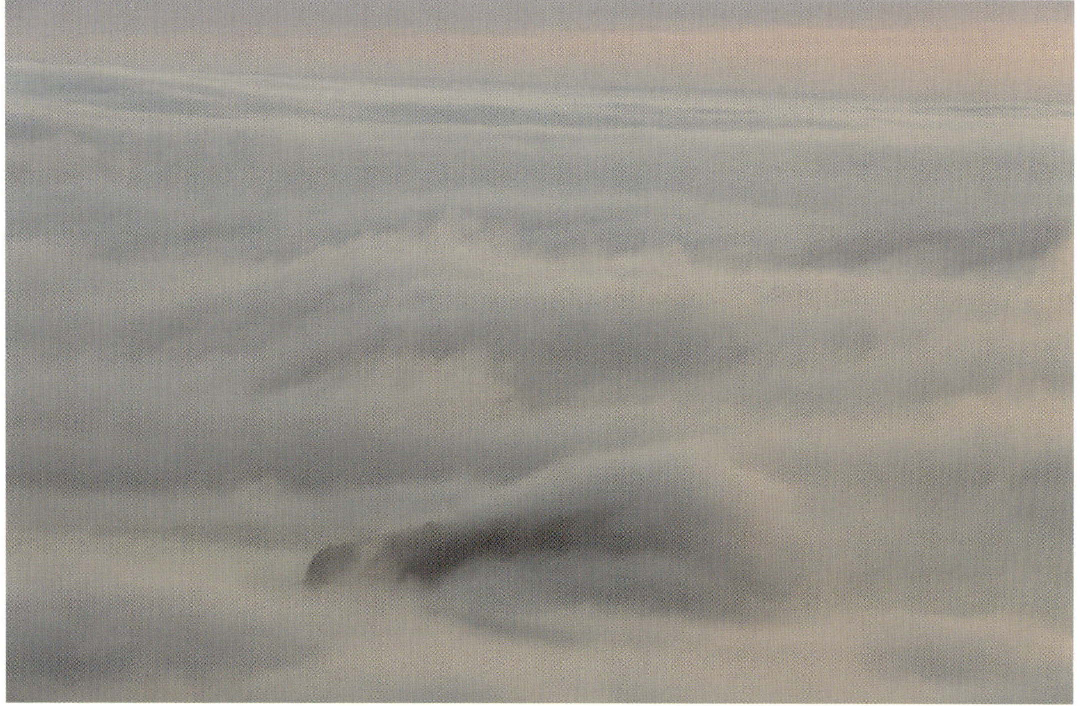

BALD PORCUPINE ISLAND IN FOG AT SUNRISE

•

For the next two hours, we were in and out of the fog as it swirled about Cadillac Mountain.

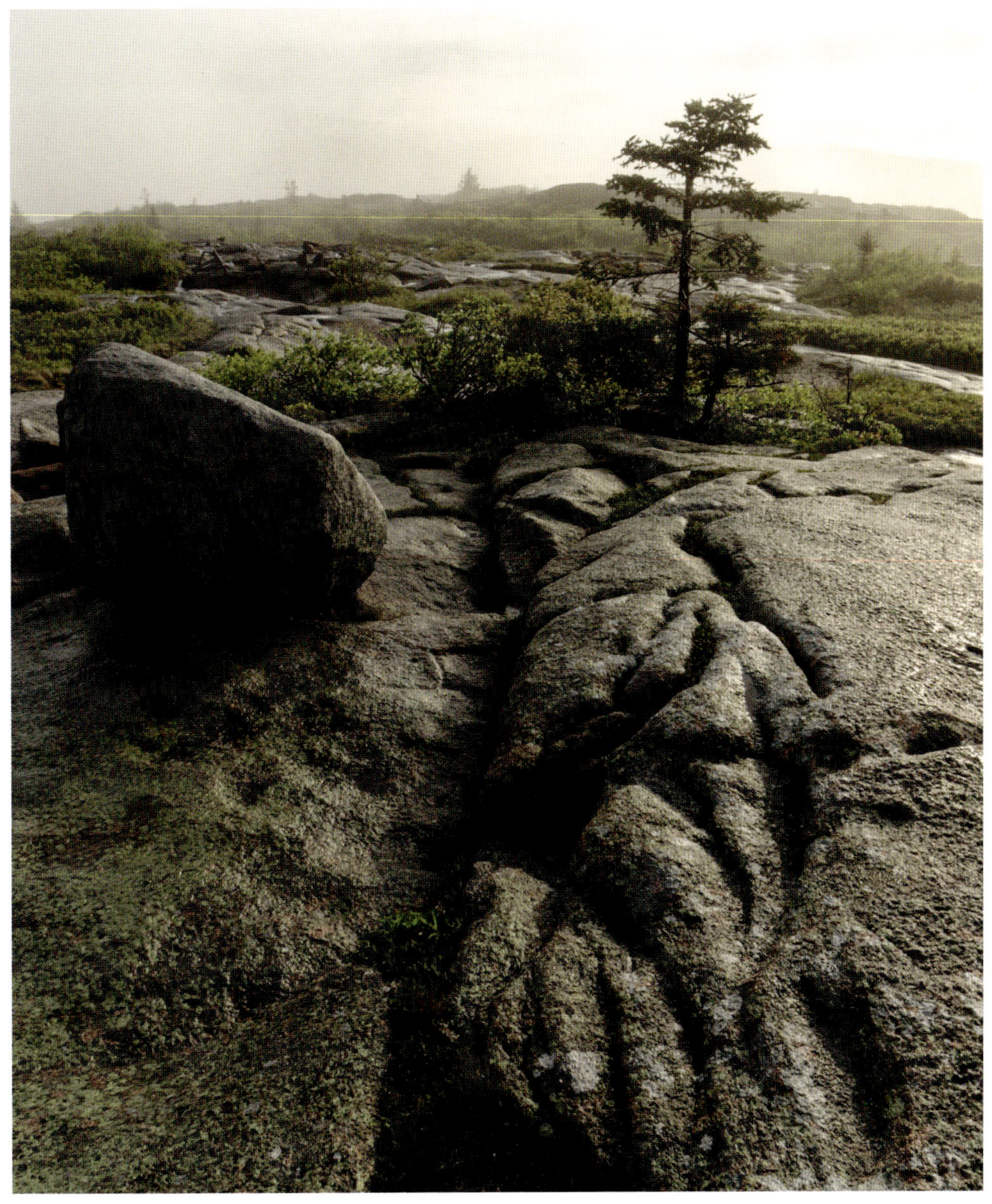

Granite and spruce in early-morning fog

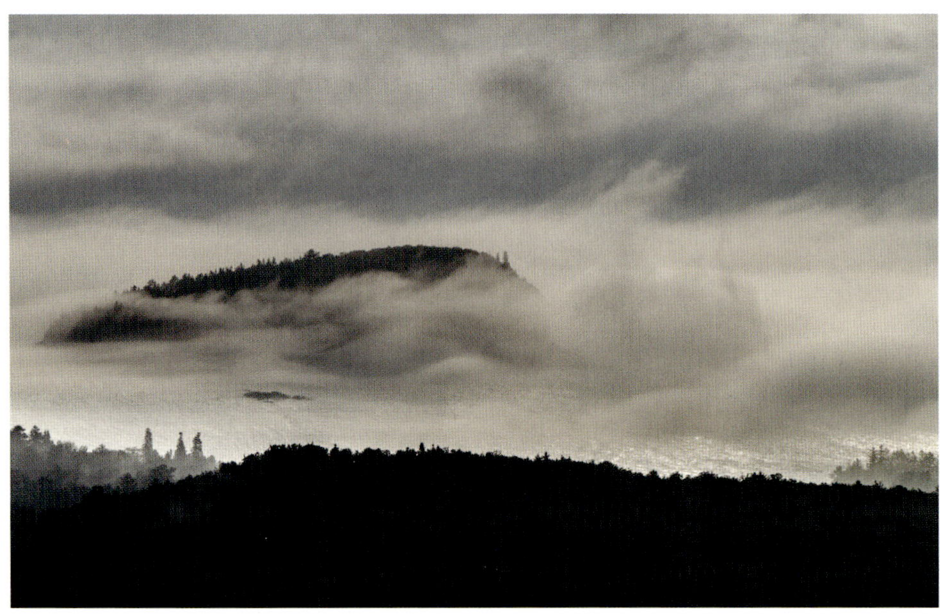

Bald Porcupine Island contours the fog shortly after sunrise.

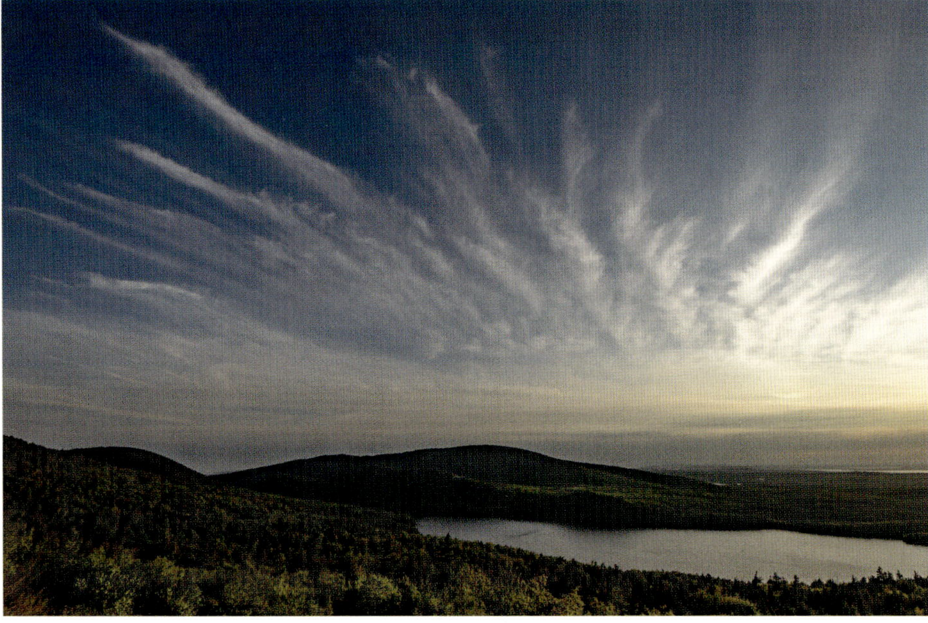

Cirrus clouds invade the sky over Eagle Lake before sunset.

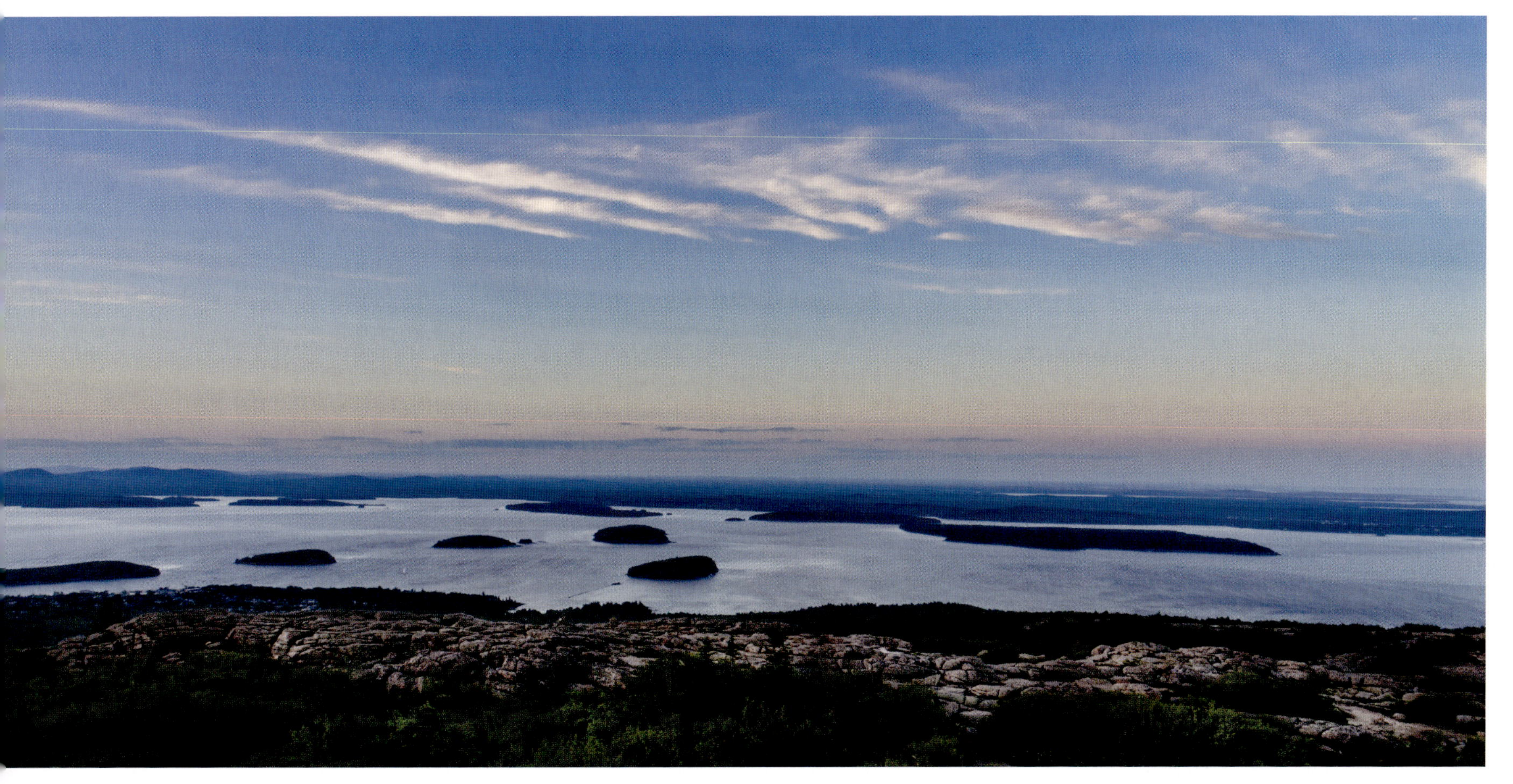

FRENCHMAN BAY TWILIGHT FROM CADILLAC MOUNTAIN

•

The one that got away back in August

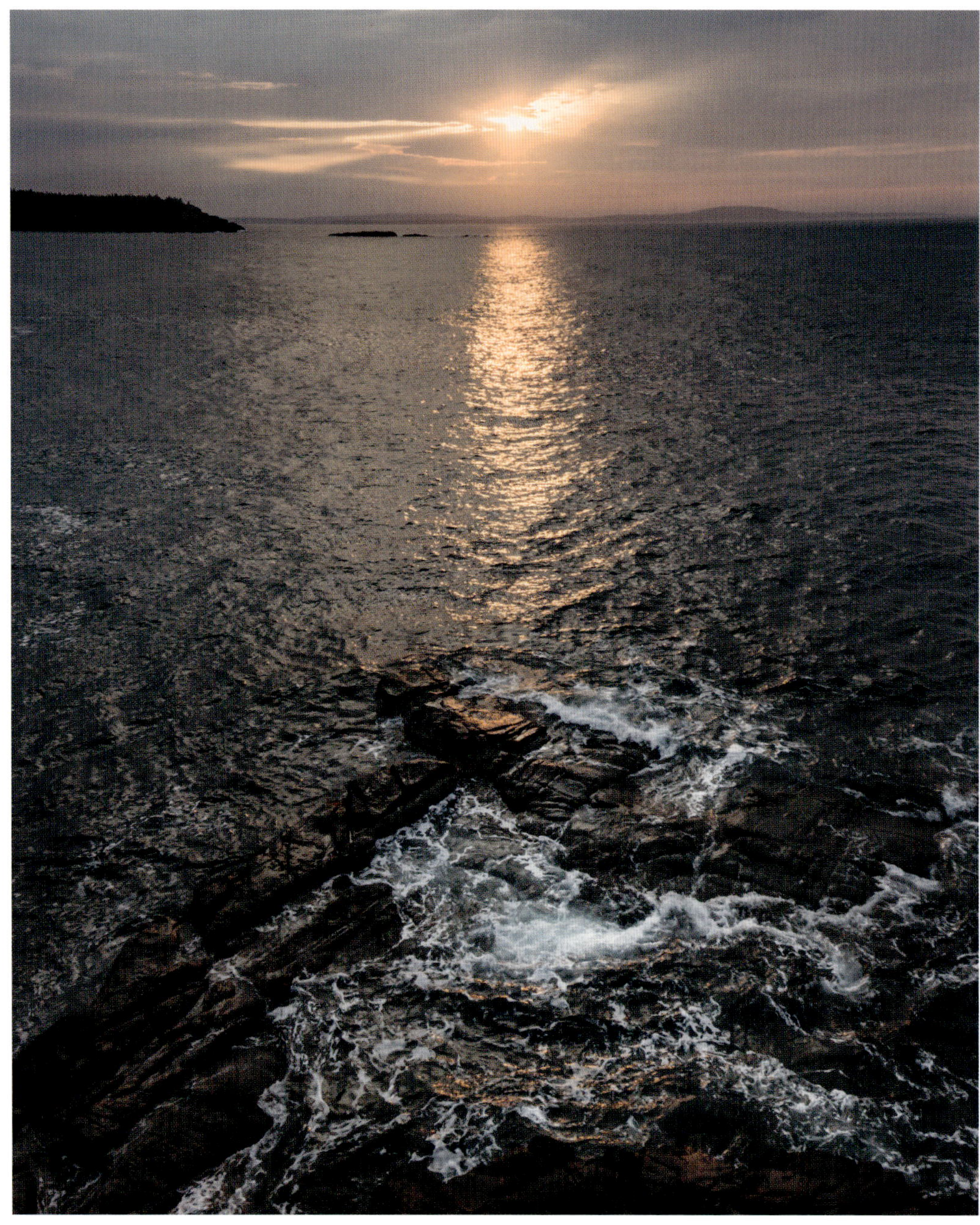

RUSH HOUR

SUNRISE OVER SCHOODIC PENINSULA FROM MONUMENT COVE

Rush hour used to have a very undesirable connotation for me. For fourteen years, I worked in downtown Boston. Although it is 35 miles from where I live, it is a two-hour or more commute each way, during the "rush hours." Doesn't matter whether one drives or takes the commuter trains; for four hours a day you're in transit. And you are at the mercy of the weather, other drivers, construction, sporting events, concerts, summer traffic heading to Cape Cod, autumn leaf peepers, Thanksgiving weekends, Christmas, Easter—you get the idea. Traffic is so heavy and roads are so inadequate that in certain areas it's permissible to drive in the breakdown lanes. Commuter trains, subways, and buses add another layer of complexity. My typical commute was to leave my house at 5:45 a.m., drive 6 miles, park, remember to pay for parking, get on the train, find a seat, and ride into town for anywhere from sixty to ninety minutes. Once in Boston it could be another thirty to forty-five minutes to get to work, either walking, riding the subway, or taking a bus. So by the time I arrived at work around 8 a.m., I felt like I had already put in two hours. All my friends and coworkers had similar feelings. Reverse the process eight hours later, and if you were fortunate you could be back home by 6:30 p.m. But stay a few minutes late, arrive at the station just as the train is pulling out, and it's 7:30 before you get home, exhausted. Just enough time to grab a bite to eat and relax for an hour or two before heading to bed to rest, so that tomorrow you could do it all over again. While I may have a forty-hour workweek, most weeks I was spending over twenty hours just getting back and forth, to a job I disliked. Any energy one had for work upon waking in the morning was greatly diminished by the time you arrived there. We all felt it—the stress, the anxiety, and we all hated commuting during rush hour. On the plus side, I wasn't driving in a car by myself (it was actually 41 miles and there were forty-one traffic lights, and a great deal of time was spent moving forward one car length at a time, sometimes for miles on the turnpike or interstate) and I made a lot of friends on the train who made the journey bearable. But, in the end, rush hour was taking a toll on all of us.

Now, standing here atop the cliffs (it's only 4:15 a.m. and I've been here for an hour already) overlooking Monument Cove at sunrise, rush hour has a completely different meaning. A subtle awakening, it starts with the anticipation of that moment when the energy rushing from the sun, 93 million miles away collides with our little piece of the universe to bring us light and warmth. The wind picks up, air currents stir and rush through the spruces and firs, damp with last night's rain, spreading the forest aroma (just a brief hint; it departs as soon as you notice it), and then the aroma returns again on the next breeze, but changed, now mixed with the salt ocean air; droplets churned up by the waves rush into the rocks below, rising on the updrafts. It's almost high tide. There is no sound but the wind, gulls, the buoy off Otter Cliffs, and waves. An old tune by the Hollies, "The Air That I Breathe," runs through my mind. Aroused by this visual, aural, and olfactory stimulation, I reflect on how fortunate I am to be standing here, and this triggers another rush—synaptic currents run the length of the nervous system, releasing a rush of endorphins, which travel to the pleasure centers of the brain. I am refreshed, revitalized, ready for whatever the day offers. I reflect on my previous life in relation to my newly discovered life, convinced I made the right decision to forgo the "other rush hour." I embrace the moments, unwilling to release them, holding on to them as long as I can. These days, a large print of this image hangs on the wall next to my bed; the first thing I see upon waking is a reminder of a more exhilarating rush hour to begin my day.

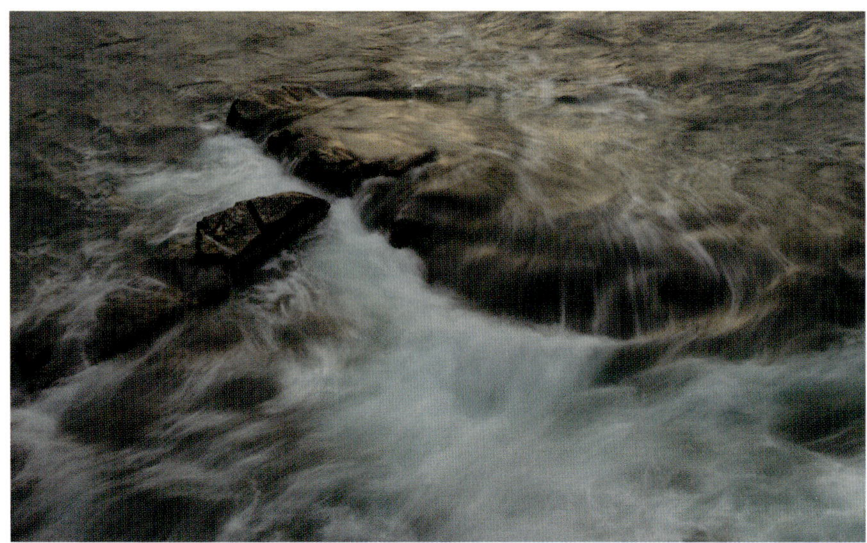

TURQUOISE AND GOLD

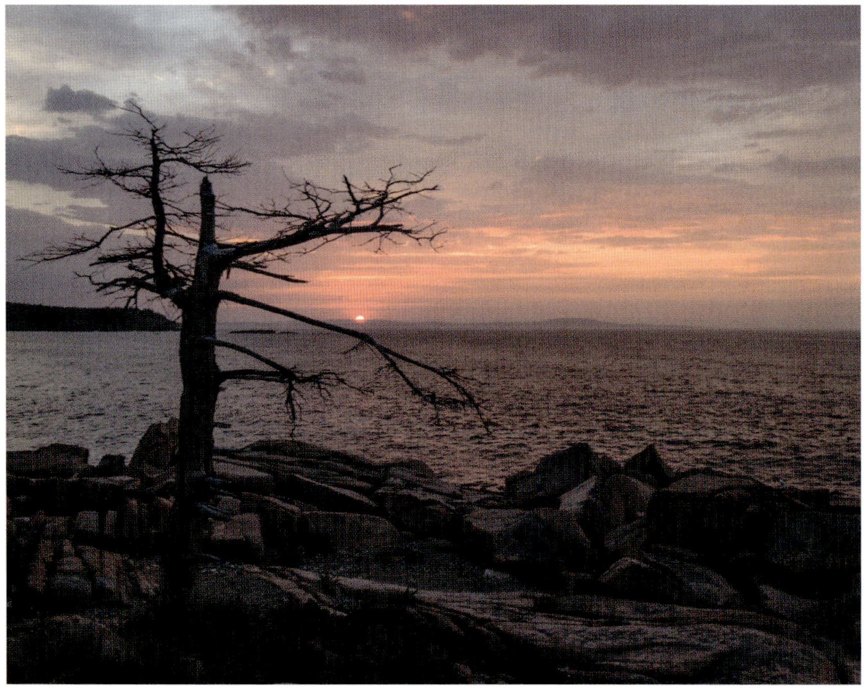

SUNRISE SENTINEL, OCEAN DRIVE

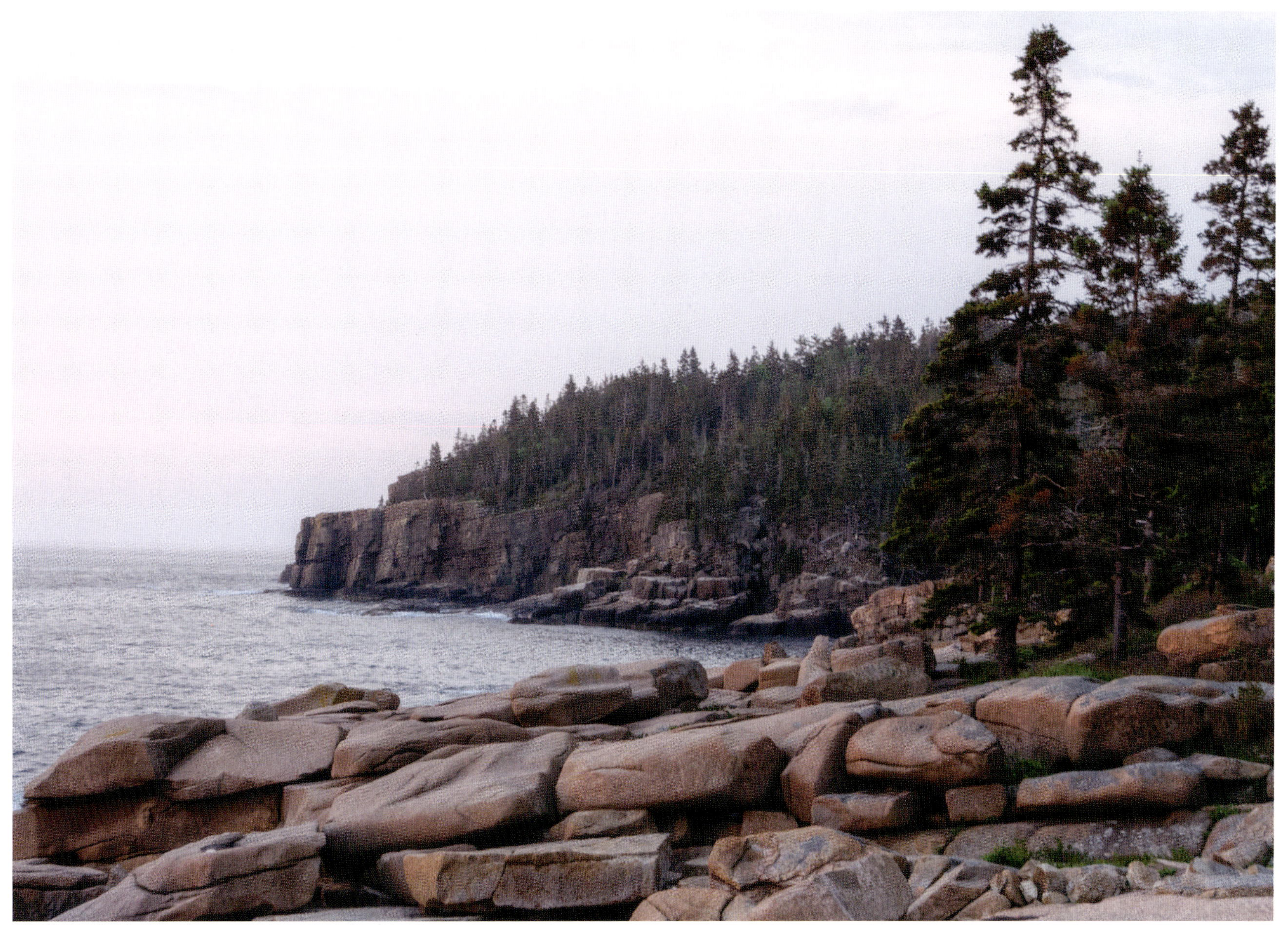

OTTER CLIFFS IN ROSE LIGHT AT DAWN

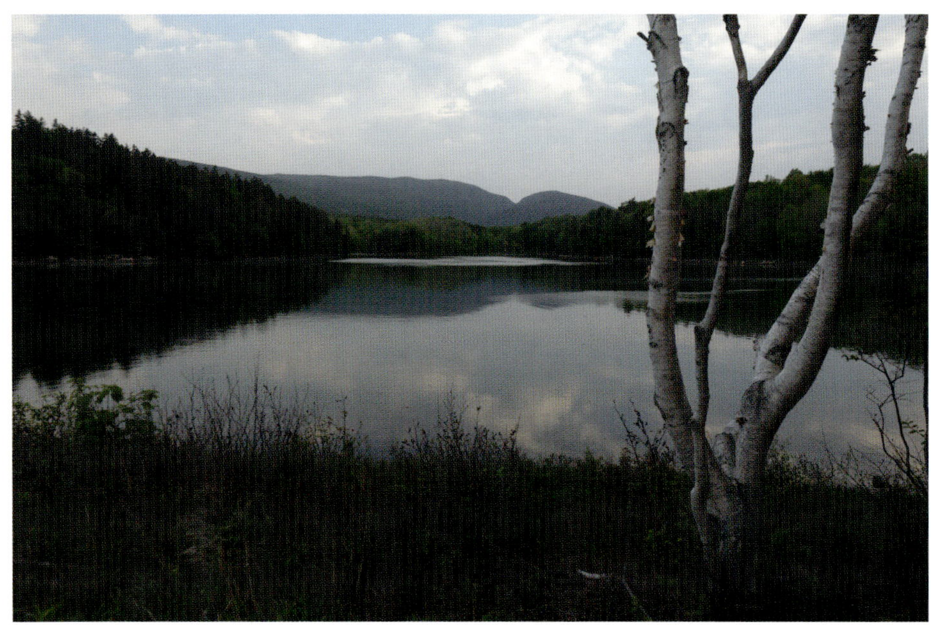

Birch trees witness the slow morning dance of the clouds over Otter Cove.

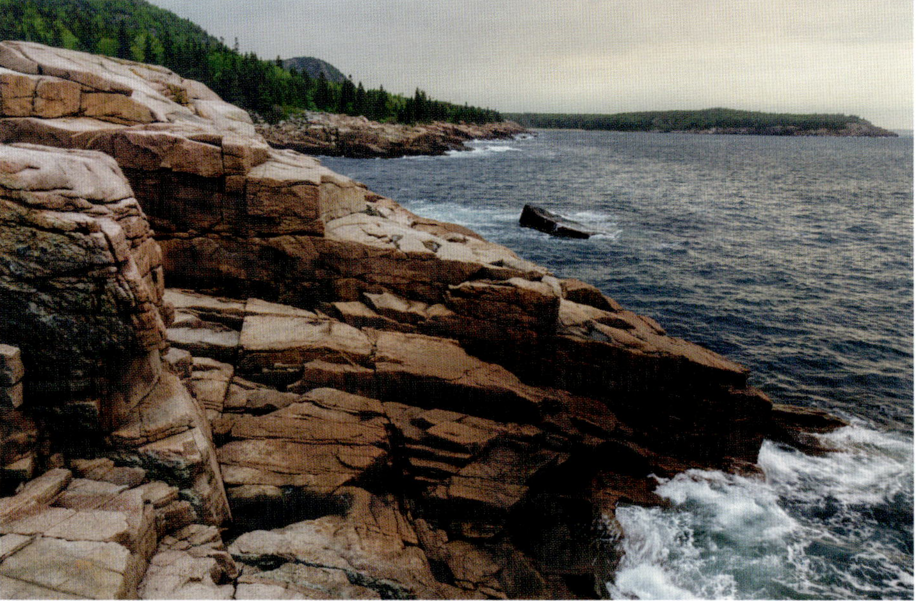

NEAR MONUMENT COVE IN SOFT LIGHT

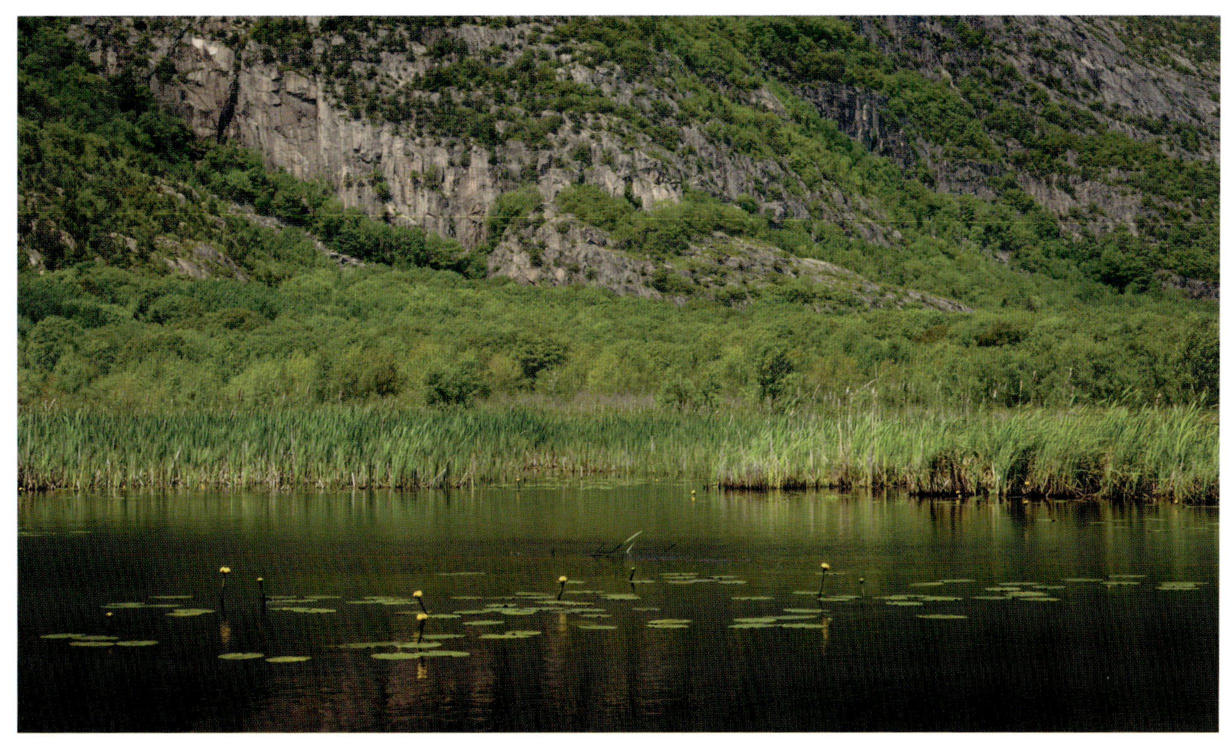

YELLOW POND LILIES NEAR CHAMPLAIN MOUNTAIN

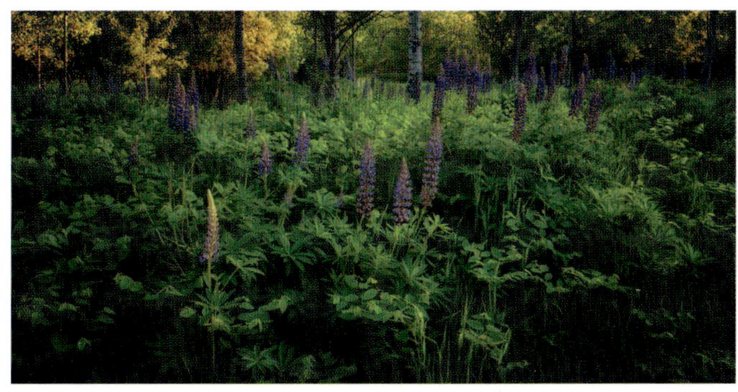

EVENING LUPINE CELEBRATION

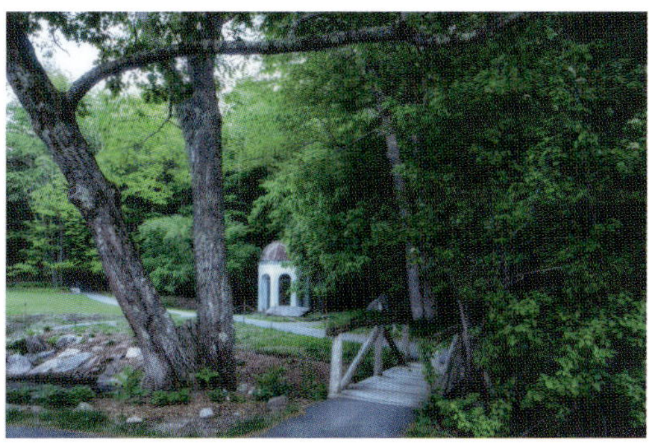

SIEUR DE MONTS SPRING AT TWILIGHT

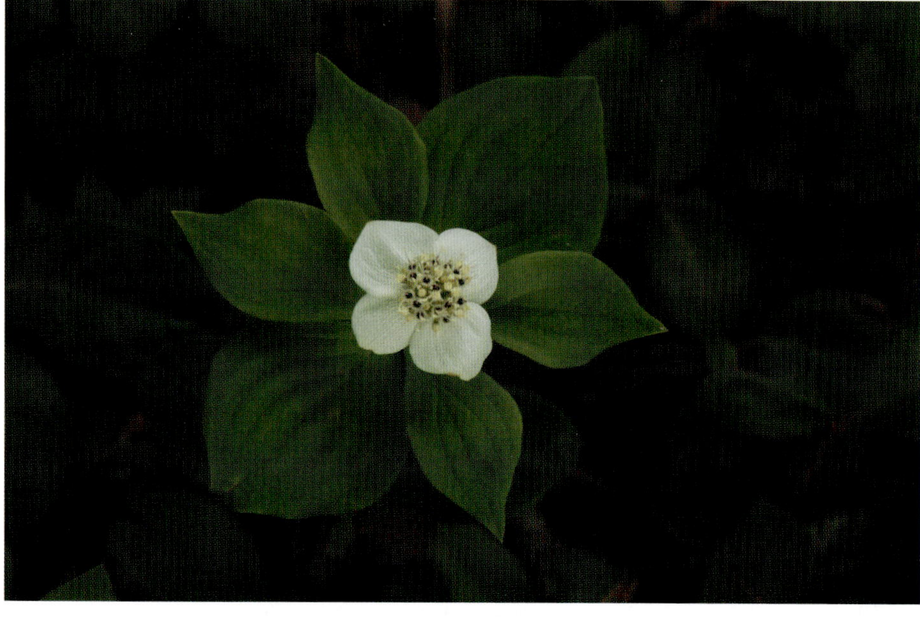

BUNCHBERRY SOLO

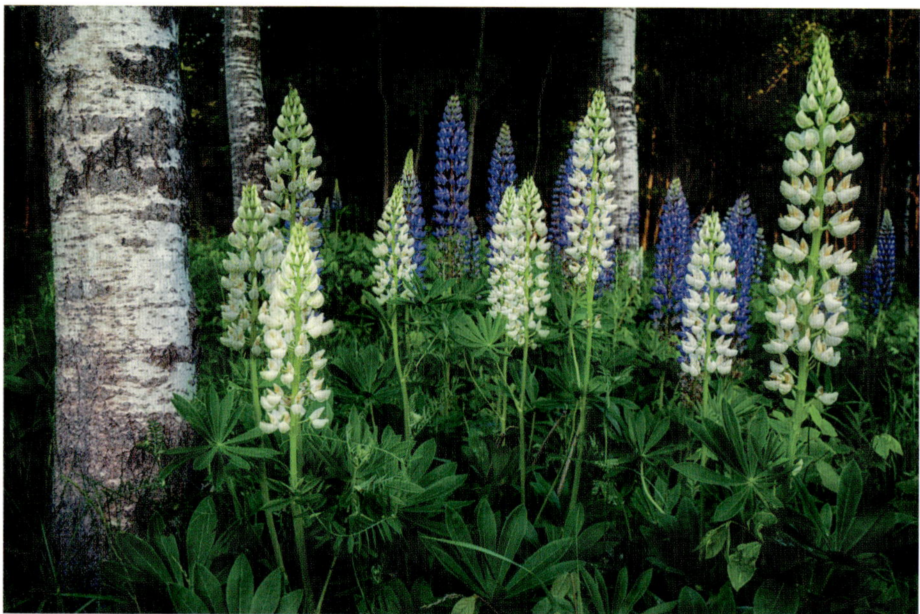

LUPINE AND ASPENS

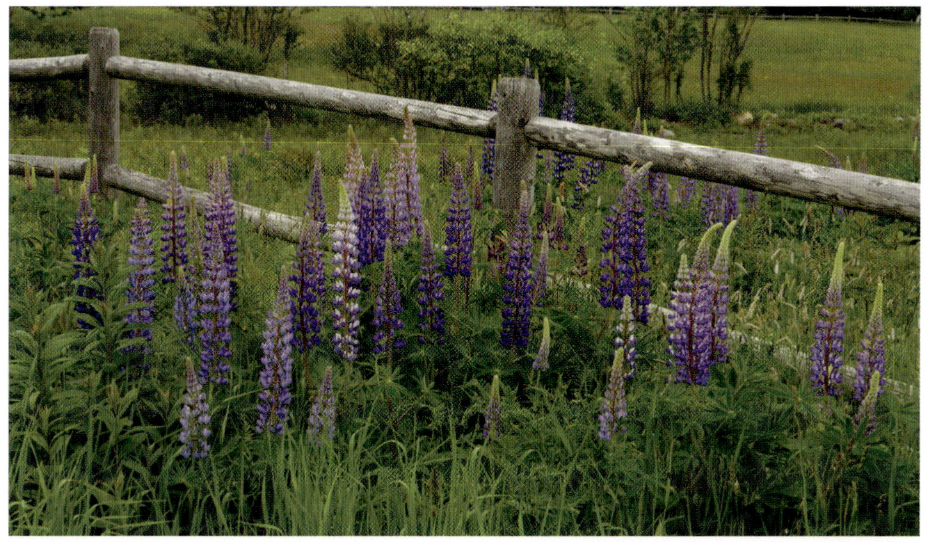

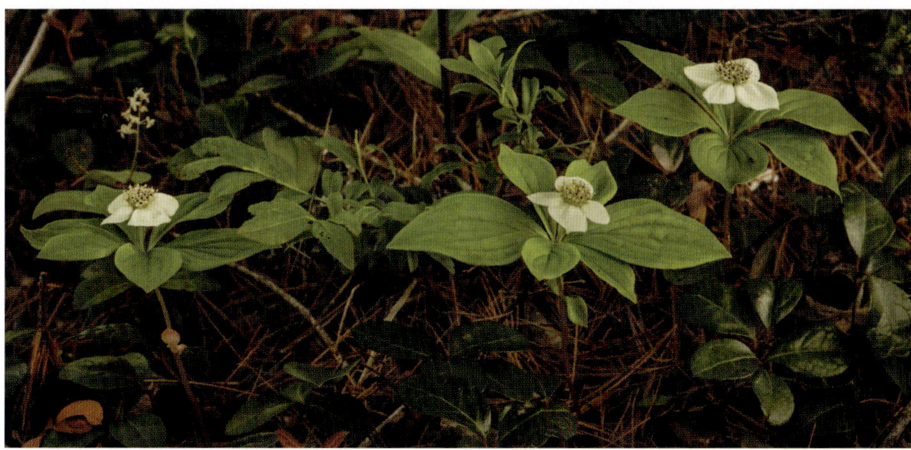

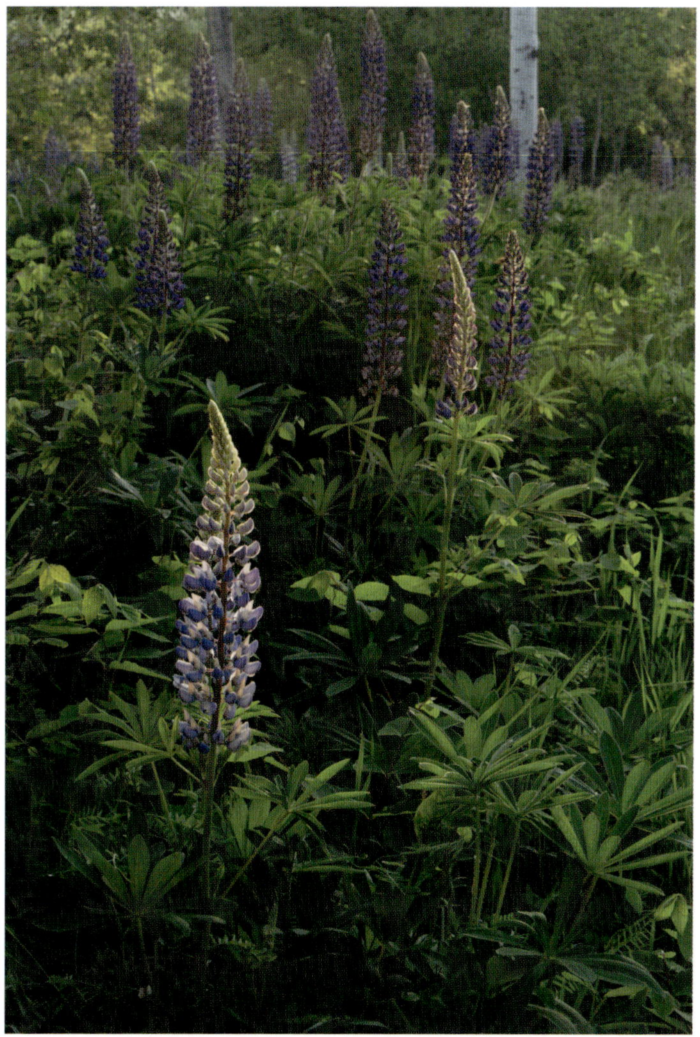

Don't fence me in. Southwest Harbor.

BUNCHBERRY TRIAD

NEAR GREAT MEADOW AT TWILIGHT

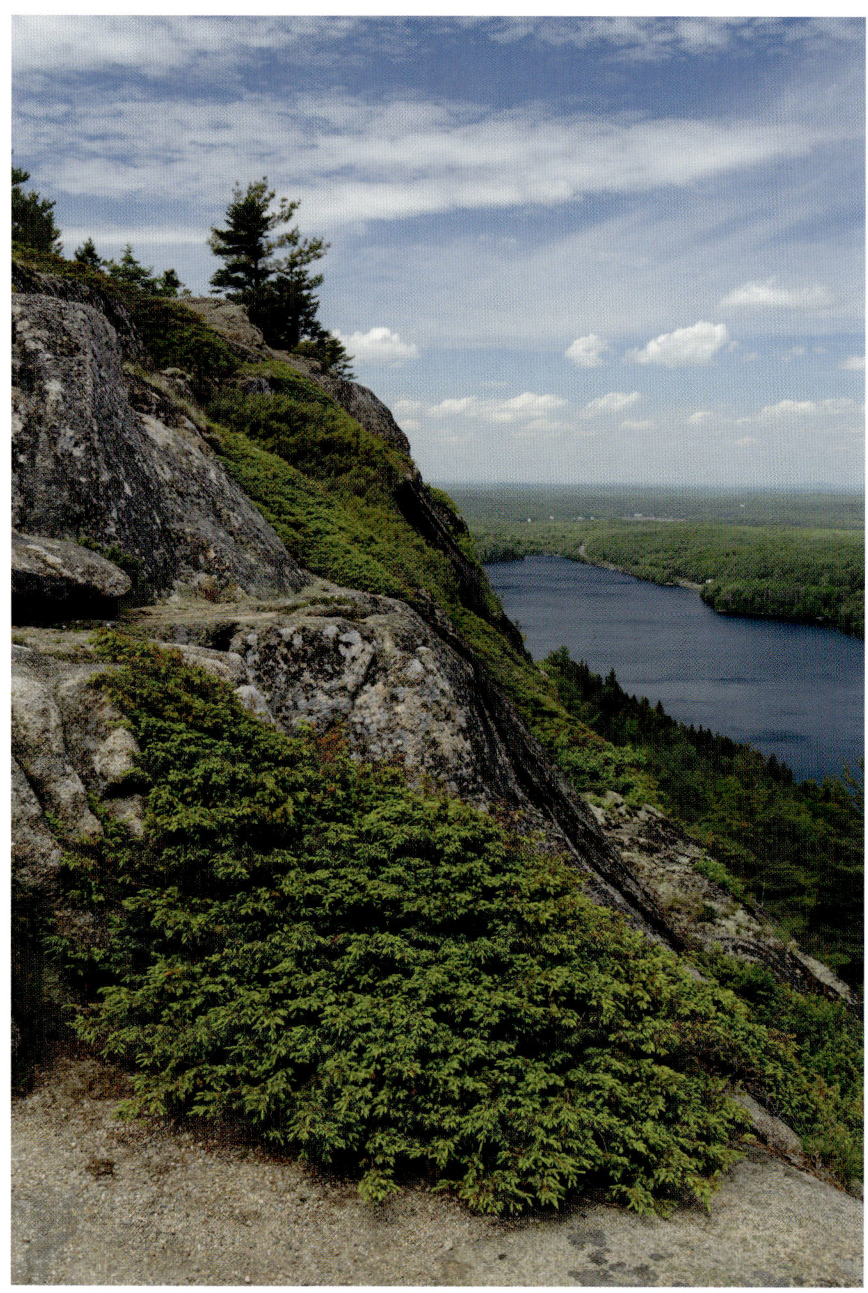

ECHO LAKE FROM THE CANADA CLIFFS ON BEECH MOUNTAIN

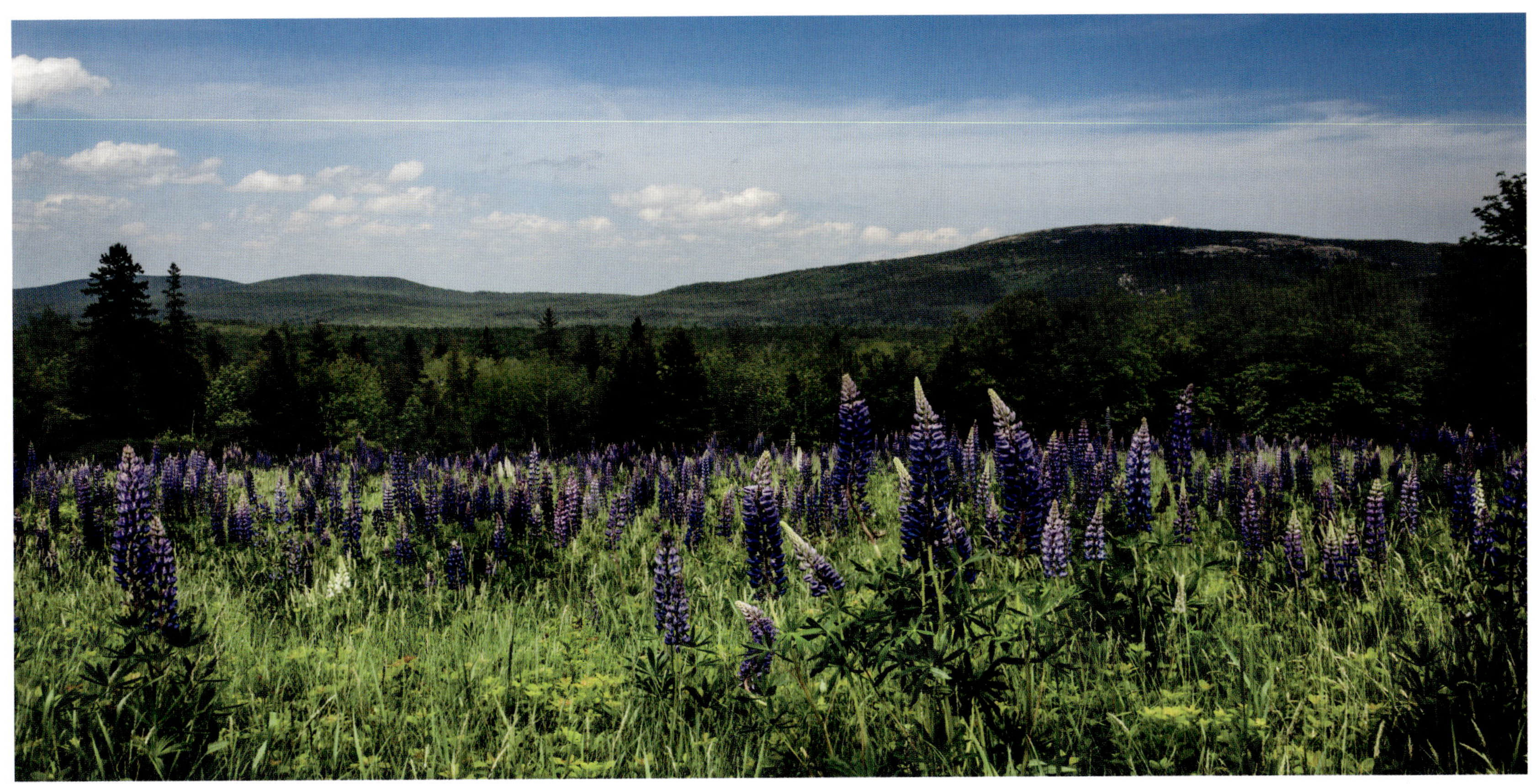

LUPINE ALONG BEECH HILL ROAD

•

The meadow stretches for about half a mile with lupine on both sides of the road.

Equipment, Gear, and Digital Darkroom

Shortly after I ended my time in Acadia, I was out photographing at Nubble Light in York, Maine. I had made several images of a reflection of the lighthouse in a tide pool. The only way to make the image was to lie flat on the rocks at the edge of the pool, with the camera directly on the ground. After I had taken a break, a couple from the Midwest, on their first visit to Maine, came by and we struck up a conversation. They asked what I was doing lying on the rocks like that, and I showed them some of the images I had made. Then came the inevitable "You must have a really good camera."

In years past, my response would have bordered on smartass superiority, like: "Well, yes I do, but more importantly, I know how to use it." Another favorite quip was "Would you tell Emeril that he must have a really good set of knives?" As if the camera, a collection of mechanical and electronic parts attached to a piece of glass, was responsible for the images, and the user just needs to point the device in a particular direction and is relieved of all responsibility other than pressing the shutter release. I've come to realize that most people aren't educated about art and the creative process, and I've gained a bit of humility as well. So now I take a bit of time to educate them and in the process make new friends.

I patiently explained to the folks that the cameras are really just tools I use to create and share what I feel about what I observe and experience. It's more about vision. If one thinks a little more about what is being photographed, the camera doesn't matter that much; it's how it's used. Great photos can be made with the most-rudimentary equipment. I asked them if they had a cell phone camera, which they did. I then brought them down to the tide pool, showed them how to set up the shot, then went back to my seat on the rocks while they played around. They both came back to show me what they had taken. Plus they had an experience they might not have had. Somewhere in my archives I have a picture of them lying on the edge of the pool, happily making images that they wouldn't have made otherwise, rather than the more typical snapshot.

With that being a long way to getting around to it, here is the equipment I used for the images in this book.

Cameras

Nikon D800. This is my primary camera, a 36 MP full-frame sensor with a fourteen-stop dynamic range. Rugged as well, since I tend to be tough on equipment. I've dropped it several times, not on purpose, and it still keeps going. Produces a 40 MB raw file. It is capable of shooting at ISO 50, which I find really useful for long

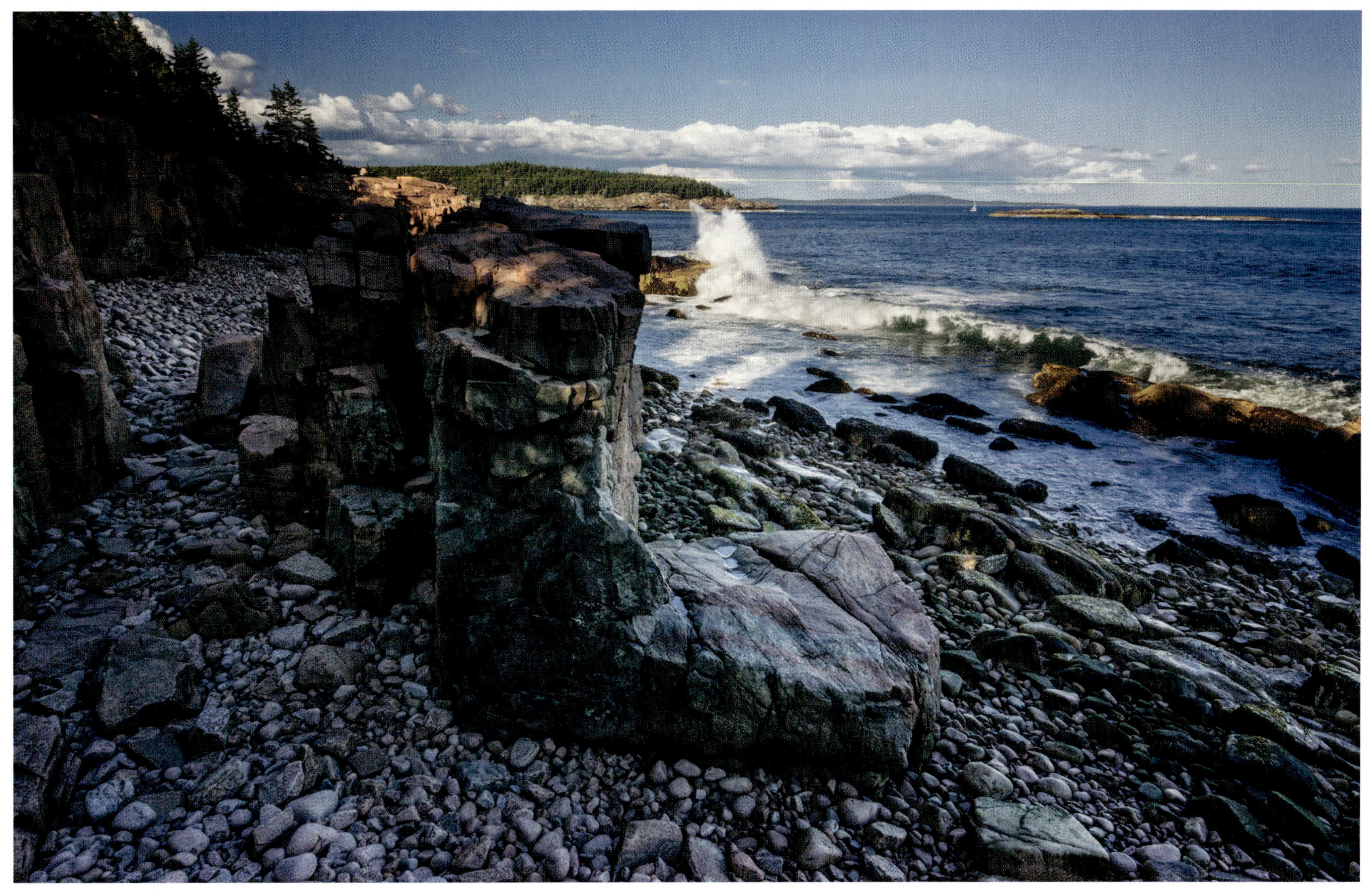

SEA STACK AND SURF NEAR THUNDER HOLE IN THE EARLY EVENING

•

Great Head and Schoodic Peninsula form the backdrop
as a sailboat passes behind the Old Soaker.

exposures, and it has the ability to bracket nine frames automatically. It is heavy, though. I also like the ability to use LiveView for fine focusing, checking composition and exposure, and eliminating vibrations due to the reflex mirror flipping up and down. LiveView enables the photographer to use the LCD screen on the back of the camera as an Electronic viewfinder.

Nikon D7000. My backup camera, a 24 MP DX sized sensor. 16 MB raw file. I use this as a walk-around, general-purpose camera and for the occasional wildlife shot, because of the 1.5 magnification factor of the smaller sensor (a 500 mm lens is effectively equal to a 750 mm lens). I also use this when I have the D800 set up on a tripod, and I'm waiting for the light to change and there are other interesting subjects to photograph. It also is LiveView capable.

Nikon D70s. My first digital SLR; 6 MP DX sensor, with a 1.5 magnification factor. Several images in the book were made with this camera. Not so rugged; I actually snapped the base plate from the body on a cold winter day, with my bare hands. However, it continued to work well. It has since been retired.

Samsung Galaxy S6 Smartphone. I use this mostly when I'm scouting a new location or see something I want to come back to at a later date. Kind of visual reminders or a digital sketchbook. Also when I don't want to carry a lot of gear. And I use it for snapshots to post on Facebook to let friends and followers know what I am up to. Two images in this book were made with the S6—I'll let you guess which ones.

LENSES

Nikon 16–35 mm F4. A great, sharp, wide-angle zoom.

Nikon 28–300 mm F5.6. A very good, all-purpose lens; tends to be on my camera most of the time. I tend to use it more for telephoto shots. If I'm working on wide images, I switch to the 16–35. I like having some overlap in the zoom lenses so I can respond to quickly changing conditions.

Nikon 18–300 mm F5.6/6.3. Used with D7000 only. There is a 1.5x factor when using this lens/camera combination, so effectively this is a 27–450 mm lens.

Sigma 100 mm Macro. Used for extreme close-up images of flowers, lichens, leaves, or rocks. Used on the D7000, it is effectively a 150 mm lens.

Rokinon 24 mm 1.4. I use it exclusively for star photography.

Tamron 500 F8 Mirror. This is an old lens from my film days, and I use it only for wildlife, usually mounted on the D7000 and attached to a tripod, which makes it equal to a 750 mm lens. It is a manual-focus lens, and it doesn't have autoexposure capabilities. It's pretty much a manual process, but I've found that if I use LiveView, magnify the image, and focus with a Hoodman HoodLoupe, I can get very good results. But it's a slow process suitable for such things as bald eagles perched in trees, but not birds in flight.

TRIPODS

Manfrotto. I have two Manfrotto tripods that I use. Both are about ten years old, made of aluminum, and very durable, if somewhat heavy. Both have legs that spread at adjustable angles, allowing me to put the camera just a few inches above the ground. This feature comes in handy when photographing in the rocks and cliffs of Acadia, since there are a lot of uneven surfaces or sometimes the best spot is standing on boulders. If I am not going too far from the car and the wind is heavy, then I'll use the heavier model, the 3221WN, for increased stability. My other Manfrotto is a early version of the 102 series, which has a center post that rotates 90 degrees. I use it mostly for macro-photography when I need to get very low to the ground and close to the subject. I rarely use the center post with the larger tripod, since it increases vibrations, not something you want when doing long exposures. I bought both these tripods several years ago; Manfrotto has since replaced them with updated versions. Both have performed well in a variety of conditions.

Induro. A few years ago I broke down and bought an Induro Carbon Fiber tripod, to use on longer treks. It weighs in about 4 pounds. It also has variable-angle legs, but I can't get as close to the ground as I need to. Everything is a trade-off. I replaced the center column that came with the tripod with a shorter one, since I don't generally use it to gain more height, because of the vibration issue. Also with the longer center column, the only way to get close to the ground is to remove the column, reverse it, and mount the camera upside down, so that it sits between the legs of the tripod. It works in a pinch, if you don't mind lying on the ground and contorting yourself to make adjustments. It does tend to vibrate in heavy wind conditions, as I found out when shooting the image of Monument Cove during a hurricane (page 78). There is a hook on the bottom of the center column, and by hanging a camera bag from this retractable hook, the additional weight and lower center of gravity help dampen the vibrations and add stability. If I am traveling by plane, this tripod will fit in my checked luggage bag, if I remove the ball head.

I also use an Induro Monopod, mostly with the D7000, when I am just walking around with no particular objective in mind, or when I have the D800 mounted on a tripod set up for a planned shot, and something interesting is occurring in another area. This way I don't have to set up and break down and set up again.

BALL HEAD

AcraTech Ultimate Ball-Head. I like the open design of this ball head, since it is easy to keep clean and moving freely. I have used other ball heads that allow dirt to get between the ball and the housing, resulting in the head locking up (which is how I came to crack the body of my D70s on a cold winter day). Also I have not had any issues with the ball head slipping out of position even with my heaviest lens/camera combination. I have even used it with my 12-pound view camera without any problems. I use the ball head together with an AcraTech Universal Extended L Bracket, so I can switch the camera from horizontal to vertical orientation quickly. Without the L-bracket, the camera ends up 3 inches to the right or left of where you started, and 3 inches lower or higher. It is then necessary to move the entire tripod left or right and raise or lower the tripod to return to the original composition. The L-bracket eliminates that process. I leave the L-bracket on my camera all the time, since it also makes it easier to hand-hold the camera. I use the ball head on all my tripods interchangeably. I also carry an extra-inexpensive ball head in my car—just in case. Finally, I have quick-release plates attached to all my camera bodies, since it is much quicker than trying to attach the camera by using a screw mount. Especially when it's 10 below and your gloves are too thick.

FILTERS

Neutral Density (ND) Filters. I use the Lee system of filters. Yes, they are expensive, but why put an inferior filter in front of a high-quality lens? I use both soft- and hard-edge filters to help balance out the exposure when the range of light is too great to obtain detail both in the highlights and shadow areas. Soft-edge filters gradually decrease the light, which is useful when you are photographing an uneven horizon, such as mountains. Hard-edge filters are best for a horizon that is straight, such as where the sky meets the ocean. I use one-, two-, and three-stop filters, and by using the filter holder that mounts to the lens, it is possible to combine filters together, as well as add a polarizer.

I also use the Lee Bigger Stopper (ten stops) and Little Stopper (five stops) to reduce the light coming into the camera, so that I can make long exposures that create a smooth, velvety look to water and clouds, blurring the motion and creating an ethereal look to photographs. For times when I am traveling light, I use a Tiffen Variable ND filter, which reduces the light entering the camera by one to ten stops.

POLARIZERS

I have a confession to make: I love saturated colors, and I hate glare. I am addicted to polarizer filters and have one on all my lenses, although I have been using them less often, or not using them at maximum strength as I have in the past. It's a hard habit to break, but slowly I'm coming around. I used to buy inexpensive ones and found the results disappointing, not because of the effect, but I was using a lower-grade filter on a superior lens, degrading the image quality. If you put a piece of $30 glass on the front of a $1,500 lens, the resulting image is somewhat degraded. I have since upgraded to a high-grade polarizer for all my lenses, and I keep them in place at all times because they also provide a bit of protection to the front element of the lens. During the production of images for this book, I was walking among the rocks along Ocean Drive with my new Nikon 18–300 zoom on the D7000 when the strap let go. As luck would have it, I didn't have the lens cap on. I watched in horror as the front of the lens nose-dived into the granite. However, I had the polarizer on, and it took one for the team, sacrificing itself to save the lens. Easier to replace a $120 filter than a $1,500 lens.

The reason for using polarizers is twofold: reducing reflections and glare on leaves, water, and other reflective surfaces, and increasing color saturation. They will darken the sky and provide more definition to clouds. Eliminating the glare and reflection on water allows us to see below the surface. A polarizer will increase exposure time by about two stops, so there is a trade-off, and it does make focusing a little harder. Also, autofocusing works only when you are using a circular polarizer. Because it decreases light coming through the lens, it can also be used as a two-stop neutral-density filter. Polarizers work best at a 90-degree angle from the direction of the light. The effect decreases as the lens angle moves toward the light source or in the opposite direction (toward 180 degrees) of the light source. I don't use them when shooting directly toward the sun, because it increases lens flares since there are more glass surfaces for light to bounce off.

Using a polarizer with a wide angle can result in uneven polarization in the sky, especially noticeable if the sky is clear blue.

I use two brands of polarizers. I have Tiffin polarizers on my lens all the time. If, however, I am using the Lee filter system, then I use the Lee 105 mm Polarizer.

BAGS

I have three bags that I use to carry my gear, depending on what I am doing on any particular day. Generally, I use a Lowepro Slingshot 302, since it is large enough to carry my D800 with my largest zoom lens attached, as well as space for two or three extra lenses, a flash unit, my Lee filter system, extra batteries, headlamp, tools, Hoodman HoodLoupe memory cards, extra cell phone battery, food, water bottle, insect repellent, hand warmers, sunscreen, and emergency blanket. When I am just out on a scouting trip or traveling or just want a lighter kit, I use the smaller Slingshot, which will hold a camera with lens, two additional lenses, and a few additional items. I use a Tenba Shootout backpack when taking extended trips. It's a heavy bag, but it holds all my gear, plus a 14-inch laptop. I put all my cameras and lenses, laptop, and extra drives in the Tenba, then throw the Slingbag into my checked luggage. Once I arrive at my destination, I redistribute the equipment to fit the day's activities.

MISCELLANEOUS GEAR

Hoodman HoodLoupe. This item comes in very handy when evaluating images on the LCD screen on the back of the camera, especially when using LiveView and performing critical focusing. I couldn't get by without this item.

CamRanger. This is a wireless device that connects to the camera and allows me to remotely control all the functions of the camera from a laptop, tablet, cell phone, or another wireless device. It creates a discreet wireless network to which you can connect. I've tried it from my cell phone, but it's a bit too small. I've also used both a 7-inch and 10-inch Samsung tablet with better results. If you need to get close to the ground or out in the water, or you need to extend your tripod up higher than eye level, it comes in handy. Range is about 300 feet, but best performance is within about 10 feet.

Headlamp. I keep a small headlamp (as well as a small Maglite®) in my bag. The headlamp has a very bright LED light, and it also has a less intense red LED, for those times when you want to preserve your night vision. I use the Maglite® to assist with focusing when the subject is in a dark area, and to do some "light painting" when shooting at night or doing star photography.

Pruning Shears. Small, plastic pruning shears come in handy for trimming away unwanted or distracting twigs and dead sticks when you are photographing flowers and other small subjects close to the ground. I use them only as a last resort when I can't bend or move the offending twigs out of the way.

Sensor Gel Stick. The Eyelead Gel Stick is another item I keep in my pack, to keep my sensor clean. I generally use it only when I am indoors, but I have had a rare need to use it outdoors to remove a piece of windblown particle that found its way onto the sensor while I was switching lenses. It requires a delicate touch to use, so I first try to remove debris with a handheld air blower (never, ever use canned air, since it has a propellant that will get on the sensor and will require professional cleaning to remove). Once I've cleared what I can with the blower, I use the gel stick, with a very light touch, and go over the sensor one section at a time.

Tripod Tools. I keep a small, 5-inch ratchet with appropriately sized socket for tightening the hex nuts on the Manfrotto tripod, since the release levers tend to loosen over time. Also, Induro provides some dedicated tools for maintaining their tripods. Allen wrenches, for keeping the quick-release plates secure to the camera, also occupy space in my bag.

PROCESSING AND PRINTING

I use Lightroom and Photoshop CC to process all images along with the Nik Software suite. I use a Dell Desktop with dual LCD monitors, which use IPS technology for the best color range and consistency. There is 24 MB of RAM, 4 terabytes of hard disk space, a dual video processor with dedicated RAM, and a huge set of fans to keep it all cool. I back up daily to a small RAID-configured NAS device. I also use a 10-inch Wacom touch pad. A Spyder4 Pro monitor calibration device is used to control monitor consistency, and Spyder Print is used to match color prints with monitor colors. Prints are made on a Canon Prograf Pro-1000 on Ilford Smooth Pearl or Red River Arctic Polar Luster Paper with appropriate ICC profiles.

Inspiration

I draw my inspiration not only from nature but from many sources in art, photography, and music. These are just a few that I would encourage the reader to take time to learn more about and to experience their work. It's pretty obvious why the photographers and artists inspire me; the composers are the ones who provide the soundtrack for my life, which plays through my mind when I am still and contemplating the moment.

PHOTOGRAPHY

Ansel Adams
Eliot Porter
David Muench
Joe Cornish
David Ward
William Neill
Kurt Budliger
Guy Tal
Jack Dykinga
John Shaw
John Paul Caponigro
Q. T. Luong
Michael Frye

ART

Frederic E. Church
Claude Monet
Andrew Wyeth
Edward Hopper
Georgia O'Keeffe
Alfred Bierstadt
Hudson River School of Artists
Vincent Van Gogh

MUSIC

Mozart
Beethoven
Brahms
Bach
Chopin
Vivaldi
Tchaikovsky
Smetana
George Winston

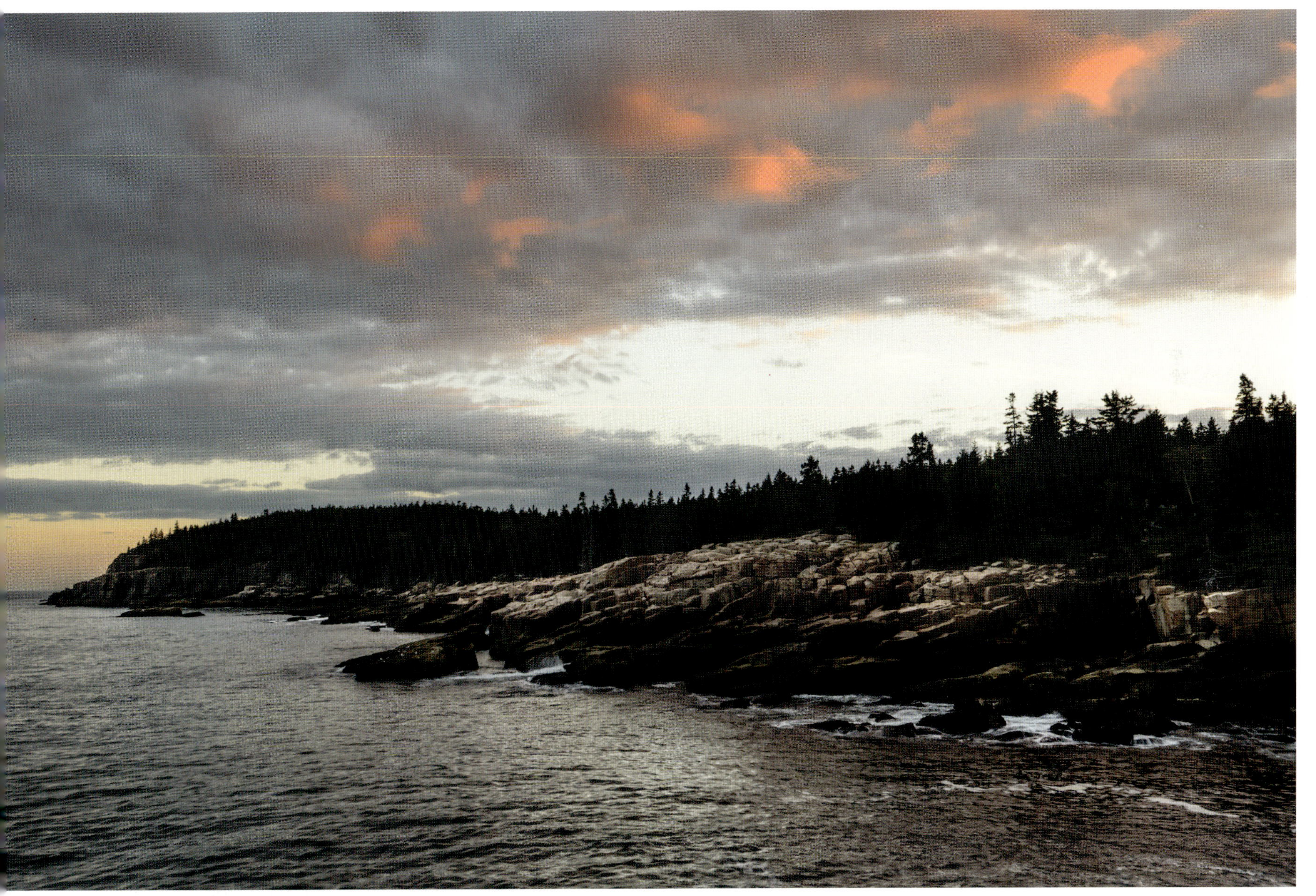

SUNSET COLOR FROM THE ENTRANCE TO MONUMENT COVE

Logistics and Practical Considerations

Getting There. I love the drive to Acadia, especially once I cross the Piscataqua River, which forms the boundary between New Hampshire and Maine. I usually leave my home early in the morning, before 3 a.m., not only to avoid the traffic on I-495 around Boston, but so I can watch the transition from dark to dawn as I travel north and east. By the time I get to Portland, the city is just starting to wake up as we drive through on I-295. Staying on I-295 keeps us near the coast. Once we get to Brunswick, it's on to Route 1, the more scenic route, although it can be a bit slower and somewhat congested in Wiscasset, Rockland, and Camden. It's a two-lane road, but the extra time spent, for me, is more invigorating than blasting past interior Maine farmland and forests on the Maine Turnpike. Only if I'm pressed for time will I stay on the interstate to Bangor, before taking Route 3 to Ellsworth and Bar Harbor. Traveling on Route 1 also provides the opportunity for side trips to L.L.Bean in Freeport (open 24/7; rumor has it they lost the key to the front door a long time ago, so they just stayed open), Pemaquid Light, Boothbay Harbor, and several other Maine oceanside destinations. Along the way, you see forests, lupine, farmland, small fishing villages, and outstanding coastal views.

One can also fly to Portland or Bangor Airport, rent a car, and drive to Bar Harbor, or fly into Bar Harbor Airport (from Boston only) and take a taxi onto the island.

Once on the island, there are plenty of shuttle buses to help get you around if you don't have a car.

Staying There. There are numerous hotels and bed-and-breakfast establishments in Bar Harbor, in all price ranges. I generally stayed at the Atlantic Oceanside, since they are open all year round, have a great location, and are very accommodating. Breakfast is also complimentary. In the winter there are only three places to stay, and they are the only ones that have a private power generator, since power interruptions occur frequently during winter storms. There are also accommodations in Northeast and Southwest Harbor, and off the island in Ellsworth. Prices vary with the seasons, and during my time there the rate per night went from $85 in December to $250 in July. We also camped (yes, in a tent, on the ground) when we were younger, and there are several campgrounds on the island. The only one I have any experience with is Hadley's Point Campground, and it has always been positive. There are also several cottages that are available for rent throughout the island. Check with the Bar Harbor visitors center (www.barharborinfo.com) for more-detailed information.

Eating There. I have a lot of favorite places to eat, but half the fun is discovering your own favorite places. Between mid-April and Thanksgiving weekend, most restaurants are open. After that, choices are extremely limited to a few bars that remain open year-round. Once we get to mid-April, places begin to open up again. Most restaurants tend to get quite busy between 6 and 8 p.m., so I usually eat outside those hours. Besides, in the summer, some of the best light for photography is after 5 p.m., and the park becomes considerably less crowded, since most visitors head into town to eat and shop. There are no fast-food franchises on the island, other than a few Subway sandwich places. It pays to plan ahead to avoid disappointment, especially if you're traveling with someone who is more interested in eating and shopping than photography, so you may need reservations.

My list of favorites by meal, in no order. Most of these are in Bar Harbor unless otherwise indicated:

Breakfast: Jordan's Restaurant, 59 Cottage, 2 Cats Bar Harbor, Great Maine Breakfast, Trailhead Cafe

Lunch: 59 Cottage, Jordan's Restaurant, Side Street Café, Route 66, the Jordan Pond House in Acadia Park

Dinner: CherryStones, 59 Cottage, Poor Boy's Gourmet, Galyn's, the Jordan Pond House in Acadia Park, Side Street Café, the Thirsty Whale, Route 66, the Asticou Inn in Northeast Harbor, the Finback Ale House, Paddy's Irish Pub, Stewman's Lobster Pound, Red Sky in Southwest Harbor

Coffee: The Trailhead Café, Coffee Hound Coffee Bar, Choco-Latte. If you want Dunkin' Donuts, you're going to have to go to Ellsworth. I don't know where the nearest Starbucks is; maybe Bangor or Waterville?

Ice Cream: Jordan Pond Ice Cream and Fudge, Ben and Bill's Chocolate Emporium, Mount Desert Ice Cream Island

There are many other places; I just haven't tried them all yet. These are just my favorites, so far.

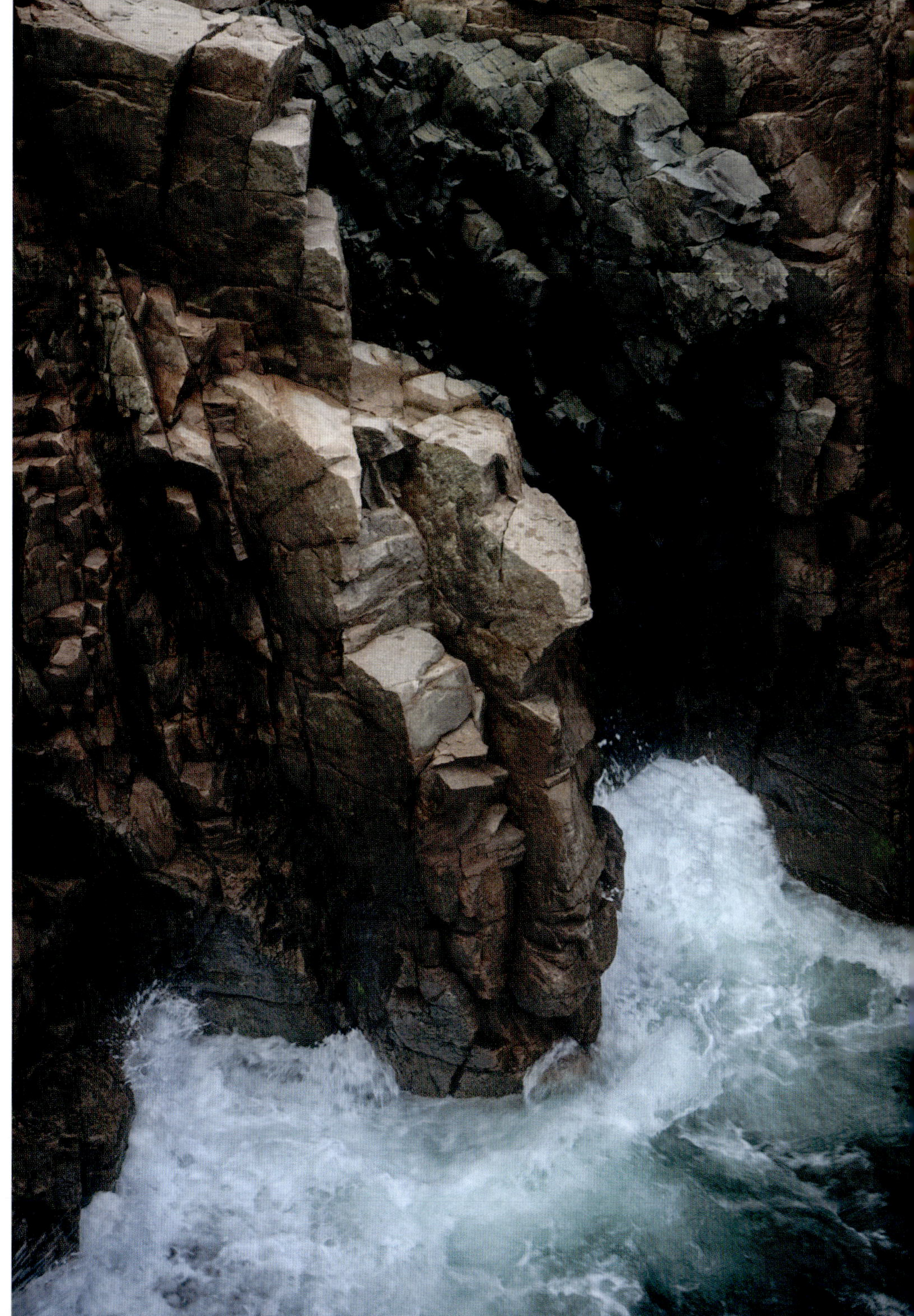

SURF AND CLIFFS NEAR THUNDER HOLE

Driving and Parking. Rule number 1: pedestrians always have the right-of-way. Always. Even if you are backing up. Driving in and around Bar Harbor requires a great deal of attention during the peak tourist season. Keep your head on a swivel and pay attention. It's crowded and congested; patience and cooperation are needed to navigate the narrow streets. There is one traffic light in town, otherwise there are only stop signs. There are three traffic lights on the entire island. Parking is limited and most of it is along the streets, so having the skills to parallel park is quite handy. There is also a two-hour limit on occupying a space. You've been warned. Otherwise you just might see your car on Bar Harbor's Famous Parking Show Facebook page.

Weather, Tides, and Waves. Mark Twain once famously said, "If you don't like the weather in New England, wait a few minutes." That is especially true the farther north you go, so it pays to be prepared. Fog can occur when least expected, and temperatures can drop unexpectedly. Tides rise or fall approximately every six hours, so having an application that will track tidal activity, such as "Tides Near Me," on your phone or device is pretty handy and will help plan your activities. Low tide provides access to tidal pools and Bar Island, but keep one eye on the ocean to avoid being trapped by rising water. One can find video clips on YouTube of people who drove out to the island and attempted to drive back through the rising water, only to lose their cars. The water is also very cold, usually never getting above 60 degrees F in the summer. Finally, if you are near the ocean, keep your head on a swivel and pay attention to the waves. Rough surf is amazing to watch, but the potential to be washed off the rocks and drawn out into the ocean is always possible—a timely rescue may not be.

Other Stuff. Along Ocean Drive it can be great fun to walk and hop and climb the rocks and boulders; however, there is a lot of poison ivy in this area, so knowing how to identify and avoid it can prevent some uncomfortable rashes. Benadryl gel is my treatment of choice. You've been warned!

In the winter, I carry chemical hand warmers, but not just for my hands; I have

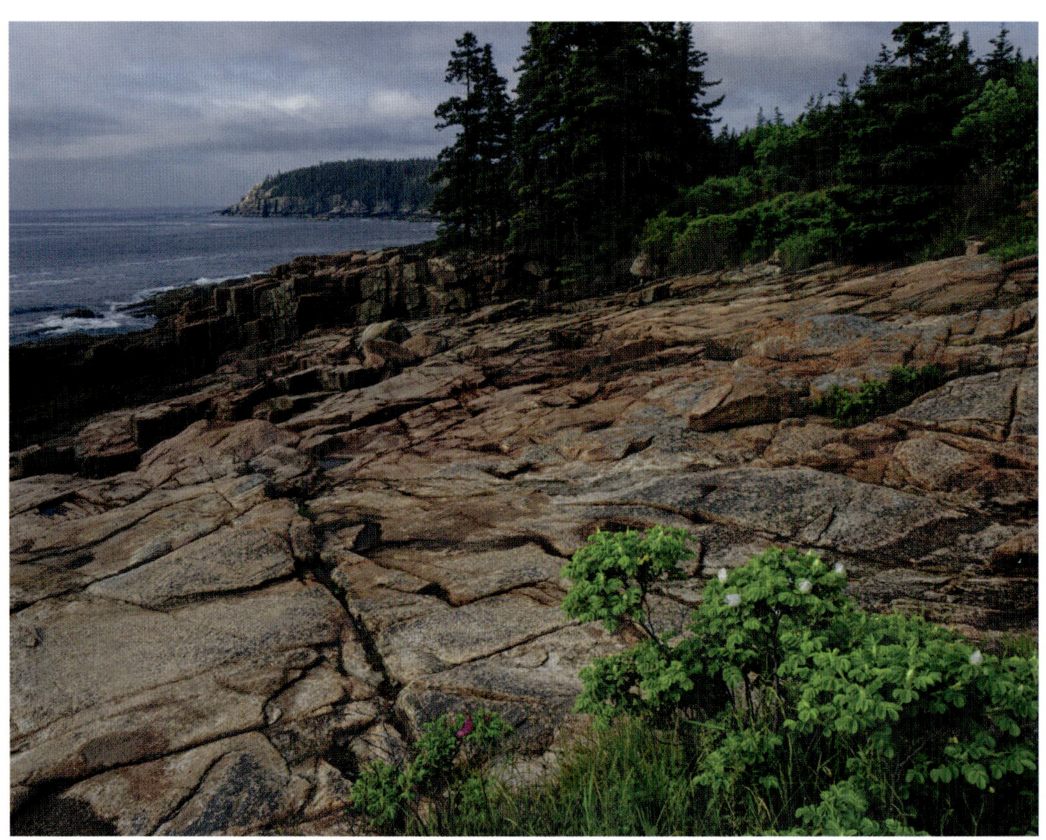

WHITE RUGOSA NEAR THUNDER HOLE AREA ON A STORMY MORNING

also used them in my boots, and if it is below zero, I'll toss one in my camera bag to keep my spare batteries warm.

Insect repellent is essential in the spring and early summer, as well as sunscreen. Beware when using products containing DEET, since it can mar the finish on plastic surfaces of your camera gear if your hands are wet with it when handling gear. Once it has dried, it's not a problem. I try not to use it on my fingers and palms of my hands. I've also found that some clothing impregnated with repellent works well for keeping the mosquitos at bay. I have an ExOfficio hat coated with Permethrin that I have used for several years that works well. I also have a few shirts with sunblock and insect repellent properties.

Getting around in Winter. Most of the Park Loop Road is closed between November 15 and April 15, as a general rule. Ocean Drive is open between Sand Beach and Otter Cliffs. Access to this area is via Schooner Head Road as you head south out of Bar Harbor on Main Street. Only one lane is kept open for vehicles; the other lane is for cross-country skiing, hiking, and snowmobiles. Parking is limited as well. One section of the Sand Beach lot is open, and there is usually enough space along the road to park. At Otter Cliffs, a gate bars access to vehicles; exit by turning right onto Otter Cliffs Road. On the left is the Fabbri picnic area, where you can find space to park as well. Restrooms are open both at Sand Beach and Fabbri. On bright, sunny days, many island residents can be found walking this section of the road. It faces south and can be quite exhilarating to be out and about on it.

A word of caution about going down to Sand Beach: Although there are stairs that lead down to the beach, they quickly become packed with snow, which turns to ice after a warm spell. It can be quite treacherous going down, and even harder to get back up. It's the only access to the beach, unless you approach from the Schooner Head area. I also don't advise going out on the rocks, since blowing and drifting snow will hide the spaces between them. Unless you can clearly see where you are putting your feet, I advise against it. As with anything in the park, conditions are subject to change, so check the Acadia National Park website for updates.

One can also access Jordan Pond from Seal Harbor on Jordan Pond Road. The parking lot at the pond is open, as are the restrooms. The Jordan Pond House area, however, is closed. Other areas that are open include the Carriage Paths at Eagle Lake, Little Long Pond, Bass Harbor Light, and Schoodic Peninsula.

Cell Phone Access. I have found that cell phone access can be spotty, depending on your service provider. It would drive me absolutely crazy to be unable to make a call home, while my friends, using a different service provider, would stand right next to me chatting away. On many nights I would drive up to the top of Cadillac and call home while I watched the stars move across the sky. It seems to be worse on the south side of the island along Ocean Drive, and between some of the mountains. This situation may have been resolved by the time you read this. But since I was there to get away from the everyday annoyances of modern life, I didn't mind too much that I couldn't constantly check or update my Facebook status. My biggest concern was getting help in an emergency.

Getting into the Park. There is an entrance fee to get into the park; at the time of this writing it was $20 for a seven-day pass. Check with the National Park Service for updates. Once in the park, make sure to display your pass. Park rangers are very friendly but will remind you if you forget to have the pass prominently displayed. There are also free annual passes for Active Duty Military and Reserve/Guard members as well.

Senior Pass. If the national parks are one of America's greatest ideas, then the Senior Pass is the second-greatest idea. Once you reach the age of sixty-two, seniors are eligible to purchase a lifetime pass for $80, valid in all National Park Service locations. Be sure to ask for it. My first two weeks on the island I had to purchase seven-day passes, but I turned sixty-two the following week, and that was the last time I had to pay for a pass, and at that time it was only $10. What a deal! Recently I visited seven national parks on a four-week road trip and did not have to pay any entrance fees.

Acknowledgments

There are a lot of folks without whom this book would not be possible. This has been a labor of love for me, and at times I felt it would never be completed. I've given up a few times, lost my way on occasions, and become frustrated on others, but somehow there were a few people behind me who pushed me to the finish line.

Donna Dufault, Scott Erb, Jeff Baker, Steve Iodarola, Missy Borgeson, Howard Kong, and the other members of the Worcester Alliance of Photographers Photo Goals group, which I am proud to belong to. Thanks for all your support, constructive critiques, observations, and motivation. You were a great help in keeping me going when I seemed to make obstacles for myself. Donna, thank you for giving me the courage to share my images; without your friendship and guidance, all of these would be sitting in my digital "shoebox" of images.

William Neill, David Muench, and Kurt Budliger, for helping me realize that I am a better photographer than I think I am. Bill, you provided the insight to think of myself as an artist, which has made all the difference in growing as a photographer. David, thanks for your gracious comments on my work, and for the time we shared in Glacier National Park. Kurt, you helped me see that it is not all grand vistas, and that we can make great images of a more intimate nature right here in New England.

My wife, Judy, for driving me, feeding me, and accompanying me when she could, and allowing me the freedom to pursue the light even when she really wanted to be dining or shopping. My children, Joe and Nikki, for listening to me obsess about small moments in the light that have excited me.

My friends and coworkers at the Jackson Laboratory, who recommended special places to visit and patiently listened to me gush about a photo session. In particular, Bonnie Lyons, Rachel Malcolm, Claudia Basso, Chuck Dangler, and Rachel Bates. Thanks to Chuck Dangler for letting me use his weekend house for a few weeks during the spring of 2015, when I was growing weary of hotel rooms and bar food.

Amy Forbes, for recommending the job at Jackson Lab to me.

Skip Geibel and Audrey Bianco, for proofreading.

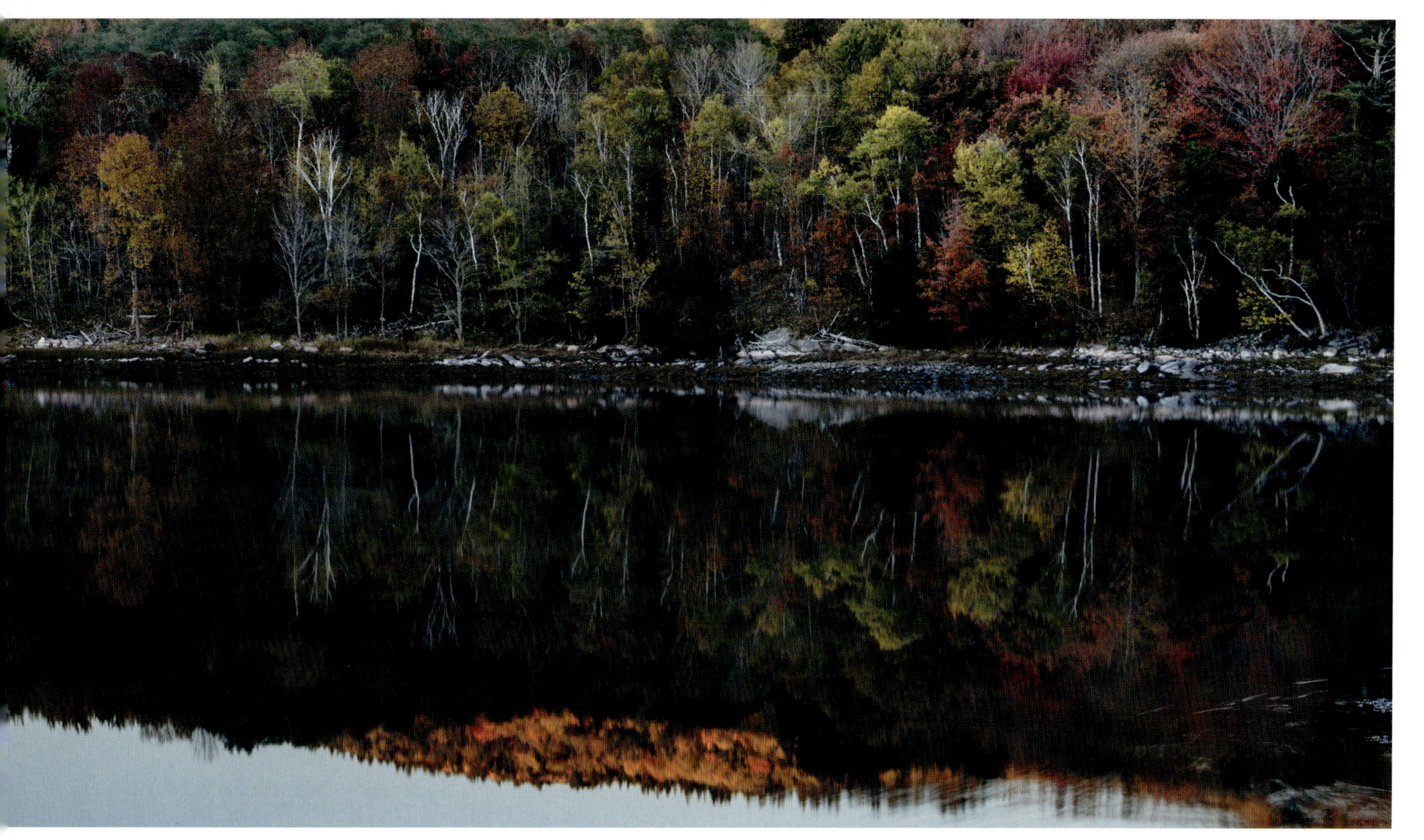

OTTER COVE, AUTUMN EVENING TWILIGHT

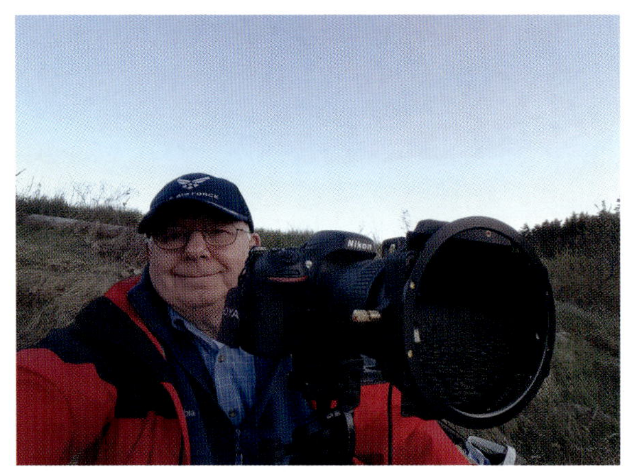

Scott Erskine is a landscape photographer who lives in central New England. He grew up in Maine and after graduating high school joined the US Air Force, where he was a medical laboratory scientist for over 20 years. After retiring from the Air Force, he has worked in healthcare informatics in and around Boston, Massachusetts. Mostly self-taught, he has photographed extensively in Maine, Alaska, Massachusetts, and Wyoming. To see more of Scott's work, visit www.scotterskinephotography.smugmug.com.